Teaching
Social Studies
in the
Elementary School

Fifth Edition

Teaching Social Studies in the Elementary School

Ralph C. Preston
University of Pennsylvania

Wayne L. Herman, Jr.
University of Maryland

HOLT, RINEHART AND WINSTON

New York   Chicago   San Francisco

Dallas   Montreal   Toronto   London   Sydney

Library of Congress Cataloging in Publication Data
Preston, Ralph Clausius
    Teaching social studies in the elementary school.

    Bibliographies
    1. Social sciences—Study and teaching (Elementary)
I. Herman, Wayne L., joint author. II. Title.
LB1584.P68   1981   372.8'3044   80-22214
ISBN 0-03-043886-1

Preface

This book offers a complete treatment of the teaching of social studies from kindergarten through Grade 8. It contains significant teaching tasks used by successful teachers of social studies at these grade levels. For many years, the textbook has been used in social studies methods courses at both undergraduate and graduate levels.

This, the fifth edition, contains a thoroughgoing revision of key chapters, and additions and rearrangements throughout most of the rest of the book including more material than before to aid the teacher of very young children. Several compelling circumstances led to the decision to publish a new edition at this time. For one thing, the dust of the curriculum ferment of the sixties and the consequent controversies and confusion of the seventies had finally settled. Elementary education today is in the grip of new forces. Among these are the back-to-basics movement, the mainstreaming of pupils, the continued rapid growth of the middle school, and the lessening of classroom improvisation and innovation in the face of widely promoted prepackaged, set curriculums and so-called "individualized" kits and workbooks. The society served by the school is also beset by new circumstances: energy shortages, alarming economic and political dislocations, and serious air and water pollution.

Prospective teachers, experienced teachers, and school supervisors are asking tough questions these days. What are the curriculum priorities? What changes are justified in social studies? How can teachers absorb the best in the avalanche of standardized teaching materials without losing their traditional role as the prime movers of classroom procedures and as the shapers of children's social concepts and attitudes?

A new edition was called for to answer such questions. In this effort, new topics have been added. Among them are what to do about values clarification; how to mediate between packaged units and teacher-made units;

capitalizing on children's massive television watching; helping children interpret, in a rudimentary way, cultural conflict; and acquainting children with the long struggle by women and minorities for their civil rights.

Fresh examples from the field have been supplied of how imaginative teachers have enlivened their social studies courses. For example: how kindergarteners acquired advanced concepts of the interaction between human beings and their environment; how a class of third-graders learned at first hand the steps by which an idea can lead to a law; how fifth-graders learned about the lives and work of United States Presidents through role play; how children in all grades, through collaborative action in school jobs and services, learned about business enterprise; and how primary-grade children produced and marketed a picture dictionary as part of their study of careers and free enterprise.

This edition also presents a breakthrough in the dilemma of teaching history to children. History has fared poorly in the elementary school, in terms of interest generated and knowledge retained, due to the practice of organizing and teaching it in the same way that it is organized and taught in high school and college. The reader will find herein a modified version of that neglected but brilliant framework proposed by Gadin, which is based on a synthesis of the principles of leading child psychologists and which bears the promise of closing the gap between the child's here-and-now orientation and a grasp of the past.

Troubles in another area of teaching have arisen from exaggerated claims of some advocates of "inquiry" and "discovery" types of teaching. Such claims made many teachers self-conscious about "presenting" or "explaining" concepts to children. Inquiry-based experiences have an important place in teaching, of course, and we have been explicit in describing workable and worthwhile forms of inquiry. But we have also indicated the limitations of such experiences and have tried to show the usefulness of expository teaching.

The chapter on reading has been completely rewritten in light of the documented, shocking revelation by Professor Delores Durkin, University of Illinois, of the paucity of teaching of reading comprehension in reading and social studies classes. This chapter now focuses entirely on procedures for teaching reading comprehension through social studies materials.

Another reorganized chapter brings together the content of geography, anthropology, and history. This is consistent with the increasing trend of social studies units to unite these fields, with emphasis on emerging cultures rather than on discrete academic fields.

Affective education has been integrated with the material on the teaching of citizenship and government. This is in harmony with the welcome tendency of educational leaders to recognize the fact that civic attitudes and behavior are tied more closely to a child's emotional development than to the intellectual content of social studies.

Although in preparing this revision, each author made contributions to every chapter, revision and re-writing were done independently. The senior author prepared Chapters 1, 2, 3, 4, 5, 6, 7, 8, 9, 10, 11, 12, 13, 19, 21, and 22. Dr. Herman prepared Chapters 14, 15, 16, 17, 18, and 20.

Many persons have contributed to this revision. Special thanks go to classroom teachers who shared with us some of their recent teaching discoveries and experiences. These include Jane Galloway, Highland Park School, Upper Darby (Pennsylvania) School District; Janet Rogers, Lucie County (Florida) Public Schools; and Covey Bryant, Lakeland School, Carbondale (Illinois) Public Schools. Teachers who contributed to past editions and whose creative ideas are again included in this edition are Charlotte Werner Bernstein, Katherine Conner, Sara N. Dalton, Sister M. Euphrosine, Helen C. Moore, Olga C. Pennacchio, Wendy Santaro, Barbara E. Smith, and Joan Willens.

For careful, critical, and helpful reading of the manuscript, we are indebted to Professors Charles M. Godwin, University of Nebraska; Robert V. Duffey, University of Maryland; and Gifford G. Hale, Florida State University. Most of their proposals have been incorporated but, since we have not adopted all their suggestions, they should not, of course, be held responsible for any errors or omissions.

Photographs used in this book come from various sources, as credited below each one. Special credit is due to the Center for Young Children, University of Maryland, and to photographer Richard Farkas; to Merrick County Public Schools, New York; to San Diego City Schools, California; to Montgomery County Public Schools, Maryland; and to Prince George's County Public Schools, Maryland, and to photographer Robert La Follette.

Once again, we are grateful to Madeline Preston for contributing her expert editorial skills with good cheer and without stint.

Philadelphia, Pennsylvania   R.C.P.
College Park, Maryland   W.L.H., Jr.

Table of Contents

Preface   v

part I   **Social Studies in the Elementary School**   1

1 The Nature and Purpose of Social Studies   1
The Nature of the Social Studies / Importance of the Social
Studies / The Social Studies and the Social
Sciences / Relation of Social Studies to the
Humanities / Aims of Social Studies Instruction / General
Objectives / Behavioral Objectives / A Proposal for
Formulating Objectives

2 The Social Sciences: Their Relation to Children
and the Social Studies Curriculum   17
The Behavioral Sciences / Political Science /
Geography / History / Economics

3 Trends in Elementary Education: Their Effect on
Social Studies   35
Back to Basics / Mainstreaming / "Individualized"
Instruction / The Middle School / The Nongraded
School / The Open Classroom / Team Teaching / Values
Clarification and Affective Education

4 The Social Studies Curriculum   52
Prevailing Practices / A Look at Some
Curriculums / Criteria for Judging Curriculum
Programs / Paper Curriculums and Curriculum-less
Classrooms / The Key Role of the Teacher

part II   **Social Studies and Children**   71

**5 Characteristics of Children: Implications for
Social Studies**   73
Childhood Traits and Social Studies / Disadvantaged
Children / Attitudes of Children Toward Social Studies

6 Stages in Social Studies Learning   84
Stages and Ages / Interpretation of Piaget's Stages /
Benefits to Teachers of Knowledge of Stages / Social Studies
Readiness

7 The Psychology of Teaching Social Studies to Children   96
Principles of Learning Social Studies / The Teaching of
Concepts / Classroom Management

part III   **Organizing and Teaching Social Studies Units**   113

8 The Social Studies Unit   115
The Content / Packaged Units and Teacher-Created
Units / The Resource Unit and the Unit Resource
Collection / Planning the Unit / Launching the
Unit / Teaching the Unit / The Effectiveness of Unit
Teaching

9 Citizenship and Government   134
Promoting Emotional Health / Providing Opportunities for
Practicing Citizenship / Teaching Citizenship Through
Following the News / Introducing Children to Government

10 Cultures Present and Past   156
The Study of Cultures / Culture Regions / The Way of
Life and the Beliefs of a Culture / A Culture's
Past / Building Global Understanding

11 Our Environment   176
A Controversial Subject / Some of the Issues / Teaching
Suggestions

12 The World of Work   195
Early Concepts / Business Enterprise in a Mixed
Economy / Consumer Education / Career Education

---

part IV **Special Teaching Strategies**   211

---

13 Promoting Critical Thinking   213
Classroom Conditions That Facilitate Critical
Thinking / The Discussion as a Vehicle for Critical
Thinking / Classification of Information / Training in
Problem Solving / The Inquiry Process

14 Managing Committee Work   232
The Function of a Committee / The Rationale for Having
Committees / Teacher Qualities That Promote Successful
Committees / Organizing for Committee Work /
Supervision of Committees / Interpersonal Problems /
Concluding Committee Work

15 Providing Creative Experiences   257
Contributions of Creative Experiences to Social
Studies / Factors Contributing to Creativity / The
Distinction Between Free Creativity and Creativity as an
Aspect of Social Studies / Creative Play and
Dramatics / Construction / Industrial Arts / Art / Music
and Dance

16 Providing Field Trips and Bringing in Consultants   279
Field Trips / Consultants / Museums

17 Using a Variety of Instructional Media   300
Guidelines for the Purchase, Use, and Evaluation of
Learning Media / Types of Instructional Media / Free and
Inexpensive Materials / Pupil-Constructed Media / Display
of Materials / Organization of Instructional Materials

18 Evaluating Pupil Performance   325
Mental Health Aspects of Evaluation / Some Characteristics
of Evaluation / Informal Evaluations / Testing Pupil
Performance / Records of Evaluations / Helping Children
Set Standards for Evaluating Their Own Performance / The
Place of Testing in Elementary School Social
Studies / Reporting Pupil Performance to
Parents / Delayed Effects of Instruction

part V **Academic Skills Through Social Studies**   349

19 Improving Reading Comprehension in the
      Social Studies   351
Why Teaching Reading Comprehension Should Be Part of
Social Studies Instruction / Neglect of Teaching Reading
Comprehension in Social Studies Classes / Techniques of
Teaching Reading Comprehension

20 Providing Writing Experiences   367
Kinds of Writing / Dictated Compositions in the Primary
Grades / Ways of Stimulating Writing / Teacher Praise
and Teacher Criticism

21 Promoting Understanding of Maps and Globes   378
Maps and Globes in the Primary Grades / Maps and Globes
in the Intermediate Grades

22 Guiding the Development of Time Concepts   411
Teaching Time Concepts / Construction of Time Lines:
Practical Considerations / Supplementary Ways of
Stimulating the Growth of Time Concepts

Index   423

part I Social Studies in the Elementary School

1 The Nature and Purpose of Social Studies

*Instruction in the social studies
ought to open up a new world of
interesting inquiry.*
Ernest Horn

In elementary schools,[1] "social studies" is the name commonly given to the curriculum area that embraces the social sciences. The field is enormous. Everything that is known and thought concerning social behavior— the institutions, the heritage, and the environment of human beings—provides potential social studies content.

Social studies offer teachers and their pupils the opportunity to learn about the world and its people—an exciting opportunity when a spirit of exploration pervades the classroom. In such an atmosphere social studies can become a fascinating part of the elementary school curriculum. The children, eager to know about the world, find in well-conducted social studies classes a natural and satisfying outlet; their curiosity is stimulated, their intellectual life is enriched, and their perception of ways in which they can occupy socially useful roles, both as children and as adults, is sharpened. Achieving these desirable ends requires lively presentations by the teacher, productive discussions between teacher and class, energetic participation by

---

[1]The term *elementary school* as used in this book designates the primary grades (kindergarten and Grades 1, 2, and 3), the intermediate grades (Grades 4, 5, and 6), and the middle-school grades (Grades 5, 6, 7, and 8).

all concerned in problem-solving pursuits, and exciting discoveries by the children. The primary purpose of this book is to suggest how such teaching and learning can be brought about.

THE NATURE OF THE SOCIAL STUDIES

A searching study, *Defining the Social Studies*,[2] identifies six "areas of evolving agreement," as paraphrased below. They sum up the most widely held conceptions of social studies specialists concerning their field.

1. The primary purpose of social studies is citizenship education.
2. The social studies field is not limited to one or even to just a few academic areas.
3. Knowledge is of prime importance.
4. Because of the importance of knowledge, the learner must know how to acquire it, how to make sense of it, and how to evaluate it.
5. The learner also needs to know how to examine values, beliefs, and attitudes, and why "caring" is important.
6. The learner needs to have practice in applying what he knows and feels by participation in civic enterprises.

Would most experienced elementary school teachers agree with these propositions? Probably so. To be sure, they would split on the interpretation of "citizenship education" in the first item. For example, some elementary teachers believe that, to serve citizenship education, social studies teaching must, above all, guide the child to become a responsible, sensitive member of the classroom and the school community. Others believe citizenship goals are served by emphasizing teaching of the "minimum essentials" in history and geography in order to give the learner acquaintance with landmarks of our past's achievements and firm knowledge of how the earth's cultures and resources are distributed. Such disparity in the interpretation of citizenship education may appear irreconcilable. Our contacts with elementary teachers, on the other hand, persuade us that the view of citizenship education held by most of them embraces elements of these seemingly contradictory interpretations. Most of them do not hold doctrinaire views on the subject. In discussions, almost all, after expressing their own preferred meanings and hearing the opinions of others, spontaneously agree that citizenship is a complex of diverse behaviors, concerns, loyalties, and knowledge. The above-listed six "areas of evolving agreement," at the very least, provide *some* points of unity that can facilitate curriculum planning by elementary-school faculties.

---

[2]Robert D. Barr et al., *Defining the Social Studies* (Washington, DC: National Council for the Social Studies, 1977), pp. 67–68.

IMPORTANCE OF THE SOCIAL STUDIES

The school, of course, is not the only place in which the child learns about society. Many children spend more time before their television sets than they do in school, and their viewing is by no means confined to children's programs. They view news broadcasts, discussions of controversial issues, travelogues, and entertainment programs featuring crime, divorce, shady business deals, and other problem situations. Children also overhear, and sometimes participate in, adult conversations about social issues.

While the school obviously has no monopoly on social studies education, it nevertheless carries a heavy responsibility for extending it. The school should help children round out their knowledge and understanding, and enable them to check the accuracy of their randomly obtained impressions and arrange their knowledge in some kind of order.

The critical problems of today are social problems. They include poverty, war and foreign relations, inequality and injustice toward minority groups, unemployment and inflation, air and water pollution, inadequate health care, corruption in public life, voter apathy, labor and consumer problems, unequal opportunities for education, and military-industrial monopolies. The list could be greatly expanded.

Obviously, then, the children in today's classrooms will live out a good part of their lives in difficult times. It is not proposed here that their teachers should set them the task of attempting to solve national and world problems in the classroom. That would be preposterous. But social studies instruction should make children aware of the problems and the reasons they are not easily solved, what values should be taken into account in searching for solutions, and possible rational solutions.

Of course, social studies are important, not just because they deal with social problems, but also because they contain the information, the ideas, and the methods of inquiry that help make possible a satisfying and creative intellectual life. Furthermore, they can provide a basis for healthful social attitudes, such as tolerance of the dissimilarities between various cultural groups.

THE SOCIAL STUDIES AND THE SOCIAL SCIENCES

As stated in the opening paragraph, the social studies are derived from the social sciences. The social sciences, in turn, comprise the specialized fields of knowledge that deal with our social behavior and our social institutions. Elementary school social studies draw generously from many of them: the behavioral sciences, political science, geography, history, and economics. All are described in general below and in detail in Chapter 2.

The Behavioral Sciences

The term "behavioral science" is fuzzy. Deciding which branches of which fields are properly classified under its rubric is not always a precise matter. The social sciences most clearly and consistently classified as behavioral are *psychology, sociology,* and *anthropology.*

Psychology is a relatively new recruit for the elementary school curriculum and the focus is upon social psychology. Social psychology, holding particular promise for society, deals with the interactions between individuals and between individuals and groups. Sociology concentrates upon the groups and institutions found in any society—family, school, church, economic system, and government; and upon social processes: cooperation, competition, conflict, assimilation. Anthropology includes the study of cultures and social systems.

Political Science

Political science embraces the structure of local, regional, and national governmental institutions, the content of state and national constitutions, contrasting types of political institutions and their functions throughout the world, and the nature of political parties, public opinion, and international law. In elementary and high school the field used to be called "civics," emphasizing responsibilities of citizenship.

Geography

Geography is the study of the regions of the earth, with special emphasis upon human relationships to habitat (land, climate, and other physical features) and how these relationships are influenced by human energy, imagination, technical skill, aesthetic instincts, traditions, and beliefs.

History

History was succinctly defined by historian Charles Beard as all that has been done and said on earth since time began. Only a small portion of history, of course, has been recorded. Even the recorded portion is too vast to be mastered by a single historian.

Economics

Economics is the study of our use of resources. It deals with the production, distribution, and consumption of *commodities* and with the utilization of *services* of all types, from the unskilled to the professional.

The Overlapping of the Social Sciences

It is apparent that the five fields of the social sciences overlap one another. Moreover, the specialists themselves, in their research and writing, cut across the boundaries freely and frequently and do not regard them as sacrosanct. The disciplines obviously merge in such subfields as economic history, political geography, and historical sociology. In addition, any given problem may be attacked independently by scholars in diverse fields. For example, public opinion is studied by political scientists as well as by behavioral scientists; tariffs and other trade policies are by no means the monopoly of political scientists, but fall within the domain of both economists and geographers; and the pollution of the environment and efforts to conserve natural resources have been investigated by scholars in all five fields. In view of such extensive overlapping, then, it would be arbitrary and artificial for the teacher to try to keep the teaching of any unit of instruction neatly within the confines of a single social science.

Example of an Interdisciplinary Study. An interdisciplinary social studies topic contains material that cuts across the boundaries separating the various social sciences. Thus, a unified third-grade study of the Plains Indian might contain the following items:

> The taboos, rites, ceremonies, and religious beliefs of the Plains Indians have counterparts in our modern society in which individual behavior is similarly influenced. (Anthropology)
> The Plains Indians were governed by local chiefs who lacked supreme authority; critically important questions were decided by councils of men or warrior societies. Today the federal government recognizes the Indians as citizens and gives them the right to establish local governments. (Political Science)
> What nature provided differed from one section of the country to another; consequently, the food, clothing, and shelter of the Plains Indians varied widely from those of Indians of markedly differing habitat. (Geography)
> The Plains Indians got their first horses from the early Spanish settlements in what is now New Mexico and Arizona. (History)
> The Plains Indians' division of labor was limited to the division of tasks between men and women (for example, men hunted buffalo, and women cut up the animals, prepared the meat, and dressed the hides); but there was no division of labor in the modern sense of mass production and specialization of occupations, with consequent interdependence of workers and regions. (Economics)

The Artificiality of the Controversy over Interdisciplinary Studies

Many words have been wasted in arguments over whether social studies should be offered on a cross-disciplinary or single-subject basis. No social scientist bothers to classify formally, according to subject, the information he uses in his search for answers to the problems he is exploring. The historian working on Lewis and Clark is concerned with the total social context of the expedition, its geographical, economic, sociological, and other aspects. What is unique is the historian's *focus* of concern, that is, the *point of view* he brings to bear upon his study, and his *methods* of work. (These are discussed for each of the social sciences in Chapter 7.) Generally speaking, cross-disciplinary studies are eminently suitable for children in the primary grades; and in the upper elementary grades most of the social studies continue to be interdisciplinary. The older the children are, the more they should learn each year about how the social sciences are differentiated, just as they should become increasingly aware in their study of science of the separate fields of chemistry, biology, astronomy, and others.

RELATION OF SOCIAL STUDIES TO THE HUMANITIES

The humanities have an indispensable contribution to make to elementary school social studies, chiefly through literature and the fine arts. One of the most faithful means of capturing the spirit of a culture—whether a contemporary culture or an ancient one—is through its literature, art, and music. Many illustrations drawn from the humanities will be given in succeeding pages.

AIMS OF SOCIAL STUDIES INSTRUCTION

George Santayana declared that "fanaticism consists in redoubling your efforts when you have forgotten your aim." Teachers who lose sight of their objectives often react similarly; they may work even harder than before, but their efforts are wastefully expended and erratic. In teaching, as in other fields of endeavor, the slighting of objectives is a calamity. A mere exertion of extra "effort," however conscientious, fails to compensate for lack of purpose and direction.

There is no dearth of statements of goals. Every curriculum guide contains them. Unfortunately, most of them have had very little effect upon instruction. The statements of aims appearing in hundreds of courses of study and curriculum guides suffer from a common shortcoming: They appear to have little relationship to the proposed content. The most noble goals are of no consequence if they remain isolated from what goes on in the classroom. The failure of these general objectives to become operational has resulted in recent years in a drive to have teachers formulate behavioral objectives instead.

It is important that teachers think in terms of both general *and* behavioral objectives. The former help teachers to obtain a depth of purpose and provide the philosophical underpinnings without which their work could readily become automatic and shallow, while the latter help them translate goals into observable performance. Each type will be discussed in turn.

GENERAL OBJECTIVES

Knowledge and Understanding

Part of our role as educators is to pass on to each succeeding generation important facts and ideas that have been received from past generations.

Thus, children come to know what adults have learned, and believe to be true, about society. Children thus gain a sense of society's continuity and stability.

Some major general objectives in social studies are the achievement by children of knowledge and understanding of:

1. The cultural history, traditions, and values of the child's own society.
2. The cultural history, traditions, and values of selected other societies, representing a variety of beliefs and practices.
3. The relation of human beings to their respective habitats.
4. The movement of the nations of the world toward interdependence.
5. Society's management and use of its resources.
6. The real world of work: blue- and white-collar occupations.

Attitudes toward Learning

As important as the acquisition of knowledge is, a spirit of inquiry, intellectual curiosity, and imagination play an equally vital role in the child's development. Many current ideas and items of information the child learns in the classroom are ephemeral. They represent the present condition of knowledge, but may not be appropriate five years from now. New discoveries are continually requiring revision of subject matter. The teacher is properly charged with bringing about a number of attitudes:

1. Toward the subjects and topics under study: curiosity about, and interest in, their subject matter.
2. Toward questions and problems: inclination to formulate hunches or hypotheses about their possible answers and solutions.
3. Toward the social studies area: desire to continue exploring it outside the classroom and to increase mastery of it.
4. Toward stereotypes: a desire to reject them and to make a fresh examination of phenomena; and a desire to form conclusions directly from raw data.
5. Toward tolerance of ambiguity: such as tolerance of partial solutions, which often are inevitable with human problems.

Social Values and Attitudes

Children, as developing citizens, require considerable guidance in interpreting what they learn about their complex world, and in acquiring a scale of values on which to base their interpretations.

You, the teacher, can realistically hope to cultivate in your pupils such general attitudes as the following:

1. Toward society: recognition of its need for justice and integrity.
2. Toward people: appreciation of human dignity, and sensitivity to the feelings of others.

3. Toward community and country: development of a sense of responsibility toward them.
4. Toward natural resources and the environment: desire to protect, conserve, and wisely use them.
5. Toward evidence: respect for it and acceptance of the rules that govern it.

Moral Character

Moral character is not the product exclusively of religious training, but an extension of attitudes and values. It is present in children who internalize (that is, adopt as their own, incorporate into their way of life) the rules of behavior of their culture.

It is true that many social scientists do not think of moral character as a goal of their field; they prefer to limit their objectives to the cognitive domain. Furthermore, many communities frown upon the school's involvement in this area. Sometimes children are precipitated into discussions beyond their depth. But moral character is generally considered to be an essential ingredient of citizenship; and citizenship education is, in turn, an indisputable part of elementary school social studies. Moral character is a long-neglected social studies objective, and little is known about how to attain it. Lawrence Kohlberg's proposal to meet it head on is described in Chapter 9.

Skills

Teaching social studies involves more than seeing to it that children amass knowledge and develop positive attitudes and social values. They must learn the requisite skills to do so. Social studies classes should provide practice and improvement of the following skills:

1. Language arts skills, including reading and interpreting books; oral communication for reporting, discussing, and interviewing; writing notes, summaries, and reports; parliamentary skills.
2. Study skills, including gathering and organizing information, checking reliability of sources, using techniques to enhance memory, and taking notes.
3. Critical thinking skills, including examining data objectively, classifying and judging the relevance of data, weighing evidence, forming hypotheses, and solving problems.
4. Map and globe skills, including interpreting map and globe symbols, estimating distances, determining directions, determining time zones, and using latitude and longitude.
5. Graphic interpretation skills, including reading and interpreting graphs, tables, charts, and time lines.
6. Cooperative group work skills, including organizing group projects, collaborating, and taking turns at leadership.

What General Objectives Do and Do Not Accomplish

The general objectives listed on the preceding pages denote an ideal scope of the social studies curriculum. Adherence to such objectives by a teacher or a curriculum worker prevents the curriculum from becoming too narrow (as it was in the days when the social studies consisted of little more than factual material from history and geography). They are useful to teachers as checklists for occasional reference to test the adequacy and comprehensiveness of the generalizations and skills they are stressing. Children will move toward the achievement of the general objectives if their teachers have thought them through beforehand and keep them constantly in mind.

Nevertheless, general objectives do have their shortcomings, some of which must have occurred to you while reading those stated in the preceding pages. First of all, they are banal to the extent that they express rather obvious ideas that have been tiresomely reiterated in education courses and books on education. They lack freshness. Second, they are nonoperational. They don't give even a hint of what specific content the teacher should use, in what manner the teacher is to perform, or what specific knowledge or ability the pupil is to attain. They are not sufficient to guide instruction. Many feel that behavioral objectives are the answer.

BEHAVIORAL OBJECTIVES

A behavioral objective describes the behavior the teacher wishes the pupil to achieve (or a task the teacher wishes the pupil to perform) following instruction. You ask yourself: What behavior do I want the child to exhibit upon the completion of this unit (or this lesson)? Here are some examples:

After Instruction:
- The pupil is able to draw a line on a community map showing the route he or she takes to school.
- The pupil is able to tell the class about one way in which our community is different from the community of an Eskimo child.
- The pupil is able to construct a graph to show the population of (a) Africans, (b) Europeans, and (c) others in the Republic of South Africa.

Note that each objective has an action-verb (*draw, tell, construct*) to describe behavior.

Advantages Claimed for Behavioral Objectives

The advocates of behavioral objectives start from the proposition that the purpose of teaching is to modify behavior—that is, to insure that the learner will be able to do something after instruction that he could not do before. Therefore, runs the argument, the sought-after behavior should be clearly defined for teachers in order that they will know exactly what content to teach and how to evaluate the effectiveness of their instruction. Thus, once the teacher completes a list of objectives for a unit, or a lesson, the curriculum is laid out! All one has to do is teach the behaviors (or tasks) contained in the list. The pupils, too, will benefit. They will know ahead of time what they are expected to learn and will consequently be able to apply themselves with greater purpose. The curriculum, having been broken down into wieldy segments arranged in a logical sequence, will be more meaningful and manageable for them.

Behaviorally defined objectives also solve the evaluation problem. As Albert Bandura states:

> When desired outcomes are designated in observable and measurable terms, it becomes readily apparent when the methods have succeeded, when they have failed, and when they need further development to increase their potency.[3]

At the completion of instruction, the teacher need only check the pupil's performance on each item in the list of objectives through observation or a paper-and-pencil test.

Precision is thus brought to both curriculum planning and evaluation, which have hitherto been extremely fuzzy. The exponents of behavioral objectives attribute this fuzziness to the teacher's reliance upon general objectives, such as "the improvement of citizenship." How, from such a value statement, they ask, can a teacher possibly know what to teach or how to determine what, if any, success he or she has had by the end of the school year? With behavioral objectives, on the other hand, pupils can demonstrate either that they can perform a given task or that they cannot. "I cannot emphasize too strongly," writes Robert Mager (often referred to as the father of the behavioral-objectives movement), "the point that an instructor will function in a fog of his own making until he knows just what he wants his students to be able to do at the end of instruction."[4]

The behavioral-objectives movement was given impetus in the 1960s by rapidly rising costs of education without a visibly commensurate improvement in the educational product. A clamor arose for schools to become accountable for "delivering the goods." Such a demand logically required that outcomes be specified in terms of objectives that describe detailed, specific performances.

Limitations of Behavioral Objectives

Despite the logical appeal of behavioral objectives, many educators and psychologists do not accept them as a final solution of either the curriculum

---

[3]Albert Bandura, *Principles of Behavior Modification* (New York: Holt, Rinehart and Winston, 1969), p. 74.

[4]Robert F. Mager, *Preparing Instructional Objectives* (Palo Alto, CA: Fearon, 1962), p. 3.

or the evaluation problem. J. M. Stephens, in an intensive analysis of the process of schooling, found that it consists largely of spontaneous, unsophisticated teacher behaviors and that the teacher's effect upon pupil learning is not likely to be improved by most deliberate innovations, including the insistence in some quarters upon behavioral objectives. He contends that teachers who have a lively interest in a subject, but who slight objectives even outrageously, would probably bring about greater subject-matter learning than teachers whose interest is less but who are punctilious about specifying objectives.[5]

Philip W. Jackson belives that advocates of behavioral objectives oversimplify what goes on in the elementary classroom, where the teacher typically handles four or five curriculum areas and where his or her work involves as many as a thousand interpersonal interchanges with pupils each school day—a situation that, he found, many teachers like! Moreover, he observes that teachers are intuitively more behaviorally oriented than they are often given credit for. He writes:

> As the teacher keeps his eye out for signs of restlessness and inattention, as he learns to discriminate between feigned and genuine involvement in a learning activity, his concern for concrete behavior is fully as great as that advocated by the proponents of behavioral objectives. Languid postures, drooping eyelids, averted gazes, these are signs that things are not going as they should. Teachers learn how to interpret this language of classroom behavior and adjust their instructional procedures accordingly. In so doing, they are about as closely attuned to the real world as they can be.[6]

The elementary teacher's major contribution, Jackson feels, lies in his or her ability to convince students that the compulsory activities facing them are worthwhile and that what they are doing is not just busy work.

David P. Ausubel and his associates point to an often overlooked weakness in the behavioral-objectives movement: ". . . an entire instructional program can be planned using Mager-type objectives without giving any consideration to concepts to be learned. . ."[7] In another comment, Ausubel held that to exhort curriculum workers to state their objectives in behavioral terms "often does more harm than good." He points out that it may lead them to "give more attention to relatively trivial but readily definable goals than to goals that are intrinsically more important but resistive to precise behavioral definition." He concludes:

---

[5]J. M. Stephens, *The Process of Schooling: A Psychological Examination* (New York: Holt, Rinehart and Winston, 1967), pp. 150ff.

[6]Philip W. Jackson, *Life in Classrooms* (New York: Holt, Rinehart and Winston, 1968), pp. 163ff.

[7]David P. Ausubel et al., *Educational Psychology: A Cognitive View*, 2nd ed. (New York: Holt, Rinehart and Winston, 1978), p. 380.

In the present state of our knowledge in educational psychology, it is probably more realistic and generally satisfactory to define educational objectives in grosser and more descriptive terms that are closer to the language of the curriculum worker than to that of the psychologist.[8]

Anthony G. Oettinger, too, reminds us: "Behavioral objectives with a strong taste of the explicit, the quantitative, and the measurable account for but a small fraction of the many effects we expect of schooling."[9]

A PROPOSAL FOR FORMULATING OBJECTIVES

Having seen that there are many disadvantages in both kinds of objectives, general and behavioral, one may wonder how to proceed in planning a social studies program or unit. Obviously, a teacher must have some goals so as not to be teaching a hodge-podge of unorganized, meaningless material. Both of these methods have strengths, and neither should be abandoned.

The solution lies in combining the two approaches. It is recommended that the teacher first prepare as many behavioral objectives as he or she can concerning the desired outcomes of his or her teaching. Even though they may be few in number, the usefulness of jotting them down justifies the effort. In listing them, the teacher should realize (1) that not all significant outcomes can be behaviorally formulated and (2) that typical elementary school teachers would find it impractical and probably impossible to write extensive sets of behavioral objectives for the several fields they teach. For these reasons, it is recommended that teachers supplement the behavioral objectives with general objectives.

The compromise offered here may not satisfy the more deeply committed adherents of the behavioral point of view, but it is probably the most realistic and satisfactory course of action. No matter how objectives—whether general or behavioral—are phrased, unless they are referred to by teachers from time to time and used as checklists and reminders, they will not be effective.

FOR STUDY AND EXPLORATION

1. Some laymen believe that educators spend too much time discussing objectives. One lay critic wrote: "Education is the only important profession whose practitioners spend much of their energy in an effort to decide just what the devil they are supposed to be doing." Is that how it seems to you? Why *are* educators so concerned about objectives?
2. Select a social studies topic you have taught or would like to teach, and use both behavioral and general objectives to indicate your goals.

---

[8]Ibid., 1st ed. (New York: Holt, Rinehart and Winston, 1968), p. 351.

[9]Anthony G. Oettinger, *Run, Computer, Run: The Mythology of Educational Innovation* (Cambridge: Harvard University Press, 1969), p. 221.

3. Visit a classroom and observe a social studies lesson. Draw conclusions concerning what objectives were probably being sought by the teacher.
4. The study of social studies teaching procedures, to be of maximum effectiveness, must be more than an armchair experience. Useful though books are, it is highly

---

BOX 1.1

Some Expectations and Activities for Fieldwork in a Social Studies Course for Elementary Education Students

By Gifford G. Hale, Florida State University

GENERAL EXPECTATIONS

The students are expected:

1. To find out the objectives for social studies and social education in the classrooms and schools visited.
2. To learn how social studies and social education fit into the total school program.
3. To examine the social studies materials available and in use.
4. To appreciate, through observing and helping teachers and children in social studies and social education activities, the work involved in planning, carrying out, and evaluating successful learning experiences.
5. To plan, try out, and evaluate at least one social studies/social education learning experience (of one attention span) selected to fit into the ongoing classroom program.
6. To assist the teacher by helping in the supervision and guidance of children, and by sharing materials obtained from the college social studies class.

ACTIVITIES

To make progress toward these expectations, the student should engage in the following activities in the cooperating school and classroom:

1. Study school and class guides for teachers.
2. Study the total school program and identify the social studies/social education aspects (duration and placement in the schedule).
3. Study materials (including texts, bulletin boards, library resources, audiovisual aids, etc.).
4. Study children—their interests, activities, and dialogue—recording examples of good learning experiences.
5. Plan a learning experience that fits into the ongoing program or one that is an acceptable and interesting experiment.
6. Try out the plan with the college instructor's and classroom teacher's guidance.
7. Evaluate children's learning resulting from the tryout of this learning experience.

desirable to supplement them with field experience. Professor Hale's plan for field work is presented with his permission in the box that follows. He has used it successfully for several years with his own classes, and it is recommended as a guide to any field work which may be planned to accompany the reading of this book.

FURTHER READING

Robert D. Barr, James L. Barth, and S. Samuel Shermis, in *Defining the Social Studies* (Washington, DC: National Council for the Social Studies, 1977), have produced a lucid summary of the social studies field. Their major contribution is in identifying areas of agreement as well as of disagreement, and in thus drawing attention to elements of order that are emerging in this complex field.

John Jarolimek has summarized the shifting emphases in elementary social studies from 1960 on, in "Social Studies for the Elementary School: Where Have All the Flowers Gone?" *Childhood Education*, 55 (October 1978), 26–31.

A forthright "position statement" on the social studies curriculum, dealing in large part with objectives, has been prepared by a committee of the National Council for the Social Studies and is published in *Social Education*, 43 (April 1979), 261–273. Page 276 contains a checklist for assessing the adequacy of the teacher's (or the school's) objectives.

An able defense of continued use of "general" objectives is made by John A. Zahorik, "The Virtue of Vagueness in Instructional Objectives," *Elementary School Journal*, 76 (April 1976), 411–419.

Chapter 11 in Robert M. Gagné's *The Conditions of Learning*, 3rd ed. (New York: Holt, Rinehart and Winston, 1977) continues to be one of the most persuasive arguments available for using behavioral objectives. A keen analysis of the behavioral approach is offered by Morton and Neil Botel, *A Critical Analysis of the Taxonomy of Educational Objectives, with a Sidelong Glance at Behavioral Psychology and Implications for Curriculum Development* (Washington, DC: Curriculum Development Associates, 1975). One of their conclusions is that behavioral objectives have "no theoretical or practical value."

Those desiring help in writing behavioral objectives will find the following books explicitly helpful:

Norman E. Gronlund, *Stating Behavioral Objectives for Classroom Instruction* (New York: Macmillan, 1970).

H. S. McAshan, *Writing Behavioral Objectives* (New York: Harper, 1971).

The student who wishes to probe some of the classic discussions of objectives will find several that are both readable and penetrating. One is Alfred North Whitehead's *Aims of Education and Other Essays*, first published in 1929 and now available in paperback (New York: Free Press, 1967). Whitehead, a philosopher and mathematician, doesn't treat social studies per se, but almost every page contains insights that are applicable. His style is vigorous and refreshing.

Charles A. Beard's *Charter for the Social Sciences in the Schools* (New York: Scribner, 1932) is thoughtful, sober, scholarly. The charter laid out by this great historian and political scientist remains applicable today. Another classic statement is by John Gardner, "National Goals in Education," which appears in *Goals for Americans: The Report of the President's Commission on National Goals* (Englewood Cliffs, NJ: Prentice-Hall, 1960).

2 The Social Sciences: Their Relation to Children and the Social Studies Curriculum

Human society is such an enormously complex subject that no single discipline can do justice to its intricacies.
Robert Bierstedt

Social studies is the name given to that part of the curriculum in which portions of the social sciences are taught. What are the social sciences? In this chapter, they will be defined and grouped under the following heads: behavioral sciences, government, geography, history, and economics. A balanced social studies program draws upon all of them, interrelating and integrating them as necessary in the organization of appropriate units for children's study.

THE BEHAVIORAL SCIENCES

The behavioral sciences are relative newcomers to the elementary school curriculum. They comprise those portions of psychology, sociology, and anthropology that deal with the behavior of individuals and groups. Because they require us to examine ourselves and our associations, it is more difficult to be objective about them than about those social sciences that deal with external entities, such as governments and treaties, and natural entities, such as climates and rivers. Yet the need for people to become objective about themselves and the groups to which they belong is obvious. Emotionalism and sentimentality often blind us. Only by stepping back and

BOX 2.1

Conceptual Structure of the Behavioral Sciences

Psychology, sociology, anthropology, and the humanities overlap considerably. This makes it possible, at least from the point of view of the elementary social studies program, to consider the fields together. We can examine concepts and generalizations relating to human behavior, and need not be concerned with their academic classification.

I. PEOPLE AS INDIVIDUALS
   A. We may logically begin with the nature of individual behavior itself. Behavior is *caused*, and is directed toward goals. Central to the behavioral sciences is this practice of thinking about causes and goals, and a disinclination to be satisfied with mere descriptions of actions, or with easily formed moral judgments.
   B. Each person is unique. Individuals differ from one another in inherited physical traits, in personality, and in behavior. These traits are the products of interaction among heredity, physical environment, and social environment.
   C. Most individuals realize only a portion of their potential. Many could increase their effectiveness by improving their self-image.

II. INDIVIDUALS AS MEMBERS OF GROUPS
   A. Each person is a member of several social groups, some of which overlap.
   B. The individual is trained to participate in a group or in society at large, and to accept its established norms.
   C. Other social processes are cooperation, competition, and methods for reducing social conflict—accommodation of some sort, such as compromise, or assimilation, such as the absorption of immigrants into the legendary American "melting pot."

III. BEHAVIORAL PHENOMENA AS CULTURE
   A. Social institutions tend to standardize behavior and stabilize society. Hence, social groups tend to become conservative and rigid—therefore, cultural lag results. Failure to make needed adaptations may result in a weakened society, internal conflict, and social revolution.
   B. A culture is dependent upon language for its development and perpetuation. Music and art also act as important transmitters of its essential spirit.

IV. BIOPHYSICAL PHENOMENA (RACE) AND CULTURE
   A. The races of mankind are differentiated by inherited physical traits that merge into one another.
   B. Racism and race problems are cultural phenomena based on emotionally charged opinions, which often assume the existence of race differences that have never been scientifically determined.
   C. Both racial and cultural differences add to the variety of human life and human behavior.

viewing ourselves in a detached manner can we hope to solve our formidable problems of crime, racism, poverty, broken homes, war, etc. Through studying the behavioral sciences, children may take first steps toward gaining a measure of objectivity in assessing the human situation and human events.

Children's Concepts of Human Behavior

Although children are familiar in a general way with fear, anger, competitiveness, prejudice, courage, cowardice, love, hate, generosity, and other manifestations of behavior, they are apt to think of behavior as something that "just happens." If a classmate is competitive, they accept this fact as a trait, like the color of hair or the shape of nose, without analysis. His or her behavior pattern may reveal itself in his or her efforts to be called on during classroom recitations, to win praise from the teacher, to get high marks, or to outdo others in sports. Children normally do not think of competitiveness as a possible front against weakness, a defense against feelings of inferiority, or an extroverted relish for activity.

A similar state of affairs exists with respect to their understanding of individual differences. Children are well acquainted with the surface phenomena of individual differences in height, weight, color of skin, speed, strength, and ability, and take them for granted. Yet they know little about how such differences arise in the first place, whether popular ideas about their significance are true or false, or how they may be variously regarded in different cultures.

What accounts for children's restricted knowledge of the reasons for variations in human behavior? Part of the explanation may lie in the abstractions inherent in the analysis of human motivation, theories of cultural change, and other topics of the behavioral sciences. Primarily, however, the school's traditional and continuing neglect of these sciences must be held responsible. Arthur T. Jersild pointed out, quite accurately, that the schools in our culture have "a policy of encouraging children to evade rather than to face their personal concerns."[1] Children learn little about the defenses they and others use to cover up their real problems, defenses such as "shifting the blame to others; assuming an attitude of self-righteousness; converting a weakness into an appearance of strength; taking flight into academic arguments . . . ."[2]

Research by Ralph Ojemann and his associates has shown that intermediate-grade children are capable of increasing their awareness of the complex, multiple, causative nature of human behavior. They have shown experimentally that children can learn that (1) there are many ways in which a given behavior pattern may develop, (2) causes are complex, and (3)

---

[1]Arthur T. Jersild, *Child Psychology* (Englewood Cliffs, NJ: Prentice-Hall, 1960), p. 456.

[2]Ibid., p. 461.

before applying a strategy to deal with a human problem, one should evaluate the proposed strategy in terms of its possible effects.[3] Evaluations of anthropology projects, even in the primary grades, also point to children's capacity for growth in understanding behavior.[4] The pioneering stage is over. It is now up to schools and teachers to undertake available programs and invent new ones in this productive realm.

Curriculum Trends and Issues

Programs in Anthropology. The most conspicuous innovation in all elementary social studies is the increasingly frequent inclusion of anthropological content. In certain programs, anthropology is presented to children in a pure, straight, unadulterated form. This is true of the *Anthropology Curriculum Project.* In other curriculums, anthropology is a part of a broad social studies program. Examples of these are *Concepts and Inquiry, Family of Man,* and *Taba Program in Social Science.* All of these programs are described in Chapter 4.

There is nothing new in teaching about primitive cultures (especially the American Indian) and foreign cultures, but much of the teaching in the past utilized material that was a mixture of romance, fancy, and anachronism. Contemporary programs have a factual, scientific base and are distinguished by the attention they give to the work of anthropologists—their methods, their equipment, their use of evidence, and the generalizations arising from their work. Older programs tended to neglect these significant features.

The introduction of anthropology into the elementary school curriculum is a welcome, humanizing step. Questions need to be raised, however, when it is allowed to dominate totally the primary-grade social studies, especially in kindergarten and Grade 1:

1. Are primary-grade children sufficiently grounded in the use of the social scientist's techniques (such as they gain by exploring and surveying their own locale and by comparing experiences and analyzing selected problems in connection with their own homes, school, and neighborhoods) to be able to understand how information about other cultures, that they learn at second hand, is gathered?
2. What opportunities can be provided for primary-grade children in the study of foreign cultures to gather and examine data, discover generalizations, and consider applications of the generalizations?
3. Is there a tendency for these studies to select unduly shallow

---

[3]Ralph H. Ojemann et al., "The Effects of a 'Causal' Teacher-Training Program and Certain Curricular Changes on Grade School Children," *Journal of Experimental Education,* 24 (December 1955), 95–114.

[4]Frances Emmons and Jacqueline Cobia, "Introducing Anthropological Concepts in the Primary Grades," *Social Education,* 32 (March 1968), 248–250.

generalizations for teaching? Consider the following, for example: "People everywhere must have food for life, but different people meet this necessity in different ways." Ought not children to know that the world is developing into a place of haves and have-nots, that half the world may go to bed hungry, that overpopulation and underdevelopment of technology are responsible, and that cultural mores make change difficult?

Programs in Social Psychology.   In the elementary school, programs in social psychology are fewer than those in anthropology. Two programs in current use set a high standard for others that will undoubtedly follow. One of these is *Social Science Laboratory Units*, described in Chapters 4 and 10, which emphasizes how the behavioral scientist works. The other is *A Teaching Program in Human Behavior and Mental Health*. More rigorously evaluated than most innovative curriculum programs, the latter is a simple attempt to help pupils undestand why people act as they do. It will be described in Chapters 4 and 9.

Studies of Foreign Cultures.   Most, if not all, elementary school curriculums include units on foreign cultures. The commonest practice has been to teach them in the intermediate and junior high school grades, primarily from the geographical point of view, often with sufficient history to show how the cultures have developed, and also with sufficient attention to their governments, ostensibly to "round out" the picture. Most textbooks take this approach. Actually, it leaves the picture far from complete. Gradually, the content is reflecting the upsurge of interest in the behavioral sciences, with resulting inclusions of an increasing number of anthropological and sociological concepts in curriculums. But the grip of geography, history, and government on "culture studies" remains strong.

Programs in Identity Education.   An increasing number of voices are expressing the need for children to study their identity and their relationship to others. This need arises from the failure of traditional education to succeed with the urban poor. Curriculums that are strictly academic and concerned exclusively with cognitive values have not proven effective with children whose personalities have been scarred by growing up in economically and culturally handicapped homes and communities, by race prejudice, and by general neglect. But there is no reason why programs in identity education should be provided for only the underprivileged, as most of them are. A healthy society requires that *all* children learn to understand themselves better and to improve their relationships with others. Activities are described in Chapter 9.

POLITICAL SCIENCE

The crucial issues of the day are being dealt with in the halls of government. Government is a political institution, but the issues themselves may not be political and, in fact, usually are not. For example, truthfulness in advertising is a moral issue; the control of pollution is in part a health, an aesthetic, and an engineering issue; and taxation is an economic issue. Government is required to make commitments about them. Even avoiding coming to grips with an issue is in itself a way (albeit a negative one) of handling it. How the government makes and enforces decisions and how the citizen relates to government are among the most significant matters for children to explore in the entire elementary school curriculum. This does not mean that units dealing exclusively with government and citizenship are needed. What is called for is more consistent attention to this vital field in all unit teaching.

BOX 2.2

Conceptual Structure of Political Science

I. THE FRAMEWORK
   A. Governments can be usefully classified according to (1) the way power is divided between national and local governments, (2) the extent to which autonomy is granted to nongovernmental groups, and (3) the identity of the ultimate ruling power.
   B. Modern governments may be classified, though imperfectly, as either democracies or dictatorships.
   C. Political stability requires governmental flexibility to meet changing conditions. The Constitution of the United States is an example of a governmental framework that provides such flexibility.

II. IDEOLOGIES
   A. To understand a government fully, one must know far more than its framework. Key questions are: What ideology dominates the government? What ideologies may be competing for control?

III. DECISION MAKING
   A. Governmental decisions are made by legal procedures and are strongly influenced by the interaction of personal, social, economic, and other forces within society.
   B. Pressure groups are among the most influential nongovernmental forces. Some pressure groups confine their methods to lobbying, electioneering, and mass propaganda; others add to these practices strikes, boycotts, and nonviolent civil disobedience; still others resort to violence to forward their ends.
   C. Voting during elections is a means by which the individual citizen influences governmental decisions.

IV. EFFECTS OF GOVERNMENTAL DECISIONS
   A. Many governmental decisions make a marked difference in citizens' lives. Ever fresh situations and challenges require that decisions be frequently revised.

(Continued)

V. PUBLIC OPINION
  A. Public opinion, the sum of individual citizens' views, is an impor-
     tant influence on political leaders.
  B. Methods of measuring, through polling techniques measuring
     both the direction and the intensity of opinions have been highly
     developed.

VI. COMPARATIVE POLITICAL SYSTEMS
  A. Different governmental systems may be compared with respect
     to their methods of providing external security, internal order,
     justice, welfare, and freedom, and their effectiveness in carrying
     out these objectives.

VII. INTERNATIONAL RELATIONS
  A. All governments are part of a worldwide system that is
     characterized by interdependence.
  B. A nation may have goals and values that conflict with those of
     other nations, and may seek to attain its goals through coer-
     cion—that is, by war or threats of war. Its success depends
     upon geographical position, size of population, wealth, military
     prowess, and psychological factors such as internal unity and
     the loyalty of its citizens.
  C. In a thermonuclear age, war between contesting nuclear powers
     would spell disaster for the human race. Because of this, inter-
     national law and international political institutions, such as the
     United Nations, have special significance.

VIII. CITIZENSHIP
  A. The school takes responsibility for inculcating such aspects of
     citizenship as concern for the social consequences of one's
     acts, recognition of the dignity of the individual, and belief in the
     necessity of pursuing one's own freedom only as long as it does
     not interfere with the freedom of others.
  B. In a thermonuclear age such as ours, safety dictates that some
     form of world citizenship be adopted, while at the same time re-
     taining national citizenship.

Children's Knowledge and Views
Concerning the Political World[5]

Children in the primary grades possess sketchy ideas of government,
which they associate with personal figures of political authority, such as the

---

[5]The data in this section on political concepts are drawn from Merton S. Krause,
"Schoolchildren's Attitudes Toward Public Authority Figures," *Adolescence*, 10 (Spring
1975), 111–122; David Easton and Jack Dennis, *Children in the Political System* (New
York: McGraw-Hill, 1969); Fred I. Greenstein, *Children and Politics* (New Haven: Yale
University Press, 1965); and Martha Wolfenstein and Gilbert Kliman (Eds.), *Children and
the Death of a President* (New York: Doubleday, 1956).

President and the police officer. They are inclined to evaluate such figures favorably and to view government as benevolent; they do not share the widespread cynicism and distrust of adults toward politics.

Growth in knowledge of the political arrangement is evidenced by the time children reach fourth grade, but gaps in their information are still wide. Thus, most fourth-graders in one study rated the President's job as "the most important," but less than one-third of them had a "reasonably accurate" idea of the President's duties. The reactions of preadolescents to the assassination of President Kennedy were mild and brief, in sharp contrast to the intense grief found among adolescents. Such lack of involvement in a momentous but remote event may be interpreted as a sign of incomplete political socialization.

Older children are at a more advanced stage of political socialization. They have *more* political information than younger children; their information is *more accurate*; and their ideas are *more general and abstract*. They are more inclined to associate government with elected legislative bodies and their lawmaking activities, rather than with personal figures. A growth in sophistication also is evident. For example, there is a shift from the starry-eyed idealization of leaders to a more realistic view. Party partisanship declines between Grade 4 and Grade 8 among upper socioeconomic groups, while self-declared "independent" political status increases. By contrast, children in primary grades usually follow their parents' party partisanship, with little question.

Factors in the Slow Development of Political Socialization.   Two explanations have been offered to explain the näiveté and inaccuracy of the political perceptions of primary-grade children and the subsequent slow growth of accurate perceptions. One explanation is that adults keep younger children immature by shielding them from harsh political realities, such as corruption and chicanery, and by teaching about politics in an unctuous and unrealistic manner. Fred Greenstein believes that adults "more or less unconsciously sugarcoat the political explanations they pass on to children," and goes on to develop a second explanation that may be more fundamental, namely, that "young children probably are unable to engage in the abstract cognitive operations inherent in ideological thinking."[6]

Would more systematic teaching about government in the primary grades bring about earlier political knowledge and sophistication? That knowledge can be imparted was demonstrated by Melvin Arnoff, who found that after a five-week unit on government, even second-grade children were able to identify correctly definitions of terms such as "subpoena," "ballot," and "campaign."[7] But ability to identify a term does not necessarily imply depth of understanding.

---

[6]Greenstein, *Children and Politics*, p. 77.

[7]Melvin Arnoff, "Added Depth to Elementary-School Social Studies," *Social Education*, 28 (October 1964), 335–336.

Curriculum Trends and Issues

As a school subject that is required by law in most states to be a part of children's education, government is taught in a remarkably patchy manner in the elementary school. Surprisingly, evidence shows, the lower grades may receive the most thorough citizenship training of the elementary grades.

Content.   In the primary grades, a class may look at the presidency in connection with the commemoration of Washington's and Lincoln's birthdays, discuss traffic safety laws, survey the work of governmental employees (librarians, policemen, teachers, and others), and learn how the post office, fire department, and other public agencies are supported through taxation. During election campaigns, many teachers discuss elections and voting with their pupils, and some classes conduct their own polls. A number of teachers see an opportunity for children to learn about governmental processes by having their own officers and by participating in classroom "town meetings." It is no exaggeration to say that responsible civic behavior is a major objective of most primary-grade teachers. They exhibit a genuine concern that their pupils learn to respect the rights of others, refrain from violating the personalities of their classmates, and recognize their own civic obligations. In fact, general observation leads many educators to conclude that primary-grade teachers are the most successful instructors of citizenship in the entire range of educational practice.

Study of government and citizenship increases in the intermediate grades. Courses or units labelled "civics" (a study of government intended as training for citizenship) have declined; frequently, portions of this field are taken up in connection with the study of history and, less frequently, with the study of anthropology and the community. Topics customarily touched upon (and "touched upon" is the right phrase) include the United States Constitution; the structure of federal, state, and local government; how a bill becomes a law; the role of the government in protecting health and in fostering recreation; civic-beauty education; law enforcement; the process of naturalization; the responsibility of the citizen for voting, serving on juries, and taking part in other civic work; and government and citizenship in primitive societies. Government is also lightly treated in most studies of foreign cultures.

In the junior high school, we again find government taken up in courses in United States history and culture regions of the world, but seldom in any depth. Civics has been the dominant ninth-grade social studies subject for more than 50 years. Its content has paralleled that of the elementary school and has been criticized for being woefully shallow for ninth-grade students.

Renewal of Old Insights Applied to Civic Education.   Several forces are leading to changes in the quality of the teaching of government and citizenship. While they appear new, these changes are derived from ideas that were vigorously advocated long ago during the era of progressive education.

The current interest among teachers in stimulating inquiry and critical thinking (see Chapter 13) is moving the teaching of government and citizenship from a largely descriptive treatment (with large chunks of moralizing added) to a treatment in which live problems are dealt with. Current issues on which children can cut their political teeth abound: the wisdom of using nuclear power for energy, school busing, the preservation and use of wilderness areas, and new urban-suburban patterns, to mention a few. This newer approach encourages pupils to dig below the surface of political issues and phenomena in search of possible causes and motivations.

Educators have lost faith in the traditional formal civics class, with its large doses of indoctrination and moralizing. It has seemed to lack significant impact. Its rejection is supported by studies of character training through character-education classes, Sunday school, and Boy Scouts. These studies have found little relationship between such training and results shown on behavioral tests of honesty or service on the part of children who participated in such programs.[8] (On the other hand, learning effects are often delayed, and the behavioral tests may have been given too soon after training.) This does not mean that we should therefore plump for the solution proposed by the "spare the rod and spoil the child" advocates in their view that character is best formed through early training involving punishment. Conditioning preschoolers in this manner at best brings about short-run conformity.[9] Implications are set forth in Chapter 9 where Kohlberg's suggestions for advancing morality are presented.

One of education's most productive assumptions is that children learn what they live. There are many fresh attempts today to provide children with opportunities to participate in their classrooms and schools as members of a democratic community. It is difficult to see how social responsibility and social sensitivity can be developed on a large scale without planning this type of experience for all children.

GEOGRAPHY

Geographical concepts inevitably form a part of every social studies unit, for in every unit the child learns about interrelationshps among a society, its culture, and its environment, and about differences and similarities between places. These relationships are the nub of geography.

---

[8]Lawrence Kohlberg, "Development of Moral Character and Moral Ideology," in Martin L. Hoffman and Lois Wladis Hoffman (Eds.), *Review of Child Development Research*, Vol. 1 (New York: Russell Sage, 1964), p. 388.
[9]Ibid., p. 389.

BOX 2.3

Conceptual Structure of Geography

I. OUR HABITAT

   A. The earth is divided into natural regions created by latitude, altitude, prevailing wind directions, atmospheric moisture, and other factors. In various combinations, these factos produce the earth's great regions of desert, tundra, permanent snow, prairie, steppe, rain forest, savanna, and various transitional types of regions.

II. HABITAT AND CULTURE

   A. The physical environment has no human significance per se; its significance is determined by the cultural group inhabiting it, and it is used accordingly.

   B. Although the culture of primitive people is sharply conditioned and restricted by their environment, in their more advanced stages people clearly dominate many aspects of their surroundings. They are not always wise in their manipulation, but they succeed in changing and utilizing their habitat in ways they believe will serve their needs.

   C. What people can accomplish depends on their drive, imagination, caution, energy, and technical skill.

III. NATURAL RESOURCES: THEIR USE AND CONSERVATION

   A. Our culture is dependent upon our natural resources. Some resources, such as metals, are in limited supply—a fact that the "recycling" movement dramatizes. Others, such as coal, oil, and other fuels, are destroyed after one use. Timber, soil, and game can also be depleted, although they can be restored through scientific management. Resources such as air and water are abundant, but, if polluted, can impair all forms of life.

   B. Among the destructive agents that cause environmental imbalance are industrial and home wastes, the exhaust of motor vehicles, reckless spraying of forests and farm crops, nuclear radiation, and building of highways and housing developments without consideration of ecological costs. The problem has been intensified by an energy shortage, resulting in construction of nuclear power plants and drilling for offshore oil—potentially damaging to people and their environment.

IV. AREAL VARIATION

   A. Areal variation refers to differences between places. The study of areal variation is geography's principal objective and its unique contribution to the social studies.

V. AREAL INTERACTION

   A. Peoples in diverse regions interact with each other. They exchange commodities, inventions, technologies, ideas, and customs.

Children's Geographical Concepts

As we mention in Chapter 6, children up to about seven years of age have limited ability in exercising certain cognitive skills central to geographic thinking. They make judgments in terms of how things look to them. For instance, they have difficulty in answering a question about a picture, spread out on a table, from the point of view of someone opposite, who is looking at the picture from a different perspective. Children find it difficult to understand multiple classification, which involves, for example, thinking of a person who lives in Omaha as living in Nebraska at the same time. Not until later do they discover the concept of hierarchy, such as that involved in city-county-state-nation-hemisphere relations.

It appears not at all certain, as is sometimes asserted, that children reared in our television culture are more precocious in their knowledge and interests than children of the generation preceding television. The evidence on this will be cited in Chapter 6. In one study, for example, first-grade children, in answering the question, "In what city do you live?" typically responded by naming a street or a state.[10]

Children also appear to grow slowly with respect to grasping the spatial relationships required for understanding maps. In a well-known experiment conducted by Piaget and Inhelder, children up to age seven were unable to tell how a set of cardboard mountains (on a table at which the child was seated) looked to a doll that was placed on another chair at the table. Even subjects at the operational stage (seven to eleven) performed on a mediocre level. John O. Towler and L. D. Nelson found that children also had difficulty with the concept of scale, so essential to map learning. These and other studies that reveal limitations of children's spatial concepts are discussed also (and footnoted) in Chapter 21.

Earlier training could possibly bring about readiness for certain skills, and more adultlike interests, sooner than they normally occur. If this were accomplished, however, there would be other matters to consider. Would there be an element of waste in such early training—that is, would most children learn these skills with greater ease a few years later? Many educators feel that there are no clear advantages, and there may even be possible dangers (inducing verbalism and anxiety) in trying to promote interest in remote subjects before the child has explored with satisfaction the more proximate aspects of his environment.

Curriculum Trends and Issues

Geography is taught in some schools as a separate subject, but more typically geographical content is included in studies of culture regions,

---

[10]Dorothy J. Mugge, "Are Young Children Ready to Study the Social Studies?" *Elementary School Journal*, 68 (February 1968), 732–737; see also a report by the same author in *Eementary School Journal*, 74 (April 1974), 399–407.

together with the content of their history and government. In these unified treatments, geography appears to be the leading element.

Studies of the Homeland.   Studies of the home and the local community are commonly taken up in the primary grades, sometimes making contrasts with community life in foreign cultures. Some schools provide surveys of the state or province in Grade 3 or 4. The entire homeland is commonly studied in both Grades 5 and 8.

Culture Regions.   Various ways of dividing the world into culture regions have been devised by geographers. One scheme consists of 11 major culture areas. Textbooks customarily reduce the number of areas by combining some of the 11. Thus, one widely used college textbook is organized around the following eight areas: (1) Europe, (2) Soviet realm, (3) Middle East, (4) Orient, (5) Pacific World, (6) Africa, (7) Latin America, and (8) Anglo-America.[11] This is essentially the grouping generally found in materials prepared for the elementary school.

HISTORY

The study of history gives the adult a needed perspective, a distinctive framework, for looking at and thinking about the present. The extent to which it has value for the elementary school child has been questioned, but the issue is by no means a settled one.

Children's Readiness for Learning Time Concepts

It stands to reason that the study of history will not have much value for children until they are able to acquire concepts of time. Time concepts include the *meaning* and *significance* (not definitions learned by rote) of terms such as *yesterday, century, era,* etc., and of abstractions such as a historical *movement,* a historical *period,* historical *change* (in customs, spirit, and values), *causes* of historical change, historical *sequences,* etc.

One study with exceptionally practical implications was conducted over a generation ago by F. Pistor. It deserves resurrection and attention. Pistor studied two groups of children, one of which pursued history in Grades 4, 5, and 6 with emphasis on chronology. The teachers of this group made extensive use of time lines and other time devices. The second group was not taught history in those grades except as it was informally introduced in connection with geography. Upon entering Grade 6, time-concept tests were administered to both groups. Quite surprisingly, the first group of children did no better than the second group. When examined again at the beginning of the seventh grade, both

---

[11]Jessie H. Wheeler, Jr. et al., *Regional Geography of the World,* 3rd ed. (New York: Holt, Rinehart and Winston, 1975).

BOX 2.4

Conceptual Structure of History

Most historians are far from certain that their subject has a structure beyond the chronological arrangement of events and the identification of historical periods. They sometimes refer to their field as man's organized memory and deny that it is a "science" like psychology or economics, governed by general laws or principles that make possible the prediction of events. Historians content themselves with carefully studying, explaining, and interpreting unique situations in the past.

If we think of history in terms of what we hope it may do for the child, we can at least conceive of a *teaching* structure. Thus, the child may acquire the following two concepts and their attendant generalizations:

1. Chronology. Space and time form a framework within which all events can be placed; events occur in a sequence, past ones influencing present ones.
2. Change. Change is continually taking place; not all change is progress; most changes are gradual.

The child can also begin to develop a few elements of historical-mindedness like the following:

1. Sufficient curiosity to wish to know causes of certain events.
2. Acceptance of the inevitability of change.
3. Willingness to brush aside wishful thinking and examine the facts.
4. Knowledge that the future cannot be predicted with certainty.

---

groups showed substantial gains. The difference between the scores of the two groups was not significant.[12] Other studies also furnish evidence that growth in time concepts is at least in part a matter of maturation.[13]

More recent studies have been reviewed by William J. Friedman[14] and by Michael Z. Zaccaria.[15] They, too, report slow growth of time concepts during childhood. Roy N. Hallam found that his British subjects reasoned about historical content at levels several years below those at which Piaget's child sub-

---

[12]F. Pistor, "How Time Concepts Are Acquired by Children," *Educational Method*, 20 (November 1940), 107–112.

[13]Paul Fraisse, *The Psychology of Time* (New York: Harper, 1963); K. C. Friedman, "The Growth of Time Concepts," *Social Education*, 8 (January 1944), 29–31; E. C. Oakden and M. Sturt, "Development of the Knowledge of Time in Children," *British Journal of Psychology*, 12 (April 1922), 309–336.

[14]William J. Friedman, "Development of Children's Understanding of Cyclic Aspects of Time," *Child Development*, 48 (December 1977), 1593–1599.

[15]Michael A. Zaccaria, "The Development of Historical Thinking," *The History Teacher*, 11 (May 1978), 323–340.

jects had reasoned about mathematical and science content.[16] All of the foregoing studies, old and new, point to the doubtful readiness of children of elementary school age to deal profitably with the systematic study of history. A few investigators have concluded that training does accelerate an understanding of chronology, at least at the sixth-grade level, but their evidence that the training produced much more than recall of chronological facts is unconvincing.[17]

The question is: How can the introduction of historical material be selected and paced in harmony with the child's slow, gradual development of time concepts? A curriculum plan that aims to do this is proposed in Chapter 10.

Curriculum Trends and Issues

There is greater emphasis now than formerly upon the cultural life of peoples of the past—that is, upon how people lived—and lesser emphasis upon political and military events. Many historians have been unhappy with the great stress that elementary textbooks traditionally placed upon political history. Charles Guzzetta submitted a list of historic persons named in fifth-grade social studies textbooks to a panel of 15 historians. The historians criticized the list's omission of representative Americans from the broad spectrum of cultural fields, and its overweighting with political personalities.[18] This is a situation that textbook writers should seek to correct.

A more fundamental trend is the decreasing emphasis in the elementary school upon formal history of any sort. Some radical proposals are in the wind. One historian recommends that, in the elementary school, we content ourselves with having children study the concrete present, and during the beginning years do little more than teach them to make careful observations and to examine evidence.[19] Another historian thinks that the practice of "covering" a period should be abandoned and that students should be invited to frame their own questions and to search for answers to them.[20] Still another proposal is that history be abolished as a series of courses and hereafter be viewed as a source in the learning of social studies.[21] These three

---

[16]Roy N. Hallam, "Thinking and Learning in History," *Teaching History*, 2 (November 1972), 337–346.

[17]Val E. Arnsdorf, "An Investigation of the Teaching of Chronology in the Sixth Grade," *Journal of Experimental Education*, 29 (March 1961), 307–313; O. L. Davis, Jr., "Children Can Learn Complex Concepts," *Educational Leadership*, 17 (December 1959), 170–175; and Edith L. Dodds, "A Study of the Sequential Development of Time Sense and Chronology in the Elementary School," *Dissertation Abstracts*, 24 (June 1964), 5075.

[18]Charles Guzzetta, "Children's Knowledge of Historically Important Americans," in Wayne L. Herman, Jr. (Ed.), *Current Research in Elementary-School Social Studies* (New York: Crowell-Collier-Macmillan, 1969), pp. 392–400.

[19]George E. McCully, "History Begins at Home," *Saturday Review*, 53 (May 16, 1970), 74–75, 86–88.

[20]Charles G. Sellers, "Is History on the Way Out of the Schools and Do Historians Care?" *Social Education*, 33 (May 1969), 509–516.

[21]Edgar B. Wesley, "Let's Abolish History Courses," *Phi Delta Kappan*, 49 (September 1967), 3–8.

proposals, it will be observed, are mutually supportive. They mark a tendency among thoughtful educators that is now having a small but unmistakable impact on the social studies curriculum.

ECONOMICS

Economics is an area from which many elementary school teachers shy away. Their intellectual interests tend to center around those aspects of life that deal with human involvement in social relationships, in language, in literature and the other arts, and in human development, particularly that of children. Elementary school teachers find the study of marginal utility, business cycles, monopolies, and other abstract economic concepts to be uncongenial.

In recent years, however, an ever-increasing number of teachers have learned to look at the field in a more favorable light. Pioneers in the field of economics education, such as Lawrence Senesh, have been largely responsible for this awakening interest—by providing for the first time appealing and teachable methods and materials. It has become evident that children's lives include some experiences that have prepared them for the study of economics.

BOX 2.5

Conceptual Structure of Economics

I. PRODUCTION AND MARKETING
   A. A society's income is determined by the total output of goods and services that are created to meet the wants of its members. Its market value is referred to as the Gross National Product (GNP).
   B. Only by increasing the GNP is it possible to increase the standard of living of a society.
   C. Potential GNP is limited by the availability of (1) natural resources, (2) industrious workers, (3) capital for investment, (4) technological knowledge, and (5) opportunity for economic initiative.
   D. Division of labor and specialization are features of the modern production system. They have resulted in interdependence, making it unnecessary for people to strive to be self-sufficient.
   E. Supply and demand determine price and are guides to production. High prices of a product attract others to produce the same product, whereas low prices discourage new enterprises.
   F. Banks perform an indispensable function in production. A manufacturer or other producer may not have enough money on hand to buy what his business requires, such as additional merchandise or new machinery, so he applies to a bank for a loan.

(Continued)

II. CONSUMPTION AND THE DISTRIBUTION OF INCOME
   A. The most basic economic wants are food, clothing, and shelter.
   B. Income received from wages, dividends, and rents determines the size of the consumer's claim to goods and services.
   C. Consumer decisions concerning spending and saving determine what and how much is produced.

III. ROLE OF GOVERNMENT
   A. Government influences economic life through manipulating a number of mechanisms: fiscal policies, regulations affecting foreign policy, domestic loans, public ownership, operation of schools, and many others.
   B. Taxes are the main means of diverting income from private hands to government.

Children's Economic Concepts

A number of reports on the teaching of economic concepts in the primary grades indicate that many children are capable of learning aspects of the economic system, and are interested in doing so.[22] On the other hand, children also exhibit difficulty in abstract analysis, as brought out in Chapter 6. Most economic processes and problems call upon the learner for more than average use of logic and systematic thought, and more than average persistence. All of these traits are correlates of both age and intelligence.[23] Even high-school students who have studied economics show but a slight grasp of the principles they are taught; in one study, high-school students knew fewer than one-third of the test items and, following a six-week unit on economics, still could respond correctly to fewer than half of them.[24]

Curriculum Trends and Issues

Most of the economics studied by children is of the descriptive variety. In a study of agriculture, for example, they learn about the proportion of the working population that is engaged in farming, and the transportation and marketing of crops. Seldom do they analyze the interaction phenomena such as supply, demand, and prices, or the law of diminishing returns as it affects the worker's productivity in developing countries.

---

[22]Marilyn Kourilsky, "The Kinder-Economy: A Case Study of Kindergarten Pupils' Acquisition of Economic Concepts," *Elementary School Journal*, 77 (January 1977), 182–191; and Karen F. A. Fox, "What Children Bring to School: The Beginnings of Economic Education," *Social Education*, 42 (October 1978), 478–481.

[23]David P. Ausubel et al., *Educational Psychology: A Cognitive View* (New York: Holt, Rinehart and Winston, 1978), pp. 256, 576.

[24]Edward G. Sewell, "Effects of Classwork in Economics on Attitudes and Understanding of a Select Group of Secondary School Pupils," *Journal of Educational Research*, 57 (November 1963), 131–136.

Yet evaluations of the Senesh textbook series, *Our Working World* (see Chapter 4), has shown that many children are capable of performing simple economic analysis.[25] The secret appears to be that the situations to be analyzed have been presented by Senesh in simple, interesting, concrete form.

FOR STUDY AND EXPLORATION

1. Select a topic you have taught or would like to teach. List some items of its content, indicating the disciplines with which each item is primarily associated. Plan how the social sciences from which the content is drawn can be presented in intellectually honest form and yet be comprehensible to children.
2. Do the curriculum trends as indicated in this chapter suggest a move toward traditional emphases of the past, or do they suggest movement toward innovation? Give supporting evidence for your answers.
3. For which of the five subject areas do children of five or six years of age appear to have the greatest readiness? What is the evidence? How compelling is the evidence? What are the curriculum implications?

FURTHER READING

See the penetrating articles on trends in the social sciences which take up most of one issue of *Society*, 15 (March/April 1978), 18–54. They are written by leaders in the fields of sociology, comparative politics, psychology, and economics.

Many natural scientists used to scoff at the social sciences, believing the term "science" to be pretentious, if not, indeed, a travesty. Today, however, the National Academy of Sciences includes an "Assembly for Behavioral and Social Sciences" (ABASS) within its organization. This new development is described by Constance Holden in "ABASS: Social Sciences Carving a Niche at the Academy," *Science*, 199 (March 17, 1978), 1183–1187.

Differences and common bonds between science and social science are brought out by George P. Zimmer (a scientist) in "Personal Reflections in Science and Social Science" in *Social Education*, 41 (February 1977), 128–131.

A critical view of social scientists is taken by Russell Kirk in "Narrow Vision," *Society*, 15 (March/April 1978), 52–54, who, with considerable justice, calls attention to their disregard of the role of religion in society, their lack of historical perspective as they focus upon present issues, their ignorance of humane learning, and their lack of vision.

---

[25]A. Guy Larkins and James P. Shaver, "Economics Learning in Grade One: The USA Assessment Studies," *Social Education*, 33 (January 1969), 958–963; and Sol Spears, "Children's Concept Learning in Economics under Three Experimental Curricula," *Dissertation Abstracts*, 28 (January 1968), 2462-A.

3 Trends in Elementary Education: Their Effect on Social Studies

> *We can no longer speak of "the slow change of time."*
> **Carl Bridenbaugh**

We live in an era of change, so it should not be surprising that the elementary school, along with other social institutions, is in flux. It has been receptive to many new ideas over the past 20 years, and it continues to be modified through innovations and shifts in emphases. Some of the movements dealt with in this chapter, such as the nongraded school, may already have peaked, but it is a rare school whose practices have not been shaken up in one way or another by the forces that created these movements. This chapter will show how social studies may function under the new arrangements and emphases.

BACK TO BASICS

Our schools are under public pressure to drop the frills and take the curriculum "back to basics." A Gallup poll determined that 83 percent of the public familiar with the movement to return to basics were in favor of it.[1] To most of the people polled, back to basics meant primarily a return to teaching the three Rs.

---

[1]*Gallup Opinion Index*, Report No. 151, February 1978. Surprisingly, 57 percent of those queried had never heard of the term "back to basics."

Indeed, many people believe that to return to basics means teaching the three Rs exclusively and in isolation. Such a practice would be regrettable. While some children can learn the skills of "reading, writing and 'rithmetic" as isolated subjects in this way, most learners need to learn them partly in isolation, to be sure, but also partly in contexts in which the skills can be used in practical ways. The farther a tool is taught from its practical application, the less securely does it become established in the learner's repertoire. Mastery of the three Rs usually requires the motivation and insight that come from *using* and *applying* them.

Application of Reading Skills in Social Studies

What gives social studies a special significance in any program devoted to developing children's academic skills is its ample provision for use and application of those skills. The social studies create a *need* among children for using the three Rs. In social studies, children develop a feeling of responsibility for finding an answer to a question or for getting needed information for their committees or for reports, which of course requires reading. Such reading introduces children to new words, to the table of contents, to the index, and to maps, charts, and graphs.

In the process, children frequently pick up books which normally would be too difficult for them, and are propelled into reading situations which advance their vocabulary and reading skills by leaps and bounds. One fourth-grade teacher was surprised to find a youngster of mediocre reading skill, during a unit on Switzerland, reading the difficult Spyri book, *Heidi*, and another child using an adult encyclopedia to track down information about the timberline of the Alps. The readability level of a book is often not as reliable an indicator of the child's success in reading it as strong motivation to read it, background of experience for understanding it, and skill in using the context to predict the meaning of whatever "difficult" words and phrases it contains.[2]

Application of Writing and Math Skills in Social Studies

Situations arise in which children find they must learn how to write a business letter to secure information for preparing a report, or a thank-you letter following a trip (Chapter 20). Other situations call for meaningful use of math, such as measuring in constructing an exhibit or stage sets (Chapter 15), using ordered pairs of numbers when working with latitude and longitude (Chapter 21), drawing a time line to scale (Chapter 22), or computing costs and profit (Chapter 12).

---

[2]P. David Allen and Dorothy J. Watson (Eds.), *Findings of Research in Miscue Analysis: Classroom Implications* (Urbana, IL: National Institute of Education and National Council of Teachers of English, 1976); A. M. Williams, *Children's Choice in Science Books*, Child Development Monographs, No. 27 (New York: Teachers College, 1939); Karl F. Nolte, "Simplification of Vocabulary and Comprehension in Reading," *Elementary English Review*, 14 (April 1937), 119–124, 146.

Part V of this book, "Academic Essentials through Social Studies," contains four chapters on subjects that are "basic." Those who define "basics" narrowly, in terms only of literacy and mathematical competence, run the danger of denying other important skills, or increased practice in the basic skills themselves.

MAINSTREAMING

Mainstreaming is providing the least restrictive environment for all children, regardless of their abilities, strengths, and handicaps. It is the procedure whereby mildly handicapped children are moved from special classes to regular classes. It applies to all categories of handicapped, including educable mentally retarded, emotionally disturbed, learning disabled, and physically impaired. Mainstreaming is a policy that has been backed by court decisions and law during the 1970s. It implies acceptance of the view that handicapped children should not be denied access to free public schools—that their education is a responsibility of every school system.

Research on Mainstreaming

Research has verified the feasibility of mainstreaming. It has shown, for example, that emotionally disturbed children assigned to special classes held no advantage over emotionally disturbed children with regular classroom experience only, either in academic performance or in social adjustment.[3] Countering the predictions of opponents to mainstreaming that handicapped children would prove disruptive in the regular classroom and would be rejected by normal children, it has been found that their frequently bizarre behavior is not necessarily disruptive; that, with continued exposure to the regular classroom, they can win positive acceptance by normal children, and show improved attitudes toward school and more positive perceptions of self.[4]

The chief problems with mainstreaming arise because most teachers of regular classes are reported not to support mainstreaming and are resistant to taking courses or attending in-service training in special education.[5] Furthermore, adequate teaching materials for the handicapped and adequate support personnel are often lacking.[6]

---

[3]Daniel J. Macy and Jamie L. Carter, "Comparison of a Mainstreamed and Self-Contained Special Education Program," *Journal of Special Education*, 12 (Fall 1978), 303-313; Nicholas A. Vacc and Nancy Kirst, "Emotionally Disturbed Children and Regular Classroom Teachers," *Elementary School Journal*, 77 (March 1977), 308-317.

[4]Macy and Carter, ibid.

[5]Vacc and Kirst, "Emotionally Disturbed Children and Regular Classroom Teachers."

[6]Ellen Kavanagh, "A Classroom Teacher Looks at Mainstreaming," *Elementary School Journal*, 77 (March 1977), 318-322.

On the other hand, some teachers who have taught social studies to mainstreamed groups believe that benefits accrue to all children. They contend that both groups benefit by simply rubbing elbows while on field trips and while engaged together in map making and other projects. It is probably true that normal children tend to develop empathy and learn how to be helpful without being bossy or intrusive, and the handicapped tend to learn the need to develop independence in the regular world.

Examples of Social Studies under Mainstreaming

Consider the case of mildly retarded children during a social studies discussion. Contributions of the nonhandicapped pupils are, more often than not, stimulating to the handicapped and arouse interest and curiosity that a teacher alone could not produce. A handicapped pupil, on the other hand, may raise questions that bring the class back to fundamentals and provide an opportunity for normal pupils to explain situations and principles. During one discussion, for instance, a handicapped pupil asked that an explanation of a flow chart be repeated. In another classroom, a normal child advanced the understanding of a learning disabled classmate by explaining to her how to select the volume in an encyclopedia set which would contain an article on wheat, while at the same time developing his own expository skills. Other ways in which normal and handicapped have profitably collaborated in social studies include teaming together in explaining frames of a filmstrip, serving on a committee to arrange a bulletin board exhibit, taking part in a Columbus Day dramatic skit, supplying examples of how names of newly born are sometimes selected, and reviewing a field trip.

Essentials for Successful Mainstreaming

Successful programs for improving the functioning and adjustment of handicapped children depend upon personal warmth and patience on the part of the teacher, small classes, intimate personal relations between teacher and pupils, and a family-type climate in the classroom. These conditions, beneficial to children at all levels of intellectual, emotional, and physical functioning, appear to be absolutely critical to the success of mainstreaming.

"INDIVIDUALIZED" INSTRUCTION

Critics of education are increasingly insistent that schools become accountable for the outcomes of student learning. The most direct response to this demand has been widespread use of a variety of devices for individualizing instruction—workbooks, work sheets, programmed materials, learning kits, and computer-assisted instruction.

Forward-looking educators think of individualized instruction as providing custom-tailored activities to individuals or small groups in order to meet their specific learning needs. The present tide of individualized instruction, however, is quite different in nature. It may merely make it possible for each pupil to proceed at his own pace, with the activities and exercises precisely the same for all. Discriminating educators look askance at this brand of individualized instruction, some even regarding it as a travesty of the term individualization. That is why the term has been placed within quotes in the heading of this section.

Individualized Instruction in Action

In its simplest form, each student is provided with a workbook to be gone through systematically at his or her own pace. A typical workbook begins each lesson by informing the student of that lesson's purpose. It may state: "This lesson will tell you how crops are affected by rainfall." A printed description of the relationship between rainfall and crops follows. When the lesson is completed, the workbook may present a test designed to evaluate the student's success in meeting behavioral objectives determined for that lesson. One item in the test may call for filling in blanks: "Land which has less than 10 inches of rainfall in a year is called _____." Multiple-choice test items are also used: "Of the following two crops, which requires less rainfall than the other? _____ (a) rice; _____ (b) wheat." The student then consults an answer sheet, thus receiving immediate feedback. If correct answers fall below 90 percent of the test items, the student either repeats the lesson or is put on a different "track"—i.e., a page which presents the lesson more simply and assumes less background or ability on the part of the student. Eventual mastery is insisted upon, and the teacher's and the school's accountability is thus theoretically assured.

In a more sophisticated form, a computer-based program is used. The teaching materials are carefully programmed—that is, the content or skill to be learned is arranged in sequential steps, each a little more advanced than the one before. The program provides video displays, and feedback includes direct instruction to each student, such as an explanation of why an incorrect answer is wrong. A record of each student's performance is automatically maintained. If the range of pupil ability in a class is wide, a large number of computer programs may be generated so that all pupils are able to achieve the same objective. Theoretically, a computer-based system can be constructed that contains as many programs as there are combinations of pupil ability, learning style, and background of knowledge.

Individualized instruction is most readily applied to the learning of skills, and it is in the skills area that it most frequently operates in the elementary school.[7] Students are exposed to a series of fragmented goals. It is evident that the teacher's traditional role of presenting information to the

---

[7]For an informative and interesting account of how it was adapted to teaching spelling and math in second grade, see Thomas J. Werner and Stephen F. Bono, "The Application of PSI to a Second Grade Classroom, or, The Lone Ranger Rides Again," *Educational Technology*, 17 (September 1977), 20–24.

class shifts radically. Teachers become advisers and consultants. The teaching-learning process is depersonalized. Individualized instruction makes no provision for supplying nurturance to immature or dependent students who may need it. On the positive side, individualized instruction is clearcut and efficient and allows for self-pacing by students.

Limitations of Individualized Instruction in Social Studies

Karen Kepler and Jill W. Randall bring out some harmful distortions of education that occur when individualized instruction is applied to social studies: (1) The content of social studies becomes divorced from children's more immediate social studies experiences and interests. (2) The content is that which is most easily translated into kit form, such as map skills, and not that which could provide insights into social relationships and social processes. (3) A "fill-in-the-blank, circle-the-answer" mentality sets in—and vast boredom! "The teacher simply plugs the child into the right workbook, the right kit, or the right worksheet."[8]

Programmed and computer-assisted social studies are being developed that can be carried out with remarkable (if dehumanized) efficiency. It is important to heed the caveat of David P. Ausubel that such "individualization," the use of programmed and computer-assisted instruction, "cannot constitute a complete and self-contained program of individualization, since it does not provide for pupil-pupil and pupil-teacher interaction. In addition, those aspects of instruction in which knowledge is less well defined and in which the acquisition of independent and critical thinking ability is a major goal obviously require more class discussion and direct teacher participation."[9] Social studies is such an area, and requires the categories of experience mentioned in our discussion of the back-to-basics movement such as independent investigation, committee work, browsing among social studies books, drawing time lines, and writing for information.

THE MIDDLE SCHOOL

The middle school is a separately housed institution that incorporates pupils from Grades 5 or 6 through Grade 8. Their number doubled between 1968 and 1975,[10] and, arrording to one estimate, there may be more than 10,000 middle schools by 1986.[11]

---

[8]Karen Kepler and Jill W. Randall, "Individualization: The Subversion of Elementary Schooling," *Elementary School Journal*, 77 (May 1977), 358–363. Support for individualized social studies is given by Anthony E. Conte and John D. McAulay, "The Need for Individually Guided Social Studies," *Social Studies*, 69 (March/April 1978), 52–55.

[9]David P. Ausubel et al., *Educational Psychology: A Cognitive View* (New York: Holt, Rinehart and Winston, 1978), pp. 296–297.

[10]Paul S. George et al., "Middle School Teacher Certification: A National Survey," *Educational Leadership*, 33 (December 1975), 213–216.

[11]Robert E. Fiedler, "A Solution to the Middle School Problem," *Clearing House*, 51 (March 1978), 322–326.

Purpose of the Middle School

The middle school was created as an alternative to the junior high school, which many believe has been a failure. The junior high school, embracing Grades 7 to 9, was founded in the early years of the twentieth century to give students during early adolescence an opportunity to explore their aptitudes and select their careers before entering senior high school, where they were to receive training in the fields of their choice. Not long after its birth, however, the junior high school abandoned the model that was originally advanced and took over the pattern of the senior high school. Its exploratory function declined, and increasingly heavy emphasis was given to the traditional academic subjects. This was due in part to the anomalous position of Grade 9. The subjects taken in that grade carried Carnegie units needed by students planning to enter college. A few junior high schools acted logically and dropped their ninth grades, thus becoming two-year institutions. Unfortunately, two years allowed insufficient time for students to establish themselves with their teachers and their peers. But the old junior high school, with Grades 7 to 9, persisted and in most places became an anachronistic institution. It seems now to be giving way to the middle school.

The middle school is a strange mix of 10- to 14-year-olds. To many, this grouping appears inappropriate. Its supporters, however, believe that the physical and psychological differences between students in Grade 5 and Grade 9 tend to be exaggerated. They point out that the age of the menarche has dropped from 14 in 1900 to slightly less than 13 today, that more boys and girls reach puberty in Grades 5 and 6 now than a generation ago, and that those who do not are at least more mature psychologically and socially than youngsters of their age were formerly. These adherents believe that because of the psychological makeup of this age group, consisting as it does of those who are either about to reach puberty or are already in its early stages, the group's members ought to be housed together so they can be placed with teachers who are specially trained and temperamentally equipped to teach them in this difficult transitional period. They contend further that, with the ninth grade turned over to the high school, the middle grades are freed from high school domination and can restore the abandoned concepts of self-exploration and establishment of personal identity.

Grounds for Concern about the Middle School

Educators have grown accustomed to organizational changes that promise much but fail to live up to the promise once the novelty wears off. There are grounds for skepticism in the case of the middle school. Its success will depend not upon a mere rearrangement of grades, but upon the depth of understanding on the part of principals and teachers and their commitment to helping pupils exlore their potentialities and find themselves. The maturational argument cited as the rationale for the middle school is not compelling. Despite the earlier physiological maturation of children, it cannot be claimed that many fifth- and sixth-grade children have reached puberty[12] or have attained the social maturity commonly found among eighth-grade pupils. Moreover, with respect to intellectual development, a more natural break would be between ages 11 and 12 (Grades 6 and 7) than between ages 14 and 15 (Grades 8 and 9). The former corresponds more closely to the transition between the concrete operational stage of cognitive development and the abstract logical stage, as described in Chapter 6.

Whether or not the middle school is able to provide the revitalization of learning that its advocates predict is yet to be seen. The evidence, based on comparisons of middle school and nonmiddle school academic achievement, student attitudes, and student self-concept, is inconclusive.[13] Middle school teachers, recruited from elementary and high school faculties, are not trained for the most part to focus on the developmental characteristics and the learning problems evidenced during this critical period.[14]

Improvements Needed in Middle School Social Studies

Despite its shaky theoretical underpinnings and its as yet unimpressive outcomes, the middle school is with us and will doubtless remain. There is a need for more teachers who can teach social studies with enthusiasm, who are student-oriented, and who know how to make appropriate use of the facilities in the new middle school buildings. These include space for independent and small-group study activities and social science laboratories. Older buildings can be adapted to provide such facilities. The opportunity is present for rethinking and restructuring the social studies curriculum so that it may be more challenging to children in preadolescence and early adolescence than current middle school social studies programs.

THE NONGRADED SCHOOL

The purpose of the nongraded school is to change the prevailing practice of uniform instruction to children in a given classroom—a practice that flies in the face of the well-known fact that children differ widely in

---

[12]Only 22 percent of girls reach menarche by age twelve. Ernest H. Watson and George H. Lowrey, *Growth and Development of Children*, 5th ed. (Chicago: Year Book Medical Publishers, 1967), p. 319. See also S. R. Berenberg (Ed.), *Puberty: Biological and Psychological Components* (Leiden: Stenfert Kroese, 1975), pp. 268–269.

[13]Jon W. Wiles and Julia Thomason, "Middle School Research 1968–74: A Review of Substantial Studies," *Educational Leadership*, 32 (March 1975), 421–423.

[14]Fiedler, "A Solution to the Middle School Problem;" George et al., "Middle School Certification." It is interesting to note that the British are experiencing similar difficulties in their middle schools. The British middle school is constituted somewhat differently (including children as young as eight and nine), but the purpose is the same—to offer a distinctive transitional program to bridge elementary and secondary schooling. See "Middle School System in Chaos" and "The End of the Middle?" in *Times Educational Supplement* (London), May 7, 1976 and November 26, 1976, respectively.

academic achievement. The nongraded school abolishes grade designations. Pupils are encouraged to proceed at their own rate without risking failure. The teacher provides learning experiences consistent with each child's state of readiness. For subjects such as reading and arithmetic, which are tightly structured, pupils are formed into subgroups according to level of achievement. The grouping is flexible so that children may be shifted from one subgroup to another if their progress either outstrips or falls below that of the majority in their subgroup. It is thus evident that, when the nongraded plan is limited to the first three years of school (the commonest occurrence), some children may require four or more years to complete the requisite amount of work. Consequently, the pupils in a given class are of varying ages.

Teaching Problems in the Nongraded School

Teaching in the nongraded school is difficult. It entails a curriculum that is vertically structured, with a sequence worked out in each area of instruction so that the teacher is never in doubt about the next step for a given pupil. Providing individualized instruction is doubly difficult in schools that combine nongradedness with the self-contained classroom, in which a single teacher is given total responsibility for the instruction of a group of children in a variety of subjects throughout the day. It places a staggering burden upon such a teacher, both in day-by-day planning and in attending to the various levels of achievement and different paces within the class. One solution is to reduce the class size. A second solution is to modify the self-contained classroom with some form of team teaching. These measures give the teacher time to take part in group discussions and to direct such social studies activities as problem solving, discovering new knowledge, thinking through alternative social behaviors, role playing, and dramatics.

Wide differences in the meaning of nongradedness among principals who call their schools "ungraded" may be a major reason for conflicting evidence concerning this innovation's impact on pupil achievement.[15] Many a nongraded school has adopted only surface features, causing John I. Goodlad, one of the founders of the nongraded concept, to comment that "there are, indeed, precious few nongraded schools."[16]

Place of Social Studies in Nongraded Schools

How may the social studies curriculum function in the nongraded school? There are several possibilities. For one, children may be grouped ac-

---

[15]One review of the research in this area concludes that pupils in programs that are labeled "nongraded" "perform as well as, and often better than, graded groups." Lyn S. Martin and Barbara N. Pavan, "Current Research on Open Space, Non-Grading, Vertical Grouping, and Team Teaching," *Phi Delta Kappan*, 57 (January 1976), 310–315.

[16]John I. Goodlad, "Editorial," *National Elementary Principal*, 47 (November 1967), 2–3.

cording to their breadth of background and their facility in acquiring new concepts. A different sequential arrangement of concepts may then be worked out for each group.

In a more promising plan, however, a single theme or topic is selected for study by the entire class. Everyone participates in discussions, dramatics, field trips, film-viewing, and other activities. In this way, social studies becomes a unifying experience, cultivating mutuality and *esprit de corps*. Opportunities for sharing experiences and for the expression of group feeling are highly desirable in a nongraded class, for the bulk of instruction divides the class into small groups. Social studies can thus bring the class together. There are, however, times when social studies, too, need to be individualized, such as when the learning of certain specialized concepts and skills are encountered—e.g., learning about the purpose and symbolism of map legends, time zones, and chronological relationships.

THE OPEN CLASSROOM

The teaching-learning methods of the open classroom are open-ended and the atmosphere informal. Children spend much time in small groups at tables, at the chalkboard, and at learning centers with all kinds of materials. At these and other places, alone or with others, children investigate concepts and develop skills. While at work, they are at liberty to talk with one another and to exchange ideas. So, unwittingly, they teach each other.

The open classroom may also be "open" architecturally, with unencumbered open space and portable walls. These commodious, adjustable quarters make it easier to carry out the flexible teaching-learning curriculum. But specially designed architecture is not a necessary feature of the open classroom. In an antiquated Philadelphia school building, for example, two enterprising teachers pooled their classes of 30 pupils each and obtained three contiguous classrooms that opened into each other. The two teachers met each Sunday to plan the learning centers for the ensuing week. They arrived at school early Monday morning to arrange the equipment and materials and to post accompanying sets of instructions and questions. Their plans covering a seven-week period are presented in Box 8.2.

Learning Centers in the Open Classroom

The "activity-center structure" described in Box 8.2 probably offers an open-classroom model that more fully lends itself to enriched social studies learning than do the more child-centered models. A classroom built upon this model may contain from 15 to 20 learning centers, replaced each week by another set, each of which offers something of fresh interest and challenge to pupils and has the potential of teaching an important concept or skill.

For designated parts of the school day the pupils move in small groups from center to center, undertaking each activity in turn. Directions and questions for each activity are either explained orally by the teacher or are given on a posted bulletin on the site of the center. One center, with a wardrobe of costumes and a box of props on hand, may be for dramatics. The three or four children who visit that center together are directed to dramatize a story, event, or situation. An additional center may contain various objects and a scale. The children are instructed to estimate the relative weights of each object and to check their estimates by weighing each on the scale. At another center a large map of the community may be posted, on which a pupil is asked to locate his or her home, trace the customary route to school, and identify the cardinal directions with reference to the locations of home and school. At still another center, children with headsets hold books in their hands and follow with their eyes the lines of print as a story is read by the teacher's tape-recorded voice.

There are no standard or approved activities. They are as varied as are the age, maturity, and needs of the pupils and the imagination and resourcefulness of the teacher. A learning center may contain an encyclopedia, a spelling test, mathematics problems, a writing assignment, objects with contrasting odors, books for browsing and reading, art and construction materials, classifying exercises, or a plant to be observed and nurtured. All such activities are used as tools of learning, as specified by the teacher-formulated instructions. Thus, the pupils spend part of the day in

FIGURE 3.1.   The open classroom is characterized by a variety of learning centers, small groups of children, and attention to individual differences in learning. Courtesy of Prince George's County Public Schools, Maryland.

small groups, handling materials, testing themselves, demonstrating things to one another, teaching each other, raising questions with each other, and critically appraising each other's responses.

Teachers bear a heavy responsibility throughout. They plan and supply the learning environment and see that it is constantly renewed and kept challenging. They move about the room to help as required. They supply feedback to pupils as needed, so that they may evaluate the accuracy or appropriateness of pupil performances. They keep a record chart, which shows activities completed by each pupil. They determine which children need special help in developing reading, writing, and other skills, and teach them in small groups that are relatively homogeneous with respect to academic achievement. In some open classrooms, teachers allot approximately half the day to learning centers and associated activities. The balance of the day is used for art, music, discussions, role playing, literature, and skill periods.

Evaluation

The open classroom was brought to the United States from England in the expectation that it would increase motivation for learning among children and would promote academic growth and creative thinking. Subsequent research shows mixed results. Considered as a whole, the open classroom appears to have no consistent or clearcut advantage over conventional classrooms in these respects, and some disadvantages have been reported.[17] The conflicting findings may be attributable to the inability of conventional tests to measure the broad cognitive growth that the open classroom aims to produce. Presumed gains in motivation, confidence, and independent thinking apparently have not been adequately looked into. It may be that such gains could not be expected to manifest themselves in test scores for years to come.

Many teachers like the teaching-learning format of the open classroom and have faith in it. Visitors have generally been favorably impressed by the positive spirit, vigor, and industry of its pupils. It is a format and a method of teaching in which the social studies can be appealingly taught.[18] Whether or not it yields superior learning has yet to be determined.

TEAM TEACHING

Team teaching is an effort to create a richer school program through the cooperative planning of a team of teachers. Its usefulness as an adjunct to the open classroom has already been shown.

---

[17]Paul S. George, *Ten Years of Open Space Schools: A Review of Research* (Gainesville, FL: University of Florida, 1975); and Ann Lukasevich and Roland F. Gray, "Open Space, Open Education, and Pupil Performance," *Elementary School Journal*, 79 (November 1978), 108–114.

[18]Evelyn Berger and Bonnie A. Winters, *Social Studies in the Open Classroom: A Practical Guide* (New York: Teachers College Press, 1973)

How Team Teaching Works

The team members, with a leader, collaborate in mapping out and coordinating the work of the pupils, each teacher seeking to supplement and reinforce to a significant degree the work of his or her colleagues. Class schedules and the grouping of pupils are kept flexible. Although normally a teacher works alone with a group of pupils, sometimes situations arise in which groups are brought together and two teachers work simultaneously with them in agreed-upon ways. One asset of team teaching is the opportunity afforded for a broader-based evaluation of pupil performance than is possible when a single teacher is called upon to make his or her sole judgment—the usual situation in a self-contained classroom.

The frequently made objection to departmentalization, namely, the threat to the children's security when they must adapt to several teachers each day, applies with less force to team teaching. Although departmentalization tends to chop up the curriculum into unrelated fragments, team teaching aims to unify the curriculum and to coordinate the work of each pupil.

Both students and teachers say they like the team-teaching arrangement.[19] The findings concerning its merits, however, are mixed, due in large part to the wide range of variables that are inevitably involved.[20] Its success depends, of course, upon the degree of harmony existing between or among the team's teachers, and the care with which each makes preparations for the daily program.

Place of Social Studies under Team Teaching

One of the members of a teaching team should be a person with special background and interest in the social studies—one who will accept responsibility for directing the social studies program. The field's diversity in content, materials, and activities, not to mention its central importance, justify having a teacher who will devote a major part of his or her time to building units and conducting discussions and other activities with small groups and the entire class, and who will see that social studies give ample outlet for the practice of basic skills in reading, writing, and math.

VALUES CLARIFICATION AND AFFECTIVE EDUCATION

The idea of incorporating the clarification of students' values in the curriculum stems from the work of Louis Raths.[21] Raths attributed certain well-known characteristics of contemporary youth (apathy, drift, overconfor-

---

[19]Lyn S. Martin and Barbara N. Pavan, "Current Research on Open Space, Nongrading, Vertical Grouping, and Team Teaching."

[20]Ibid.

[21]Louis Raths et al., *Values and Teaching* (Columbus: Merrill, 1978).

mity, cynicism, and contentiousness) to confusion about values. He developed "values clarification" procedures—a set of teaching strategies designed to help students select their own values and develop more purposeful lives. The procedure directs the teacher to elicit from students their value preferences and to encourage them to share with one another those values they prize and what they are doing, or planning to do, by way of applying them to everyday life. The teacher makes no attempt to impose values upon the student.[22]

Although values clarification was intended for use in high school, some educators have adapted it for use with younger children. John J. Cogan and Wayne Paulson give examples of its application to children in the primary grades. The teacher selects a value-laden subject such as fighting. Children may be asked, "How do you feel when you see two people fighting on the street?" Or they may be asked to put their feelings about fighting on a continuum that ranges from "fighting is fun" to "fighting is awful." Still other approaches are suggested by Cogan and Paulson. Then there is discussion and sharing.[23]

Teaching Values Clarification through Affective Education

More appropriate to the elementary school and more thoroughly developed at that level than values clarification is the "curriculum of affect." It includes consideration of children's values, but its aim is broader, encompassing all affective areas, and it is better suited than is values clarification to the young child's level of cognitive and emotional development.

"A Curriculum of Affect" is the subtitle of a Ford Foundation report.[24] It describes what was observed and learned in Ford's action-oriented Elementary School Teaching Project, expressing with clarity and vigor the view that education of the intellect alone falls short of engaging children, particularly the disadvantaged, and fails to modify their behavior in any profound way. Sensitive teachers everywhere have been exploring ways of capitalizing on children's beliefs, feelings, experiences, and interests. They are asking such questions as: To what extent are the affect elements of a

---

[22]Some critics of values clarification object to the ethical relativism or nihilism that is apt to emerge—i.e., the idea that one person's values are as good as another's, that it's just a matter of personal taste. See Alan L. Lockwood, "A Critical View of Values Clarification," *Teachers College Record*, 77 (September 1975), 35–50. Lockwood suggests how this objection could be offset by the teacher's setting a framework within which the values are shown to function, such as the framework of a democratic society, of the concept of justice, or of empathy. See also Joshua Weinstein and Marilyn S. Schwartz, "Values Education without Indoctrination," *Educational Forum*, 42 (January 1979), 203–211.

[23]John J. Cogan and Wayne Paulson, "Values Clarification and the Primary Child," *Social Studies*, 69 (January/February, 1978), 20–24.

[24]Gerald Weinstein and Mario D. Fantini, *Toward Humanistic Education: A Curriculum of Affect* (New York: Praeger, 1970).

child's life worth serious study by children, despite the subjectivity and parochial nature of such experiences? How can these experiences be discussed by children so as to lead to greater self-acceptance and improved self-image? Can they be used as stepping-stones to an objective academic analysis of society and its problems? The Ford report deals with these questions forthrightly, masterfully, and practically. A rather free rendition of major points of the Ford report, with added applications to the social studies, follows:

1. If social studies content is not related to the child's feelings and attitudes, it will have little impact upon the child's behavior.
2. The curriculum reform programs (such as those presented in Chapter 4) have not touched the problem of how to modify behavior. They have missed fire, despite their talk about behavioral objectives, which often amounts to little more than the child's ability to perform paper-and-pencil exercises. They have not dealt with the central issue of how to make the content more meaningful—not only to the disadvantaged, but also to more privileged children.
3. The way to test the validity of a social studies curriculum is to determine how meaningful its content is to children—how it stimulates self-examination of their attitudes and feelings.
4. A social studies unit of learning should begin with an examination of children's own statements and questions, particularly those that reveal feelings that could conceivably range over the entire realm of children's living and thinking: opinions on the personal status gained through fighting, reactions to conflicts with parents, disillusion over a friend's betrayal, feelings of futility in trying to effect changes for the better in one's condition, and so forth.
5. A social studies curriculum should systematically help a child to understand him- or herself better. Children need assistance in establishing a more constructive relationship between social groups (class, ethnic, and other), improving their own self-concept and personal behavior, understanding the reasons for social tensions, and determining the relative accuracy or inaccuracy of reports they have had about themselves, their race, or their parents' occupations.

Applications of the curriculum of affect are described in Chapter 9.

FOR STUDY AND EXPLORATION

1. Locate schools that have adopted some of the innovations mentioned in this chapter. Visit them to see how they operate and how the social studies are handled. Find out from the principal or a teacher why and how the scheme was inaugurated, and what he or she feels are its chief assets and limitations.
2. Draw up a plan of how you as a teacher in a self-contained classroom in a traditional school could adopt in part some of the newer approaches in your own classroom, particularly as they apply to the teaching of social studies.

3. Read Raymond English's "Ten Discoveries about Basic Learning" in *Social Education*, 41 (February 1977), 105–107. The "discoveries" relate to basic learning in the social studies. Following English's style, add a few of your own discoveries.

FURTHER READING

Many books and articles have been published on the movements and changes reported in this chapter. Among them are:

Back to Basics

Barry K. Beyer, "Teaching Basics in Social Studies," *Social Education*, 41 (February 1977), 96–104.

M. Hanif et al., "Open Education Versus Back to Basics: An Analysis of the Issues," *Contemporary Education*, 50 (Winter 1979), 104–109.

Ellen V. Leininger, "Back to Basics: Underlying Concepts and Controversy," *Elementary School Journal*, 79 (January 1979), 167–173.

Mainstreaming

Anne Adams et al., *Mainstreaming Language Arts and Social Studies: Special Activities for the Whole Class* (Salt Lake City: Goodyear, 1976).

Susan R. Bookbinder, *Mainstreaming: What Every Child Needs to Know about Disabilities*, Guide for Grades 1 to 4 (Boston: Exceptional Parent Press, 1978).

Patrick O'Donnell and Robert H. Bradfield (Eds.), *Mainstreaming: Controversy and Consensus* (San Rafael, CA: Academic Therapy, 1976).

Marion B. Stroud, "Do Students Sink or Swim in the Mainstream?" *Phi Delta Kappan*, 60 (December 1978), 316.

Individualized Instruction

Helen F. Durio, "Toward Personalized Instruction," *Intellect*, 102 (February 1974), 297–299.

Elisabeth S. Hirsch, "Accountability: A Danger to Humanistic Education?" *Young Children*, 31 (November 1975), 57–65.

Karen Kepler and Jill W. Randall, "Individualization: The Subversion of Elementary Schooling," *Elementary School Journal*, 77 (May 1977), 358–363.

T. F. McLaughlin, "Personalized Instruction at the Intermediate Grade Level: Some Suggestions," *Educational Technology*, 17 (September/October 1977), 25–26.

Middle School

The Middle School We Need (Washington: Association for Supervision and Curriculum Development, 1975).

Louis G. Romano et al. (Eds.), *The Middle School* (Chicago: Nelson-Hall, 1973).

Alice Stelle and Helen Wallace, "Meeting Learning Needs of the Young Adolescent," *Thrust*, 8 (January 1979), 25–27.

Nongraded School

Edward G. Buffie, *Curriculum Development in Nongraded Schools* (Bloomington: Indiana University Press, 1971).

Evelyn M. Murray, *The Flexible Elementary School: Practical Guidelines for Developing a Nongraded Program* (West Nyack, NY: Parker, 1971).

Betty H. Yarborough and Roger A. Johnson, "Relationship Between Intelligence Levels and Benefits from Innovative, Nongraded Elementary Schooling and Traditional, Graded Schooling," *Education Research Quarterly*, 3 (Summer 1978), 28–38.

The Open Classroom

Evelyn Berger and Bonnie A. Winters, *Social Studies in the Open Classroom: A Practical Guide* (New York: Teachers College Press, 1973).

Muhammed Hanif et al., "Open Education versus Back to Basics: An Analysis of the Issues," *Contemporary Education*, 50 (Winter 1979), 104–109.

Marie E. Hopke, "A Review of the Literature on the Open-Concept Elementary School," *Oregon ASCD Curriculum Bulletin* (Salem, OR 97308), 30 (March 1976), entire issue.

L. Stephens, *The Teachers Guide to Open Education* (New York: Holt, Rinehart and Winston, 1974).

Joy Taylor, *Organizing the Open Classroom: A Teacher's Guide to the Integrated Day* (New York: Schocken, 1974).

Team Teaching

Elizabeth G. Cohen, "Technology and Teaming in the Elementary School," *Sociology of Education*, 52 (January 1979), 20–33.

Jean E. Davis, *Team Teaching* (Washington: National Education Association, 1975).

Norman Evans, *Beginning Teaching in Professional Partnership* (New York: Holmes and Meier, 1978).

Values Clarification

William E. Collie, "Institutionalization of Values Education in Elementary and Secondary Public Education," *Counseling and Values*, 23 (February 1979), 68–72.

Robert C. Hawley and Isabel L. Hawley, *Value Exploration Through Role Playing* (New York: Hart, 1974).

Howard Kirschenbaum et al., "In Defense of Values Clarification," *Phi Delta Kappan*, 58 (June 1977), 743–746.

Louis E. Raths et al., *Values and Teaching*, 2nd ed. (Columbus: Merrill, 1978).

"Values Clarification" (symposium), *Curriculum Review*, 18 (February 1979), 8–34.

4 The Social Studies Curriculum

It is probably easier to say something foolish and harder to offer any wisdom in the area of curriculum than in any comparable specialty within the domain of pedagogy.
George W. Hartmann

"War is much too important a matter to be left to the generals," said Georges Clemenceau, the French premier who led France through the critical days of World War I. It may be said similarly that curriculum is much too important to be left to the curriculum makers. Teachers should be on guard when reading what even the experts have to say about it. In the first place, they don't agree with each other, and in the final analysis, only the teacher, working with a class, knows what curriculum will work.

This chapter will describe current curriculum practices, identify a few published curriculum programs, propose ways of analyzing the suitability of a curriculum, and indicate the teacher's role in developing a curriculum.

PREVAILING PRACTICES

Dominant Position of Commercially Produced Curriculum

A nationwide survey of the practices of 12,000 teachers revealed that an overwhelming proportion of their classroom teaching time (90 percent or more) involved use of commercially produced instructional materials in social studies as well as in other fields.[1] Reports based on classroom observation also indicate that the earlier practice of a faculty to develop its own course of study in social studies has approached the vanishing point.[2]

Fifteen years ago, anyone wishing to find out what was going on in curriculum development in the United States would need to collect courses of study or curriculum guides from several hundred representative school districts. Today, one need only examine the teacher's guides, pupil textbooks, and pupil workbooks of recently published or revised programs. In social studies these programs number probably no more than 30 or 35. The summary which follows in this chapter is based on an analysis of 27 of them.[3]

Components of the Programs

A typical published program today consists of more than a teacher's guide and a textbook and workbook for the pupil. With some exceptions, it is "pre-packaged"—that is, it includes varying combinations of filmstrips, audio cassettes, phonograph records, study photoprints, simulation games, duplicate masters for tests, and other ingredients designed to lighten the teacher's preparation.

Goals

Most of the published programs are explicitly aimed at (a) developing well informed and responsible citizens; (b) providing learning that will enable children to formulate concepts and generalizations derived from the various social sciences; (c) teaching how to seek answers to questions and solutions to problems; (d) building attitudes and values consistent with democratic living; and (e) establishing skills such as those involved in using maps, reference work, reporting, and acquiring and classifying data.

Inquiry Learning

Inquiry learning is a process by which children discover answers to questions by bona fide investigation (not by looking up answers in a book). Most of the programs claim adherence to inquiry learning. The process is discussed with examples in Chapters 7 and 13.

Inquiry can be conducted with children through group thinking and group discussion. It is not something that a published program can "provide," though it can help by supplying questions for investigation and by giving suggestions to the teacher. Some programs seem to regard any act of processing information as inquiry learning, from interviewing a resource person to organizing information, omitting some of the crucial steps that are

---

[1]Educational Products Information Exchange, *Selector's Guide for Elementary School Studies Programs*, EPIE Report No. 84m (New York: EPIE Institute, 1978), p. 5.

[2]Karen Kepler and Jill W. Randall, "Individualization: The Subversion of Elementary Schooling," *Elementary School Journal*, 77 (May 1977), 358–363.

[3]Twenty-three of the programs are those listed in *El-Hi Textbooks in Print—1978* (New York: Bowker, 1979).

described in Chapter 13. It is fair to say that more programs give lip service to inquiry learning than promote it in a practical way, and some define it so loosely that it becomes a meaningless cliché.

Scope and Sequence

In the 27 programs examined, the following "central tendencies" stand out:

Kindergarten	Children's home and school relationships and responsibilities. A few programs include an introduction to children of other lands through pictures.
Grade One	Families and communities. Compared to offerings of 10 years ago, an increasing number of programs include brief comparisons of families in the United States with those in selected foreign cultures.
Grade Two	Neighborhoods and communities in contrasting environments, usually in the United States, but in a growing number of programs in foreign environments also.
Grade Three	Communities here and abroad, with attention given in varying degrees of thoroughness to community resources, community needs (food, clothing, and shelter), forms of communication and transportation, and urban-suburban living.
Grade Four	Selected world regions and cultures. In some cases, emphasis is upon the cultures, in others upon selected communities within the cultures, and in still others upon geographical features. A minority of programs confine the study of regions and cultures to those in the United States.
Grade Five	United States history and geography, including some sociology and anthropology. A few programs add a study of Canada or Latin America, and occasionally both.
Grade Six	The history, geography, and cultural features of selected areas of the world, chiefly a sampling of nations in the Eastern Hemisphere, in other instances a sampling of nations in Latin America, plus all of Canada. A minority of programs offer broad studies of cultural, social, political, and economic developments and problems.
Grade Seven	Eastern Hemisphere or Latin America, sometimes straight global geography, sometimes studies of economics merged with bits of sociology.
Grade Eight	United States history. Some programs provide global geography.

It is evident that the formerly widely adopted "expanding environment" principle has been modified. That principle has a logical enough basis: school beginners learn about their immediate environment; as they advance in school, they study consecutively larger segments of the world. But many educators believe that rigid adherence to it is not in keeping with the rapidly expanding horizon of today's child. The expansion, it is believed, is not only rapid, but it is no longer neatly concentric. It seems reasonable that children's relentless exposure to television and increased family travel has made many distant features familiar to five- and six-year-olds. As a consequence, the "expanding environment" idea is now rarely followed in unmodified form.

A LOOK AT SOME CURRICULUMS

The preceding section suggests not only that commercially produced curriculum programs are the dominant ones, but also that in a number of respects they tend to be remarkably similar. Those described in this section are but a light sampling of those that stand out because of their originality and imaginativeness. They are not the nine most widely used programs—indeed, a few of them have not been commercial "successes" at all.[4] They do not have a monopoly on distinctiveness. Along with the others, they have strengths and weaknesses. Most of these nine have broken new ground in one respect or another—ground which will probably be tilled in some way in the years ahead by enterprising publishers and by resourceful teachers.[5]

Comprehensive Social Studies Curriculums

The *Concepts and Inquiry* curriculum is for Grades K to 12. Its outstanding characteristic is the solidity and depth of its content and its heavy emphasis on history—even in the lower grades. Uses of the globe and information about children of contrasting cultures are taught as early as kindergarten. The first-grade studies include maps, transportation, and biographies of Americans. Second grade takes the pupil to communities of various types here and abroad. United States history is taken up in Grade 3. Grade 4 explores agriculture and industry in contrasting areas of the world, business organization under a free economy, and India. Grades 5 and 6 deal with aspects of history. For example, one of the units examines four world views—Confucianism, Buddhism, Judaism, and ancient Greek civiliza-

---

[4]But then, when was commercial success a necessary attribute of merit? Consider the slow acceptance, following initial outright rejection, of the work of Copernicus; the angry protests that greeted the first edition of Malthus' *Essay on the Principle of Population*; the century-long delay before the greatness of J. S. Bach's music was recognized; the initial failures of Gounod's opera *Faust*, Bellini's opera *Norma*, and a long series of other important creative efforts.

[5]The curriculum programs described in the subsections are arranged alphabetically.

tion—and raises questions such as why civilizations rise and fall, and whether or not civilization is in danger today. The Grade 7 program introduces principles of sociology, anthropology, and economics. In Grade 8, United States history is the chief subject of study.

Several books and pamphlets have been prepared for each grade level. Available also are filmstrips, puzzles, and games. Suggestions are given to the teacher for questions that are calculated to elicit analytical, evaluative thinking.

This is a full program and a healthy challenge to the more able student, but teachers may well question the intellectual readiness of many of their pupils for some of the studies slated for their grades. The concept load is heavy. Child development data have apparently not figured significantly in designing the program.

The program, produced by the Educational Research Council of America, is published by Allyn and Bacon, Boston, MA 02210.

The *Family of Man* program covers Grades 1 to 4. It is based on the curriculum development work of the University of Minnesota's former Project Social Studies Center, a curriculum that ranged from K to Grade 12. The original program, directed by Edith West, was designed by a distinguished interdisciplinary team of social scientists and educators, who jointly drew up a list of basic concepts, generalizations, skills, and attitudes before constructing the curriculum.

Briefly, Grades 1 and 2 concentrate on family studies, including families of the Hopi Indians, Japanese, and early New Englanders. Grades 3 and 4 study various communities (contrasting communities in the United States, an early California gold-mining camp, a village in India, and others). The program has unity and continuity. If one can accept the heavy concentration on foreign cultures at the beginning levels, it also has appropriateness to children. It is a good example of a carefully worked out interdisciplinary program. Appealing kits are provided, each of which contains a teacher's resource guide, study prints, trade books for pupil use, filmstrips, artifacts, games, songs, and cassettes.

The curriculum is produced by Selective Educational Equipment, Newton, MA 02195.

The *Holt Databank System*'s content has a welcome simplicity of organization: Kindergarten—Myself; Grade 1—People; Grade 2—Communities; Grade 3—Cities; Grade 4—Cultures; Grade 5—American History; Grade 6—Technology. Some of the units are outstanding, such as those on pollution and city planning in third grade, and the program's case studies in most of the units in sixth grade. The kindergarten program, organized by the months of the year and with a set of a dozen activities for each school month, is splendidly formulated. The activities in Grades 3 to 6 of data-gathering, data-organizing, and data-using are well thought through and stimulating, though to classify them all as "inquiry" processes, as is done in the program, may be misleading.

The quantity and spread of content in the upper grades appear excessive. The conscientious teacher who feels each unit must be "covered" will have to move very rapidly from one topic to another and will have to be satisfied with superficial learning. Some of the items in the kits (called "databanks") are ingeniously designed and vie with the series' textbooks as major sources of learning. For example, one foldout (Grade 3) is a fine aid in explaining the reason for the location of cities on the lower Mississippi River, and the audiovisual materials (Grade 5) are effective in illustrating the nature of historical evidence.

The series, edited by William R. Fielder, is published by Holt, Rinehart and Winston, New York, NY 10017.

The *Taba Program in Social Science* is in large part the legacy of one of the keener minds engaged in curriculum work in our time—the late Hilda Taba. It is the very embodiment of analytical logic applied to curriculum design. Each aspect of the curriculum rests upon a carefully considered principle. The lesson plans in the teacher's edition are explicit and helpful to anyone wanting to know how to conduct a productive discussion with children. Learning objectives are stated explicitly, in behavioral terms, and the recommended evaluation procedures are based largely upon the attainment of the behaviors thus identified. The components of effective thinking are made clear, as are the teaching strategies that are recommended to bring about the thinking. The grade-placement of themes is probably the least innovative aspect of the curriculum; its presence in this curriculum shows how relatively unimportant is the selection of themes when one's main intent (as it was Taba's) is to get away from covering detailed facts and to move instead toward stressing the more durable knowledge and promoting analytical thinking by having children use facts and generalizations to hypothesize solutions to problems. The themes follow the expanding-environment concept, ranging from family and school in Grade 1 through communities here and abroad, the state, the nation, and the western hemisphere, ending with the eastern hemisphere in Grade 7.

The program is published by Addison-Wesley, Menlo Park, CA 94025.

Programs in the Behavioral Sciences

The *Anthropology Curriculum Project* produces exactly what its name implies: a straightforward curriculum in anthropology. Beginning in kindergarten, pupils learn the basic vocabulary of anthropology (*artifact, culture, enculturation, archaic, participant observer*—examples of the easier terms), the methods used by anthropologists in their field work, and basic concepts. The content is arranged in cycles:

CYCLE 1	THEME	CYCLE 2
Kindergarten and Grade 1	Concept of culture	Grade 4
Grade 2	Development of man and his culture	Grade 5
Grade 3	Cultural change	Grade 6

The content in Cycle 1 differs from that in Cycle 2 in being more descriptive and less analytical and abstract. Also available is a curriculum for Grade 7, dealing with the life cycle of selected peoples of the United States, Nigeria, and China.

The approach is deductive. The pupils are presented with generalizations and the data upon which the generalizations are based. Pupils have only occasional opportunities to make discoveries. Teachers who are inquiry-oriented may be disappointed by this approach, but the program is so packed with meritorious material that it is worth a tryout. Its creators deserve credit for fashioning a program straight and clean from their own experience and intuition, without trying to conform to any pedagogical cult.

The program, developed at the University of Georgia by Marion J. Rice and associates, consists of one unit for each grade, each unit requiring from one to two months. The materials include pupil texts, workbooks, tests, teacher's guides, and background information for the teacher. They may be obtained from Anthropology Curriculum Project, University of Georgia, Athens, GA 30602.

The program, *Human Behavior and Potential*, deals with the dynamics of human behavior. One of the characteristics of most social studies curriculums is their tendency to present society in a purely descriptive way. Events, institutions, and human actions are given as fixed. Even when pupils are encouraged to discover generalizations from these static data, as is frequently the case, they may analyze the facts but fail to dip below the surface. *Causes* of human behavior tend to be only vaguely explored, and there is also little systematic effort to have pupils think of alternative behaviors that might be pursued. For example, a major cause of crime may be vaguely identified as poverty. But usually neglected are such questions as why some persons living in poverty become criminals and some do not, and what alternatives are available to those about to perpetrate a crime.

This neglect was challenged by the late psychologist Ralph H. Ojemann, whose experimental work and that of his students laid the groundwork for *Human Behavior and Potential* for Kindergarten through Grade 6. Antisocial behavior, such as lying and stealing, is presented as a means of solvingpersonal problems that could be solved in alternative and more acceptable ways. This type of knowledge, Ojemann believed, will help children feel more at home in their world and will reduce many strains and conflicts. Ojemann and his associates conducted experiments in which they compared the attitudes of children who were taught to examine causes and consequences of behavior and alternative behaviors, with those of children who were not given this instruction. They found that the attitudes of the instructed children become significantly less arbitrary, less judgmental, less authoritarian, less intolerant of ambiguity, and less anxious.

For each grade there is a handbook for teachers and an array of booklets with titles such as "Why People Act as They Do" for pupil use. Each grade's program deals with human behavior; in Kindergarten, stories and role playing, to develop what Ojemann calls "a causal orientation," are employed, and in the later grades the causal view of social studies content is applied: for example, slavery in Grade 4, social growth of a city in Grade 5, and understanding foreign peoples in Grade 6. The program's materials are distributed by Educational Research Council of America, Cleveland, OH 44113.

Man: A Course of Study is a year's program for Grade 5 or 6. It focuses on three questions: What is human about human beings? How did human beings get that way? How can they be made more human? In order to provide a background against which these questions can be examined, the pupil studies the life cycle of the salmon and the behavior patterns of herring gulls and baboons. The study of man is centered on Netsilik Eskimos. In answering the questions about human beings, pupils compare their own lives with those of the Eskimos, with respect to work patterns, child rearing, family structure, cooperative activities, values, and the like. What makes the program unique and exciting is the high quality of its source material. Its color films, which were photographed explicitly for the program, are the central source of data. In viewing them, the children vicariously participate in the field work involving animals and Eskimos. They examine the raw data and are encouraged to discover generalizations on their own.

Twenty-three booklets differing in style and readability constitute the reading. To illustrate, there is a book of field notes by an anthropologist, and a book on Netsilik Eskimos, adapted for children from the work of a Danish explorer-anthropologist. Phonograph records, films, filmstrips, maps, games, and other learning devices are of a quality unmatched by any other program. There are several guides for the teacher, including one devoted exclusively to evaluation strategies.

The program, developed with grants from the National Science Foundation, was sharply criticized a few years ago in Congress and in school board sessions because of its mention of Netsilik social standards at variance with ours—for example, wife stealing and the fate of old people in winter when food is scarce. A question that arises is: Are elementary school children able to understand moral dilemmas occasioned by exceptional environmental pressures and social traditions? One view is presented by Brand Blanshard:

For the advanced student it undoubtedly has its value. For the beginner the value is more questionable. If the student is as yet unskilled in ethical analysis, such study may easily mislead him. It is likely to suggest that . . . the principles of ethics somehow rest on anthropological fact . . . and . . . since every practice seems to have found favor somewhere, that morals are a matter of fashion.[6]

On the other hand, teachers who have taught from *Man: A Course of Study*, and who continue to teach from it, report that children learn that Netsilik morals are *not* "a matter of fashion"—that senilicide, for example, is attributable to the extremely precarious survival in the Arctic for a primitive culture. Furthermore, the booklet containing such information is one of 23, and could be eliminated by any teacher desiring to do so. It should also be stated that features of Netsilik culture that have raised the controversy play a small part in the study and one that is presented in a natural, prosaic fashion. For a positive view of *Man: A Course of Study* and its merits, see Douglas R. Lewis' stout defense of it after six years of its use by teachers in his school.[7]

The program was developed by Educational Development Center, Cambridge, Mass., and is distributed by Curriculum Development Associates, Washington, DC 20036. Preservice or in-service teacher training is a requisite for the use of *Man: A Course of Study*.

The *Social Science Laboratory Units* were developed for Grades 4 to 6. Their purpose is to teach children how the behavioral scientist works—how he gathers his information, how he establishes cause-and-effect relationships, and how he draws conclusions. They are taught how to use interviews, questionnaires, and observation forms, and how to tabulate and analyze results. The pupils apply the instruments and methods of analysis in their study of hypothetical case studies. The word "laboratory" in the title of the units is a misnomer, for the pupil is not given experience in carrying out one of the most important steps in the laboratory of the behavioral scientist, namely, using the data to formulate and test hypotheses. Rather, the program provides that the pupils compare their approaches with those of established social scientists. Needless to say, teachers could use procedures of their own to overcome this limitation. The materials are fresh and intriguing, and lead the way in developing a systematic plan for carrying out in the classroom what has long been advocated: teaching children some of the methods by which knowledge in the social sciences is advanced.

There are seven units ("Learning to Use Social Science," "Discovering Differences," "Friendly and Unfriendly Behavior," and so forth), each planned for one or two months of instruction. The materials, developed at

[6]Brand Blanshard et al., *Philosophy in American Education* (New York: Harper, 1945), p. 223.

[7]Douglas R. Lewis, "Anyone for MACOS?" *Independent School*, 36 (December 1976), 40–43.

the University of Michigan by Ronald Lippitt and associates, include a text-book, project books, phonograph records, and teacher guides. The units are published by Science Research Associates, Chicago, IL 60611.

A Program in Economics

The important concepts of economics have been almost totally absent from the elementary school curriculum, partly because of the virtual monopoly exercised by geography and history, and also because of a lack of imagination on the part of educators as to how economics might be taught to children. One program, stunning in its originality, its child-centered ap-proach, and the richness of its content, will be cited—the Senesh program.

This program, *Our Working World*, designed for Grades 1 to 6 by Lawrence Senesh, was developed in the classrooms of Elkhart, Indiana. It was originally conceived as an economics program. The material was varied and lively—replete with case studies, plays, stories, poems, suggestions for role playing, and so on. Senesh assumed that children in every grade, with proper motivation, can become excited about the abstract ideas underlying their economic experiences and can acquire an understanding of the basic ideas of economics. He showed that economic ideas and relationships, so long neglected, are well within the grasp of even first-grade children.

The revised edition of *Our Working World* has diluted the economics content and is being marketed as a general social studies series. It has thus lost its distinctiveness. Its economics orientation, however, is still discern-ible, and it is still, if used selectively, the most reliable and most imaginative guide to acquainting children with the field of economics. Books for pupils, teacher's guides, filmstrips, cassettes, and kits are available from Science Research Associates, Chicago, IL 60611.

CRITERIA FOR JUDGING CURRICULUM PROGRAMS

In this section, we shall present standards for evaluating curriculum programs. Teachers, by checking a program against the criteria, will be reminded of needed adjustments in teaching to offset the program's weaknesses, such as the common tendency of many programs to provide an overload of content.

Conformity to Maturity Levels of Children

Is the arrangement of content, and are problems and questions pro-posed for children's discussion, consonant with the stages of children's development? Unfortunately, most programs seem more sensitive to educa-tional fads than to the principles of child development developed by Piaget and others (see Chapters 5 and 6). To illustrate, one current fad is to in-troduce the primary-grade child to faraway places and early periods of history. This fad is an excessive reaction to the valid recognition that the ex-panding environment theory (which had its heyday, too) underestimates the young child's intellectual capacity. Joseph Featherstone's criticism of the curriculum reform efforts of the 1960s still applies to many of the recent editions of those curriculums: "They concentrated on content . . . and ignored the nature of children and their ways of learning. Too often children were regarded as passive recipients of good materials, and teachers as passive conduits."[8]

While most programs make an obvious attempt to proceed from simple-to-complex and concrete-to-abstract within a lesson and from lesson to lesson, there are numerous lapses. Teachers often need to substitute their own oral expositions for sections in the textbook, or precede reading in the textbook with a preliminary discussion.

Recycling of Ideas

The ideas of the social studies are complex and, for mastery, require recycling (reintroduction). The Taba program does this with striking and deliberate regularity. For example, the theme of interdependence is presented in a fresh context and with new content in each grade. Every year, the curriculum builds further upon it. Every year, the idea of interdependence is broadened and deepened through study of new and successively more complex applications.

Balance of Content

Balance is achieved by seeing to it that pupils at each grade level have contact with what the faculty or the curriculum maker believes to be important. Balance is planned through a scope-and-sequence framework which organizes teaching plans in a way that shows the emphases of the program. There should be balance within a single grade (see Chart 4.1) and in the total range of educational experience (see Chart 4.2).

Readability of Textbook

If children are expected to do independent reading in a social studies textbook, it is obvious that vocabulary should be simple, the style should be appealing, and major concepts should be enriched through detailed examples. Many textbooks for children do not meet these standards.

Depth of Content

Sages over the years have maintained that it is better for learners to dwell in detail on a few significant areas rather than to spread out superficially over many. They have argued that you will make more of an hour if you concentrate on a few facts or ideas, learning them in their varied interrelationships, than crowding your hour with a multitude of unrelated or loosely related facts or ideas.

---

[8]Joseph Featherstone, "Open Schools II: Tempering a Fad," *New Republic*, 165 (September 25, 1971), 17–21.

When children are expected to learn something, they should be given whatever time is necessary to have them make it their own. They need time to fit the new learning into already existing knowledge and to have it become organized there, where it is likely also to modify the existing knowledge. To clinch the learning, they need additional time to see how it is applied to their here-and-now world.

Including too many topics necessitates skimming the surface, and scatters effort. Alfred North Whitehead wrote:

> Do not teach too many subjects. . . .What you teach, teach thoroughly. . . . Let the main ideas which are introduced into a child's education be few and important, and let them be thrown into every combination possible.[9]

Nothing defeats this simple truth as effectively as requiring that a class cover massive subject matter. Comprehensive study can be self-defeating. Edgar Dale reported:

> Some of these orientation courses have been like the Powder River in Montana, a mile wide and a foot deep. They do not really orient and are quickly forgotten. Certain so-called broad courses have been unsuccessful because they have attempted to cover the ground rather than to uncover it.[10]

One way to achieve the depth is to select segments of the topic for intensive treatment—a procedure recently called "postholing." Instead of trying to cover all of Europe in detail, for example, nation by nation, the class identifies major culture regions, surveys one region, and then concentrates upon one or two places in the region for detailed study. For example, Norden (Scandinavia plus Finland and Iceland) would be overviewed as a whole, but perhaps only Sweden would be singled out for detailed study. The other regions of Europe would be similarly studied.

The "covering ground" obsession is slowly passing as a result of educators' growing awareness of two phenomena. First, it has become apparent that much of the information is obsolete-prone. A startling amount of the factual material absorbed in one decade is out of date by the next decade. Laws change, political regimes topple, birth and death rates shift, the population rank of cities alters, economic theories come and go, and changes in technological procedures often cause the bottom to drop out of the demand for certain time-honored resources and occupations. Public moods, life styles, habits of consumption, are evanescent. Even place names change. The child struggles to retain information that is in almost immediate need of revision.

---

[9]Alfred North Whitehead, *The Aims of Education and Other Essays* (New York: Macmillan, 1929), p. 2.

[10]Edgar Dale, "Generalized Education," *The News Letter*, Ohio State University, 16 (7) (April 1951).

CHART 4.1. Scope and Sequence Chart for Grade 3:* Inquiring about Cities

UNIT	TOPICS	CONCEPTS	SKILL DEVELOPMENT GOALS	INQUIRY GOALS	AFFECTIVE GOALS
I	City Life	cityness	Reading 6 Listening 1, 4, 7 Observing 1	Observing 2, 3, 4 Counting 10, 11 Experimenting 2 Comparing 3, 10 Modeling 8 Generalizing 11	Valuing (es) 2, 4, 9 Self-concept 1, 6, 7, 11 Attitudes 2, 3, 4, 5, 8, 9, 10
II	Were These Cities? Case studies: Tikal Zimbabwe Mohenjo-daro	cityness maps	Reading 1, 3, 4, 7, 8, 9, 10, 11, 15, 17, 18, 19, 22 Writing 8, 13, 15, 18, 27 Listening 12, 15 Mapping & Globes 1, 2, 3, 6, 15, 16, 21	Observing 5, 16, 27 Counting & Quantifying 5, 7, 24 Classifying 22, 23 Comparing 5, 7, 8, 11, 12, 20, 25, 26, 27 Modeling 14, 19 Inferring 10, 14, 16, 17, 18 Deducing 8, 10, 16, 20, 22, 26, 28 Generalizing 12, 20, 23, 25, 29 Explaining 13 Hypothesizing 7, 15	Valuing 4, 8, 10, 14, 20, 28 Self-concept 1, 2, 3, 5, 6, 7, 10, 15, 16, 20, 23, 27 Attitudes 4, 5, 7, 8, 11, 13, 17, 26, 28
III	Where on Earth? Case studies: Cairo London Denver Chicago New York	maps city site and situation	Reading 3, 6, 7, 10, 13–14 Writing 12 Mapping & Globes 1, 2, 4, 8, 9, 10, 11, 13–14	Classifying 11 Comparing 7 Mapping 15–17 Generalizing 6, 11, 12 Explaining 4 Hypothesizing 15–17	Valuing (es) 1, 5, 11 Self-concept 3, 8, 9, 13–14 Attitudes 15–17
IV	Cities from the Inside Out: The Central Business District Population and Density	maps suburbs central business district population	Reading 3, 6, 7, 8, 9, 12, 14, 15, 16 Writing 9, 13 Listening 5, 13 Speaking 8, 10 Mapping 1, 2, 3, 4	Observing 5 Experimenting 9, 12 Comparing 4, 5 Defining 2, 12 Modeling 11, 13 Deducing 13, 16	Valuing (es) 9, 13, 14, 15, 16 Self-concept 3, 4, 5, 13, 17 Attitudes 1, 11, 12, 14, 15, 16

64

V	Where Are the Edges? Case studies: Bangor, Maine Atlanta, Georgia Omaha, Nebraska Los Angeles, Ca. Honolulu, Hawaii Nome, Alaska	hinterlands megalopolis	Reading 3, 5, 7, 8, 9, 10, 11, 12–13 Writing 11 Listening 1, 5, 7 Mapping 4, 9, 15	Observing 6, 7, 14, 16 Comparing 5, 8, 10 Modeling 4 Deducing 11, 12–13 Explaining 11, 14 Predicting 16	Valuing (es) 4, 9 Self-concept 1, 3, 12–13, 17–18 Attitudes 4, 7, 10, 11, 17–18
VI	Tin Lizzie: Horseless Carriages The Model T Cars Changed the City	producer & consumer goods & services assembly-line production	Reading 1, 6, 8, 9, 14, 15, 16, 17, 18 Writing 5, 14 Listening 10, 13, 15 Speaking 15	Observing 2, 4, 10 Counting & Quantifying 16 Experimenting 7, 9, 13, 18 Classifying 8 Comparing 3 Modeling 10, 11, 12, 13, 17 Deducing 1, 2, 3, 4, 5 Generalizing 13 Explaining 14	Valuing (es) 2, 4, 9, 14, 16, 17 Self-concept 2, 3, 5, 6, 7, 8, 9, 10, 12, 16, 18 Attitudes 11, 12, 13
VII	River and Cloud: Water Air pollution Waste removal	pollution resources	Reading 2, 4, 6, 7, 15, 16, 18, 19 Writing 14 Listening 12 Mapping 6	Observing 3, 8, 13 Counting & Quantifying 1 Classifying 5 Graphing & Charting 8, 13 Inferring 4, 6, 9, 10, 11 Deducing 127 Explaining 2, 7, 14, 18	Valuing (es) 4, 6, 16, 17, 19 Self-concept 4, 5, 12, 19 Attitudes 1, 3, 7, 9, 10, 11, 14, 15, 18
VIII	City Planning	city planning	Reading 1, 3 Writing 10–11 Listening 1, 3, 10–11 Mapping 6, 7, 8, 9 Space 5	Observing 1, 3, 5, 10–11 Comparing 1, 4 Modeling 5 Inferring 2	Valuing (es) 3, 5, 6, 10–11 Self-concept 5 Attitudes 1, 7, 8

*Chart 4.1 is only one segment of *Databank's* comprehensive framework for Grades 1 to 6. Each grade's program is similarly charted.
Source: Holt Databank System: A Social Science System (New York: Holt, Rinehart and Winston).

CHART 4.2.   Scope and Sequence Framework—Based on Goals and Objectives*

	ILLUSTRATIVE OBJECTIVES		
GOALS	KINDERGARTEN THROUGH GRADE THREE	GRADES FOUR THROUGH SIX	GRADES SEVEN AND EIGHT
I. Interdisciplinary Concepts 1. Citizenship *(followed by 17 additional concepts)*	1. Students will accept the idea that every student has certain rights and responsibilities.	1. Students will understand that present, past, and future life in California necessitates active participation of citizens in the processes of decision making.	1. Students will explore the effects of tradition and contemporary values on shaping the lifestyles of people in various subcultures in the United States and in the emerging nations.
II. Social Science Skills 1. Help students develop and use the skills involved in critical thinking. *(followed by 4 additional concepts)*	1. Students will discriminate between fact and fancy.	1. Students will state a variety of generalizations describing the effects of the actions of different groups on the use of land and resources in California.	1. Students will make and test hypotheses, use relevant information, develop generalizations, and avoid overgeneralizations.
III. Diversity 1. Help students understand and appreciate the world as a multiracial, multicultural, multilingual and multinational phenomenon. *(followed by 5 additional concepts)*	1. Students will, after having identified cultural differences in the makeup of the class, discuss likenesses and differences in the way peole satisfy basic needs.	1. Students will identify on a world map the regions from which racial minorities now in the United States came and will give a brief report on one aspect of the original culture of these minorities.	1. Students will understand that the United States had a multicultural beginning with the development of Native American cultures across the continent; Indian, Spanish, and Mexican cultures in the Southwest; and European cultures in the colonies along the Atlantic seaboard.
IV. Social Values 1. Help students become aware of their own value positions and the positions held by other individuals and groups. *(followed by 4 additional concepts)*	1. Students will listen to the thoughts of fellow students, family members, and members of the larger community in which they reside.	1. Students will examine a selected issue as to the viewpoints of cultural and ethnic groups in California toward the issue and will compare those viewpoints with their own.	1. Students will explore and examine their own value positions to foresee the probable consequences of acting upon such positions.

CHART 4.2.   Continued

GOALS	ILLUSTRATIVE OBJECTIVES		
	KINDERGARTEN THROUGH GRADE THREE	GRADES FOUR THROUGH SIX	GRADES SEVEN AND EIGHT
V. Social Participation 1. Help students analyze social situations, determine value issues, and prepare appropriate solutions upon which the students are willing to act. (followed by 3 additional concepts)	1. Students will study their behavior in the classroom and will formulate an appropriate set of classroom rules.	1. Students will examine reasons why fighting sometimes takes place on the school grounds and will work cooperatively to develop a plan for resolving conflict.	1. Students will identify ecological issues and will participate in community projects designed to improve the environment; for example, service in a recycling center and in antilitter campaigns.

*Chart 4.2 is only part of California's comprehensive framework for Kindergarten to Grade 12.

Source: Abbreviated from *Social Sciences Education Framework for California Public Schools* (Sacramento: California State Department of Education, 1975).

Second, the rapid increase in knowledge makes covering ground an impossible accomplishment, although some curriculums still attempt it. The explosion of information has made gaps in the curriculum inevitable and is forcing us to make careful *samplings* of content, and is making depth studies possible.

These two situations concerning subject matter should make us all sensitive to the need to develop a love of learning and to teach a method of study which pupils can then apply to other processes, regions, periods, and problems throughout life.

PAPER CURRICULUMS AND CURRICULUM-LESS CLASSROOMS

Leaders in curriculum theory state that the real curriculum is the sum total of children's school experiences, not the curriculum as set down in curriculum guides, courses of study, or textbook programs. There is evidence, already cited, that published textbook programs are currently the dominant curriculum influence. How pervasive is that influence—does it permeate the experiences of children, or do the programs contain exercises that the children perform nominally but that leave the children untouched in a real sense? Or are the programs taught half-heartedly?

The most complete survey of the current functioning of social studies curriculums is not encouraging to those who believe in the central importance of the field. It reports that elementary teachers "are backing away from the social studies." In two states 70 percent or more of Kindergarten to Grade 4 teachers "were doing little or nothing with social studies."[11] In another state, elementary teachers in two districts were devoting, on the average, one hour per week to social studies. In still another state, fewer than half of the Kindergarten to Grade 5 teachers regularly taught social studies.[12]

These findings were generally confirmed in a more modest survey conducted by the senior author of this book, conducted by correspondence with personally known supervisors and teachers. Typical information came from an interview with an assistant principal in charge of curriculum in a school district of a western state:

> There is a chaotic situation in the social studies area. In the early days of the district, there were certain areas assigned to each grade; for example, the local community was taught in second grade and state history in fourth grade. Teachers followed the official county guide, drawing on various materials in addition to the state-adopted textbooks, which were used in all classrooms.
>
> Gradually, over the years, various study guides were handed down from the state, county, and district. The more recent guides tend to be less specific, concentrating on skill-development levels rather than on specific content required for each grade. Teachers and administrators alike tend to file away the study guides and disregard them.
>
> At present, teachers are feeling pressured. There are state-mandated programs which involve mounds of paperwork for both principal and teachers. There are reading and math programs adopted by districts which require massive record-keeping and many hours of labor. Many teachers admit to "forgetting" about social studies. Others teach individual units about which they are personally excited, encouraged to do so by the fact that the district no longer sets certain specific content aside for each grade.
>
> I do not have a curriculum guide or course of study for social studies nor do I know anyone who has one. A committee is being formed to set up a district course of study for social studies, as it is uniformly acknowledged by all that a new realistic program needs to be worked out so that social studies will not be taught in a hit-or-miss fashion.

It is doubtful if social studies will resume its former commanding position in the elementary curriculum until the public and school administrators relax their fervor for a narrowly conceived back-to-basics movement, which severely cuts back on time allotment for social studies and the arts, and until they modify their concept of teacher accountability so as to reduce the magnitude of unproductive paperwork.

---

[11]Richard E. Gross, "The Status of the Social Studies in the United States: Facts and Impressions of a National Survey," *Social Education*, 41 (March 1977), 194–200.
[12]Ibid.

THE KEY ROLE OF THE TEACHER

This chapter has made it clear that pre-packaged programs are an increasingly prominent part of the school curriculum picture. But a curriculum cannot be planned entirely in advance and packaged. Much must be planned and created by the teacher on a day-by-day basis.

It is regrettable when teachers look upon themselves as mere executors of a curriculum prepared by others. The extent of their creative participation in the curriculum will vary, of course, depending upon the richness of their background in the social sciences, their interest in teaching social studies, and their desire to try out their own ideas. Many teachers do not attempt to discover their own potential contributions, however, and are content to let a pre-packaged program take over.

But no matter how full and excellent a pre-packaged program may be, it should not be considered complete and self-sufficient. It is essential that the teacher personally discover, each day, just how much of the content the children understand. Successful teachers give every child the chance on certain days to react to the study or to raise questions. At the beginning of each session, they try to bring out the children's unanswered questions through discussion, relate the subject matter to that of the day before, and cultivate pupil curiosity about what is to come.

Some teachers have a special knowledge of one of the social sciences or of children's literature. No matter what program or textbook they are following, they will normally find opportunities to draw upon that knowledge to provide an enrichment that the curriculum-maker never had in mind.

Wise school administrators know that creative teachers enjoy the freedom of selecting and experimenting in connection with the social studies curriculum. They realize it is a mistake to place a ceiling above those who would fly. Some teachers would like to try out an unconventional program. Others may see possibilities in combining elements from a variety of programs. Still others may wish to develop programs that are entirely their own. No curriculum plan will succeed unless it is executed by a teacher who believes in it. Teacher interest and initiative should be prized, and, where it exists, the administrator's word should be: "Go ahead!"

FOR STUDY AND EXPLORATION

1. Interview a teacher who uses one of the programs described in this chapter to obtain his or her judgment of the readability of its components for children's reading, the comprehensibility of its concepts and generalizations, its appeal to children, and the value of its activities. Compare the teacher's experience with the program with your own reaction to it.

2. Add to the criteria given here for judging curriculum plans. Justify your additions.
3. Construct your own ideal curriculum for a specified grade for one year's work in social studies. Explain your selection of themes and topics and your sequential arrangement of them.

FURTHER READING

Early versions of most of the curriculum programs described in this chapter were produced during the early 1960s and climaxed in the early 1970s, a period characterized by curricular ferment in all academic fields. This creative span of years is described by John D. Haas in *The Era of the New Social Studies* (Boulder, CO: The Social Science Consortium, 1977).

Trends in curriculum are reported by Richard E. Gross in "The Status of the Social Studies in the Public Schools of the United States," *Social Education*, 41 (March 1977), 194–200; by John Jarolimek et al., in "The Status of Social Studies Education Throughout the Nation," *Social Education*, 41 (November-December 1977), 574–601; by John Jarolimek in "Where Have All the Flowers Gone?" *Childhood Education*, 55 (October 1978), 26–31; and by Mark M. Krug in "The Social Studies—Search for New Directions" in Mark M. Krug (Ed.), *What Will Be Taught—the Next Decade?* (Itaska, IL: Peacock, 1972), chap. 6.

A miscellany of thoughts and suggestions appears in *Social Studies and the Elementary Teacher: Promises and Practices*, edited by William W. Joyce and Frank L. Ryan (Washington: National Council for Social Studies, 1977).

An efficient way to keep up-to-date with regard to curriculum programs and publications is to consult on a regular basis the monthly journal, *Curriculum Review*. Publishing events in the social studies are well represented.

part II   **Social Studies and Children**

5 Characteristics of Children: Implications for Social Studies

> *Knowledge of human nature is necessary if educational changes are to be made economically, securely and without secondary ill effects.*
> **Edward L. Thorndike**

The teacher who learns what makes children tick will seldom be completely at a loss to know what teaching procedures to employ. This chapter brings together information about children that has special relevance for social studies instruction.

CHILDHOOD TRAITS AND SOCIAL STUDIES

Each child is a unique learner, possessing a singular personality, a distinctive background of experience, and a preferred mode of learning. Keen observation by the teacher reveals these idiosyncrasies. But children also widely share characteristics that a teacher can capitalize on in planning social studies.

The Child Responds to Varied Aspects of the World

Children spontaneously seek orientation to many aspects of the world. Their curiosity is diverse and shifting. During a stage when they are seemingly totally preoccupied by some specialized interest (caring for a pet, jumping rope, or collecting stamps), they normally have, more subtly expressed, a host of simultaneous subsidiary interests.

The range of children's interests is well known. Kenneth D. ann studied the interests of children aged three to five and described them as "global, even universal in scope."[1] Children in Grades 1 and 2 in 12 schools were asked by Dorothy Kirsch to draw pictures showing what they would like to read, after which they were interviewed to further identify their interests. These were found to cover 22 to 25 topics.[2] In another experiment, Sylvia M. Carter had more than 500 pupils also draw pictures of what they wished to read or have read to them. Their interests were found to range over a wide field, ranked in the following order of frequency: realistic fiction, modern fantasy, traditional fantasy, information, poetry, biography, historical fiction, and science fiction.[3] In the upper grades, another investigator of children's social studies interests reported a distribution among six social science disciplines.[4]

Such evidence supports an interdisciplinary approach to the social sciences and argues against sampling just two to three of them, which has been done so often through an exclusive diet of geography, history, and sometimes civics. Balance and variety are needed to satisfy what appears to be a pressing intellectual need of children for broad orientation to their world.

The Child Is an Investigator

A desire to find out how things work is one of the strongest drives of children. Although their most active investigations are directed toward objects and ideas found in their environment, it should be noted that they are also curious to explore the remote, the unfamiliar, and the antiquated.[5]

However, as children advance to the intermediate grades and on to high school, their intellectual curiosity and zest for inquiry declines. This is undoubtedly due in part to the demands placed upon them to retain information from books and teachers, with the inevitable result that their opportunity to explore, discuss, discover, and create grows less and less. Ways to counteract this decline are presented later in the chapter.

---

[1]Kenneth D. Wann et al., *Fostering Intellectual Development in Young Children* (New York: Teachers College, 1962), p. 18.

[2]Dorothy Kirsch, "From Athletes to Zebras—Young Children Want to Read About Them," *Elementary English*, 52 (January 1975), 73–78.

[3]Sylvia M. Carter, "Interpreting Interests and Reading Interests of Pupils in Grades One Through Three," *Dissertation Abstracts International*, 37 (January 1977), 4113-A.

[4]Frederick E. Green, "Elementary-School Children's Interests in the Social Sciences as Revealed by a Forced Choice Questionnaire," *Dissertation Abstracts*, 29 (September 1968), 760-A.

[5]See the books by Muller, by Smart and Smart, and by Arasteh and Arasteh described under "Further Reading" at the end of this chapter.

The Child Is a Doer

The child is characterized by action. This creates a problem in teaching social studies. Unlike science, in which children and teachers can demonstrate and examine phenomena through lab experiments, social studies provide fewer opportunities to learn by doing. Children cannot manipulate social phenomena except when reduced to the level of their own relations with other people. At the community, national, and world levels, obviously they are unable to experiment with, say, labor negotiations, elections, inflation, or corruption. The social studies, clearly, are more abstract than other studies.

Nevertheless, there are ways of introducing "doing" activities to help make social studies less a textbook and an armchair subject and more a concrete one. Many of these activities will be described in later chapters. A few are indicated in Box 5.1.

BOX 5.1   **VARIOUS GRADES**

Examples of "Doing" Activities in Learning Social Studies

- Reproducing arts, crafts, and dances of other cultures.
- Corresponding with children of other lands.
- Participating in school and community service projects.
- Modelling and mapping local areas.
- Making time lines.
- Interviewing older residents for local historical information.
- Role playing for involvement (historical episodes, work processes, and political functions).
- Experimenting with alternative ways of working (division of labor vs. non-specialization, hand vs. machine, etc.).
- Collecting, classifying, mounting, and captioning newspaper clippings and pictures that illustrate current manifestations of a topic.
- Drawing explanatory diagrams and pictures.

The Child Has Strong Interest in Detail

Teachers frequently remark on children's concern with detail. Robert J. Havighurst pointed out long ago children's "preference for details rather than wholes," their interest in "sidelines, oddities, minor details," and their "avidness for detail."[6] When trying to encourage pupils to discover a significant generalization, teachers are often distressed to note that they become side-

---

[6]Robert J. Havighurst, *Human Development and Education* (New York: McKay, 1953), chap. 7.

tracked by some insignificant feature. For example, a child may wonder more about why a caboose is red than about the purpose of a freight train. By extrapolating a bit from Jean Piaget's findings, we may conclude that this tendency arises from the young child's predisposition to center attention on one or two specifics of a subject, and "his inability to shift his attention to other aspects of a situation."[7] The child also shows difficulty in seeing a state of affairs or an event from another's viewpoint.[8]

When such an impasse is reached, teachers need not scuttle the lesson, but may need to revise their expectations of its outcome. Through a varied supply of verbal and visual illustrations to insure the presence of specifics, teachers will meet young children on their own ground and within the limited framework of their developmental stage.

The Child Has a Rich Imaginative Life

Imaginative play and make-believe are prominent in the life of a young child. Such behavior declines in outward expression during the elementary school years, but in revised form it continues to occupy a significant role in the child's development. Its more obvious expressions are drawing, painting, creative writing, music, role playing, and creative dramatics. These are the means to a closer understanding of a people or a period—by identification with them or by representing details of their life and work.

Another channel for children's imaginative impulses is the formulation of hypotheses or hunches to explain events and processes they are studying. Teachers can stimulate children in this activity by having them tackle questions that call upon imaginative thought and the discovery of new relationships. By way of illustration:

- How can you tell that trees are living things?
- Why should children help parents with their work at home?
- What does this picture of the South Pole region tell us about that part of the world?
- Why does lace made by hand cost more than lace made by machine?
- Why could corn and rice not be grown on the same plot of ground?

Answers to such questions should be viewed as hypotheses to be explored by teacher and class and checked with books and other sources. A regular diet of such searching and discussion helps lay the basis for a thoughtful, creative intellectual life.

---

[7]John L. Phillips, Jr., *The Origins of Intellect: Piaget's Theory* (San Francisco: Freeman, 1969), p. 63.

[8]Ibid., p. 84.

DISADVANTAGED CHILDREN

"Disadvantaged," as used here, refers to children who, in addition to being socially and economically handicapped, are also lagging in educational achievement. The term "disadvantaged" does *not* apply to personality attributes, latent ability, or quality of personal relationships, or any single racial or ethnic group, for in these areas socially and educationally disadvantaged children are often average or even superior. Approximately 15 percent of the United States population of school-age children and youth may be described as disadvantaged. Disadvantaged children enter school below grade expectations and fall further behind with the passage of time. What are these children's needs that are so obviously not being fulfilled?

Background of Disadvantaged Pupils

Much has been written about the alleged "lacks" of disadvantaged children as viewed in terms of the demands of our predominantly middle-class educational system. They enter school handicapped by deficiencies in home background such as minimal family conversation; few, if any, trips to historical sites, zoos, museums; lack of experience in being read to and being taken to the library, having questions answered, and receiving explanations of how things work; lack of books; lack of educational toys. They may come to school each day with primary needs unsatisfied—hungry, ill-clothed, and below par physically.

Less has been written about the strengths and assets of disadvantaged children. Such children tend to be cooperative, patient, refreshingly relaxed about prestige as a goal, independent (the latter trait possibly springing from the absence of overprotection at home), and they enjoy music, companionship, and other humanistic experiences.

Approaches to Teaching Disadvantaged Children

1. Look upon the child's cultural background with respect. Idiosyncratic traits are often enriching differences to be valued rather than defects to be deplored. When children speak, accept their language and ideas sympathetically. Read to the class, organize reading circles or clubs, encourage the telling of stories and experiences, and plan excursions.
2. Avoid setting up middle-class standards of verbalization and behavior that you expect the children to observe. Such a procedure cuts children off from successful, satisfying participation in classroom learning experiences.
3. Remember that many disadvantaged children are from authoritarian homes. This does not imply that the teacher should assume an authoritarian manner; to the contrary, children should be

encouraged to take part in decision-making activities and democratic give-and-take. This requires patience on the part of the teacher and the provision of practice with democratic procedures on a small scale in small groups within the class.

4. Relate unfamiliar concepts and generalizations to concrete experiences that the class has recently had or that you can supply. Nothing alienates disadvantaged children from school so much as their being precipitated into difficult, affectively sterile content, top-heavy in abstractions and lacking in concrete references.

5. Expect the same variations among the disadvantaged as among any group of persons. Most writing about disadvantaged children overgeneralizes. This is true of the present treatment, too. Disadvantaged children are not all alike. While the above leads furnish valid guidelines, they can be harmful if they suggest a stereotype. Be attentive to disadvantaged pupils as individuals who require separate consideration.

Social Studies for the Disadvantaged

It is argued sometimes that the elementary school's program for disadvantaged pupils should be devoted entirely to the basic skills, especially reading and writing. However, the plan has not changed substantially the customary pattern of lagging test scores in the "basics" in these schools. The ineffectiveness of crash programs in reading is due partly to excessive time allotments for reading, paradoxical though that may seem. Observation reveals that many pupils experience ennui well before reading lessons are ended. Reading (a subject with no cognitive content of its own) can be taught to the point of diminishing returns. While success in school depends partly upon mastery of skills, such as those involved in reading, it depends at least equally upon cognitive development (that is, growth toward an orderly organization of knowledge).

The curriculum fields most likely to stimulate children's cognitive development are the social studies, science, and literature. Broadening children's horizons and building their interest in these fields provide precisely the kinds of stimulation that will benefit their academic progress most. Their concepts will be enlarged, the number of understood generalizations increased, vocabulary enriched, and curiosity about peoples, places, social processes, and natural phenomena aroused. Such all-around intellectual expansion produces an innate desire for more information. Self-propelled practice in reading ensues and typically increases skill even more than does formal instruction in reading. The amount of time allotted to the latter can then be reduced. In a classic investigation, with reduced instruction in reading per se and increased social studies projects, a group of slow learners "apparently acquired as much reading ability as equivalent pupils in the conventional school. The children established habits of wider reading and enjoyed reading more."[9]

In short, forcing children to overconcentrate on developing proficiency in reading, divorced from interesting content, may well teach them to dislike it. Conversely, an absorbing social studies program that gradually introduces reading as a purposeful tool for learning may gain more converts to reading than programs that overdo reading instruction seemingly for its own end.

Programs Designed for the Disadvantaged

A class of disadvantaged pupils may benefit from the same social studies content as do advantaged pupils, provided their greater need for the concrete and the relevant is kept in mind. Some programs have been designed explicitly for the disadvantaged. One of these is the Wilmington, Delaware, *Adventure in Human Relations* (see Chapter 9). It succeeds impressively in tying hard, everyday realities (broken homes, the inability of small family incomes to meet nutritional needs, gaps between standard English and dialect speech, and so forth) to mind-stretching, academic learning. Another program, *Human Behavior and Potential—Behavior Science* (see Chapter 4), stresses the importance of eliciting children's feelings and attitudes in order that their interests and behavior may be modified by the curriculum. Affective education projects (see Chapter 9) and the open-classroom unit described in Box 8.2 are further examples of content that have helped disadvantaged children come to a firmer grip with everyday life and to greater realization of their own potential for growth.

ATTITUDES OF CHILDREN TOWARD SOCIAL STUDIES

James H. McMillan cites 17 studies that seem to demonstrate the importance of positive attitudes for school success.[10] We are justified in having concern that surveys of subject preferences reveal that the social studies are relatively unpopular among children. They were unpopular over a generation ago, and surveys conducted since then show that the situation has not changed. All studies of subject preferences since 1937 known to the authors indicate that social studies rank below most other subjects, or are among the

---

[9]Arthur I. Gates and Miriam C. Pritchard, *Teaching Reading to Slow-Learning Children* (New York: Bureau of Publications, Teachers College, 1942), p. 62.

[10]James H. McMillan, "Factors Affecting the Development of Pupil Attitudes Toward School Subjects," *Psychology in the Schools*, 13 (July 1976), 322–325.

least liked.[11] In one study, almost twice as many children mentioned social studies unfavorably as mentioned them favorably, and the social studies field was not one that many children indicated they would like to learn more about.[12]

Factors Accounting for Low Interest in Social Studies

There are several probable reasons for the unpopularity of social studies. First, many parents and teachers believe that the three Rs are the most important school subjects. Through their anxiety about their children's progress in those subjects, they transmit their feelings and values to the children and undoubtedly influence their preferences.

Second, many children like the three Rs and spelling because of their clearcut, precise nature. They find security in having an immediate check upon their success, such as they receive on an answer to an arithmetic problem or their spelling of a word. It is unequivocally either right or wrong. By contrast, social studies problems are often less concrete, and their solutions are less definite and often controversial. In fact, to enjoy social studies requires the ability to accept partial solutions to problems with equanimity. This is not easy for all children. Many become vexed with indefinite and ambiguous generalizations, with obscure cause-and-effect relationships, and with the numerous maybes, buts, and ifs. Furthermore, today's difficult problems—nuclear dangers, racial problems, energy shortages, pollution of air, food, and water—may cause anxiety in children as well as in adults.

Third, the social studies are replete with abstract concepts (for ex-

---

[11]Ethel E. Holmes, "School Subjects Preferred by Children," in *Sixteenth Yearbook of the National Elementary Principal* (Washington, DC: National Education Association, 1937), pp. 336–344. Howard H. Mosher, "Subject Preferences of Girls and Boys," *School Review*, 60 (January 1952), 34–38. Joseph P. Rice, Jr. "A Comparative Study of Academic Interest Patterns among Selected Groups of Exceptional and Normal Intermediate Children," *California Journal of Educational Research*, 14 (May 1963), 131–137. Robert L. Curry, "Subject Preferences of 1,111 Fifth-Graders," *Peabody Journal of Education*, 41 (July 1963), 23–27. Lelon R. Capps and Linda S. Cox, "Attitude toward Arithmetic at the Fourth and Fifth-Grade Levels," *Arithmetic Teacher*, 16 (March 1969), 215–220 [includes data on social studies]. E. L. Greenblatt, "An Analysis of School Subject Preferences of Elementary School Children of the Middle Grades," *Journal of Educational Research*, 55 (August 1962), 554–555. Wayne L. Herman, Jr., "How Intermediate Children Rank the Subjects," *Journal of Educational Research*, 56 (April 1963), 435–436. Robert W. Wood, "An Investigation of School Subjects Preferred by Elementary School Children in South Dakota," *Education*, 99 (Fall 1978), 77–84.

[12]Arthur T. Jersild and Ruth T. Tasch, *Children's Interests and What They Suggest for Education* (New York: Teachers College, 1949), p. 77. In this same study it was also reported that when children were asked to name topics they would like to learn more about, some mentioned social studies topics. Hence, a part of their dissatisfaction may have been with social studies *as taught*, not necessarily with social studies content per se.

ample, "responsibility," "progress," "climate") that do not have the clean, tangible, physically demonstrable character of, say, the abstractions of science, such as magnetism, osmosis, relative humidity.

Fourth, some curriculums and some teachers omit controversial topics on the ground that children are not mature enough to deal with them. Children who study their local community, for example, may not be given an opportunity to find out why so many blacks live in ghettos or the causes of corruption in local government. As a result, the study may seem flat and not have much to do with the real world around them.

Fifth, many textbooks are hard to read, are crowded with too many topics, and are dehumanized. Social studies become a dreary, colorless field. To make matters worse, such inadequate books are often not supplemented, and there is an overemphasis on remembrance of highly condensed information.

Sixth, many social studies classes are poorly taught. They are teacher-dominated, seat-centered, and textbook-centered.

Overcoming Lagging Interest

Teacher enthusiasm has often been called the key to favorable pupil attitudes. This view was corroborated by A. L. Egan's intensive study of the interests of children in Grades 3 to 6. They tended to mirror the genuine interests of their teachers.[13] McMillan reviewed 124 research studies on interests, most of which seemed to show that strong teacher enthusiasm generally could be counted on to generate enthusiasm in pupils. He also found that the students' previous backgrounds, including their previous attitudes toward subjects, also contributed to their present attitudes.[14] On the other hand, one group of teachers with strong interest in the social sciences were unable to transmit their interest to their pupils any more successfully than did teachers whose interest in the social sciences was weak.[15] We can only conclude that, while teacher enthusiasm *may* promote pupil interest, it is not always sufficient.

Strong interest on the part of the teacher usually needs to be buttressed by teaching procedures that actively involve children in their learning. This was demonstrated in a unique study of 20 classrooms by W. Linwood Chase and Gilbert M. Wilson. In 10 of these, a majority of pupils said they pre-

---

[13]A. L. Egan, "Incidental Living: A Study of Attitudes," *Education*, 93 (April/May 1973), 314–321.

[14]McMillan, "Factors Affecting the Development of Pupil Attitudes."

[15]Mark E. Stedman and Michael J. Breen, "Teacher Interest and Pupil Attitudes," *Educational and Psychological Measurement*, 37 (Winter 1977), 1091–1094. Mention should also be made of failure to find a significant correlation between the preferences of pupils and preferences of teachers by James Inskeep and Monroe Rowland, "An Analysis of School Subject Preferences of Elementary School Children in the Middle Grades: Another Look," *Journal of Educational Research*, 58 (January 1965), 225–228.

ferred social studies to other subjects; and in the other 10, no child accorded first choice to social studies, and few accorded it second choice. All 20 teachers reported that they preferred to teach the social studies over all other subjects. Sharp differences were found in the teaching in the two sets of classrooms. In brief, where social studies were popular, Chase and Wilson found ample opportunities for pupil participation, a wide range of activities (trips, committee work, dramatics, interviewing resource visitors, and so on), and instruction in study and research skills. These conditions were not typical of the classrooms in which the social studies were unpopular.[16] How to provide such opportunities is treated in subsequent chapters. In fact, the question of how to teach social studies so as to create strong pupil interest is the subject matter of this entire book.

FOR STUDY AND EXPLORATION

1. Give further implications for social studies instruction of children's characteristics named in this chapter.
2. Add other childhood characteristics than those discussed in this chapter that might have a bearing on social studies instruction.
3. Administer to a few children an interest inventory such as *What I Like to Do* (Science Research Associates) or *Inventory for Elementary Grades* (Center for Psychological Services, George Washington University) or *Personality and Interest Inventory* (Teachers College Press). Summarize the extent to which their interests include topics and activities that are embraced by social studies.

FURTHER READING

There is no dearth of books on child development. Among the more readable of those showing special sensitivity to the role of the school are Helen Bee's *The Developing Child*, 2nd ed. (New York: Harper, 1978); Betty Rowen, *The Children We See: An Observational Approach to Child Study*, especially chap. 10, "Knowing the School-Age Child" (New York: Holt, Rinehart and Winston, 1973); and Mollie S. Smart and Russell C. Smart, *Children: Development and Relationships*, 3rd ed. (New York: Macmillan, 1977).

Ever since the heightened interest in cognitive development and in Piaget's work in particular, it has been hard to find impressionistic reports on children's proclivities, preoccupations, "developmental tasks," and similar topics of importance to the teacher, that characterized the work of Arnold Gesell a generation ago. Nevertheless, see Phillipe Muller, *The Tasks of Childhood*, especially chap. 9, "The School Child and His Developmental Tasks" (New York: World University Library, 1969); Smart and Smart, *Children* (cited in preceding paragraph), chap. 11, "Increasing Competence as a Learner and Doer"; and Harold W. Bernard, *Human Development in Western Culture*, 5th ed. (Boston: Allyn and Bacon), 1978, chaps. 8–11.

---

[16]W. Linwood Chase and Gilbert M. Wilson, "Preference Studies in Elementary School Social Studies," *Journal of Education*, 140 (April 1958), 26–27.

To delve further into children's creative and imaginative impulses, the reader is referred to A. Reza Arasteh and Josephine D. Arasteh, *Creativity in Human Development: An Interpretive and Annotated Bibliography* (Cambridge, MA: Schenkman Publishing Company, 1976), chap. 1, "Creativity and Related Processes in the Young Child." Besides discussing originality, fantasy, curiosity, and related subjects, the authors describe methods for increasing creativity. See also Mark A. Barnett, "The Role of Play and Make-Believe in Children's Cognitive Development," *Journal of Education*, 159 (November 1977), 38–48; and Robert D. Strom, *Psychology for the Classroom* (Englewood Cliffs, NJ: Prentice-Hall, 1969), chap. 5, "Educating for Creative Behavior."

An absorbing account of what is known about pupils' attitudes toward school and about their attentiveness during classroom instruction appears in chaps. 2 and 3, respectively, of Philip W. Jackson's *Life in Classrooms* (New York: Holt, Rinehart and Winston, 1968).

6 Stages in
Social Studies Learning

*Knowledge of the timetable of intellectual
development should theoretically make
possible, for the first time, the scientific,
as opposed to the arbitrary or traditional,
grade placement of subject matter.*
David P. Ausubel

Someday we may have the "time table of intellectual development" which Ausubel refers to in the above quotation. We do not have a precise schedule today, but much more is known about developmental sequences than is reflected in today's largely arbitrary and tradition-based curriculum. The best place to start looking for information about stages of growth is in the work of Jean Piaget, a Swiss psychologist.

STAGES AND AGES

Piaget has provided us with a realistic picture of the intellectual development of children in the Western world. Although more data are needed to substantiate certain features of the picture and to clarify details, numerous investigators and observers of children in Europe and America have verified, in general, Piaget's developmental sequences. These sequences offer teachers a meaningful framework of the child's development.

The stages are age-related, not age-determined. That is, there is a probability that a child of six or seven years is likely to reason about a problem in a particular way and that the young adolescent will employ very different thought processes. Piaget has described the characteristics of thought at different stages. Of course, individual differences exist within an age group, with some children being more advanced than others because of such factors as heredity and opportunities for learning.

Sensorimotor Period

The first stage in the development of intelligence is the *sensorimotor*, lasting from birth to about 18 months. During this period, infants are carrying on countless transactions with the physical world as they look, suck, grasp, and experiment with objects in the environment. They assimilate information from these transactions—that an object continues to exist even when it is out of sight, for example—and their developing mental structures change to accommodate the new information. "Thinking," however, is action-oriented; the infant does not have the capability for representational thought and so can only *act out* what is going on in his mind. If asked, "Where is your teddy bear?" the child can look at the teddy and lift it up, but cannot visualize or think about the action before carrying it out.

Period of Preoperational Thought

The next stage, *preoperational thought*, is of concern to the primary school teacher, for it typifies most children in kindergarten and first grade. Thought is termed preoperational because the child lacks the ability to perform operations of thought upon data. Instead, the following characteristics describe the thinking processes:

1. Children are perceptually oriented; each child makes judgments of how things look to him or her. If the child has made a map on the classroom floor and is looking north on the map, he or she cannot answer a question from the point of view of an observer looking south. The answer will depend on how things look to him or her, for children cannot turn the map around in their minds. By way of another example, if parents point out to their child the long shadows cast by the sun as it sets, the child's teacher may find it futile to try to explain that a photograph with long shadows, taken at dawn, is indeed a morning scene. We can give the child a logical explanation of why long shadows occur at both morning and evening by going into how the earth turns, why the sun appears to move, and why both the morning and the evening sun throw long shadows. But the perceptual, real-life experience means more to children than a logical explanation. Expanded perceptual experiences are required at this stage.

2. Children center on one variable only, usually the one that stands out visually; and they lack the ability to coordinate variables. For example, a kindergarten child is pouring juice into paper cups. The standard-size cups run out, and the teacher substitutes some that are

much taller, but also smaller in diameter. As the children drink their juice, several comment that Jimmy, Eddie, and Danny have more juice. Why? Because those children have cups that are taller. The dimension of height, not width, stands out. Children's thinking is rigid; they do not perform operations on what they see. Later, they will reason that "higher than" is compensated for by "skinnier than" and that both kinds of cups may hold the same amount of juice. Similarly, when a first-grade boy was shown a map of the United States and was asked which of two indicated areas (Florida and Georgia) was larger, he immediately pointed to Florida. (The two states have approximately the same area.) When he is older, he will see that the elongated thinness of Florida's conspicuous peninsula is compensated for by Georgia's chunkiness. This abilty to see reciprocal relationships in two sets of data is an important logical tool available to older chidren, but not to the preoperational child.

3. The child has difficulty in realizing that an object can possess more than one property and that multiple classifications are possible. It is hard for a child to see that one can live in Los Angeles and in California at the same time, that the city is contained in the state, and that, since there are cities in the state in addition to Los Angeles, there are logically *more* people in the state than in any one city in that state. The operation of combining elements to form a whole and then seeing a part in relation to the whole has not yet developed, and so hierarchical relationships cannot be mastered.

So far, this consideration of preoperational thinking has been largely negative. We have seen that the child lacks the ability to combine parts into a whole, to put parts together in different ways, and to reverse processes. What, then, *can* the child do? The development of logical processes is not at a standstill during this period; there are some positive accomplishments. We see, for example, the rudiments of classification: The child can make collections of things on the basis of some criterion. Thus, if we present a first-grade girl with pictures of stores and ask her to sort them into two piles, those in each pile being alike in some way, she can do this. Some children may put the pictures of food stores in one pile, all other stores in another. Others may classify the stores differently, in terms of their products. A few children, if previously introduced to the concept of general versus specialized stores, may place pictures of general stores (for example, supermarkets and department stores) in one pile and pictures of specialized stores (for example, auto supply store, book shop, bakery) in another. A few children will discover a third criterion, such as size, or perhaps architectural features. The ability to classify, of course, is essential to the formation of classes and, eventually, a hierarchy of classes.

Children are also beginning to arrange things in a series. They can compare two members of a set that are in a consecutive order; they know that

Tuesday comes after Monday, for instance. But since Friday comes after Tuesday, does Friday also come after Monday? This operation, involving seeing logical relations among things or events that are arranged in a series, is not yet possible to the preoperational child, but simple experiences with seriation prepare the way for the development of such thought processes.

These include daily marking of the calendar, making a record of the day's class schedule, learning to read the scale of a thermometer, maintaining and referring to a chronological file (such as a file of class-dictated experience records or a file of *My Weekly Readers*), and noting such sequences as the numbered buildings on a street, the procession of the seasons, and the call numbers of library books.

Period of Concrete Operations

Between the ages of 7 and 11, on the average, as children assimilate information from their actions and accommodate mental structures to new information, thinking processes change. Children abandon their perceptual judgments, and thought takes on certain logical properties. Piaget calls this the stage of *concrete operations*, because, while children use logic, the content of their thinking is concrete rather than abstract. One of the mental operations that develops is the combining of elements; children begin to put two and two together, figuratively as well as literally. They use this combining operation to discover (although not until toward the end of this stage) the concept of a hierarchy, and so the relationships involved in city, county, state, nation, and hemisphere begin to become clear.

Another property of logical thought is the recognition that one can manipulate elements of a whole in various ways without changing the total. An urban renewal project may change the appearance of a community beyond recognition; yet the total area of the community remains unchanged. The political boundaries within Europe may change many times, but the total area of Europe remains the same, or is *conserved*.

A third property of logical thought is identity, which is basically a null operation. An application of the identity operation to social studies is the one-to-one correspondence a pupil carries on to establish identity between two sets. Is Darby, Pennsylvania, a city or a town? To answer that question we have our students find an acceptable definition of a city and then compare each of its characteristics with corresponding characteristics of Darby. Was the Eskimo belief in Sedna, goddess of sea animals, a *religious* faith? First we must help the pupils define religion, then compare each characteristic of religion with the Eskimo belief in Sedna. Is Sweden an archipelago? The pupil must compare each characteristic of archipelagoes with each characteristic of Sweden on a one-to-one basis to answer the question.

Of all the properties of logical thinking, one of the most critical to develop is reversibility. Every change that the mind makes upon sensory data is reversible. The child can mentally rearrange a winding street shown on a map leading from Point A to Point B by thinking of it as stretched out in a straight line, in order to estimate its length by reference to the map's scale of miles. After making the estimate, the child turns his or her attention again to the winding arrangement as depicted on the map. The child understands that the length is conserved. Similarly, he or she can solve the problem of whether or not matter in a total system (say, a river system) is conserved when a river carries away soil and deposits it in the river delta by reversing the depositing process.

Period of Formal Operations

The fourth and last stage in the development of logical thinking, *formal thinking*, begins roughly at 12 years of age. According to Piaget, most adolescents are capable of doing an "if this happens, then that is likely to happen" kind of thinking. They can identify variables in a problem and examine them critically. They can understand and appreciate the irony of political cartoons, such as one of Herblock's in which a dwarf, labeled "Minority Rule," is shown pointing a large pistol, labeled "Filibuster," at a group of normal-sized adults and saying, "Sure I'm for equalizing things." They can also reason logically from contrary-to-fact propositions, such as "Suppose each of the 50 states was a sovereign nation with independent power to establish its own tariffs, its own postal rates, its own flag, and the like; how would it change our society?"

INTERPRETATIONS OF PIAGET'S STAGES

Some American educators and psychologists have been critical of Piaget's formulation of stages. They allege that he makes it appear that the transition between stages is abrupt rather than gradual; that each stage is distinct and does not possess characteristics that overlap with other stages; and that intellectual growth is the product of inner maturation, free of cultural and environmental influences. The superficiality of such criticisms and the extent to which each merely demolishes a straw man has been pointed out by a number of distinguished psychologists. "Actually," points out Ausubel, "developmental stages imply nothing more than identifiable sequential phases in an orderly progression of development. . . . there is no reason why their *manner of achievement* must necessarily be abrupt. . . . a certain amount of overlapping among age groups is inevitable. . . . Piaget's age levels, like Gesell's, are nothing more than *average* approximations set for purposes of convenience. . . . Neither is the concept of developmental states invalidated by the demonstration that they are susceptible to environmental influence,"[1] a susceptibility pointed out by Piaget himself and

---

[1]David P. Ausubel et al., *Educational Psychology: A Cognitive View*, 2nd ed. (New York: Holt, Rinehart and Winston, 1978), pp. 225–227.

his followers. Despite cultural variations, it is interesting to note that a number of investigators in the United States and elsewhere have drawn conclusions quite similar to Piaget's with respect to the developmental sequences (but not always in terms of age levels).

Nevertheless, as Helen Bee points out, there remain certain unresolved problems with Piaget's theory: (1) Not all children develop at the same rate; (2) a child is not at a given stage on every task or in every situation; and (3) some of the ages proposed by Piaget for the onset of a given stage appear to be high.[2] Specifically, with respect to Bee's third point, some believe that Piaget underestimates the preoperational child's ability to deal with certain abstractions. It is important to give examples of this possibility. Two follow.

A. H. McNaughton reports success in making it possible for a group of 10- to 12-year-olds to move a step or two from operational thinking toward abstract thinking. He exposed them to successively enriched teaching about African bushmen. The pupils' ability to supply abstractions in their responses to questions increased in proportion to the degree of in-depth information they had access to.[3]

David P. Ausubel gives as an example the possible development of the concept of "work," which a preoperational child may acquire from the experience of seeing cars repaired, housekeeping chores performed, his or her parents employed at their occupations, and the like. Children may discover attributes of work (work is necessary, work is useful, and so forth), or they may have these attributes pointed out to them. The child checks each activity against the attributes, and thereupon forms the abstraction "work"—built from the raw materials of direct experience.[4] Once formed, an abstraction becomes part of the child's mental apparatus. Younger children can deal even with contrary-to-fact propositions if they have been introduced to, and have become familiar with, the abstractions that are involved. Thus, if a first-grader in the city has learned the meaning of work through observation and other direct experience and has studied farming in school with films, pictures, stories about farms, perhaps even a trip to a farm, he or she could probably handle such a question as: What problems would a city man have if he were suddenly to switch jobs with a farmer?

We thus conclude that acceleration is indeed possible. Concepts could probably grow in complexity at a more rapid rate than they customarily do. That would require teachers who know how to, and who would in actuality, provide their classes with an abundance of observational and direct experiences and other forms of enrichment. Teachers with the requisite skill, energy, and devotion have always been in short supply.

---

[2]Helen Bee, *The Developing Child*, 2nd ed. (New York: Harper, 1978).

[3]A. H. McNaughton, "Piaget's Theory and Primary School Social Studies," *Educational Review*, 19 (November 1966), 23–32.

[4]Ausubel et al., *Educational Psychology*, p. 234.

BOX 6.1   GRADES K–3

Applications of Piaget's Findings to Primary-Grade Social Studies

Piaget has never tried to apply his findings to teaching procedures or to curriculum, but a number of educators have. Kathleen E. Metz is one of the very few who has ventured to draw implications for teaching primary-grade social studies.* Among her inferences are the following:

1. Limit any study to a small geographic area, one that is "spatially accessible to the child."
2. Keep the content largely contemporary.
3. Avoid tasks that require children to undertake classification that requires them to make "class inclusion." (Class inclusion is the ability to form subclasses, and to include subclasses in a larger class. For example, up to age 10, most of Piaget's subjects denied the possibility of a person's being both Genevan and Swiss at the same time.) Thus, avoid as a major goal the identification of similarities and differences among cultures. Differentiation is a normal process among six-year-olds, but the ability to identify commonalities usually comes later.

*"Children's Thinking and Primary Social Studies Curricula," *Elementary School Journal*, 79 (November 1978), 115–121.

BENEFITS TO TEACHERS OF KNOWLEDGE OF STAGES

The teacher who is aware of stage characteristics is in a position to diagnose pupil thought and ask the kinds of questions that will help children to think more logically. The teacher can also plan learning activities suited to the developmental characteristics of the class. Most important of all, knowledge of stages makes teachers sensitive to published programs that are topheavy with information, are affectively sterile, overlook the need for concrete experiences, and have little relevance to children's concerns. Stagesoriented teachers see through the inadequacies of such programs and quickly eliminate them from consideration.

SOCIAL STUDIES READINESS

When children have sufficient maturity, preparatory training, and interest to engage profitably in learning a skill or a concept, they have achieved the requisite readiness for it. In other words, readiness is a particularly favorable point in the development for their learning of the skill or concept. There are no tests in social studies, as there are in reading, to determine when this point is reached for a given child, so just what does readiness for learning a social studies concept mean? How do we know, for example, whether or not a first-grade child is prepared to learn about faraway regions and faraway times? When is a child prepared to move from concrete matters (specific and particular events, places, people, items) to abstract matters (justice as a human aspiration, crime as a form of inadequate socialization, "expensive" as a relative term and a point on a continuum from "economical" to "extravagant")?

We have very little information about readiness for social studies concepts. As already shown, Piaget has furnished data on various types of thinking that we can reasonably expect at various stages. But in only a general way and through inference can we draw conclusions from his data or from the work of others concerning appropriate subject matter. In the absence of adequate information, curriculum-makers have had to work from assumptions of their own. It was indicated in Chapter 4 that proponents of the expanding-environment curriculum assume that children are not ready for making systematic study of foreign cultures until about age nine (Grade 4), and that it is more reasonable before that age to have them confine their study to the here and now. Educators today generally reject that view. Another quite different assumption was made by Bruner in his widely quoted, startling assertion that "any subject can be taught effectively in some intellectually honest form to any child at any stage of development."[5] With this statement as a spur, a number of curriculum-makers have introduced concepts into the primary grades that have traditionally not been introduced until the intermediate grades, high school, or even college, such as cultural universals and factors determining prices and wages. This trend raises two important and interesting questions: *Can* any subject be taught at any age? Are today's children more precocious than those of the past?

Can Any Subject Be Taught at Any Age?

There is no evidence that the quantity theory of money, for example, can be satisfactorily taught to kindergarten children. Furthermore, Bruner himself recognized limitations to his celebrated statement in the very book in which he made it. He wrote:

> . . . It is only when we are equipped with such knowledge [as produced by Piaget in the study of physical causality, of morality, of number, and the rest] that we will be in a position to know how the child will translate whatever we present to him into his own subjective terms.[6]

There is a sense, however, in which the proposition that anything can be taught at any age is acceptable. For example, kindergarten teachers can assume that the geographical theme of the use of land can be taught to their

---

[5]Jerome S. Bruner, *The Process of Education* (Cambridge: Harvard University Press, 1961), p. 33.

[6]Ibid., p. 53.

pupils as well as to those in the upper grades. But they know that they would need to emphasize those applications the child can observe first hand (lawns, playgrounds, roadways, and so on). They would leave for subsequent teachers such topics as how the cultivation of land is subject to the law of diminishing returns, and how the shadoof (a bucket device common along the Nile, operated by hand) is used to irrigate crops in Egypt.

Are Today's Children More Precocious Than Those of a Generation Ago?

A number of educators believe children today are more precocious than formerly (and hence ready for learning at an earlier age). They point to the heavy use made of television, expanded family travel, and increased numbers and availability of children's books. They conclude that children have wider frames of reference and more sophisticated knowledge than children of the pretelevision era.

Most of the evidence does not support this view. Eleanor E. Maccoby, in her review of research on effects of the mass media upon children, points out that although television has made "very substantial inroads upon children's time, . . . it has not appreciably broadened children's knowledge or interests, at least not so far."[7] Paul A. Witty and Mary Ellen Batinich found that new vocabulary acquired by children via television disappears quickly.[8] Robert C. Hornik, in his review of research on the subject and in his own study, found that the effects of televiewing are either nonexistent or slightly negative.[9]

The most convincing evidence that we can easily mistake children's apparent sophistication and fund of ideas acquired from television for precocity is found in Dorothy J. Mugge's studies of first- and second-graders whose mean intelligence and socioeconomic status were above average. She asked the first-graders questions about simple social studies concepts. The average child could respond to only 25 percent of the questions. In answer to the question, "Where do you live?" pupils typically responded by naming a street or a state. Several said they did not live in a city, but on a street. They were stumped by questions requiring multiple classification such as "What do you call your father's mother?"[10]

---

[7]Eleanor E. Maccoby, "Effects of the Mass Media," in Martin L. Hoffman and Lois W. Hoffman (Eds.), *Review of Child Development Research*, Vol. 1 (New York: Russell Sage Foundation, 1964), pp. 330, 345.

[8]Paul A. Witty and Mary Ellen Batinich, "A 1967 Study of Televiewing," in J. Allen Figurel (Ed.), *Reading and Realism*, Proceedings of the 13th Annual Convention, International Reading Association (Newark, DE: International Reading Association, 1969), pp. 732–737.

[9]Robert C. Hornik, "Television Access and the Slowing of Cognitive Growth," *American Educational Research Journal*, 15 (Winter 1978), 1–15.

[10]Dorothy J. Mugge, "Are Young Children Ready to Study the Social Studies?" *Elementary School Journal*, 68 (February 1968), 232–240.

Mugge's second-graders lacked precision of knowledge with respect to important aspects of the community. In regard to the postal service, for example, very few children could tell how much it costs to send a letter or why a stamp is canceled. Like the first-grade pupils, they had difficulty in keeping cities, states, and countries in their proper hierarchical relationship. Those children who traveled did not know significantly more than those who had not traveled. Mugge found a sea of empty concepts beneath a facile surface.[11]

If contemporary American children were exceptionally precocious, one would expect to find them exceeding Piaget's norms. A number of investigators, however, have compared their data on children's thinking with those of Piaget and have found them strikingly similar. Millie Almy studied several hundred children of diverse socioeconomic backgrounds from kindergarten to Grade 3, focusing on their transition from the preoperational to the operational stages. Her findings generally conform to those of Piaget.[12] John D. Towler and L. D. Nelson studied the ability of pupils in Grades 1 to 6 to understand the concept of scale. Each pupil was shown a three-dimensional model of a farm, five features of which (barn, lake, and so forth) were each reproduced as a cardboard cutout in five sizes. The pupil was to choose the correct size to fit a blank cardboard that was to serve as the base of a map of the farm. Except for the sixth-graders, the children's mean scores were low. These findings closely approximate those of Piaget, who reports that full understanding of scale does not emerge until the ages of 11 or 12.[13]

Instances of Early Readiness

If it is doubtful that children today are more precocious than their peers of earlier times, it is nonetheless true that young children are able to learn concepts previously considered too difficult for them. This is partly because the concepts are probably not as inherently difficult as once believed, but it is mainly because of superior teaching materials, a generous use of concrete demonstrations, and imaginative use of dramatization and role playing. Thus, first-graders demonstrated in a series of related studies that they were able to learn "at least some of the content" in economics in the vivid and imaginative *Our Working World* program (see Chapters 3 and 12). (Children of lower ability, however, were unable to score better than chance on the economics test used.)[14]

---

[11]Dorothy J. Mugge, "Precocity of Today's Young Children: Real or Wishful?" *Social Education*, 27 (December 1963), 436–439.

[12]Millie Almy, *Young Children's Thinking: Studies of Some Aspects of Piaget's Theory* (New York: Teachers College, 1970).

[13]John O. Towler and L. D. Nelson, "The Elementary School Child's Concept of Scale," *Journal of Geography*, 67 (January 1968), 24–28.

[14]A. Guy Larkins and James P. Shaver, "Economics Learning in Grade One: The USU Assessment Studies," *Social Education*, 33 (December 1969), 958–963.

Disadvantaged kindergarten children, in another study, were taught about spatial relations, earth-sun relationships, day-night relationships, and seasonal characteristics. A diagnostic testing device was administered before and after the instruction. The results showed a significant gain. The distinctive characteristic of the program was the use of demonstrations and manipulative activities with concrete materials.[15]

Other studies, too, have shown that children seem able to learn much about the world at an early age. We know little, however, about the depth and performance of early academic learning or the amount of the chidren's true understanding. Parents, teachers, and research workers are sometimes misled by the glibness of middle-class children into believing that their understanding equals their array of information. One of Piaget's contributions has been to show the deceptive nature of children's facility with language. We are also well warned by Ausubel: "When abstractions are introduced prematurely, some children become quite adept at mouthing them and, at the same time, concealing their lack of true understanding."[16]

What to Do About Readiness

The message for teachers conveyed by the bulk of data reported in this chapter is clear: Proceed slowly! It is so easy for us to be deceived by children's superficial maturity and sophistication and to believe them "ready" when they may not be ready.

Curriculum writers have tended to overestimate children's readiness. They have given expert attention to the logical organization and balance of subject matter, but they have neglected, except in general and obvious ways, attention to the child's ability at a given stage to profit advantageously and economically from the subject matter. This point is further documented in Chapter 7 where the content of each of the social sciences is examined from the point of view of the child's ability to assimilate it. History fares particularly badly.

Our best protection against wasteful teaching of concepts beyond the child's grasp is a habit of finding out, on our own, what our pupils already know about the concepts slated for development each week, or even each day. We can do this through questioning and discussion, and sometimes through informal pretests. If discussion reveals that the background of a large portion of the class is weak, the theme may have to be abandoned, or at least expectations of the outcomes may need to be changed. If, on the other hand, the pupils show advance evidence of being well informed and in fair command of the concepts to be learned, again teachers may need to revamp their plans, this time to provide more challenging material.

---

[15]Dora Portugaly, "A Study of the Development of Disadvantaged Kindergarten Children's Understanding of the Globe," *Dissertation Abstracts*, 28 (April 1968), 4056-A.

[16]Ausubel et al., *Educational Psychology*, p. 113.

FOR STUDY AND EXPLORATION

1. Visit three classes, one with children at the preoperational level, one at the stage of concrete operations, and one at the stage of formal operations. Note performances and responses during social studies instruction that verify, or vary from, Piaget's formulations.
2. With one or two other students, study Lavatelli's activities to aid in the child's acquisition of classification concepts (consult Lavatelli's book listed under "Further Reading"). Carry them out with a small group of kindergarten or first-grade children, and evaluate your results.
3. Construct a set of questions similar to Mugge's (see footnotes 10 and 11) and use them in interviews with a sampling of first- and second-grade children. What social studies experiences do you conclude, on the basis of the children's responses, would be most appropriate?

FURTHER READING

Piaget's own writings tend to be technical and lacking in the capsule summaries that busy teachers would like to have. Fortunately, his findings and theories have been summarized ably by others:

Dorothy J. Mugge, "Social Studies Beginnings: Piagetian Theory and Sensitive Periods," *Elementary School Journal*, 74 (April 1974), 399–407.
Helen Bee, *The Developing Child*, 2nd ed. (New York: Harper, 1978), chap. 9.
Hans J. Furth and Harry Wachs, *Thinking Goes to School: Piaget's Theory in Practice with Some Additional Thoughts* (New York: Oxford University Press, 1975).
John L. Phillips, Jr., *The Origins of Intellect: Piaget's Theory*, 2nd ed. (San Francisco: Freeman, 1975).
Norah Rosenau, "The Sources of Children's Political Concepts: An Application of Piaget's Theory," in David C. Schwartz and Sandra K. Schwartz (Eds.), *New Directions in Political Socialization* (New York: Free Press, 1975), chap. 6. Piaget's theory is well described on pp. 164–172.

Teachers who wish to tackle Piaget's own works might begin with Barbel Inhelder and Jean Piaget, *Early Growth in the Child: Classification and Seriation* (New York: Harper, 1964). It presents evidence on children's acquisition of logical relationships. The discussion of "all-some" relations in chap. 3 has particular implications for the social studies.

A Piagetian program for children in kindergarten and first grade has been developed by Celia Stendler Lavatelli and is described in her *Piaget's Theory Applied to an Early Childhood Curriculum* (Cambridge: American Science and Engineering, 1970). Lavatelli tells how the child may be helped to acquire the mental processes that compose classification, space and number, and seriation through concrete materials and through key questions asked by the teacher.

An attempt to show similarities among the developmental theories of Piaget, Freud, Erikson, and Kohlberg has been made by John F. Lavach and Roger R. Ries in "Ages and Stages: Child Development Revisited," *Social Education*, 42 (May 1978), 375–377.

7 The Psychology of Teaching Social Studies to Children

The important thing is not that every child
should be taught, but that every child
should be given the wish to learn.
John Lubbock

The description of the nature of childhood in the preceding two chapters *implies* much about how the child learns. But to be of maximum benefit to the teacher, such description needs to be supplemented by explicit knowledge of how learning takes place, and of what teachers can do to have it take place so that the child will discover learning to be attractive and even exciting. Incomplete though our understanding of classroom learning is, research has established a sufficient basis for citing some principles that are important in teaching social studies. This chapter will present the major principles and will also take up the teaching of concepts, and the thorny problem of classroom management.

PRINCIPLES OF LEARNING SOCIAL STUDIES

Thousands of learning experiments with children involving all subject areas and skills have been conducted in laboratories and classrooms. Yet, after eliminating those yielding ambiguous results and those without discernible classroom implications, we are left with a scant handful that yield useful principles. Those selected for inclusion here are those that have proved workable in classroom practice and that are especially applicable to teaching the social studies.

The Child Requires a Suitable Background of Information

David P. Ausubel, preceding the preface of his *Educational Psychology*, states: "If I had to reduce all of educational psychology to just one principle, I would say this: The most important single factor influencing learning is what the learner already knows. Ascertain this and teach him accordingly."[1] The importance of this principle in teaching social studies cannot be exaggerated.

Teachers need to determine frequently what their pupils know about the themes, generalizations, and concepts embodied in the content they are about to study. This can be accomplished through direct questioning and class discussion. In Grade 3 and above, informal teacher-made tests can be useful.

In conducting a study of national forests as part of a larger study of recreational areas, one teacher discovered that some of her pupils had visited a national forest, responded with apparent awe to its beauty, used its camping facilities, and learned about the Forest Service's aim of "multiple use." These pupils were obviously prepared to plunge into the study. Most of the class, however, lacked such background. The teacher built it up through vicarious means. Nature magazines and a filmstrip were introduced. The class also learned from verbal descriptions given by their experienced, informed classmates.

Sometimes teachers find that their pupils' knowledge of the planned lesson content is considerable. In that case, it may be a waste of time to pursue the lesson. It is unnecessary to teach concepts that children have already mastered.

Motivation Increases the Effectiveness of Learning

Motivation is an individual's inner drive toward a given goal. Although learning can take place in the absence of motivation, strongly motivated learners throw themselves into the work at hand, giving it their sustained attention and obtaining satisfaction from it. Children's natural desire for knowledge as evidenced by their curiosity and their drive to exlore provides motivational power that "is at least potentially the most important kind of motivation in classroom learning."[2]

Teachers can set the stage so as to increase the likelihood that motivation will develop. First, they can help a class identify and clarify learning goals, both for the long-term unit of work and for individual lessons. They can ask the children: "What are some of the questions about this subject that we ought to try to find answers to?" "In what ways will the subject be useful to us?" "How does the subject tie in with your interest in photography (or

[1] David P. Ausubel, *Educational Psychology: A Cognitive View* (New York: Holt, Rinehart and Winston, 1968), p. vi; 2nd ed. (1978), with others, p. iv.

[2] Ibid. (1978), p. 403.

stamp collecting, dressmaking, fishing, and so forth)?" If answers are shallow the teacher can restate them or shift them. Questions can help the class to develop a sense of direction. Clarity concerning the subject and its relationship to their present interests enable children to incorporate the new learning into their present fund of knowledge.

Second, when new facts or ideas are to be presented, it is preferable for teachers to "take charge" rather than let the textbook assume dominance. Most children require a generous amount of time to assimilate new concepts. Textbooks are in a hurry and keep beckoning the class to move along. The wise teacher has the books put away for a while and will devote one or two sessions to whole-class and small-group discussion of the topic. He or she challenges the class to find nontextbook materials, and encourages children to make their own drawings, stories, or dramatizations to enlarge their thinking about the concepts.

Third, active pupil participation in learning can be planned. Subsequent chapters illustrate how participation may occur in discussions, committee work, formulation of goals, construction activities, role play, excursions, evaluation activities, and other undertakings.

Fourth, learners may be motivated through being presented with facts or ideas that are in conflict with commonly accepted beliefs. Conceptual conflict follows, causing surprise, perplexity, or bafflement. The learners are thus motivated to search for a resolution that will eliminate the contradiction or at least lessen the discrepancy.[3]

It is not difficult for teachers to find ways of jarring children's conceptual complacency. This is because much of children's knowledge of the social sciences is naive and stereotyped. The class is studying deserts. The teacher discovers they have a narrow view of deserts—as endless stretches of sand with, perhaps, camels and Bedouins scattered about. The teacher presents a contrasting picture, displaying photographs of desert shrubs with their thick leaves and stems, and in bloom; also a heavy desert rainfall. The teacher reads a description from T. E. Lawrence, the adventurer and archeologist, in which the range of desert temperatures is revealed, another from Edward Abbey's *Desert Solitaire*, and others from Joseph Wood Krutch's *Desert Year* and *Voice of the Desert*.

At the outset of a study of American Indians, the teacher may find that children have the stereotyped notion, perpetuated by television Westerns, of Indians as wicked, ruthless, and unprincipled. Moreover, they may have the common mistaken idea that there is one American Indian culture that cuts across all tribes. The teacher may then read or have children read an authentic account of an Indian culture which presents valid and typical characteristics for that culture.

---

[3]Daniel E. Berlyne, "Curiosity and Education," in John D. Krumboltz (Ed.), *Learning and the Educational Process* (Skokie: Rand McNally, 1965), chap. 3.

Fifth, the teacher may stress the fun of learning social studies, the satisfaction of knowing a topic well, and the pride one can take in being able to read maps and use reference books in running down facts. Teachers should never underestimate the power and the contagion of their own attitudes toward learning.

Lastly, plain, unadorned, energetic teaching often proves to be surprisingly productive in building interest. Some teachers feel, mistakenly, that until children are well motivated, there is little use in beginning the study of a new social studies theme. But getting involved in a learning situation induces its own motivation. In the words of Ausubel: "Frequently, the best way of teaching an unmotivated student is to ignore his motivational state for the time being, and to concentrate on teaching him as effectively as possible."[4]

Knowing the Structure of a Topic Facilitates Understanding, Retention, and Transfer

Every unit of learning, from a day's lesson to a year's curriculum, has basic, essential ideas that constitute its structure. But unless the teacher emphasizes the structure, it may become obscured by a jumble of facts and concepts. There are at least three reasons why a child should know the structure of the topic he or she is studying: (1) The lesson or curriculum is easier to understand. (2) The details can be more readily remembered. (3) The child has a durable model available for use in understanding related things (in other words, structure facilitates the "transfer of training").[5]

Key Generalizations.   It follows that teaching should be organized around the basic ideas of a subject—its key generalizations. For example, one of the major generalizations of the development of transportation, a subject commonly taught in the elementary school, may be stated thus:

Topographic features have played a role in the history of transportation.

Two items of information which illustrate this generalization are:

The Baltimore and Ohio Railroad, in laying its first rails to the west, had problems in getting over the hills of the Potomac Valley and the mountains of West Virginia.

Before the day of steel bridges, it was necessary to ferry railroad passengers across wide rivers, such as the Delaware.

These two facts draw their significance from the major generalization cited.

---

[4]Ausubel et al. (1978), *Educational Psychology*, p. 401.
[5]Jerome S. Bruner, *The Process of Education* (Cambridge, MA: Harvard University Press, 1961), pp. 23–25.

If the teacher stresses the generalization, helping children put it in their own language, making sure they recognize it as one of the pegs on which to hang the details, then the subject becomes comprehensible. Without such pegs (really more than "pegs," for they are the *pillars* of the structure), the subject easily ends up as a jumble of items of information that do not add up to any significant understanding.

On the other hand, once the structure is grasped, not only is the subject revealed in its full meaning, but the children remember the details better because they fit into a structured pattern. When the children review the foregoing generalization, the details about the engineering difficulties in laying tracks westward are brought to mind because they so vividly illustrate the generalization.

Advance Organizers.   Another way of calling the pupil's attention to the structure of a new subject is through advance organizers. An organizer is a statement that resembles an overview. Whereas an overview simply condenses the subject matter to be studied, an advance organizer guides the learners from what they already know to the new material. It does this by telling them, in advance of the study, what the new material is like, and how it differs from something that was previously learned. It thus lends familiarity to the new material.

Here is an example of how this works. A class is about to begin a study of trade between nations. The class has already learned, in previous years, or perhaps in a previous study in the current year, about the operation of interdependence at simple and unsophisticated levels—interdependence of members of the family and interdependence of community institutions and agencies. The teacher prepares an advance organizer. It is fashioned to remind the pupils of what they know about interdependence at the family and community levels. It then introduces the new subject, world trade, which is based on the interdependence of nations. It explains that some people, maybe some of the pupils themselves, have the idea that our nation is not dependent on any other nation, that we can exist untroubled, as a nation, without looking to other nations for cooperation and without aiding other nations. An effective organizer attempts explicitly to extinguish such existing misconceptions, which are likely to inhibit the learning of sounder concepts.[6]

The organizer explains that resources essential for modern living are not available in all nations (as illustrated by our present shortage of oil) and that world trade and cooperation benefit all. The teacher presents the organizer to the class orally and clarifies and expands upon it through class discussion. The teacher may also type it up and duplicate it so that each pupil has a copy to read.

---

[6]Ausubel et al. (1978), *Educational Psychology*, p. 373.

Learning Occurs through Both Reception and Inquiry

One way of classifying learning is according to whether the pupil *receives* the generalizations to be learned (by being told, by reading, or by observing demonstrations or pictures) or whether the pupil *discovers* them through a problem-solving approach called inquiry. Reception learning is so well known that it need scarcely be described. Learning through inquiry, on the other hand, is less familiar, though it has approached the fad stage in some quarters. Even so, or perhaps because of this, its role in learning is widely misunderstood. It is treated at length in Chapter 13. Here it will be merely introduced.

The idea of having pupils learn through inquiry is not new. It was advocated by Jean-Jacques Rousseau, Herbert Spencer, and John Dewey. Fifty years ago, the eminent social studies educator, Lucy Sprague Mitchell, expressed the view that "children grow in mental maturity from the very beginning by the active process of discovering relationships" and that the school, therefore, should operate "essentially as a laboratory where such discoveries may be made."[7]

Bruner gives an example of learning by inquiry from the practice of a fourth-grade teacher whose pupils were asked to figure out why civilizations have most often begun in fertile river valleys.[8] In reception learning, the pupils would have been told by their teacher or textbook that the river valleys' fertility encourages agriculture and settlement; and that a settled life in place of nomadic wandering led to the establishment of an elaborate government and the exploitation of mineral resources.

The advantages of teaching that encourages inquiry are perhaps self-evident. Pupils are motivated to see how close they can come to a workable solution or hypothesis. They work eagerly, putting their best thinking into the process. It develops their powers of independent, creative thought, and gives them a tool (the technique of problem solving) applicable to their future attacks on other problems.

A word of caution is in order, however. The inquiry approach slows up learning. A child would never be able to acquire all he needs to know about his heritage or his environment if this were the sole method at his disposal. Obviously, there would not be enough time even in a long life to rediscover all that man has learned over the ages. Moreover, learning through inquiry often involves much blind groping and random guessing. "Telling" the learner a generalization is certainly quicker than having him discover it through inquiry, and it is often more effective and appropriate. A leading psychologist writes:

---

[7] Lucy Sprague Mitchell, *Young Geographers* (New York: Basic Books, 1963; original printing, 1934), p. 11.

[8] In Richard C. Anderson and David P. Ausubel, *Readings in the Psychology of Cognition* (New York: Holt, Rinehart and Winston, 1965), pp. 80–81.

After all, one should not forget that man is a verbal animal, and there are marvelous shortcuts in learning to be achieved by the use of language. The chances are that . . . telling the learner the principle verbally is much quicker than any other method, and may well be as effective.[9]

Finally, too much has been claimed for inquiry learning. Ausubel, in his extensive review of the research, concludes that "the various enthusiasts of the discovery method have been supporting each other researchwise by . . . citing each other's opinions and assertions as evidence and by generalizing wildly from equivocal and even negative findings."[10]

The need today is for teachers to recognize that both inquiry and reception learning are available and that they need to be kept in balance. Teachers of younger children have ample justification for giving heavy emphasis to inquiry learning. As verbal facility grows, however, including growth in vocabulary and reading ability, children become increasingly capable of assimilating knowledge through reading and listening, and reception learning is increasingly appropriate. This should not be viewed as regrettable. Reception learning can be attractive and exciting, too.

Learning Is Promoted by Reinforcement

One factor in determining the quality and permanence of the insights acquired by the child as he or she undertakes a given task appears to be the promptness and strength with which his or her performance is *reinforced*. (When a pupil gives a correct answer or otherwise performs satisfactorily, and the teacher strengthens the correct response with a smile of approval or a reward of some other type, the child's learning is said to be reinforced.) Praise, high marks, gold stars, the tokens of behavior modification systems, and special privileges are venerable reinforcers for successful school performance.

By offering their classes a steady diet of material rewards and prized privileges, teachers encourage an undesirable competitiveness among children. This promotes the "grade-hound" psychology in which accumulating rewards takes precedence over the interests and other satisfactions that accompany successful learning. A more valuable and socially defensible kind of reinforcement than exaggerated reliance upon material rewards is prompt confirmation of the correctness of the child's performance or prompt help in overcoming failure.

Practice and Review Contribute
to Mastery and Durable Learning

The goal of practice and review (either oral or written) is to add to the clarity of the learned material and to aid in its retention. Practice and review

---

[9]Robert M. Gagné, *The Conditions of Learning*, 2nd ed. (New York: Holt, Rinehart and Winston, 1977), p. 58.

[10]Ausubel et al. (1978), *Educational Psychology*, p. 554.

are necessary because the child's initial exposure alone to a body of information or a new skill seldom yields durable acquisition. Practice provides additional interaction with the material to be learned. During the second and third exposures, the child can note points missed the first time and consolidate bits and pieces of detail that he or she had not fitted together during the first exposure. In rote learning (memorizing dates, length of rivers, the four time zones of the United States, and so forth), practice (often called "drill") is commonly and successfully provided by teachers. Practice is less often used for meaningful learning (understandng why policemen, dentists, and other service workers, as well as workers in manufacturing and agriculture, are considered producers of national wealth; understanding the limitations of the "Great Man theory" of history; and so forth).

Two important methods of practice and review are *self-recitation* and *rereading*. Self-recitation is the more useful form. It consists of attempting to recall facts or ideas, usually by paraphrasing them. The act of recalling may be performed either to one's self or by speaking or writing them. Self-recitation may follow the reading of a passage of a book, the viewing of a film, a class discussion, or the completion of a unit of study. Having one child recite before the class may be useful on occasion in demonstrating the process, after which the class may recite quietly to themselves, or in unison, or to one another in small groups. Self-recitation is not impaired—in fact it may be helped—by referring to books or notes during the process or by receiving prompting from others. Rereading is not so effective as recitation in maintaining learning; it is too easily performed passively. If, however, the initial reading was superficial or was interrupted by distractions, a second reading is essential.

Researchers have attempted to determine optimal conditions of practice and review and have drawn the following conclusions: (1) Practice and review are helpful, whether performed immediately following the initial exposure or delayed. (2) It is desirable to spread practice or review of a given body of material over several days or even several weeks. (3) Overlearning—practice carried beyond the point where the material has been adequately learned—is beneficial. (4) When the material to be learned can be recited comfortably and meaningfully in one sitting, and when it is an integrated whole, it is better to review it as a whole in each practice session.

THE TEACHING OF CONCEPTS

Everyone needs a rich stock of concepts for effective thinking and communication. A concept refers to a class of things one can think about and that can be distinguished from other classes of things.

Examples of Concepts

"A class of things" is an abstraction that embraces many specific instances. For example, take the concept of "family." It embraces a large number of specific instances such as: "There are three in our family—mom, dad, and me," "The family next door," and "The country's first family." An adult's concept of family may include figures of speech, as in the statement: "The UN aims to build a family of nations." In each of the foregoing cases of "family," it is unnecessary to identify the family by the name of its members, its size, its religion, or any other attribute. The concept becomes a quick, handy way of classifying ideas.

A verb (or any other part of speech, for that matter) may also stand for a concept. "To bargain" means to haggle over something. It is a concept that includes all types of haggling—negotiating a management-union contract, trying to arrange an exchange of prisoners of war, seeking a settlement over the use of property, bargaining for jewelry or other goods at Cairo's Musky, and horse trading by ranchers.

The Importance of Concepts in Thinking and Communication

Having a good stock of concepts makes it possible for children to catalogue promptly things they see, hear, read, or think about. A fifth-grade class reads about wheat and corn as important products of the North Central States. The pupils in most schools can quickly classify them as crops, a concept previously learned, without having to focus tortuously on all the peculiar properties—first of wheat, then of corn. Concepts are categories, and when children use them, they are automatically and unconsciously clarifying their thinking and improving their ability to communicate ideas to others. They drive past a farm containing a variety of flourishing crops, some or all of which they cannot identify. It is nevertheless possible for them to describe the experience by saying, "We drove by Mr. Clay's farm. His crops look green and healthy." It saves having to name each type of crop by describing its leaves and other characteristics. Just as being able to say "crop" reduces the complexity of the farm and makes it easier to deal with, so every concept reduces the complexity of the world.

Suggestions for Teaching Concepts

In a reasonably stimulating environment, children learn concepts spontaneously, but the growth of concepts can be enormously augmented through teaching. First, when an important concept is unknown or is known only in a narrow context, the teacher can supply or extend it by applying it to familiar instances and in as concrete a form as possible. It is initially through knowledge of concrete instances that concepts take root. If a class seems unfamiliar with the concept "crop," the teacher proceeds to teach its meaning through a simple definition of the term ("a crop is something that a farmer grows and harvests"), but mainly through giving numerous examples.

Second, the class can be asked to supply examples from their own backgrounds. In learning the concept of "family," one child may say: "A family of birds are in a nest in our backyard." Another child: "Some families live in houses, others live in apartments." When children are able to supply additional instances, we can assume they are learning the rudiments of the concept. The more instances they can supply, the more securely we can assume they are clinching it.

Third, the teacher can, when necessary, help children learn words or terms to apply to their concepts. A kindergartener may differentiate a square from a triangle, but remain unable to name either. The teacher can teach those names. The chairman of a committee of children may be dictatorial; another chairman involves all members in decision making. Each style of leadership is known to the pupils, and they know the concepts, but they lack suitable vocabulary. Their teacher has an opportunity here to teach the terms "undemocratic" (or "autocratic") and "democratic."

Fourth, we can do something about empty concepts held by children—terms that they employ glibly, but with minimal understanding. Teaching the vocabulary of concepts is futile if the learners have no concrete referents in their experience. "Learning can become ororverbalized, which means that the concepts learned are highly inadequate in their references to actual situations."[11] The prevalance of empty concepts is the main reason for making frequent use of pictures, films, tapes, field trips, discussion, and other means for providing perception of varied exemplars of the real world.

Finally, we must often set aside the textbook and teach concepts directly, with emphasis on their interrelationships (such as between "monsoon," "floodwaters," and "dams" in a study of India). A common fault of social studies textbooks is their provision of more concepts on a page than the typical class can possibly acquire in a single lesson—sometimes more than can be acquired in a week of lessons. Shoveling new concepts into a pupil without enough time for assimilation (through examples, pictures, films, and the like) makes social studies fuzzy and dull. When children meet a new or unfamiliar concept, it is necessary for them, through discussion, to relate it to other concepts already known, in order to make it stick. *Multum non multa* (much not many) should be the teacher's guiding principle. The learning by a child who is exposed to 20 loosely related concepts in a week will lag behind the learning of one who is taught merely five concepts, but in their various permutations and combinations.

The first page of a chapter on early man in an all too typical textbook has a total of 19 lines which contain the following concepts (among others!): "two billion years old," "layers of rock," "age of dinosaurs," "many centuries," "skeletons," "extinct," "civilized." The concept density is obviously excessive for the nine-year-olds for whom the book was written. The teacher's first task is to decide which of the concepts are most essential. For one lesson, it might be sufficient to take "age of dinosaurs," "extinct," and

---

[11]Gagné, *The Conditions of Learning*, p. 124.

"centuries," and to teach them—in all their interrelationships. An alternative would be to find another book, or to write one's own unit on early man.

Concepts are the building blocks of learning, and the need to introduce new concepts with deliberation and skill cannot be exaggerated.

BOX 7.1   **ALL GRADES**

Teaching the Concept "Harbor"

1. Select and show the class a picture of a *harbor*.
2. Point out the critical attributes (necessary characteristics) of *harbor*—e.g., is situated along a coast; has a surrounding land form that provides shelter for ships from storms.
3. Show the class pictures of different *harbors*—e.g., some harbors offer protection by natural or artificial jetties; some harbors are often closed by ice and require ice-breaking equipment (such as Arkhangelsk, Soviet Russia).
4. Give examples of varied uses of a *harbor*—e.g., a harbor with dry docks such as at Halifax, Nova Scotia; a harbor with shipbuilding activity such as at Bremerhaven, Germany; a harbor with great fish-processing facilities as at Gloucester, Massachusetts; and a large commercial and industrial seaport as at Seattle, Washington.

The Relationship of Concepts, Facts, and Generalizations

We have seen that a concept is the name given to a class of things, events, or actions that have certain common attributes. "Family," "bargain," and "crop" have been given as examples. Concepts are obvious building blocks in the statement of a fact, as in the sentence, "Our boat arrived safely in a snug harbor."

Concepts are also components of generalizations as illustrated in the sentence, "A harbor is a stretch of water on the coast, such as a bay, which gives shelter to boats." A generalization is a proposition that has broad application. This generalization about harbors is true of any harbor. It clearly differentiates a harbor from a stretch of water along an even shoreline that provides no protection. (See Box 7.1.)

Generalizations are learned both deductively and inductively. These two methods of learning may be diagrammed as follows:

Deductive method:	Generalization ⟶ Facts
Inductive method:	Facts ⟶ Generalization

Children learn by both methods. They need experience with the thinking peculiar to each type.

In applying the deductive method, the teacher presents a generalization for the class's consideration. The generalization might be this:

Our city's location has helped make it an important industrial center.

The teacher directs the class to find examples of the generalization—from books, parents, or other sources. They pool their data which includes such facts as the following:

Our city is located on a large river.

Our city is in the North Temperate Zone.

Our city is near coal and iron mines.

The inductive method starts with a problem such as: "What has made our city an important industrial center?" The pupils start collecting facts about the city's location, its climate, its proximity to resources, and so forth. From these facts they form generalizations in an effort to solve the problem.

Both deductive and inductive methods are useful, in fact necessary, in learning social studies.

CLASSROOM MANAGEMENT

Classroom management lies at the heart of social studies. It is a means of assuring optimum order in the classroom to yield maximum learning and productivity. It is only secondarily a set of methods and techniques for avoiding trouble or salvaging order and decorum. It is a social studies problem—perhaps the most important one. Pupils may learn to live and work together in better ways through social studies.

The Teacher's Responsibility for Management

The social studies period often hums with activity. It is potentially noisier than other periods. As will be seen later, unit teaching in the social studies, with its learning centers, committee work, and individualized projects, means pupils moving about and frequently conferring together. Some pupils are better able to use this freedom responsibly than are others. To keep learning at a productive, efficient level, there must be rule to insure order, minimize noise, and prevent confusion. The maintenance of these rules constitutes management.

The teacher is "a leader, a superior officer, a responsible head meant to inspire confidence. He is, or ought to be, the captain of the ship."[12] This statement suggests the desirable posture of the teacher, a posture that is the

---

[12]Jacques Barzun, *Teacher in America* (New York: Doubleday Anchor Books, 1945), p. 95.

basis of successful management. To be "captain" does not imply authoritarian behavior. The maintenance of discipline may be rooted in a democratic setting, and indeed should be.

Making Rules

Group formulation of rules or standards is desirable ("only four children may be at the reference table at a time"; "committees at work—keep your voices low"; and so on). There is evidence that children even as young as kindergarten age can participate in making and helping to maintain rules.[13]

Students should understand that the purpose of abiding by rules is not to please or ingratiate the teacher, but to create the kind of classroom in which learning can take place. Once the rules are made, discussed, and accepted, they should be posted and frequently referred to. The teacher should encourage the pupils to improve or add to them as the year proceeds.

Maintenance of Rules

Rules and restrictions are a part of life, and they are obviously necessary in the classroom. It is good for children to know what their teachers expect of them. Teachers must step in when rules are broken, when noisy discussions take place; when there is horseplay, or when any untoward behavior erupts and produces a poor atmosphere for work. They should invite the class (1) to help determine the probable cause of the unruly behavior, (2) to consider the undesirability of a recurrence of the incident, and (3) to make suggestions of what needs to be done to prevent its recurrence.

Such discussions are often a successful and adequate means for maintaining discipline, but their success cannot be guaranteed. Attempting to enforce rules is easier in some communities than in others. One class may differ in its responsiveness from another class in the same school. What is a teacher to do about pupils who are not ready to share the teacher's attitude that rules are important, or who lack the responsibility to help enforce them? "I let an insult pass," wrote Herbert R. Kohl in his account of his early teaching experiences.[14] This is often the path of wisdom. Sound teacher-pupil relationships are not threatened when a teacher overlooks petty infractions, whether they be acts of insubordination, impudence, or rule breaking. The secure teacher can afford to eschew petty infractions, and the insecure teacher gains strength by learning to ignore them. Easily harassed teachers who make an issue of every minor violation are not in a position to form a warm relationship with the class or to create a productive classroom climate. They may be so fearful of being regarded as permissive that they violate common

---

[13]Marion E. Turner, *The Child within the Group: An Experiment in Self-Government* (Stanford, CA: Stanford University Press, 1957).

[14]Herbert R. Kohl, *36 Children* (New York: New American Library, 1967), p. 20.

sense. Tough attitudes and pettiness in maintaining rules imperil the teacher's chance of having a psychologically robust classroom with the favorable work-atmosphere that teachers desire.

Teacher Planning as an Element in Management

A carefully planned unit is conducive to a disciplined climate. A group of new teachers in Philadelphia reported that their chief problem was class management. When they discussed their joint problem with a supervisor, it became apparent that the breakdown was in large part the product of inadequately planned lessons. The teachers later reported a vastly improved situation when they made it a practice to know, precisely, at the start of each school day what questions they wished to raise to guide discussions, what materials to distribute, and what special tasks to assign to individuals and groups. They attributed their greater skill in class management to the establishment of a routine, the alternation of "intake" activities (such as listening and reading) with "outgo" activities (such as problem solving and creating), and the maintenance of a brisker tempo of instruction.

Rewards and Punishment

Some children who continue to be disruptive despite the teacher's observance of the foregoing suggestions do respond if materially rewarded. This proved to be the case in a group of hyperaggressive boys. Praise had no effect in halting their disruptive, destructive behavior. When food was used as a reward, however, they attended to the task at hand, and they continued their constructive behavior even after the reward was gradually reduced and eventually discontinued.[15] Success has been reported by teachers of normal elementary school classes with rewarding desirable behavior with tokens (plastic discs or even slips of paper) that can be exchanged for special privileges. Under any such "behavior modification" system, the ultimate test of success is whether or not the tokens can be phased out in time without the reoccurrence of the undesired behavior.

There are times when punishment, too, is effective. Segregation ("social exclusion") of the disrupter is widely practiced in elementary schools. The child in question is required to work in an alcove or nook of the classroom. Albert Bandura states: "The effectiveness of [social] exclusion procedures can probably be greatly enhanced if, in addition to the punishment contingency, the child is provided with certain privileges and rewards for each class period during which he or she does not engage in disruptive behavior."[16] The teacher should certainly let the offender know how his restoration to the class can be achieved.

---

[15]Albert Bandura, *Principles of Behavior Modification* (New York: Holt, Rinehart and Winston, 1969), pp. 226–227.
[16]Ibid., p. 345.

Treating disruptive behavior in the above ways, by either reward or punishment, is at best a temporary expedient. It deals with only the symptoms of behavior. Teachers with pupils who persist in such behavior require all the insight of principals, guidance counselors, and school psychologists in uncovering causes of the behavior and suggesting ways of coping with it.

Self-Discipline

One of the main reasons for maintaining discipline is to teach children to internalize it, that is, to become self-disciplined. Children who are accustomed to externally imposed, reasonable discipline at home and at school, and who observe the behavior of disciplined adults, come to accept discipline as part of life. When granted increasing amounts of freedom as they develop, they learn to impose restraints over their own behavior. Through trial and error, they learn to forego indulgences of the moment in favor of greater satisfactions over the long haul. Thus, children learn the techniques and advantages of discipline through first being subject to external discipline; then through seeing self-discipline modelled in the lives of adults whom they admire; and finally, through testing and sharpening it in their own daily pursuits.

This assumes that in the homes children come from and the schools they have attended there is a reciprocal bond of affection between children and adults, children are accepted for what they are, and they are neither overindulged nor discriminated against. Where these and other conditions of sound mental health do not exist, children tend to resist discipline and to make a game of flouting authority. They may never learn to discipline themselves. Pupils of overly strict teachers lack the chance of developing their own standards. They become so dependent upon being told what to do that they fail to learn how to plan and think for themselves or how to order their own lives.

Overly indulgent teachers are equally ineffective in enabling their pupils to develop self-discipline. The teachers' intentions may be to avoid the tyrannical pattern that may have been imposed upon them in their own childhood. But, as a result, the discipline in their classrooms becomes so lax that their pupils find it difficult to distinguish democratic living from anarchy.

During their development, children naturally seek greater independence and wander from their earlier identification with adults. They pay closer heed to the standards of their pals. One of the outcomes is a seeming disregard for standards of work, from which may result a conflict between child and teacher. Teachers can put children on their own through assigning special individual tasks: interviewing a local authority on a topic being studied, constructing a special-purpose map, doing library research on a topic, preparing a report, and so on. Having responsibility for carrying out such a project will make it seem less important to children to exhibit their independence through recalcitrant behavior.

FOR STUDY AND EXPLORATION

1. Draw up a plan for introducing conceptual conflict for the purpose of having students reexamine a common stereotype.
2. Construct an advance organizer for the study of any commonly taught subject.
3. Select a major concept contained in a social studies program with which you are familiar and plan in detail for its introduction and expansion.
4. In your experience of long ago as an elementary school pupil, what effective approaches to discipline were used by your teachers that are not mentioned in this chapter? Evaluate them in terms of their probable effectiveness.

FURTHER READING

This chapter makes several references to *Educational Psychology: A Cognitive View* by David P. Ausubel and associates (New York: Holt, Rinehart and Winston, 1978). Ausubel's honesty and independence lead him to conclusions that are sometimes at odds with fashionable viewpoints in psychology and education. He is not awed by sacred cows; he rides roughshod over many of Brunder's interpretations, modifies Piaget's stages, and exposes the flimsy ground sometimes taken by advocates of discovery (inquiry) procedure, behavioral objectives, and other popular schemes. He gets into the nooks and crannies of classroom learning, examines the relevant data mercilessly, and flushes out unsupportable views. His chapter, "Learning by Discovery," should be read by all who teach social studies. His discussion of school discipline in the chapter on "Teacher Characteristics" also deserves wide reading.

Robert M. Gagne's *The Conditions of Learning*, 3rd ed. (New York: Holt, Rinehart and Winston, 1977), written from a different theoretical perspective from that of Ausubel and associates, is another valuable guide to teaching, containing a particularly lucid treatment of concept formation.

The importance of active student involvement in various aspects of their learning is pungently stated in David Nyberg's *Tough and Tender Learning* (Palo Alto: National Press Books, 1971), chap. 10, "Preliminaries of a Learning Theory."

"Much research indicates that teachers who are good classroom managers also tend to produce more student learning," write Jere E. Brophy and Joyce G. Putnam in "Classroom Management in the Elementary School" in Daniel L. Duke (Ed.), *Classroom Management*, 78th Yearbook of the National Society for the Study of Education (Chicago: University of Chicago Press, 1979), chap. 6. Brophy and Putnam identify characteristics that make for good management and stress the importance of smoothly-flowing, coherent lessons.

part III

Organizing and Teaching Social Studies Units

8 The Social Studies Unit

The unit is a way of organizing learning experiences. Briefly, it consists in providing a wide range of learning experiences for the pupil concerning a topic or problem, and planning active pupil involvement in each phase of the teaching process. A unit is an organized collection of information, ideas, and activities for teaching a topic in the social studies, and includes objectives, activities, learning materials such as books and audiovisual materials, and plans for evaluating how learning is progressing. Examples of units include "The Supermarket," "The Industrial Revolution," "Switzerland," and "Colonial America."

The unit method is one of the substantial contributions of the educational experimentation of an earlier generation. Its success can be attributed to several factors:

1. It is flexible, allowing teachers to develop fully their own unique teaching style.
2. It conforms to the psychology of childhood, permitting teachers to work *with* children rather than administer the tedious social studies "recitation," still too commonly conducted.
3. It provides opportunity for spirited application in a real-life context of language skills, math skills, and creative arts.
4. Teaching that is based on the unit plan yields superior learning (a proven advantage discussed toward the end of this chapter).

115

Teachers, of course, need to steep themselves in the unit topic. That calls for wide reading. Teachers need to plumb deeper than their pupils can be expected to. They should obtain as firm and scholarly a grasp of the subject as time permits. Teachers with a rich store of knowledge are able to know whether or not their pupils are obtaining a well-rounded picture, and they are able to supply information to which pupils do not normally have direct access.

THE CONTENT

A unit may be organized around any significant content. Unit topics are sometimes worded as problems ("Finding Ways to Conserve Our Natural Resources") or as questions ("How Did Mexico Become a Nation?"). Such unit titles are misleading when, as is often the case, they denote a focus that is narrower than the planned scope of the unit. A straightforward statement of a topic is to be preferred, such as "Our Natural Resources" and "The History of Mexico." Problems and questions can be introduced as the unit progresses.

Scope of the Unit

The suitability of the scope can be judged by the ability of the class to encompass the unit as a whole during an orientation period—that is, before engaging in its systematic study. In the unit plan, children are able to discern the "forest" before they analyze the separate "trees." They get a general, overall picture of the community, of farming, or of a nation, whatever the topic may be, before they are confronted with masses of detail.

Teachers should guard against including loosely related material in a unit, keeping in mind children's limited background and their confusion when presented with much disconnected content. It is well to remember that the child's experience will not end with this one unit; the subject will be encountered again in different form, perhaps in high school. Furthermore, too comprehensive a study that appears to present all that is worth knowing about a subject, may give the child a false sense of thoroughness and discourage further thinking in the area. If, on the other hand, the teacher concludes the unit with the frank statement that study of the topic has been merely begun, that the information is far from complete, and that many questions remain to be answered, the door is left open for future inquiry.

Unity of the Unit

The central feature of a unit is that the diverse aspects of its content are tied together. For example, colonial life, when organized as a unit, is pursued intensively in many relationships. The class investigates colonial commerce, schools, recreation, ideas about government and education, housing, agriculture, crafts, and transportation as they interact with one another, as they are pervaded by common motives and values, and as parts of community life. Thus, the content grows into a web of connecting threads. It is this which forms the closely knit internal structure of the unit—in a word, its *unity*.

The premise underlying the idea of the unit is that the child who learns only a few distinct, well-rounded concepts, but learns them intensively in their interrelationships, has learned to better purpose than one who memorizes a host of independent concepts that fail to cross-fertilize each other.

Relation of the Unit to Its Concepts and Generalizations

Most published social studies programs give suitable titles for their units, and pupils learn the underlying concepts and generalizations through a variety of learning experiences. The relationship in typical programs may be illustrated as follows:

1. The year's theme for the first-grade program of *Our Working World* is "Families at Work."
   a. The title of its only unit: "Families at Work."
   b. One of its concepts: Division of Labor.
   c. One of its generalizations: Division of labor gets the job done faster and better.
2. The year's theme of the *Social Science Laboratory Units* for one of the intermediate grades is social psychology.
   a. One of its units: Friendly and unfriendly behavior.
   b. One of the unit's concepts: Cause-and-effect relationships.
   c. One of its generalizations: Causes of behavior are multiple.
3. The year's theme of *Culture Regions in the Eastern Hemisphere*, a seventh-grade textbook program, is "Culture Regions in the Eastern Hemisphere."
   a. One of its units: The Middle Eastern culture region.
   b. One of the unit's concepts: The influence of religion in a culture.
   c. One of its generalizations: Different religions may share in shaping a region's culture.

PACKAGED UNITS AND TEACHER-CREATED UNITS

An increasing number of social studies units are "packaged," as was noted in the case of some of the programs described in Chapter 4. Packaged units provide the teacher with a combination of teaching materials. One that is well stocked may consist of a pupil textbook, supplementary reading materials, films, maps, posters, educational games, recordings, pupil workbooks, and a teacher's guide. The teacher is thus amply supplied, and the unit's scope and sequence are already worked out. The teacher need not comb libraries, film catalogues, and other sources of information in search for available learning materials. The better designed programs contain unit materials that would be impossible to match through an individual teacher's search. *Man: A Course of Study*, for example, provides a series of color films, with natural sound, that simulate with remarkable fidelity what pupils might see and hear on field trips.

While teachers may become the executors of a complete program, ready-made, it is nevertheless essential that they retain the indispensable role of creative artist. It is up to the teacher to arouse curiosity, conduct class discussions, lead the class in thinking about controversial issues, provide for differences in reading ability, and manage other phases of instruction. The loss would be grievous if packaged materials discouraged teachers from deepening their own scholarship in the unit's topic through reading and study, and adding directly to their pupils' knowledge and understanding.

THE RESOURCE UNIT AND THE UNIT RESOURCE COLLECTION

A "resource unit" is a compilation of promising ideas for teaching a unit. It functions as a reservoir from which the teacher draws, and contains many more ideas than he or she is likely to use in any single presentation of the unit.

Teachers' guides that accompany textbooks are sometimes resource units. They contain suggestions on how to present each unit, list books that the teacher may want to consult, and suggest books, films, and other materials for the classroom. They then take up each section of the textbook that could serve as a convenient lesson. They state the generalizations that emerge and give suggestions for presenting the lesson, questions for discussion, and activities that would enrich the lesson.

Teachers who construct their own units or who anticipate teaching a given unit in subsequent years will find it worthwhile to compile their own resource units. A loose-leaf notebook is handy for this purpose. As new ideas occur to teachers and as they discover projects that work well, they can write them up for future reference.

Many teachers supplement the notebook with a "unit resource collection"—an accumulation of newspaper clippings, mounted pictures, magazines, scale models, slides, and other useful teaching aids. These they classify by subject and file in a drawer or box.

PLANNING THE UNIT

Assessing Pupil Background

Before launching a unit, the teacher should take steps to learn what the pupils already know about the topic—about its concepts and generalizations. This may be done through asking questions and talking over the subject with the class. In the case of children who have learned to read and write with a fair degree of fluency, discussion can be supplemented by a teacher-constructed test.

Assessment of background often reveals that much of the content is already well known to the pupils. Primary-grade children in particular know many of the concepts of a unit prior to formal instruction. Although teachers should begin with what the class already knows, they should move on quickly to what the pupil do not know.

On the other hand, some children offer glib answers or comments that seem to indicate wider knowledge than they actually possess. When one teacher announced to her class that she would like to have them study the United Nations, a child sardonically observed: "Oh, we already know about the United Nations." A quiz by the teacher revealed that the pupils knew only two facts about the United Nations: that its headquarters were in New York, and that "a lot" of countries belonged to it. Not a single pupil appeared to know its purposes, the scope of its work, or its organization, or could give examples of its successes and failures.

It is evident that probing ahead of time is necessary to determine which concepts the teacher can take for granted and which will need to be stressed.

Planning the Content

Planning a unit involves identifying objectives, outlining content, planning the learning experiences, lining up resources and materials, and roughing out a scheme for evaluating the unit at various stages of its development.

The following outline indicates major steps that need to be taken in unit planning.

    I. Title and overview of unit.
   II. Outline of content.
 III. Objectives (stated behaviorally where possible).
      A. Cognitive goals: knowledge and understanding (generalizations, concepts, and facts).
      B. Affective goals: attitudes and values (spirit of inquiry, appreciation, respect for evidence, and so on).
      C. Performance goals: skills (classification skills, map skills, study skills, reference skills, critical thinking skills, and so on).
 IV. Introductory learning experiences (materials, activities, questions for discussion, stories to read, and so on).
   V. Developmental learning experiences (surveys, interviews, trips, learning centers, industrial arts, and so on).

    VI. Culminating learning experiences (major summarizing activity
      or activities: art project, writing project, dramatics, and so on).
  VII. Resources and materials.
    A. Audiovisual materials (mounted pictures, films, filmstrips,
      tapes, records, and so on).
    B. Books and other reading materials for children (classified ac-
      cording to subject and reading level).
    C. Books and other reading materials for teacher (for reference
      and for culling passages to read to class).
 VIII. Evaluation (teacher-made tests, questions for review, drill exer-
    cises, rating scales (see Chapter 18), and so on.

The amount of content in a unit is, of course, dependent upon the
number of units planned for the school year. A tentative time schedule is
desirable, yet teachers should avoid rigidity in executing it, for the proper
pacing of a unit can be known only after it gets under way. An examination
of eight widely used programs shows that their units per year in the primary
grades range from three to seven with an average of five, and in the intermediate grades from four to twelve, also with an average of five. Many experienced teachers believe that four or five units per year is optimum. This
allows a month to six weeks for a unit, offering adequate balance and variety
without sacrificing depth. Programs with as many as 10 or 12 units per year
lead to superficial skimming of content and, contrary to the advice of Lord
Bowen quoted in the epigraph at the head of this chapter, requires that instruction be "ladled out in a hurry." The Greek word from which our word
"school" is derived meant leisure. "There must be an atmosphere of leisure if
there is to be a truly liberal or free education."[1]

LAUNCHING THE UNIT

Introducing the Class to the Unit

    Before systematic study begins, it is a good idea to spend several days
acquainting the class with the topic. During this period of initial exposure,
most teachers present an overview of the new topic and encourage their
pupils to make comparisons between it and topics they have already studied.
    You might also present glimpses of part of the content of the unit in
order to arouse interest and curiosity. This can be done through projecting
slides, reading or telling authentic stories, and displaying pictures or posters.
    The introduction to the topic need not be elaborate. For example, in

---

[1]John Dewey and Evelyn Dewey, *Schools of Tomorrow* (New York: Dutton, 1962), p. 168.

presenting the third-grade unit on the Norwegian community in the *Taba Program in Social Science*, one teacher accomplished the following:

1. Placed on the bulletin board a set of pictures showing distinctive features of the Norwegian landscape and culture.
2. Read aloud a portion of Hopp's *Great Day in Norway*.
3. Posted some questions for speculation and inquiry. For example, under pictures of mountains rising from a glacially eroded valley, coastal islands, and a fjord: Why are parts of Norway so bare of trees? Another poster: What do these Norwegian words mean? *Ja! Nej! Hjelp!! Kald! God Morgen! Luftpost.*
4. Showed Coronet's film, *Life in Northern Lands: Norway*.

Inviting Pupil Input in Defining the Unit's Scope

After introducing the unit, show the class a plan for the study of the unit derived from your own tentative outline. However, merely to be handed an outline, already cut-and-dried, can have a stultifying effect on your pupils. Encourage them to regard it as a piece of unfinished business, and invite them to suggest additional topics that are of special interest to them. Record them on the chalkboard. You and the class should consider each topic on its merits and obtain a consensus regarding its inclusion.

One class, in studying transportation, wished to add as a subtopic the difference between a diesel and other types of engines. So a new topic, "The Engine," was inserted in the outline.

Some class-initiated questions and suggestions may appear to be trivial or based on misconceptions. In a unit on Norway, one pupil wanted the following question added to the outline: Are there any Vikings left today? The teacher wisely included it. Before the unit was over, she made sure the class understood "Vikings" to be a name for the Norsemen of long ago. Another pupil wanted to know how many whales Norwegian whalers used to get on one trip. While such a question may seem of small importance to an adult, it can be useful in at least three ways:

1. It is a reminder of children's preoccupation with concreteness and detail.
2. It suggests where the unit might be broadened to include a matter close to the interests of one or more members of the class.
3. It may lead to significant concepts and generalizations. The question about whales suggests a study of the ecology of the sea and the need for regulating the whaling industry on a worldwide basis.

Pupil input is important in every stage of the unit, as shown throughout this book. Here in the present section, we have illustrated its role in getting the unit under way.

BOX 8.1   **GRADES K–3**

Informal Units in the Primary Grades

Some primary-grade teachers have expressed a preference for a more informal approach to units than that presented in this chapter. One teacher planned the following units for a first-grade class, which illustrates the informal primary-grade unit: (1) machines, (2) the school plant, (3) licensing. They were developed over the entire school year, leisurely and intermittently.

Unit on machines. The teacher aimed to bring her class to a realization of the significance of the machine as a labor-saving mechanism. Attention was called to the pencil sharpener, lawn mower, paper cutter, typewriter in the school office, electric saw and joiner in the school shop, and other machines that could be directly operated or observed. The teacher was constantly alert to experiences that would enlarge the concept of the meaning of technological advance that the unit was designed to build.

Unit on the school plant. Every few weeks, the teacher planned a trip to widen the children's knowledge of their school building, increase their familiarity and security concerning it, and build an appreciation of certain differences between maintaining a large public building and a house. Many features of the plant were explored, mapped, and discussed, including the basement, furnace, overhead pipes, fuse box, storage rooms, assembly room, library, and the locations of key personnel including custodian, principal, and nurse.

Unit on licensing. The teacher's objective was to bring her class to an appreciation of the extent and purpose of certain requirements of organized society. The unit began during the hunting season for pheasants, which had significance for the children because some of their fathers hunted these birds. Discussions were conducted concerning the need for, and merit of, licensing hunters. A child whose father was a barber told about the license a barber must obtain. This started a rapid expansion of the theme, which continued throughout the year. Specimens of licenses were brought in—expired licenses for driving, dogs, and retail selling were among those collected, and their need was discussed.

TEACHING THE UNIT

Since most of this book is devoted to details of unit teaching, the present section will merely provide an overview of unit teaching. Many essentials of unit work will be described in subsequent chapters, including inquiry procedures (Chapter 13), pupil committees (Chapter 14), creative activities (Chapters 15 and 20), field trips (Chapter 16), instructional media (Chapter

17), testing (Chapter 18), books (Chapter 19), maps and globes (Chapter 20), and time lines (Chapter 22).

Preparing Daily Lesson Plans

Teachers differ widely in their methods of planning the day's work. Some find security in planning in great detail, others merely rough out their ideas and prefer to leave room for some improvising as they go. Regardless of individual style and preference, careful advance thought needs to be given to sequence of activities, selection and wording of questions and explanations, and what equipment and materials will be required. A written plan indicates precisely what has to be done to insure a smoothly flowing and effective lesson.

Four sample lesson plans follow:

Example 1

Objective:
To develop appreciation of two additional types of work that keep people in our community safe and well.

- Review Wednesday's lesson on hospital work. Have two or three kids recall Wednesday's summary.
- Exhibit chart showing pictures of workers replacing light bulb in street light, repairing damaged lamp post, etc.
- Form small groups, each to make list of ways in which well-lighted streets are safer than unlighted ones. Have a child from each group report his or her group's findings to entire class. On chalkboard, record a master list, eliminating duplications, and have class discuss importance of each "way."
- If time allows: Repeat procedure, with attention centered on how garbage and trash collections help keep community safe and well.

Example 2

Purpose:
To develop greater intimacy of students with child life in 19th century midwest.

- Read to class the well-drilling episode in John Muir's *The Story of My Boyhood and Youth.*
- In small groups, students will be asked to imagine they are to make a filmstrip for the Muir story. Re-read the episode if students think they need to hear it again.
- Each group will be asked to decide jointly what scenes to use, and what title to give each. Then have them divide the job, each member to do at least one picture. Use oaktag and crayons.
- Have an exhibit of "filmstrips."

Example 3

Objectives:
At the conclusion of the lesson, the children should be able to state in their own words these generalizations, and should be able to give examples:

1. There are many ways to earn an income.
2. Most workers today are specialized.

Discussion:
Have children tell of kinds of jobs they know. Make list on chalkboard.

Questions to ask:
• Which of these jobs usually require a uniform? Why?
• Which of these jobs are usually held by men? Why? By women? Why?
• What abilities are needed for these jobs?
• What kind of education and training is needed?

Work period:
Children in small groups, and individually, continue their reference work, writing, and craft projects from where left off yesterday.

Example 4

Aim:
To develop further understanding of fire insurance.

Presentations:
1. Have Arthur present his picture-chart showing how fire insurance works.
2. Explain to class the law of large numbers.

Dramatization:
Have six children role-play contrasting situations: In one home, insurance salesman visits, there's a fire, insurance company investigates and estimates loss. In contrasting situation, owner declines to buy insurance, there's a fire, all is lost.

Discussion:
Does fire insurance prevent fires? What *does* it do? Encourage children to think of dangers other than fire (lightning, lost luggage, accidents, illness) that could be covered by insurance.

If a discussion opens up a significant side issue which was not anticipated in the lesson plan but which has gripped the class, most experienced teachers would let it be pursued and the remaining part of the lesson plan postponed. A lesson plan should be a useful, flexible guide—never a straitjacket.

Daily Planning with the Class

A planning session at the start of each social studies period enables pupils to orient themselves to the social studies undertaking of the day and facilitates the creation of a state of readiness and anticipation. Planning sessions are also in order in other situations, a few of which are: To obtain pupil reactions to the unit's outline, as suggested earlier in the chapter; to prepare for a film or a field trip; to divide assignments for special investigations or reports; to arrange small group discussions; to work out solutions to problems arising from study of the content; to organize data-collecting activities.

Teachers are often tempted to short-circuit the process of planning by "selling" their own ready-made conclusions to the class. If the temptation is yielded to, the purpose of group planning is defeated. On the other hand, teachers should consider themselves members of the class and, as captains of their respective ships, not hesitate to bring up points overlooked or to offer suggestions.

Providing for Pupil Record Keeping

Many teachers have their pupils keep logs in loose-leaf notebooks and make entries in them as the class accumulates information, extends its concepts, and learns new generalizations. Time should be set aside every week for this task. The log of a kindergarten or first-grade child may be a series of drawings with simple captions. When writing skills advance, pupils may record major learnings of interest to the individual, questions explored, titles of books and films used, and accounts of any trips, dramatizations, or other activities that were carried out. The logs may be illustrated with drawings, graphs, maps, time lines, and reports. Individual children should have wide latitude in executing and organizing their logs. The recording serves several purposes. It constitutes a form of recitation that helps fix learning, it provides pupils with a feeling for the unit's movement and direction, and it often becomes a valued possession of the child.

BOX 8.2   **GRADES 3–6**

A Fourth-Grade Unit, "The City," Taught in an Open Classroom

Taught by Katherine Conner and Joan Willens

By Joan Willens

Here is a week-by-week account of a unit on the city in which the teaching of map skills played a major role.

In a team situation with two teachers and about 60 children we have found that we need about 20 centers available each week. Not all of the children are in the centers area at the same time. One teacher directs the centers while the other teaches groups in the adjoining classroom.

The centers are specific areas in the room, scattered about the edge and at tables in the middle. The activities at each have directions, either specific or very open-ended.

(Continued)

The activities are from all areas of the elementary curriculum and include affective and developmental skills at all levels. Thus, we may have large blocks and dress-up clothes, as well as charts, graphs, and maps at a rather sophisticated level. The children are allowed to make choices from the centers available, but also must complete tasks at specified "required" centers. These are individualized and posted on a large chart. As each requirement is completed and checked by the teacher for a given child, it is marked off the chart opposite that child's name. The chart is changed each week.

Thus, the pupil must gauge his time over a period of a week. Some will do all their requirements first and spend the end of the week with free-choice centers. Others will pace themselves at one a day and have some free time each day, and some will be interested in new materials and will not be willing to limit themselves to the teacher's requirements until late in the week.

This format does ask that the child budget his time, and yet the teacher, having some control, can see that the child is exposed to a variety of activities on his level.

The following is a series of centers in the area of social studies. Each center is set up for a week. Certain ones may be a requirement for some of the pupils, but may be free choices for others. The pupil is expected to go to the area in which the center is located, read the directions (the teacher may have to help the poorer readers), and complete the task. His work is then checked by the teacher, and he goes to another center.

Following are the printed directions that we supplied for the pupils at each center. (Explanations and instructions for the teacher are in parentheses.)

OCT. 2–6

MAP SKILLS
Copy the designs. (Designs of increasing complexity are arranged in a series on the chalkboard or on large cards.)

THE CITY
Pretend your group (three or four children from the class) is making plans for a new neighborhood in the city. You are to decide where all the buildings should go.
1. Copy the map on the bulletin board onto a large piece of newsprint.
2. Label the buildings—church, school, hospital, Acme, fire station, movie theater, Gino's, Penn Fruit, Woolworth's, junior high, gas station, and several stores—on squares of con-

(Continued)

struction paper. Make small red squares to show houses.

3. Choose a place for a park, and draw trees there.
4. Put the houses and other buildings where you think they should go in the neighborhood.
5. Show the teacher, and tell her why you put things where you did.
6. Paste the buildings in place.
7. Sign your name to your plan.

OCT. 9-13

MAP SKILLS

(Place strips of masking tape on the floor in squares to represent city blocks. Place toy blocks in each square to represent buildings. Have the children stand above the squares with pads of paper and pencils and draw the blocks in exactly their position within the tape square. In thus drawing a diagram of the layout from above, they are learning to make a map.)

THE CITY

(Use one of the city plans from the previous week. Ask each pupil to put his name on one of the houses and pretend he lives there. Have him answer these questions in writing, if he can write, or orally if necessary.)

1. How many blocks do you have to walk to school? Does it seem too far?
2. How many blocks is it to the nearest grocery store? Is this too far?
3. How far are you from the hospital? Is this too far, or O.K.?
4. How far are you from the fire station? Is this too far, or O.K.?
5. How far are you from a park? Is this too far, or O.K.?
6. How far are you from a laundry? Is this too far, or O.K.?
7. Name the ten buildings that are closest to your pretend house. Are most of them the kind of buildings you would like to live near?
8. Do you think you picked a good place to live, or a bad one? Give three reasons.

(Continued)

OCT. 16-20

MAP SKILLS

(Make a one-room doll house, with furniture, that is open at the top. Ask the children to draw a diagram of the room as it looks from the top, with the furniture properly placed.)

THE CITY

(Use another large sheet of blank newsprint.) In front of you is a diagram of part of a city. It shows streets, schools, stores, and movies. Can you find them?

1. Pretend that the tiles in the box are houses. Put as many houses as you can on the diagram, along the streets.
2. Use a *red* crayon to draw an arrow from each house to the school you think the children in that house would attend.
3. Use a *green* crayon to draw an arrow from each house to the store at which the people in that house would shop.
4. Use a *black* crayon to draw an arrow from each house to the movie to which the people in that house would probably go.

Now answer these questions:

1. Would everyone who goes to the same school go to the same store?
2. Where would there be a lot of traffic on your diagram?
3. Where would children meet friends?
4. Where would grownups meet friends?
5. Where would you need police?
6. Where would gangs hang out?

OCT. 23-27

MAP SKILLS

(Have a basic floor plan of the classroom, showing doors, windows, bulletin boards, and chalkboards around the edge. Give the pupil a box of inch-square tiles and a few cardboard rectangles with labels such as "teacher's desk," "supply table," "science table," "metal closet.") Put the

THE CITY

Cities have lots of people in a small amount of space. When you put lots of people in a small space, there may be problems. Can you think of five problems that cities have because of having so many people crowded together?

Put a group of white mice

(Continued)

cardboard pieces in place on the diagram as they are in the room, and then place a tile for each pupil's desk.

(classroom pets) into a small cage so that they are crowded, but not in an inhumane fashion. How do they act? Do people ever act this way when they are crowded together? Look at the mice an hour later. How are they acting then? Now return the mice to their regular cages.

OCT. 30-NOV. 3

MAP SKILLS

Draw a floor plan of the room you are sitting in, and diagram all of the furnishings.

THE CITY

You are the mayor. Think of three things you dont like about living in the city. Describe why you don't like them. As mayor, what do you think you could do to change these three things to make them better?

NOV. 5-9

MAP SKILLS

(Teach north, south, east, and west with a grid game.) On the grid, put your finger on block 1, and count 3 blocks south, 2 blocks east, and 1 block north. Where are you? Now begin on block 100, and go 6 blocks north, 5 west, and 3 north. Where are you?

THE CITY

(Bulletin board project. Have each child find a picture from a magazine showing something good about a city and write under it why he thinks it is good. Then have him find a picture of something bad about a city and write why he thinks it is bad. Make two bulletin boards, one showing positive aspects of a city and the other showing negative aspects.)

N

1	11	21	31	41	51	61	71	81	91
2	12	22	32	42	52	62	72	82	92
3	13	23	33	43	53	63	73	83	93
4	14	24	34	44	54	64	74	84	94
5	15	25	35	45	55	65	75	85	95
6	16	26	36	46	56	66	76	86	96
7	17	27	37	47	57	67	77	87	97
8	18	28	38	48	58	68	78	88	98
9	19	29	39	49	59	69	79	89	99
10	20	30	40	50	60	70	80	90	100

W ... E

S

(Continued)

Follow these directions, and show where you would end up each time:

Begin on 1	Begin on 90	Begin on 10
3 S	3 W	6 N
4 E	2 S	5 E
2 S	1 W	2 N
1 W	2 E	1 W
You are now on	You are now on	5 S
		3 E
		You are now on
_____	_____	_____

NOV. 12-16

MAP SKILLS

(Attach strips of masking tape to the chalkboard to represent streets. Have about five streets going north-south and five going east-west, with names for each. Tape several "houses" on this map, labeled with the names of children in the class.)

Answer these questions:

1. What three children live on Pine Street?
2. What two children live beside the park?
3. Who lives at the corner of Spruce and 4th Streets?
4. Who lives three blocks east of Cynthia?
5. Who lives four blocks south of Tong?
6. Who lives on the south side of Market Street?
7. Tell how you would go from Robert's house to Michael's house.
8. Tell how Mary Ann walks to Linda's house.

THE CITY

Draw a picture of a power plant spewing smoke into the air, and show lines running from the plant to the buildings in the city. It is evening, and the lights of the houses are on. The power plant that runs these lines gives the electric power that runs lights, T.V., radio, electric stoves, irons, refrigerators, and everything else that uses electricity. The power is carried to the city through the lines. This power plant also makes all the smoke you see in the air. Pretend that you are the mayor of this city. The people need the electric power, but they don't like the pollution. What would you do?

Concluding the Unit

There are various ways to finish a unit that will review and summarize the high points in an impressive manner.

The Culminating Activity.   The unit may be brought to a climax through a pageant, a play, a festival, the painting of a mural, the preparation of a book, or some other joint enterprise. Such activities are described in Chapter 15.

Summarizing the Logs.   The pupils' logs provide excellent materials for review and summary. Pupils may write summaries (or dictate them to the teacher, teacher aides, or their parents if they are too young to have learned to write).

Oral Summaries.   An oral summarizing session may be held, in which each pupil is given particular aspects of the unit to recapitulate briefly to the entire class.

Tests.   The teacher may prepare tests such as those described in Chapter 18. The results will inform the teacher what misconceptions or gaps in knowledge or understanding continue to exist; and a profitable discussion of these can then be conducted.

Group Evaluation of the Unit.   It is advantageous to conduct a discussion in which the class evaluates the success of the unit. The teacher questions the children about what they found of interest in the study, what content and activities they found valuable, what additional content and activities they wish had been included, and which methods of work they found satisfying or they feel might have been improved upon. Criticisms and suggestions coming from these evaluations are often invaluable in planning future units.

THE EFFECTIVENESS OF UNIT TEACHING

In the 1930s and 1940s, in order to determine how effective unit teaching was, investigators studied types of teaching that possessed some of its major aspects and found them to possess superiority over routine recitation procedures.[2] Interest in this type of research subsequently declined, largely because of the difficulty in drawing definite conclusions from it. It became evident that the unit method and the recitation method could not be clearly differentiated from each other, because both were characterized by a host of similar activities. For example, devices such as films, textbooks, and discussion periods were observed in both types of teaching.

Nevertheless, the old research, in exploring certain variables, did show that pupils taught by means of units were superior to pupils taught by means of formal recitations in good work habits, ability to apply new generalizations in social studies, creativity, use of reference materials, and scope of out-of-school pursuits. Thus, there was some favorable evidence which accounted to a considerable extent for the acceptance that unit teaching subsequently received.

---

[2]Leaders in this work were J. Wayne Wrightstone, Arthur T. Jersild, and Frederick Pistor.

Second, informal reports of the unit method from observers of the method in action continue to supply strong empirical evidence of its success in the hands of talented teachers. Third, unit teaching emphasizes critical thinking (see Chapter 13), long a desired goal of educators. Fourth, unit teaching accords with the psychological principles that tend to view active pupil participation and the provision of realistic, concrete experiences in the learning process as favorable ways of increasing understanding.

TEACHING COMPETENCIES

This chapter has described how to perform the following tasks that are basic to the social studies. The teacher should be able to:

1. Construct a unit that is unified and compact, built around closely knit concepts and generalizations.
2. Adapt a commercially produced packaged unit so that it may take advantage of local resources and of the teacher's own background of scholarship and interests.
3. Construct resource units and an individual collection of teaching materials.
4. Explore a class's readiness for a given unit through questions, discussion, and pretest in order to adapt the unit to the class's capacity and background.
5. Construct a detailed outline of steps to be taken in teaching the unit.
6. Introduce the class to the unit.
7. Involve pupils in defining the unit's scope.
8. Write a daily lesson plan.
9. Orient the class to each lesson.
10. Provide for pupil record keeping.
11. Bring the unit to an orderly, comprehensive, and impressive conclusion.

TRYING OUT SOME OF YOUR COMPETENCIES

1. Construct a unit, following Parts I, II, and III of the outline in this chapter of major steps in unit planning.
2. Write up a plan for introducing your unit to children of a specified age.
3. Prepare a lesson plan that would be suitable for the unit currently being taught in a class to which you have access. Try it out with the class.

FOR STUDY AND EXPLORATION

1. Examine a commercially produced packaged unit and evaluate it. Where can a teacher's creativity enter?
2. Write a constructively critical review of a teacher's description of a unit—perhaps one of the five mentioned under "Further Reading."
3. With a unit on transportation in mind, name 10 or 12 items that could be appropriately included in a unit resource collection. Identify how each could be useful in teaching specified concepts or generalizations.

FURTHER READING

Among reports by teachers of their experiences with units designed and executed by themselves are:

Thomas Bernagozzi, "If I Were Columbus: Third-Grade Unit Combines Maps, History, and Large Doses of Imagination," *Instructor*, 87 (October 1977), 170–172.

Dorothy Needham, "Kids Dig Egypt," *Teacher*, 95 (April 1978) 82–86.

Jane Ehemann, "Globe Trotting from the Classroom: Unit on International Travel," *Learning*, 6 (November 1977), 92–94.

Charles Klasky, "Another Way to Teach That State History Unit," *Social Studies*, 68 (July/August 1977), 164–166.

Dorothy Levensen and Bruce Davis, "Family History Projects Are in Schools from Coast to Coast," *Instructor*, 87 (October 1977), 96–104.

For many years, teachers have been assisted in unit teaching by *Unit Teaching in the Elementary School* by Lavone A. Hanna et al., renamed in its most recent edition *Dynamics of Elementary School Social Studies*, 3rd ed. (New York: Holt, Rinehart and Winston, 1973).

How to increase student involvement in the unit is described by Barbara G. Olmo, "Determining Effective Teaching Techniques in Unit Development," *Social Studies*, 69 (March/April 1978), 77–80. High-school oriented, it nevertheless describes techniques that are readily applicable to elementary schools, including case studies, folders provided with data for small group study, and role play.

Ineffective expository teaching is often caused by poor listening habits on the part of children, a condition that may be overcome through training. The standard teacher's guide is *Listening Aids Through the Grades* by David H. Russell and Elizabeth F. Russell (New York: Teachers College Press, 1979).

Additional approaches to learning centers are given in:

John I. Thomas, *Learning Centers: Opening Up the Classroom* (Boston: Holbrook, 1975).

Ralph C. Voight, *Invitation to Learning: The Learning Center Handbook* (Washington, DC: Acropolis, 1971).

9 Citizenship and Government

If we want children to be creatively participating members of their democratic communities when they are adults, we must help them live as creatively participating members of their communities today.
John H. Niemeyer

Good citizenship is built on sensitivity and responsibility. These qualities are fostered through emotional health. It is logical, therefore, that this chapter should begin with describing social studies experiences that are deliberately planned to promote mental health. The provision of opportunities for practicing citizenship in classroom and community are then taken up. Next, attention is turned to the teaching of current affairs as a means of advancing citizenship. Finally, suggestions are given for conducting formal study of government.

PROMOTING EMOTIONAL HEALTH

Introducing Affective Education

Teaching that includes children's feelings and values as a legitimate part of their learning is sometimes called affective education. Its purpose is to have children confront their emotions, motives, and moral and aesthetic sensibilities in a way that will bring about positive attitudes about themselves. Proponents of affective education do not assert the primacy of the child's affective learning over his or her cognitive learning. Rather, they take the position that "unless knowledge is related to an affective state in the learner, the likelihood that it will influence behavior is limited."[1] The concepts of the program are built around three major concerns of children: how to enhance one's self-image, how to become integrated with the larger society, and how better to control one's own life. The content is drawn from the children's own experiences and their feelings about them, and whatever items of information they have garnered from their social environment. Strong emphasis is placed upon the skills of "learning how to learn,"—how to analyze a problem, how to deal with someone who holds a different point of view, and how to devise and try out alternatives in a problem situation.

Tying Personal Experiences to Curriculum Topics. Having children relate personal experiences to curriculum topics is a widely practiced procedure, but it probably has never been developed more carefully or more convincingly than in an older experimental project in Wilmington, Delaware.[2]

In the Wilmington project, first-grade children who studied home and family life were, in one activity, asked to draw pictures on themes such as "the time I had the most fun with my whole family," and "things my parents ask me to do that I do (don't) like to do." These suggestive themes added a personal, emotional dimension to what is often a formal, cut-and-dried, academic study of the family. After completing their pictures, the children told the teacher the content of their pictures, and the teacher wrote it down.

Intermediate-grade children, in a study of early settlers in their state, wrote paragraphs on "a time my family moved: what made it hard to feel at home in our new neighborhood," and "a visit to another city: what helped make me feel at home." The pupils shared one another's written work through reading it. The experience enabled them to identify with the early settlers and to appreciate the differences and similarities between the settlers' motivations and experiences and those of their own families when on the move. But beyond this, they examined their own feelings and values and came to a closer understanding of themselves.

The Wilmington experiment was years ahead of its time. It deserves recognition and emulation today. Its chief pedagogical device, the open-ended question, will be described in Chapter 13.

Teaching a Unit on Individual Differences. A white second-grade teacher initiated a unit on individual differences in an urban school whose pupils were black.[3] The pupils were inclined to be critical and hostile toward

---

[1]Gerald Weinstein and Mario D. Fantini (Eds.), *Toward Humanistic Education: A Curriculum of Affect* (New York: Praeger, 1970), p. 28.

[2]Muriel Crosby, *An Adventure in Human Relations* (Chicago : Follett, 1965).

[3]This section describes the work of Wendy Santaro in the Philadelphia public schools.

classmates who were "different." The teacher's aim was to have her pupils become aware of the numerous traits in which people differ; become sensitive concerning differences in feelings; appreciate the value of having any society accept and prize individual differences; and increase mutual respect among themselves.

The unit began by having children in the class become aware of physical differences. Each child was measured. The teacher raised such questions as: "Are children of the same height the same in other ways?" "Can all children who are the same height wear the same clothing?"

Then each child was weighed. Similar questions were asked, and also: "Do all children of the same height weigh the same?" "In what ways do children of the same height and weight look different?"

Differences in skin color were taken up—the various shades of brown and differences between the children's skin color and that of the white teacher. The skin color of Native Americans (Indians) and Orientals was introduced through pictures, and their facial features were discussed.

Differences in abilities were then considered: "Which of these differences in abilities are due to differences in size? in sex? in talents?" "Do children of all heights, weights, abilities deserve to be treated fairly and kindly?"

The subject then shifted to differences in reactions to emotion-filled situations in the classroom—generous acts, hostile acts. How did different children in the class react in a specified instance? The emotions they acknowledged in the discussion that followed ranged from indignation to indifference, from sympathy to hostility. Other questions were asked: "Which way do you think you would have felt if you had not been so excited?" "Which ways do you think might have been the 'best' ways to react? Why?"

The class then discussed fighting: "What makes children fight?" "Does fighting make you feel better or worse?" "What other ways than fighting could you try when you disagree with someone?"

Many children reported their first day in a new school was especially difficult. "How did you go about making friends?" "What do you look for in a new friend?" "What do friends fight about?" "How do you make up?" "Can a person have more than one good friend?" "In what ways are your friends like you?" "In what ways are they different?"

The unit covered much ground. In the teacher's observation and judgment, it resulted in less impulsive behavior and fewer acts of hostility and intolerance on the part of many children.

Improving Self-Concept.   One lesson growing out of the *Elementary School Teaching Project's* curriculum of affect (see Chapter 3) was taught to fifth-graders whose learning appeared to be blocked by their poor self-image. Each child was given a photograph of himself and urged to see himself as someone who was "special." The members of the class decided to put all their photographs into a booklet, and wrote stories and poems to accompany them on the subject, "I am special."

In the same project, a series of lessons to enhance self-concept among children seven to nine years of age began by the teacher's reading aloud to the class from the Bradfield's *Who Are You*—a book that considers ways in which children differ from one another. Each pupil then turned his attention to what made *him* or *her* unique, drawing a picture of himself or herself to emphasize some personal characteristic particularly prized, adding explanatory notes, and using these as the first of a series of pictures and notes to bring out special traits.

In their description of the project, Gerald Weinstein and Mario D. Fantini tell of still another approach to helping children establish their identity.[4] This strategy, based on the idea of "one-way glasses," was used with children aged 10 and 11. The aim was to have them discover that there are different ways of seeing a given situation. The teacher had two pairs of glasses, one of which he called "suspicious" glasses. Children who wear them, he said, interpret the statements and actions of others with suspicion. The other pair was "rose-colored," the wearers of which, he said, interpret the statements and actions of others favorably and optimistically with relation to themselves. It is clear that splendid role-playing opportunities were present. The children thought of other types of glasses: show-off glasses, gloomy glasses, and the like. After several lessons, the children came to see that just one way of looking at the world limits a person and that trying to find positive qualities in oneself and others is desirable.

Probing Prejudice.   Another lesson in the project was aimed at having fifth-grade children understand what it means to be treated unfairly or unjustly. Children with blue eyes were arbitrarily subjected by the teacher to segregation and other forms of discrimination. Thus, the teacher provided the content. The class analyzed the discrimination and compared it with that encountered by them in their own experiences. They also considered how one can most effectively protest discrimination.

Applying Affective Education through Role Playing and Fantasy Trips.[5] Schools have long paid lip service to the moral and social education of children, but it is only recently that educators have written concrete curriculums with the *affective* domain in mind. Many of the techniques that have been developed are especially relevant to the social studies area.

Role playing. One of the techniques used in many formats is role playing. For example, the teacher may be conducting a unit on the family, Kids easily pick up typical stiuations and act them out. Of course, the action is more interesting and creative if it presents a conflict: The mother does not want the child to go out, but the child wants to go out and play with his or her friends. When two pupils role-play these parts, then switch them with

---

[4]Weinstein and Fantini, *Toward Humanistic Education*, pp. 71–99.
[5]This section was written for this book by Joan Willens.

each other, they learn to understand the feelings of both people on a very immediate level. Children can work through teacher-pupil, parent-child, gang-police, and boyfriend-girlfriend situations and perhaps come away with a deeper understanding of another person's feelings and actions. Once the technique is mastered, it can be used in the classroom when conflicts arise, to emphasize both points of view.

The fantasy trip. One of the affective techniques that emphasizes creativity and imagination is the fantsy trip. Here, the room is darkened and pupils are asked to close their eyes. If the floor is carpeted, they may be permitted to lie down and get truly relaxes. The teacher or leader then "takes" the group on a trip, only the outlines of which are given, and each individual is asked to use his imagination to fill in the details. Here is a teacher taking a class on a "trip" to school:

> Relax; close your eyes. . . . Let your whole body sink down and relax. . . . You are asleep at your house. You hear someone calling. Who is calling you? They say it's time to get up. You move. You get out of bed. How do you feel? . . . You get dressed. What do you put on? You eat something, say goodbye to your mom, and then go out the door. What kind of a day is it? . . . You are walking toward school. Are you alone or with somebody? . . . What are you talking about? What are you thinking about? You see the school ahead of you. It looks different. . . . It has become a school of the future. . . . You go inside. There is a lot of light. Are there windows? . . . Are the rooms round or square, tall or small? Where do you sit? . . . What color is the floor?

The trip continues, and ends this way:

> It is time to leave. You go back home. You are telling someone about your new school. Would you like to wake up and tell us about your school?

This technique can be used to "transport" children to other times and other cultures and to encourage them to explore emotions about themselves and the goals they hold.

Teachers attempting an affective approach are the navigators of the class. They encourage exploration and discovery as the most meaningful ways of learning, even if these ways slow it up, and they legitimatize the expression of emotions in the classroom and encourage effective ways of dealing with them.

Approaching Human Behavior Through a Causal Orientation

The late Ralph H. Ojemann and his associates were pioneers in opening up the field of human behavior as an aspect of elementary school social studies. They have prepared an original, intriguing set of teacher handbooks and pupil workbooks on human behavior, covering kindergarten through grade 6.[6] (A specimen workbook page is shown in Figure 9.1.) The books provide a structure that is welcomed by teachers who have had no training in teaching human relations and who feel the need of the sort of guidance they offer. But the books are not essential. Other programs could be developed, utilizing the findings of Ojemann's many years of research and his formulation of a point of view on how to teach about human behavior.

Ojemann's basic purpose was to help pupils develop what he called a causal orientation toward their social environment. He believed that our attempt to have children learn about causes of physical phenomena should be extended to the study of people. He searched the scientific literature on stealing, lying, shyness, overagressiveness, cooperativeness, and other forms of behavior in order to discover the situations that give rise to them. He pointed out that few adults are trained to think in terms of causality; in fact, there is evidence that most people have instead been taught a judgmental, nonunderstanding, surface approach.

Ojemann's suggestions to the teacher are these:

1. Establish a model of causative behavior by avoiding arbitrary decisions and choosing the understanding, causative approach.
2. Read to the children, and have them read, narrative material that contrasts judgmental procedures and understanding procedures by story characters in interactions with each other.
3. Include among the readings nonnarrative material that will help children understand the work and problems of the teacher and other adults, and material that will bring out problems and cultural idiosyncrasies of people in other parts of their own community and of the world.

Approaching Human Behavior Through Moral Education

The ultimate test of a child's attainment of mental health is the quality of his or her moral behavior. Lawrence Kohlberg, in reviewing the history of moral education, has documented the apparent ineffectiveness of exhorting children to perform good deeds and to practice the moral virtues.[7] Defining a morally mature person as one who is governed by the principle of justice, he finds this principle present in some form at each of six stages of moral development. The stages range from the child's conformity to rules in order to avoid punishment, to the capacity reached by adulthood for decisions of conscience and for mutual respect and trust. Kohlberg has found that the

---

[6]The basic manual for use with handbooks for teachers at the various grade levels is *Developing a Program for Education in Human Behavior and Potential* (Cleveland: Educational Research Council of America).

[7]Lawrence Kohlberg, "Stages of Moral Development as a Basis for Moral Education," in Clive M. Beck, et al. (Eds.), *Moral Education: Interdisciplinary Approaches* (Toronto: University of Toronto Press, 1971).

CASE A

Tim's family is happy and loving. He has plenty of food, rest, and physical activity. But he isn't popular at school. He thinks he would feel secure if_____

_____

CASE B

Lucy always has friends who think she is great. She loves to go to school because her friends are there and she can do her schoolwork well. But her father has left the family and her mother is away at work most of the time. She thinks she would feel more secure if

_____   _____

_____   _____

CASE C

Mr. Cook is the richest man in town. He had to go to work when he was very young, so he didn't get to go to school very long. Now he finds that most of the people he knows are well educated. Sometimes he thinks they laugh at him behind his back because he doesn't speak English very well and doesn't have fine manners. He thinks he would feel more secure if_____

_____

FIGURE 9.1   From the workbook, *Needs and Feelings*, Program in Human Behavior and Potential, produced by permission of the Educational Research Council of America, Cleveland, Ohio.

creation of conceptual conflict in the child (a process described in a different context in Chapter 7) is an effective means for "teaching virtue." This method consists of exposing children to moral conflict situations for which their present stage of moral development has no ready answers. They discuss these dilemmas and argue about their solution with one another, including some children who are apt to be at the next moral stage. Kohlberg reports that they all tend to advance toward the next stage.

Legitimate questions have been raised about the practicality of Kohlberg's procedure for the classroom teacher and about the universality of the stages.[8] Furthermore, the possibility that the moral discussions may demand tasks beyond the child's cognitive ability has been pointed out.[9] Nevertheless, experimentation with Kohlberg's approach is justified. Interested teachers are directed to the Fenton-Kohlberg teacher preparation kit[10] and Beyer's transcript of a moral discussion by junior high school students.[11]

PROVIDING OPPORTUNITIES FOR PRACTICING CITIZENSHIP

Promoting Citizenship in the Classroom

The vitality of our democratic government flows from its grass roots. Its quality can only reflect the quality of democracy operating in the home, the school, and the community. Hence, it is of critical importance that teachers make their classrooms places where children develop a sense of involvement, where children feel that their ideas will be given a respectful hearing, and where they know that part of the responsibility for evaluating their learning will be placed upon them. There should be daily occasions to ask pupils what *they* think, how *they* propose a problem be solved, what features *they* think should be labelled on a class-constructed map, and so on. In such a classroom environment the meaning of involvment is learned, and goodwill and mutual respect are observed and experienced.

Since children learn what they live, and since we want children to learn the satisfactions of participatory democracy, we should look for concrete ways in which pupil input has a better-than-even chance of influencing policy. Surely, as a minimum, children can help set up schedules for service jobs, such as "librarian" for the classroom book collection, "curator" for a

---

[8] Jack R. Fraenkel, "A Response to Edwin Fenton," *Social Education,* 41 (January 1977), 57, 59–61.

[9] David Elkind, "Humanizing the Curriculum," *Childhood Education,* 53 (February 1977), 179–182.

[10] Edwin Fenton and Lawrence Kohlberg, *Learning to Lead Moral Discussions: A Teacher Preparation Kit* (Pleasantville, NY: Guidance Associates, 1976).

[11] Barry K. Beyer, "Conducting Moral Discussions in the Classroom," *Social Education,* 40 (April 1976), 194–202.

science or museum corner, caretaker of classroom plants and pets, and the like.

Where civic sensitivity and responsibility are nurtured, children tend to develop a feeling of loyalty and protectiveness toward their class. This sometimes expresses itself in surprising, rewarding ways. One elementary school in an economically depressed urban area was the victim of rock-throwing by older youths attending a nearby high school. The elementary school's principal was assured by an official that screens would be placed on the windows to protect the children. The screens failed to appear, even after the teacher and the pupils wrote letters to the board of education, explaining the urgent need. Finally, one of the pupils, on his own intiative, wrote the following letter to one of the city's newspapers:

> I'm nine years old and in the fourth grade and I wrote this to help my school. On Friday, November 20, at 10:30 a rock was thrown through a window in my room in the _____ School on _____ Street.
> It was not the first time this has happened. The rock nearly hit a girl in the room.
> Miss _____, my teacher, and the children of Rooms 3, 4, 5, wrote a letter to the Board of Education about the screens we are supposed to be getting. Mr. _____, our principal, asked the Board of Education to get the screens three years ago, and we never got them. I wish you would help us get them.
>
> Robert Smith

The letter was published, and the following week the screens were installed. The potential influence of action by a single individual provided a valuable learning experience for all the children in the class.

Directing Service Projects for the School

Citizenship training opportunities that benefit the entire school abound, but, aside from the safety-patrol jobs found in most schools, they remain for the most part unrealized. Some projects that have been successfully carried out in schools are the following:

- Organizing and operating a school supply store.
- Building bluebird houses where the bluebird population is declining (information available from North American Bluebird Society, Silver Spring, MD 20906).
- Planting seedlings on an eroding hillside.
- Building bicycle parking facilities at the school.
- Conducting a campaign to reduce Hallowe'en vandalism.
- The classroom business enterprises described in Chapter 12 in the section, "Teaching the Role of the Entrepreneur."

In one school, a class was interested in marking trees on the school grounds with metal tags giving the common and scientific names of the trees. The class decided which trees to mark, purchased the tags, and obtained the help of a botanist to help identify unknown species.

Another class planned and planted flowers and shrubs around its unsightly school building. It asked the local garden club for advice about what plants would be best suited to the particular types of soil and exposure of various locations.

An illustration of how one fifth-grade class organized and operated a school lost-and-found department may further clarify some of the procedures of community service. The teacher, aware of the unsatisfactory, unorganized way in which lost-and-found items were handled through the school office, challenged the class with the suggestion that they do something about it. A large closet was turned over to the class to serve as headquarters for the lost-and-found department. A counter, shelves, and hooks were installed by a committee of children, under the teacher's supervision. Lively discussions were held on such matters as what hours to keep, how to work out a stagger system so that every child would have equal responsibility in tending the department, whether or not to penalize owners when they reclaimed articles in order to deter carelessness, how to advertise lost-and-found articles through the school at regular intervals, and what to do with unclaimed articles.

The children submitted designs for tags to a committee of classmates. Eventually, they held auctions to sell articles that had been unclaimed for over a month. This raised a host of new problems, including the determination of a starting price, choice of auctioneers, and how to dispose of articles not sold. This project ran throughout the year and was continued by the same class the following year. Then a committee of mothers took over the work, feeling that they could do the job more efficiently! They undoubtedly could and did, but at a considerable educational loss to the class. Schools and communities are still far from grasping the educational significance of having children undertake important community responsibilities.

Directing Service Projects in the Wider Community

Children in today's world can also make contributions to the larger community, beyond the home and the school. Members of one faculty with vision and imagination helped their classes to undertake the following projects:

> All the fourth, fifth, and sixth grades were invited to elect a representative to a central committee. This committee was asked to look about the town to see just where and how it could be made more attractive. At the next meeting the committee members brought lists of suggestions which were discussed as to relative merits.
>
> The suggestion which met with most approval was the purchase of trash cans for a number of spots in the business area, so we proceeded to work on this. It involved investigation of the different types of trash receptacles and their cost.

Then we had the problem of raising money, for we had none. Letters were written by the children to the various clubs and organizations of the town, explaining the project, and asking for financial support. This was forthcoming very quickly, and the cans were ordered. In due time they arrived, and have been in use ever since.

Another of the campaign suggestions was to clean up a number of vacant lots which were unsightly. Each class chose its own location, and on a given day the children arrived in old clothes and began work. This was planned just before the town clean-up day, so that borough trucks could collect the trash.

Still another suggestion was to visit all gas stations in the town and choose the most attractive one, in an effort to encourage all to improve their appearance. This was done, and the results were published.[12]

TEACHING CITIZENSHIP THROUGH FOLLOWING THE NEWS

Following the news is a habit of most concerned citizens, and talking about the news in the classroom once or twice a week can become a popular part of the school program.

Capitalizing on Children's Television Watching

Television is a dominant medium in children's political socialization. Even kindergarteners acquire information and impressions from televised news which influence their ideas and attitudes concerning government and society.[13] Older children not only spend large portions of time every day before the television set, as is well known, but they seem to prefer seeing a story (whether a news story or fiction) on television to reading it.[14]

In view of this situation, it is realistic for teachers to make the most of children's learning acquired through televised news. More than that, they have an opportunity to aid children to watch the news with heightened purpose and discrimination. For example, ask your class to watch a given news program on a given evening. All members of the class will thus have had a common viewing experience and will be able to exchange impressions the next day about the same presentation. Pupils may be asked to take notes during the presentation or to select portions of the program which might have been made clearer and easier to understand. At other times, you, the

[12]The authors are grateful to Helen Cornfield Moore for this report. With the increase in school district mergers and in efforts to increase ethnic integration of children, more and more school children are being bused from their home communities to schools in remote communities. Needless to say, it is virtually impossible for a teacher of a class whose members come from diverse and distant communities to undertake projects of this nature.

[13]"TV and Political Knowledge of Elementary School Pupils," *Intellect*, 104 (January 1976), 284–285; Sarah S. Van Camp, "The World Through Five-Year-Old Eyes," *Childhood Education*, 54 (March 1978), 246–250.

[14]Jackie S. Busch, "Television's Effects on Reading: A Case Study," *Phi Delta Kappan*, 59 (June 1978), 668–671.

teacher, might assign different children to watch the treatment of a given event (such as the launching of a new outer-space rocket or the opening of a new national park) on different channels and have them compare the varying treatments the following day.

Guiding the Use of Newspapers

Children's Newspapers.   Newspapers written expressly for children are available for pupils of all ages. (See Box 9.1.) They are simply written with a vocabulary suitable to the grade or grades for which each is prepared, and they contain child-centered features (puzzles, riddles, jokes, cartoons).

BOX 9.1   **VARIOUS GRADES**

Children's Newspapers

Grades 1–6 (a separate edition for each grade)

My Weekly Reader, Xerox Education Publications, 245 Long Hill Road, Middletown, CT 06457.

Intermediate Grades

Junior Review, Civic Education Service, 1733 K Street, Washington, DC 20006.
Newsmap of the Week, 7300 N. Linder Avenue, Skokie, IL 60076.
School Sprint, Scholastic Magazines, 50 W. 44th Street, New York, NY 10036.

Junior High School Grades

Current Events, Xerox Education Publications, 245 Long Hill Road, Middletown, CT 06457.
Junior Scholastic, Scholastic Magazines, 50 W. 44th Street, New York, NY 10036.
Newsmap of the Week, 7300 N. Linder Avenue, Skokie, IL 60076.
Read Magazine, Xerox Education Publications, 245 Long Hill Road, Middletown, CT 06457.
Young Citizen, Civic Education Service, 1733 K Street, Washington, DC, 20036.

One of the benefits of such periodicals is that they are written in simple enough language so that children can have a newspaper experience to supplement television news and adult conversation. Furthermore, all children may have access to the same news item through having a common publication and hence can contribute more intelligently to the discussion. Teachers should use the news publicaton in such a way that considerable interest in news is aroused; they should not use it for formal, round-robin reading lessons with minimal discussion or with emphasis on testing of factual information. The more informal and enjoyable the news discussion can be made, and the more it resembles a gathering of adults at which news is exchanged and discussed, the greater will be the interest and learning.

Adult Newspapers.   Adult newpapers also have a place, even in the earlier grades. Here are some suggestions for using them:

1. Bring a newspaper to school every day, and mention to the class now and then what news of interest you have found in it. Occasionally clip and post newsworthy items.
2. Encourage students to bring news clippings (even if only pictures) from newspapers at home for discussion and posting.
3. Have students bring old newspapers from home. Show them that newspapers are divided into sections. Have them list the section and find out about the content of each.
4. Call attention to the newspaper's advertisements—where they are placed, the varying amounts of space used by different firms, the kinds of products advertised. Have them compare prices of a given product.
5. Ask students to explain why certain news reports are so brief. After they discuss the problem of limited space, give them the experience of writing news reports of their own and then cutting them to fit an arbitrary word limit.
6. Newspapers give opinions as well as news. Children may make a bulletin-board display of clippings from the newspapers, classified under the headings "News" and "Opinions" (the latter including editorials, writing by columnists, political cartoons, and slanted headlines).

INTRODUCING CHILDREN TO GOVERNMENT

Presenting the Government of the School System

Complex processes of government can be understood by children when they study their operation in institutions with which they are familiar. One fourth-grade teacher in a large city described the opening of her class's study of local education as follows:

> My class undertook to learn about the school organization in our district as an introduction to its government and management. A visit was made to the district superintendent's office. Here we examined the maps and charts of our district. We located other schools and districts on the maps and made a list of them. Upon returning to the classroom, the children made a map of their district and put markers where each school is located, with a code number as to its type.[15]

---

[15]The authors are grateful to Olga C. Pennacchio for this account.

Following such a survey, units on the school usually take up the responsibilities of the teachers, principals, supervisors, superintendent, and school board; how these participants are chosen; what their legal and professional relationships to one another are; and how and by whom school policy and school rules are made.

Acquainting Children with the Local Government

Make arrangements for your class to visit the headquarters of your local government. One township manager volunteered to escort a third-grade class through the township offices himself. The tour included a visit to the tax offices, the engineer's office with its large map of the township, the offices of those in charge of garbage and trash collections, and, finally, the commissioner's room. There the children were seated, and the manager told them how their township government operated, what a commissioner was, what the commissioner's meetings were like, what the meaning of taxes was, and many other matters. The class questions and discussions inspired by this trip continued for days.[16]

Have your class compile a scrapbook on the local community. The same third-grade class constructed one, entitled "The Story of Elkins Park." It contained chapters bearing such titles as "The History of Elkins Park," "Our Community Government," and "The Future of Elkins Park." The book was complete with title page, table of contents, and an alphabetized index. It was illustrated with drawings and photographs. It was pored over repeatedly by its young makers and eventually took on a dog-eared, much-loved appearance, which betokened a well-awakened interest in the community.

Presenting the Concept of Community Planning

Have your pupils consider how the community can be improved. This will introduce them to a wide range of possible governmental concerns, such as beautification, for one. Arrange a survey of various ugly spots in the community: auto graveyards, dumps, and the clutter of commercial signs, ranging from garish to dingy, that spoil the approaches to many towns and cities. Discuss with the class how such conditions could be corrected.

Children in several elementary schools of Philadelphia made an intensive study of their community's aesthetic needs. Before the study began, teachers found that many children thought of their neighborhoods as incapable of change or improvement. It was not difficult, however, to stimulate them to think in terms of what might be done to create greater beauty and more space. Each pupil took a particular city block and made a

---

[16]The authors are grateful to Charlotte Werner Bernstein for this account.

detailed map showing land use. They placed their individual maps side by side. Then they listed both the neighborhood's assets and those spots that were ugly or detrimental to healthful living. They drew up plans for the community of the future. Thus, citizens of the future were led to think about the feasibility of improved surroundings. In view of the increased interest of all municipalities in planning for redevelopment, having students think about this concern is a significant aspect of studies of local government.

Acquainting Children with State Government

Fourth grade has been the traditional grade placement for study of the pupil's state. Many textbooks have been written at the fourth-grade readability level for most states, combining state history, state geography, and state government. Such integration of content is sensible. Unfortunately, the subject of government often is treated drably, due to an overemphasis on the structure of the government and little or nothing on the *dynamics* of the state's legislature, regulatory bodies, and agencies. Some teachers have reported excellent cooperation from legislators, game wardens, highway commissioners, and state policemen in supplying information about current activities and problems that deal with matters that can be understood by children—littering, bicycle regulations, use of fireworks, and the like. Sometimes it is possible for a class to follow a piece of state legislation that leads to an understanding of how laws are made that all citizens should have and few do. For an illustration of the possibilities, even at the third-grade level, see Box 9.2.

BOX 9.2   **GRADE 3**

Third-Graders Learn How an Idea May Become a Law

A third-grade class in Upper Darby, Pennsylvania, learned that some states had officially adopted "state insects," as most have state flowers and birds. "Why shouldn't Pennsylvania have a state insect?" they asked. The children decided they would like the firefly to be given that honor. They invited their representatives in the Commonwealth's House and Senate to discuss with them how this could be done. In consultation with the class, the legislators drafted identical bills to be introduced in the House and Senate. The class wrote letters to the members of the House and Senate urging support. They conducted a drive with bumper stickers, petitions signed by friends, and endorsements from civic organizations.

The class travelled by bus to Harrisburg, the state capital, to attend a hearing held by the State Government Committee on the firefly bill. Each child was given an opportunity to speak before the Committee. The Speaker of the House walked accidentally into the hearing, and said later

(Continued)

he had never seen more enthusiasm for any piece of legislation than was expressed by these children!

As the time drew near for a vote on the bill in the Senate, the bill approached a critical stage. It became apparent that some senators wanted to kill it by recommitting it to the Committee. They regarded it as a trivial intrusion. The sponsoring senator, a man of considerable prestige and influence, requested support for a move to put it in position for a vote. This was granted. By this time, all the pupils in the Upper Darby school knew what was happening in Harrisburg. They discussed the issue among themselves, and urged the media to give the bill a boost. Some complied.

The sponsoring senator was again told by some of his colleagues that they could not support the firefly bill. In an eloquent address before the Senate voted, he stressed the keen interest in the legislative process the bill had engendered among children throughout the state. The bill passed overwhelmingly in the Senate and later in the House.

Comment: Few children will have the opportunity of duplicating this precise experience of becoming lobbyists, but there are other ways in which an imaginative faculty may bring children into direct contact with governmental officials, usually at the local level, at least once in a given child's elementary years.

Clyde Dengler, the senator who sponsored this legislation, and an educator, made available to the senior author his manuscript on the firefly legislation, "Democracy Needs Lobbyists!" for condensation in this box.

Teaching the Structure and Functions
Of Our Federal Government

Beginning in Grade 4, it is easy and enjoyable for most children to learn how the federal government is organized and how it functions. By then they can straighten out the hierarchical arrangements of governmental units and can see how the work of local, state, and national governments sometimes overlap.

Federal Agencies.   You may have your pupils survey departments of the federal government which have nearby branch offices: the post office, a federal courthouse, a national park, a passport office, an office of the soil conservation service, or whatever other agency is present. Have your pupils consult the local telephone directory under "United States Government" for a list of federal agencies in your area. Some classes construct large organizational charts of federal agencies, marking those that have local branches. Committees of children may be assigned the task of finding out their purposes and the nature of their work.

The Presidency.   The Presidency is of special interest to children. A study of the personalities, backgrounds, and achievements of Presidents in various periods usually turns out to be a popular one. Box 9.3 tells how one such study is done by Jane Galloway, a fifth-grade teacher.

BOX 9.3   **GRADES 4–6**

Learning About Our Presidents

Presidents' Day is a federal holiday designated to be observed on the third Monday of February, but Presidents' Day as observed at Highland Park School comes later in the year and is an occasion for the culminating activity of the Government Unit conducted by Jane Galloway, fifth-grade teacher in Upper Darby, Pennsylvania. About 10 days before Presidents' Day, Miss Galloway places in a hat slips of paper on each of which she has written the name of a former President of the United States. There are as many slips (and Presidents) as there are children in the class. Each child draws a slip and notes the name of the President, but does not divulge the name of "his" of "her" President to others.

Each child then reads up on the President whose name he or she has drawn, and prepares "Presidential Papers," which include a drawing of the flag as it appeared when the President left office and a map of the United States as it then looked. On "Presidents' Day," each child comes to school wearing a few items of costume to suggest the appearance of his or her President and the period in which the President served. (See Figure 9.2.)

The day starts with the brisk "Hail to the Chief" march played on a phonograph. One child at a time stands before the class in costume and offers five clues for identification of the President. The most difficult clue is given first and the easiest last. For example, a difficult clue in the case of President Theodore Roosevelt might be, "As a child, I was not very healthy." An easier one would be, "I was Vice President when the President was killed, and that's when I became President."

After each clue, the class tries to guess which President it might be. Those who wish to offer a guess must first ask a probing question such as, "Was your family poor when you were a child?" Points are given to both "president" and "guesser" for good clues and good guesses.

It should be added that Miiss Galloway enjoys dressing up as one of our "First Ladies." She has her list of clues, too!

The Constitution.   Prepare or obtain a copy of the Constitution of the United States for each pupil in your class. Read and discuss with them passages from it, taking time to explain legal and other unfamiliar terms. Excerpts from the following passages are within the comprehension of intermediate-grade children and constitute a good introduction:

- Article I, Section 7: method of passing laws.
- Article II, Section 3: duties of the President
- Article VI, Part 2: supreme law of the land.
- First Amendment: freedom of religion, speech, and press.

Stress those features of the Constitution that have made it a universally

FIGURE 9.2.   "President Arthur" and "President Roosevelt" on Presidents' Day. See Box 9.3. Courtesy of Jane Galloway, Highland Park School, Upper Darby, Pennsylvania.

admired document. One of these is the establishment of three distinct branches of government—legislative, executive, and judicial—equal and independent, yet each restricted in its powers by the others. Have your pupils compare the provisions of the Constitution with bylaws of clubs or organizations that they or their parents belong to, and explain why the bylaws would not be suitable for operating the United States Government.

Teaching About Civil Rights

"Rights" are intangible privileges or immunities granted and protected by law and custom. They are appropriately studied when children have reached the maturity of most 10- to 12-year-olds.

Children sometimes confuse civil rights with the freedom to act as one chooses. It is important, therefore, to work out, with your class, a definition of civil rights. Have them consult dictionaries and other reference books. This will help destroy the widely held misconception that civil rights are a blank check to do whatever one pleases.

The civil rights of blacks deserve special attention. Have your class read and talk about portions of the thirteenth, fourteenth, and fifteenth amendments to the Constitution, helping them understand such concepts as "involuntary servitude," "subject to jurisdiction," and "abridged." Give illustrations of the freedom each amendment provides. Black children can often supply examples of cases in which the freedoms have been ignored or violated, citing experiences of their families or friends. Look into the Civil Rights Act of 1964, which forbade racial discrimination in schools, stores, restaurants, theaters, and other public places. Again, supply and have members of the class supply current examples of compliance and noncompliance. All this may be tied into the study of black history, to be taken up in the next chapter.

Civil rights issues, of course, are not confined to problems of minority ethnic groups. Another set of problems is related to the struggle for civil rights for women, who constitute half the nation. Landmarks in women's battle for civil rights for their sex, and suggestions for teaching about them, are given in the next chapter.

Introducing the Concept of International Law and Order

A study of government in the upper elementary grades is incomplete without a look at various steps that have been taken toward controlling international anarchy. How to reduce international conflict in today's world, bristling as it is with the nuclear capability of total destruction, is the supreme challenge for all governments.

Approaches to Peace within the State System.   Acquaint your class with approaches to a peaceful world under the present "state system"—the system in which the world is divided into separate sovereign nations. This may be done through supplying illustrations of peaceful settlement of disputes. The history of boundary disputes supplies many examples.[17]

One clearcut case is the sharp disagreement between Argentina and Chile at the turn of the century. Each was preparing for war. Each claimed territory that was also claimed by the other. Each was cocky, certain of success in a war which seemed inevitable. At the eleventh hour, they agreed to submit the problem to arbitration by King Edward VII of England, with an outcome (a peaceful one) that was mutually acceptable. The women of the two countries, collaborating, were largely responsible for having an impressive monument, "The Christ of the Andes," erected at the boundary as a symbol of peace.

The most ambitious approach ever made to peace under the state system was the creation of the United Nations in 1945. While not a panacea, it represents a giant step toward international order. Have your pupils dig into Edna Epstein's *The United Nations* (rev. ed., New York: Watts), which is appropriate for Grade 3 and up, and into children's encyclopedias. Have them diagram the United Nations structure and give reports on some of its functions and accomplishments.

---

[17]A useful source for the teacher is *International Boundaries* by S. Whittemore Boggs (New York: AMS Press, 1966). Geographical factors involved in boundary disputes are discussed in *Look to the Frontiers: A Geography for the Peace Table* by Roderick Peattie (Port Washington, NY: Kennikat Press, 1970).

The Concept of World Government.   Many thoughtful and concerned leaders of public opinion feel that the only way to save the world from destruction is to establish a world government. Older pupils should be learning, thinking, and talking about it. Long a dream of utopians, it captured the imagination of thousands through Tennyson's visualization of it in his "Locksley Hall" almost 150 years ago:

> Till the war-drums throbb'd no longer
> > and the battle-flags were furl'd
> In the Parliment of man, the Federation of the world.

Today, the idea of world government is being widely promoted by the World Federalists, who look upon the American federal system as the most hopeful model available for establishing a world government. They seek to strengthen the United Nations with ultimate authority to prevent war through a federal world structure. Leaders in the movement have worked with educators to establish global education programs.[18] A list of teaching materials will be included in a forthcoming *Citizens Handbook on Interdependence Education.*[19]

TEACHING COMPETENCIES

This chapter has described how to perform the following tasks that are basic to teacher competency. The teacher should be able to:

1. Give children opportunity and encouragement to relate personal experience to curriculum topics.
2. Raise questions in class designed to help children accept human differences.
3. Conduct lessons designed to help children improve self-concept and establish identity.
4. Initiate activities planned so as to have children discover the unfairness of prejudice.
5. Involve children in role playing and fantasizing as aids to improved civic sensitivity.
6. Help children look for causes of behavior as a basis for improved understanding of behavior.
7. Provide opportunities for growth in citizenship through classroom and community projects.

---

[18]In 1978, such programs were established in all grades in New Jersey and Minnesota. See *World Federalist Newsletter* (1011 Arlington Boulevard, Arlington, VA 22209), vol. 3, December 1978.

[19]Citizens' Committee on Interdependence Education, 1011 Arlington Boulevard, Arlington, VA 22209.

8. Use television and newspapers in guiding children in learning the scope of news reports, their variety, and how to examine contents critically.
9. Supplement children's "armchair" learning about government by providing experiences in observing governmental machinery in action and communicating with governmental officials.
10. Introduce children to government through surveys of the organization and administration of the school's government and of local government.
11. Acquaint children with the operation of state and national government, with emphasis on the dynamics of decision making rather than on the purely structural features of government.
12. Ilustrate the concept of international law and order under the state system and under a world federation.

TRYING OUT SOME OF YOUR COMPETENCIES

1. Try out with a small group of children some of the ideas described in this chapter for helping children (a) improve self-concept, and (b) establish identity.
2. Gather together a set of materials (see items 2 and 3 of Ojemann's suggestions) that could be used by children of a given age to develop a "causal" orientation toward behavior.
3. Plan a lesson for presenting the United States Constitution to intermediate-grade or junior-high pupils.

FOR STUDY AND EXPLORATION

1. Citizenship education (civics) has often been a form of indoctrination. How can you give it a solid conceptual base, while retaining its aim of developing social sensitivity and responsibility?
2. Draw up a plan for a class to study the consequences of planless urban or regional sprawl and to consider the problems of planning for orderly growth and change.
3. Examine your state's constitution with a view to selecting two or three salient provisions that you believe could be understood by children of a designated age. Build a lesson around those provisions that would introduce children to the purpose and importance of a constitution.
4. Can patriotism and world citizenship, often regarded as antithetical, be taught as complementary forms of loyalty? Why or why not?

FURTHER READING

Successful procedures with affective education continue to be reported. William Knaus in "Rational Emotive Education," *Theory Into Practice*, 16 (October 1977), 251–55, tells of his experience with his sixth-grade class. The entire issue of *The School*

Psychologist Digest, Spring 1978, is devoted to affective education. It is replete with leads for teaching. Another practical guide is *Humanizing the Classroom: Models of Teaching in Affective Education* by John P. Miller (New York: Praeger, 1976).

Teachers are wisely cautioned by David Elkind against the danger of demanding tasks beyond children's ability, when engaging children in discussions under the rubrics of affective education and moral discussions. His article, "Humanizing the Curriculum," appears in *Childhood Education*, 53 (February 1977), 179–182.

A significant conference on citizenship education, called by the Social Science Education Consortium, is reported in the Consortium's newsletter, *The Link*, 1 (September 1977). It presents basic issues discussed at the conference and indicates the areas of agreement and disagreement by the social studies educators in attendance.

Richard C. Remy gives an excellent account of children's political "world" and of the need for experience-based programs in "Citizenship Education in Elementary School," *Theory Into Practice*, 15 (February 1976), 31–36.

Three articles describing children's school-directed participation in the community appear in William W. Joyce (Ed.), "The Community: Laboratory for Social Learnings," *Social Education*, 40 (March 1976), 157–171.

Many ways of using the newspaper in the primary grades are described by Susan M. Glazer, "Learning to Think with a Newspaper: A Program for Grades K–3," in Harold Newman (Ed.), *Effective Language Arts Practices in the Elementary School* (New York: Wiley, 1972), pp. 789–798.

John J. Cogan presents a case study of international education, as carried out in all the grades of a Chicago elementary school, in *Social Education*, 42 (October 1978), 503–505; and in the same issue M. Eugene Gilliom and Richard C. Remy convincingly discuss the need for a new approach to global (cross-national) education (pp. 499–502).

10 Cultures
Present and Past

*There has never been a time when a
civilization stood more in need of
individuals who are genuinely culture-
conscious, who can see objectively the
socially conditioned behavior of other
peoples without fear and recrimination.*
Ruth Benedict

A people's culture is the sum total of their way of life. It consists of their language, social institutions, technology, beliefs, humor, and other characteristics. One of the greatest needs of our time, as suggested by the epigraph at the head of this chapter, is to help children, as the future guardians of our civilization, understand and accept peoples of other cultures. But much of this chapter will also deal with ways of helping them understand their *own* culture, for their knowledge of foreign cultures is of value only to the extent they are able to make informed comparisons with their own.

THE STUDY OF CULTURES

Cultures from Three Perspectives

In most elementary school curriculums, culture is looked at from three perspectives—that of geography (culture areas), that of cultural anthropology (customs and beliefs), and that of history (time periods). Usually these three approaches are integrated in one form or another. For example, one fourth-grade unit on Brazil contains the story of Cabral's visit to Brazil in 1500, descriptions of some of Brazil's land, rivers, climates, agriculture, and industry, and accounts of the ways of life of her diverse peoples.

Sometimes a unit is predominantly geographical, or anthropological, or historical. The study of United States history in Grade 8, for example, is usually "straight" history, and the study of primitive society is usually "straight" anthropology. But even here total divorcement from other disciplines is impossible. History has to be given a geographical setting, and a primitive society has to be shown as conditioned by geographical and historical forces.

Deciding Which Cultures to Teach

What cultures shall we choose for study? Traditional practice has been to crowd the study of most of the earth's surface into the elementary school curriculum. This means trying to cover dozens of cultures and regions before high school. The result is that interest does not hold up, and learning is superficial. If the curriculum guide or the textbook covers an excessive amount of territory, we will choose those cultures which seem most important, and limit them to a number which can be reasonably learned—that is the key consideration! Seldom can a culture be studied with proper thoroughness in less than four weeks.

The old "type-study unit" idea of McMurry's (now called "postholing") is still probably the most satisfactory compromise between the two opposed and equally undesirable tendencies of (1) rushing through a host of cultures in quick succession, and (2) tediously dwelling on one culture for an entire semester. The postholed unit provides for intensive, detailed study of an example of a type of culture, followed by brief comparisons with other examples of the same type of culture. Some illustrations are:

TYPE OF CULTURE	FOR INTENSIVE STUDY	OTHER EXAMPLES, FOR MAKING BRIEF COMPARISONS
Latin American	Brazil	Mexico, Venezuela, Peru
Indian	Woodland	Plains, Pueblo, Northwestern
Fishing	Norway's coastal regions	Labrador, Iceland
Democratic	Switzerland	Sweden, Germany, France

CULTURE REGIONS

Providing Practice in Applying Geographic Methods of Inquiry

Supply your students with experiences in their own area that parallel the professional geographer's first-hand study of the following categories:

Kinds and Amounts of Things in a Specific Place. Pupils can classify the buildings (or bodies of water, recreational facilities, factories, or any other significant feature in the network of a culture's community life).

Differences and Likenesses between Regions That Can Be Observed at First Hand or Through Pictures. Pupils can draw up lists of differences and similarities such as those between a rural area and a city area, suburbs and inner cities, mountain-top and valley, or well-irrigated area and dry area, and the like.

Man's Relationship to His Environment. Pupils can look for ways in which people seek to change the environment (such as building a highway through farmland), how they seek to control it (such as spraying trees and gardens with pesticides—often foolishly and ignorantly, without consulting ecologists), and how they are benefited by it (for example, by the proximity of the ocean for bathing and fishing, by adequate annual rainfall for crops, or by a mild climate which minimizes the expense of heating buildings).

Areal Associations. Pupils can be directed to track down examples of areal association between related geographical features. Thus, they may find points of early-morning traffic congestion near places where many people are employed, or they may locate the heaviest pollution in a highly industrialized area.

Areal Interaction. Pupils can be on the lookout for instances of the relationship between the community and the outside world. Thus, they may discover that their math books were published by a company many miles away. In studying other cultures, a list of their imports and exports supplies comparable information.

Using Home Life to Illustrate Geographic Concepts

The home is an institution with which the young child is familiar, and hence it provides a natural springboard to his or her understanding of some fundamental geographic concepts. Areal association and areal interaction are among these.

See how many related features governing home life your pupils can mention and how many instances they can give of the ways in which their homes interact with the outside world. Later, have them summarize their responses on picture charts.

You may want to try out some of the ideas developed in a study conducted by a first-grade teacher whose class observed the construction of new houses in the neighborhood. After reporting, discussing, and recording what they had seen, each child drew and painted plans of what he considered a model house. The class read about homemaking in available preprimers and in storybooks. They considered the issues of renting versus buying a place to live. They had a banker explain to them mortgages in simple terms. The teacher rated these children's understanding as high. She could probably have added the topics of building permits, building codes, blueprints, and the division of labor.

Modelling Local Areas[1]

One fourth-grade class extended its study of the community to include its history, government, important persons, and miscellaneous facts relating to its way of life. A major project was the construction of a three-dimensional, six-by-eight-foot floor map (see Figure 10.1). Its base was beaver board covered with sawdust, which was arranged to show the hills. White sand in elongated strips represented the roads; blue paper under glass, the rivers and streams; toothpicks, the railroad line; and sponges dipped in green paint affixed to twigs stuck in clay, the trees. Buildings were carved out of two-inch balsa wood. Each child carved his own house and one important building. The experience was an enjoyable one, which taught the children the layout of their community and its orientation to the points of the compass.

City children have made rough models of their city, showing areal variation within the city, such as the commercial core, industrial area, and residential area.

FIGURE 10.1.   Floor model of a community.

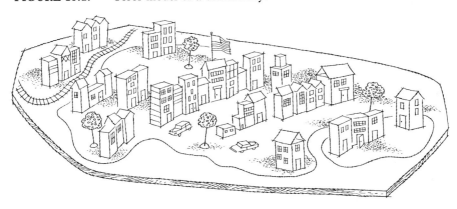

---

[1]See also the section, "Making Layouts with Blocks," in Chapter 21.

Introducing the Study of an Extensive Culture Region

In studying a large culture region have your pupils begin with a broad overview of its physical geography. Post photographs depicting the topography of the land: mountains, deserts, plains, swamps, rivers, lakes, or other prominent features. Locate these on a map that clearly shows, through shading or shaped contours, the region's relief. Have your class take an imaginary trip across the region.

Center your class's attention on salient features. For example, in approaching a study of Anglo-America (United States and Canada), you might emphasize the following:

1. The chief ranges run north and south. They are historically significant barriers to east-west travel. The long, high mountain ranges of the West force the prevailing winds into high altitudes, causing them to give up their moisture as rain and thus to irrigate the region west of the mountains, but leaving great dry stretches in those states or provinces just east of the mountains.
2. The region stretches for thousands of miles between the two largest and most important oceans in the world and contains several large rivers and lakes. Aside from their value to trade and transportation, these bodies of water have a moderating effect upon climate and supply moisture to the winds that sweep over them.
3. The region contains extensive plains with relatively fertile soil, a warm, long growing season, and adequate rainfall, all of which foster the growing of large quantities of wheat, corn, and many other crops, supplying not only the region's needs, but those of other countries as well.

Proceed from the broad overview to postholing after about a week.

Teaching Place-Location with Maps and Globes

When you first talk about an unfamiliar place, bring out a map or globe, or supply pupils with individual maps, and see if someone can locate the place. If not, point it out. Children in Grade 4 and above can learn to use the index of an atlas, with its letter-number guide system to aid in location. With sufficient practice, children acquire a mental image of a map. "No person can claim to be truly educated who does not carry such a map in his head."[2] In time, children can become "genuinely uncomfortable about studying an area they cannot visualize."[3]

Teaching about maps and globes is treated in detail in Chapter 21. You may wish to consult it at this point.

---

[2]Jesse H. Wheeler, Jr., et al., *Regional Geography of the World*, 3rd ed. (New York: Holt, Rinehart and Winston, 1975), p. 39.

[3]Edward Coleson, "The Elementary Social Studies: Sense and Nonsense in Integration," *Journal of Geography*, 57 (April 1958), 196–202.

Probing the Significance of Location

Encourage your pupils to probe the information contained on a map or globe. This involves your asking questions, usually "why" questions, about place-locations, and having children quiz one another. Some examples follow.

Why does Greenland, the world's largest island, have so few people living on it? A little research will reveal that it is almost entirely buried beneath an ice sheet (glacier) several thousand feet thick in its central areas. What if Greenland could be moved south and placed between the United States and Europe? Many children will see that the ice cap would melt and the island might then be able to support a population of millions of people. The effect upon other land areas of the melting of such a gigantic ice cap would lead to further interesting speculation.

Why is not southwestern Australia swamped with vacationers and tourists? After all, its climate is comparable to that of those popular vacationlands, Southern California and the Riviera—bright sunny weather, bringing abundant flowers and fruits, and mild winters. Pupils who look into this will probably agree that, located elsewhere, this region might indeed be a mecca for sun worshippers and that the metropolitan area of Perth, with a population of less than a million, could conceivably approach in size that of metropolitan Los Angeles (population, seven million). However, Australia's relative isolation in the vast Pacific accounts for its comparatively sparse population.

Why did the steel-manufacturing complex of Gary, Indiana, develop at this particular place, which early in the century was a sparsely settled area of sand dunes and swamp? Investigation will reveal its crossroads location for transportation and supplies: iron and limestone were accessible by lake; coal lay to the south and was easily brought by river barges and rail; Lake Michigan afforded the large supply of water needed for steel making; and both an enormous market and an ample labor supply were nearby.

You may try to establish contact with a teacher in another community and plan for the exchange of letters between your respective classes. This need not be limited to American communities. One enterprising fourth-grade teacher of Margate City, New Jersey, arranged for such a correspondence between members of her class and children in a school in Margate, England, for which the American city was named. The letters introduced the pupils in both cities to similarities and differences in community life on opposite sides of an ocean.

Areal variation can be taught with a historical dimension, too. Intermediate-grade pupils in a big city, rich in historical lore and important among the early colonies, concluded their community study by comparing their city with the small town of Williamsburg, Virginia, which had also had an early origin and was steeped in traditions growing out of a long, colorful history. A class committee wrote directly to Williamsburg for information. The current status of each of the two communities was considered in terms of population, economic importance, points of interest, and ways in which old historical sites have been preserved and restored. Then a study of the origin and early days of each of the communities was made. Questions were considered, such as why one had become a major industrial city and the other had not.

Correcting Distorted Concepts through Conceptual Conflict

Undoubtedly, occasions will arise when a teacher suspects that pupils have a distorted concept of a term, a commercial product, or a geographic relationship. In correcting them, it is well to follow the injunction of Alexander Pope: "Men must be taught as if you taught them not!" Avoid saying, "You are wrong!" Instead, quietly introduce material, preferably a picture, that will revise their idea. Review the example, given in Chapter 7, of broadening and correcting the child's narrow concept of a desert through pictures and reading selections.

Photographs, especially those in color, are all you need to demonstrate the following facts: that a live lobster is dark green, not bright red as when cooked; that bananas grow upward on the tree, not downward; that a typical Dutch landscape may not show a single windmill; and that the city of Reykjavik, Iceland, is proof that Iceland, despite its name and its location near the Arctic Circle, is not largely buried by glaciers, but that due to the relatively warm North Atlantic Drift, its southern coast has an average winter temperature only a couple of degrees lower than that of New York City. Apparent contradictions thus presented cause surprise and serve to correct a child's mistaken ideas.

THE WAY OF LIFE AND THE BELIEFS OF A CULTURE

The cultural anthropologist focuses upon customs and beliefs existing in *any* culture, whether primitive or civilized, ancient or modern, simple or complex. What customs and beliefs unite a people? How do they operate in the lives of a people? What different behaviors and values may develop in different cultures?

Emphasizing Objective Investigation

Culture units provide an ideal opportunity for teaching objectivity. Children quickly understand why we must be cautious in drawing conclusions about other peoples, and why we should avoid loose generalizations and stereotypes (e.g., "the Scots are thrifty," "Germans are autocratic," "Mexicans are lazy"). They can also learn to avoid judging another culture—that a people's behavior and values may differ from ours without making them "odd" or "wrong." Our aim should be to establish (1) objective study free of prejudice and also free of sentimentality; (2) a search for understanding, not moral judgments; and (3) recognition of changes that are taking place in customs and beliefs—how societies absorb and adopt features of another society.

Introducing the Anthropologist's Way of Working

In introducing the anthropologist's method to your pupils, you may frequently raise such questions as "How do we know this to be a fact?" "How did the people who first reported the fact get their information?" Read to your class from a book written for young people by May Edel, an anthropologist. She writes: "I can give you some idea of how an anthropologist works by telling you of what happened to me."[4] She spent a year among the Bachiga people of Western Uganda. She calls her way of working "old fashioned" and goes on to tell how, today, anthropologists use tape recorders and movie cameras.

Another absorbing account by an anthropologist (adapted for fifth-graders) is *A Journey to the Arctic* by Knud Rasmussen. It is one of the components of *Man: A Course of Study*, described in Chapter 4. Rasmussen tells of his day-by-day living with the Netsilik Eskimos in Northwest Territory, Canada—one of the most difficult places in the world for humans to live.

You may want to present the first unit of *Social Science Laboratory Units* (also described in Chapter 4), which leads children to learn the methods of behavioral scientists and to apply them in their own investigations.

Drawing upon Folklore

Part of what exists in any culture is not formally taught, but is passed on orally from generation to generation. This material, made up of accumulated knowledge and beliefs, is known as folklore. Folklore constitutes almost all of the culture of primitive peoples, but only a small part of the culture of a modern industrial society, in which most learning is transmitted through books, newspapers, TV, movies, formal educational institutions, and other means. In either type of society, however, folklore throws light on the nature of the people we are studying by enabling us to get closer to their ways of thinking and behaving than we otherwise could.

As you teach a unit on a culture, look up particular items of its folklore. A considerable body of the folklore of many countries has been published. It

---

[4]May Edel, *The Story of People: Anthropology for Young People* (Boston: Little, Brown, 1953). Other books for children about anthropologists and anthropology include Angus McBride, *The Way They Lived* (New Rochelle, NY: Soccer, 1976); H. R. Hays, *Explorers of Man* (New York: Crowell-Collier-Macmillan, 1971); Suzanne Morrow, *This Is the Way* (Encino, CA: Elk Grove, 1970); Margaret Mead, *People and Places* (New York: Bantam, 1970). See also the article for teachers by Sol Tax, "What Anthropologists Do," *Social Education*, 32 (February 1968), 132–134.

is fun just to read as recreational literature, but for children to derive the full meaning of an item of folklore, it needs to be tied in with a systematic study of the people whose culture it represents. Challenge your pupils with the task of trying to determine what it tells about the people, their culture, and their environment.

BOX 10.1   **VARIOUS GRADES**

Sources of Folklore

American Folklore

Baker, Betty. *No Help at All* (Caldwell, NJ: Morrow, 1978).
Brewer, J. Mason. *American Negro Folklore* (Chicago: Quadrangle, 1968).
    Sections on religion, superstitions, proverbs, children's rhymes and
    pastimes, etc.
Emrich, Duncan. *Folklore on the American Land* (Boston: Little, Brown,
    1971). Information about place names, cattle brands, quilt names,
    children's folklore, tall tales, etc.
Leach, Maria. *American Folktales* (Champaign, IL: Carrard, n.d.).
Lipson, Greta. *Folklore, Fact, and Fancy* (Carthage, IL: Good Apple, n.d.).

World-Wide Folklore

Carlson, Ruth K. (Comp. and Ed.). *Folklore and Folktales around the World*
    (Newark, DE: International Reading Association, 1972).
Clark, Mollie. *International Folktales Series* (Belmont, CA: Fearon, 1973).
Kamerman, Sylvia E. (Ed.), *Dramatized Folk Tales of the World* (Boston:
    Plays, 1971).

Drawing upon the Music and Art of a Culture

Portions of folklore are preserved in song and dance. They convey aspects of the spirit and mood of a culture that words alone fail to do. Set aside blocks of time in which you and your class (perhaps with the help of your school's music teacher) can sing some of the folk songs of the culture you are exploring, try out some of the folk dances, and listen to recordings.

BOX 10.2   **VARIOUS GRADES**

Sources of Folk Music and Folk Dances

Books

Gilbert, Cecile. *International Folk Dance at a Glance* (Minneapolis: Bur-
    gess, 1974).
Keller, Kate V. and Ralph Sweet. *A Choice Selection of American Country*

(Continued)

Dances of the Revolutionary Era, 1775-1795 (New York: Country Dance and Song, 1976).

Sandburg, Carl. *The American Songbag* (New York: Harcourt, 1970).

Tolman, Beth and Ralph Page. *The Country Dance Book* (Brattleboro, VT: Greene, 1976).

Records

There are hundreds of records with authentic renditions of folk dances, folk songs, and instrumental music, representing cultures throughout the world. Consult catalogues of record manufacturers (*Folkway, Indian, Canyon, Decca,* and *Columbia*).

Art, like music, is a trustworthy transmitter of a culture's spirit. Locate textbooks and magazines containing suitable pictures for a table display. The *National Geographic Magazine* is often a fruitful source. Your school or public library undoubtedly has an index to illustrations (*Illustration Index, Travel through Pictures,* or *General Index to Illustration*). Encourage your pupils to draw inferences about peoples from their art: "What does this picture tell us about the artist? About his village?"

Have your pupils express in paintings and drawings their everyday experiences at home, school, and in the community. Then send the work, accompanied by pupil letters, to a teacher in another culture with whom you have made previous arrangements whereby he or she has agreed to have his or her pupils create similar artwork and letters for exchange. An exchange exhibition with Mexico brought to the Chicago schools a fine series of paintings, in typically vivid colors, depicting flowers, sky, and inhabitants, and representations of Mexican customs, forms of recreation, and landscapes. The social studies were immeasurably enriched.

One value of having representative art in the classroom is its effect in dispelling common stereotypes we hold about a culture. An Eskimo home, for example, may be seen to be a frame house rather than an igloo, and the Eskimo may be working with implements of the machine age. Too many books depict the Eskimo and other groups as they lived 50 or more years ago. Contemporary paintings and photographs thus record the process of cultural change. It is necessary to broaden and bring up to date those pictures that depict only traditional customs and exaggerate them—such features as queues in China, boomerangs in Australia, and thatched cottages in rural Ireland and England.

Planning a Unit on Native Americans

Native American (Indian) units have been commonly taught for years. Their grade placement has varied from first grade to junior high school. They have proved popular among both pupils and teachers due to the colorfulness and dignity of the Indians' life, its closeness to nature, the beauty and simplicity of their craftwork, their ingenious use of the products of their environment, their folklore, and their intrepidity as hunters and warriors. Movies and television programs featuring Indians have captured the imagination of adults as well as children—many of them, unfortunately, lacking authenticity. Teachers have appreciated the abundance and availability of teaching materials in books and the vast collections of Indian artifacts in museums.

In planning an Indian unit, select one Native American group, or, if several are to be studied for comparative purposes, see that they represent contrasting environments (such as the Woodland, Plains, Pueblo, and Northwest groups) so that the interaction between man and his environment can be seen vividly as one conditioning factor of culture. Some teachers who prefer to study one group select the tribe that formerly occupied their local area in order to take advantage of teaching materials and services of local museums and historical societies. In such cases, it is also possible to see the same kinds of rocks, plants, and animals that the Indians were familiar with and often used. Avoid the error of combining the customs of several Indian groups and labeling them "Indian." This would create an anthropological jumble of unrelated cultural practices and would perpetuate the too-common stereotypes of "the" American Indian.

Include material that shows Indian practices that the settlers took over, some of which we still employ today. The settlers, moving into an unfamiliar environment, learned from the natives how to get along in it. They adopted Indian ways of hunting; raising and preparing food; preparing skins; clearing wooded land by ringing trees; making baskets from grass, twigs, and bark; making snowshoes, canoes, and moccasins; and adopted many other ways of the Native Americans. Note also reminders of the Indian cultures: Half of our states and many of our largest rivers have Indian names; food products such as tomatoes and pumpkins were discovered by Indians.

Plan for the reproduction by your pupils of some of the Indian handcrafts. It will help them appreciate the Indians' use of their environment and their adaptation to it. Consult some handcraft books,[5] or seek the help of art teachers and industrial arts specialists.

The mistreatment and decline of the Native Americans, and their present re-emergence, should be part of every Indian unit. History books contain vivid accounts of the white man's abuse of the red man: the encroachments on Indian lands by the frontiersman, disregard of treaties, and the slaughter of Indian men, women, and children. The Native Americans were often the attackers, but, as historians have pointed out, the westward movement of white settlers was the chief cause of hostilities.

---

[5]Julian H. Salomon, *The Book of Indian Crafts and Indian Lore* (New York: Gordon Press, 1977); Arthur C. Parker, *The Indian How Book* (New York: Dover, 1975); Marz Minor and Nono Minor, *The American Indian Craft Book* (Lincoln: University of Nebraska Press, 1978); Oscar E. Norbeck, *Book of Authentic Indian Life Crafts* (Corvallis, OR: Galloway, 1974).

BOX 10.3   **VARIOUS GRADES**
Sources of Information on Native Americans

For the Teacher

Gaddis, Vincent H. *American Indian Myths and Mysteries* (Radnor, PA:
    Chilton, 1977).
Katz, Jane B. (Ed.). *Let Me Be a Free Man: A Documentary History of Indian
    Resistance* (Minneapolis: Lerner, 1975).
Smith, Jane F. and Robert M. Krasnicka (Eds.). *Indian-White Relations:
    A Persistent Paradox* (Washington: Howard University Press, 1976).
Smithsonian Institution. *Indians* (New York: Crown, 1974). (A collection of
    impressive photographs.)
Social Education, entire issue of May 1972, contains bibliography of
    sources and materials; list of films and filmstrips; biographical
    sketches of Indian leaders.
Underhill, Ruth M. *Red Man's America* (Chicago: University of Chicago
    Press, 1971).

A CULTURE'S PAST

A Framework for History

The wisdom of teaching history in the traditional way in the elementary school is being questioned by specialists in child development and by some historians (see Chapter 7). Much of children's dislike of social studies described in Chapter 4 is probably attributable to their precipitation into historical studies for which they are poorly equipped.

The framework which follows offers a way out of the dilemma. It is a freely modified version of proposals made by André Gadin, a Brussels theologian, who synthesized, perceptively, the work of leading child psychologists.

> Kindergarten to Grade 3: During these years, history forms a very minor portion of the social studies program. The past is explored through simple stories read or told by the teacher. They are simple vignettes. They may relate to special days (such as Thanksgiving—the Pilgrim's first harvest celebration is not trite to the school beginner), or to dramatic or touching events in the life of a notable figure (such as in Benjamin Franklin's account in his *Autobiography* of his arrival as a teenager in Philadelphia, dishevelled and wet after having rowed down the river the previous night—fatigued, hungry, without lodging, and with little money). In addition to such vignettes, references to time sequences and durations are made as they enter children's lives. The calendar and the clock become concrete "props" in the development of understanding of time relationships and awareness of such abstractions as the passing of months and seasons. A program for making and introducing various props is described in Chapter 22.
>
> Grades 4 to 5: Biographical materials concerning historical figures that grow out of any culture unit are introduced. For example, in a study of India, portions of Ghandi's life are reviewed, with emphasis on the role he played in helping

gain India's independence. Time lines are introduced as props in order to support the growth of readiness for dealing with formal history in later years.

Grades 6 to 7: Selected historical periods are explored, each treated topically rather than as a continuous narrative. This approach is suited to the cognitive level of middle-school children. Periods often taught as separate culture units are the period of discovery of the Americas (from 1492 to 1550, confined to two or three of the explorers); the Colonial period; and the Western movement.

Grade 8: Straight narrative history of the United States. Time lines are needed, as explained in Chapter 22, to provide rudimentary historical perspective and a feeling for the relationships between the various stages of the country's development.[6]

Introducing Black History

Children of all races should learn about the Negro's role in our nation's past, and about the Negro as a human being with notable individual and cultural gifts and achievements.

Objectives.   Black history should be designed to improve the self-concept of black children; to help all children of all races to understand what is meant by human rights; and to bring to the consciousness of all children the contributions of black Americans to our national culture.

Black Contributions to American Life as the Core.   The contributions of individual black men and women in a variety of fields (science, education, the arts, entertainment, sports) should be the core of black history. But we must avoid what one historian calls "a succession of sugar-coated success stories, designed to give black children a more favorable and hopeful self-concept, but dangerous because they are bad history."[7] The same historian urges:

> . . . acquaint your students with the beauty as well as the pathology of black life in America by assigning them reading matter in which the Negroes speak directly. I have in mind the autobiographies of Douglass, Washington, Du Bois, and Malcolm X, the anthologies of Negro writing by James Weldon Johnson (*The Book of American Negro Poetry*), Sterling Brown, Arthur Davis, and Ulysses Lee (*The Negro Caravan*), and Alain Locke (*The New Negro*), and such classics of Negro writing as Du Bois' *Souls of Black Folk*, Richard Wright's *Black Boy*, and Ralph Ellison's *The Invisible Man*.[8]

---

[6]André Gadin, "The Historical Function," *Lumen Vitae* (June 1959), 245–265. Gadin unites findings and insights of the American Arnold Gesell, the German Heinrich Roth, the French Paul Fraisse and Philip Malrieu, the Swiss Jean Piaget, and others.

[7]Louis R. Harlan, "Tell It Like It Was: Suggestions on Black History," *Social Education*, 33 (April 1969), 390–395.

[8]Ibid., p. 395.

A Curriculum Framework for Black Studies.   A regrettable practice in many schools is to repeat identical content on black culture, grade after grade. A framework parallel to that offered earlier in this chapter would insure a freshness of content as the child progresses through the grades:

> Kindergarten to Grade 3: Simple stories, free of stereotypes, read or told by the teacher, such as Joan Lexau's *Benjie* and *Benjie on His Own* (New York: Dial, 1964 and 1970)—stories about a small black child; Miriam Cohen's *Will I Have a Friend?* (New York: Macmillan, 1967)—a story with characters from different races and backgrounds.
>
> Grades 4 to 5: Biographical material related to social studies units. In a unit on agriculture, for example, the life of George Washington Carver is eminently suitable; and in a study of government, the lives and work of Thurgood Marshall, the first black Justice on the United States Supreme Court, Andrew Young, former Ambassador to the United Nations, and blacks prominent in local government and school boards. Story material may be continued—John Steptoe's popular *Train Ride* and *Uptown* (New York: Harper, 1971 and 1970); and Natalie S. Carlson's *The Empty Schoolhouse* (New York: Dell, 1972) whose heroine is a 10-year-old black who faces a suspenseful school segregation situation.
>
> Grades 6 to 7: The study of a historical period. A useful source in study of the westward movement is Philip Durham and Everett L. Jones' *The Adventures of the Negro Cowboys* (Des Plaines: Bantam, 1969), as is Olive W. Burt's *Negroes in the Early West* (New York: Messner, 1969). For any historical period, children may draw upon Florence Jackson's *Black Man in America, 1861–1877* (New York: Watts, 1971), and Edith Stall's *Unsung Black Americans* (New York: Grosset, 1970).
>
> Grade 8: A straight narrative history of the United States, supplemented with Bryan Fulks' *Black Struggle: A History of the Negro in America* (New York: Delacorte, 1970).

Introducing the Backgrounds of Other Minority Groups

There are numerous minority groups other than blacks who have suffered discrimination and who have contributed to our culture—Native Americans, Puerto Ricans, Chicanos, Chinese, Irish, Germans among others; and some whose religion identifies them as Jewish, Amish, or members of other minority religio-cultural groups.

One widely used criterion for selection of a minority group for study is the presence in the community of sizeable representation of the group. Often minority children bring to class first-hand information about the group's history and culture. The procedure calls for skill and sensitivity on the teacher's part to see that the study is sympathetic and conducted with objectivity, without embarrassment to minority members of the class who may combine a pride in their heritage with some understandable defensiveness.

Detailed suggestions covering eight ethnic groups will be found in *Teaching Strategies for Ethnic Studies*.[9]

Introducing the Struggle for Women's Rights

The subjugation of women has a long history. It was advocated in ancient religious documents and enforced in ancient law. It has come down to our day and is unwittingly perpetuated by adult attitudes toward girls: as compared to boys, girls receive less encouragement to be independent and are subject to greater parental protectiveness.

> As a result they develop neither adequate skills nor confidence, but continue to be dependent upon others. Thus, while boys learn effectiveness through mastery, the effectiveness of girls is contingent on eliciting the help of others.[10]

While the feminist movement has brought about many changes in attitudes, women continue to be handicapped by inequities in law and custom regarding marriage and divorce, and many find themselves even denied participation in family decision making. Some women must often put up with such indignities as imposed sterilization and imposed motherhood.[11] We suggest a curriculum plan for acquainting children with the history of the role of women corresponding to the "Framework for History" presented earlier in this chapter. That framework is paced to the child's slow, gradual growth in ability to handle time concepts.

> Kindergarten to Grade 3: Simple stories told or read by the teacher that bring out the variety of jobs that women have undertaken successfully, and the versatility and solid nature of their achievements. These might include Betty L. English's *Women at Their Work* (New York: Dial, 1977); Gloria and Esther Goldreich's *What Can She Be? A Farmer* (Caldwell, NJ: Lothrop, 1973), . . . *A Lawyer* (1973), . . . *A Police Officer* (1975), . . . *A Geologist* (1976); Katherine Leiner's *Ask Me What My Mother Does* (New York: Watts, 1978); Meredith Powell and Gail Yokubinas' *What to Be?* (Chicago: Children's Press, 1972); and Inez Maury's *My Mother the Mail Carrier* (Old Westbury, NY: Feminist Press, 1976).
>
> Grades 4 to 5: Biographical material to enrich whatever social studies or science is currently studied. For example, the lives of the following would be natural subjects: In a unit on transportation, Amelia Earhart, pioneering aviator; in a unit on government, Golda Meir, former prime minister of Israel,

---

[9]James A. Banks, *Teaching Strategies for Ethnic Studies* (Boston: Allyn and Bacon, 1975).

[10]Lois Wladis Hoffman, "Early Childhood Experiences and Women's Achievement Motives," *Journal of Social Issues*, 28 (No. 2, 1972), 129–155.

[11]Diana E. H. Russell and Nicole Van de Ven (Eds.), *Proceedings of the International Tribunal on Crimes against Women* (Millbrae, CA: Les Femmes, 1976).

and Nellie Ross and Miriam (Ma) Ferguson, the first women to become state governors; in a unit on journalism, Katherine Graham, publisher of the *Washington Post*, and Gloria Steinem, cofounder of *New York* magazine and *Ms.* magazine; and in a unit on anthropology, the pioneering of Margaret Mead, Ruth Benedict, and May Edel. Invite two or three women who have achieved success and expertise in their occupations (physicians, bus drivers, etc.) to discuss with pupils their education, training, and work experience. See also the book list in Box 12.3, "Biographies for Children on Capacities and Achievements of Women."

Grades 6 to 7: Pertinent information about the role of women woven into units that are centered upon a historical period. Useful sources include Elizabeth Anticaglia's *Heroines of Seventy-Six* (New York: Walker, 1975); David K. Boynick's *Women Who Led the Way: Eight Pioneers for Equal Rights* (New York: T. Y. Crowell, 1959); and Ida S. Meltzer's *Significant American Women* (Chicago: Children's Press, 1976). The teacher from his or her own reading brings in additional information about women's denied opportunities during the period under study, their views as revealed in letters and diaries, their contributions to public life, and their organized efforts to secure greater equality.[12]

Grade 8: The social studies curriculum centers upon United States history. A number of events provide natural openings to reading and discussion on women's role. For example:

Origin of "The Star Spangled Banner." Other national anthems include "The Battle Hymn of the Republic" by Julia Ward Howe, a writer, suffragist, peace worker, and vigorous lecturer on behalf of the causes she championed.

Abraham Lincoln's candidacy for the Illinois legislature. Lincoln announced his support of women's suffrage.

The Civil War. Harriet Beecher Stowe wrote *Uncle Tom's Cabin*, "probably the most widely reprinted and reread novel ever written."[13] Despite alleged literary and other alleged defects, one renowned critic avers it remains "a great folk-picture of an age and a nation."[14]

Civil Rights. Today, many think mistakenly of civil rights as an issue concerning only ethnic minorities. The Woman's Rights Convention of 1848, a stirring affair, brought the subject of women's civil rights to the fore. Continuing discrimination against women in the job market, in training, hiring, and promotion makes civil rights for women a most relevant topic.[15]

---

[12]Leading sources are Eleanor Flexner, *Century of Struggle: The Women's Rights Movement in the United States*, rev. ed. (Cambridge: Harvard University Press, 1975); Renate Briden and Claudia Koonz (Eds.), *Becoming Visible: Women in European History* (Boston: Houghton, 1977); and Selma R. Williams, *Demeter's Daughters: The Women Who Founded America* (Paterson, NJ: Atheneum, 1976).

[13]Robert E. Spiller, *The Cycle of American Literature* (New York: Macmillan, 1955), p. 97.

[14]Van Wyck Brooks, *The Flowering of New England* (New York: Dutton, 1936), p. 432.

[15]Kathleen Preston, "Women, Employment, and Public Policy: What Are the Options?" Public Forum Series on Humanistic Perspectives on Unemployment Policy (Arcata, CA: Humboldt State University, 1979). Suggestions for teaching about discrimination in employment are given in chap. 12.

BUILDING GLOBAL UNDERSTANDING

Beginning in Grades 3 or 4, a large part of teaching effort should be to develop in children an understanding of various cultures of the world. Such understanding involves not only an assimilation of information, but a sympathetic acquaintance and a feeling of kinship with peoples of other lands.

Corresponding with Children of Other Lands

A beginning point for children is the establishment of first-hand contacts with children of the cultures they are studying. Exchanging letters with them can be fun, and is sure to enhance understanding. The youthful correspondents exchange information about family and school life, and also may swap toys, scrapbooks, photographs, and other tokens of their respective cultures. Names of "pen pals" may be obtained from one of the agencies shown in Table 10.1.

Interpreting Cultural Differences

In discussing cultural differences with your class, advises the anthropologist, Frederick O. Gearing, encourage your pupils to assume that the "odd" customs are reasonable and make sense when enough is known about the culture, and then, in continuing their study, see if that seems to be

TABLE 10.1. Agencies Providing "Pen Pals"	
AGENCY	YOUNGEST AGE SERVED
World Pen Pals World Affairs Center University of Minnesota Minneapolis, MN 55455	12
International Friendship League* 40 Mount Vernon Street Boston, MA 02108	7
The League of Friendship** P.O. Box No. 509 Mount Vernon, OH 43050	10
Student Letter Exchange R.R. No. 4 Waseca, MN 56093	10

*The International Friendship League, the oldest and largest organization doing this work, is in touch with every nation in the world where there is a postal system.

**The League of Friendship has a service charge of 50 cents for each request.

NOTE: All the agencies require a stamped, self-addressed envelope for each request.

the case.[16] Successful inculcation of the attitude that "different" ways may be the "right" ways for a given culture, as a working assumption, is a positive, important gain. This idea provides a basis for unprejudiced observation by your pupils whenever they encounter other cultures. In the words of Gearing, a child will remark in these future encounters, " 'I wonder why those people are doing that,' rather than saying, 'Look at those crazy people.' "[17] What a step toward world understanding it would be if an entire generation of children could acquire such respect for other peoples!

Gearing points out another value gained through cross-cultural comparisons. When children study peoples of another culture, they learn to see themselves more objectively. "Comparison," he writes, "assists powerfully in unclouding the senses."[18]

Units on a foreign culture should introduce activities that will capture the culture's spirit and provide experiences that will enable your pupils to empathize with features of the culture's way of life. Children may paint murals of a selected countryside that they have never seen, sample a meal prepared in the culture's style, and improvise articles of the culture's dress in a play. Children will make comparisons, and it is inevitable they will engage to some extent in "we-they" thinking. But by means of thoughtful discussion of differences, guided by the teacher, along the lines suggested by Gearing, the very act of making comparisons will lead to improved understanding.

TEACHER COMPETENCIES

This chapter has described how to perform the following tasks that are basic to the social studies. The teacher should be able to:

1. Use postholing procedures in the selection of cultures to include in a given unit.
2. Supply pupils with first-hand experiences for applying geographic methods of inquiry.
3. Develop geographic concepts in the study of home life.
4. Broaden the study of the community to include its relationships with the outside world.
5. Supply experiences that extend pupil consciousness of areal variation, broad features of a region, place location, and the significance of location.
6. Correct distorted, stereotyped, or immature concepts through introducing "conceptual conflict."

---

[16]Frederick O. Gearing, "Why Indians?" *Social Education*, 32 (February 1968), 128–131, 146.

[17]Ibid., p. 129.

[18]Ibid., p. 131.

7. Introduce studies of primitive cultures by acquainting children with the work of the anthropologist.
8. Teach children how to interpret cultural differences through investigating the folklore, music, and art of the culture under study.
9. Select historical materials according to the age of the pupils—story material in the primary grades, biography in the early intermediate grades, and material that conforms to standard social studies topics in the upper grades.
10. Present the history of minority groups by having their contributions to American life serve as the core.
11. Arrange international "pen pal" correspondence to promote understanding of another culture.
12. Employ a strategy that leads children to conclude that a culture's unfamiliar customs are reasonable when enough is known about that culture.

TRYING OUT SOME OF YOUR COMPETENCIES

1. Plan and conduct a trip for primary-grade children to illustrate areal variation and interaction.
2. Plan and teach a lesson on the work of a geographer, an anthropologist, or a historian for pupils of a specified age or grade.
3. Organize a set of historical materials for use in a unit on a foreign culture with children of a specified age or grade.

FOR STUDY AND EXPLORATION

1. Select a social studies textbook for children that deals with one or more foreign cultures. Evaluate it in terms of the contribution it makes to children's understanding of (a) culture regions, (b) customs and beliefs, and (c) the past.
2. Outline a unit for exploring the background and contributions of a specified minority culture.
3. Give several illustrations of how "conceptual conflict" (conflict due to an apparent contradiction) may be induced in social studies teaching.

FURTHER READING

Teachers will gain helpful and original ideas from Florence Krall et al., "Hooking the Geographer in Children with Field-Based Studies," *Journal of Geography*, 77 (March 1978), 94–99.

Teachers who have never studied anthropology may be hesitant about conducting units containing anthropological material. Their reluctance may disappear after reading an introductory textbook in the field, such as *Anthropology: The Study of People* by John Friedl and John E. Pfeiffer (New York: Harper & Row, 1977), or an engrossing classic, *Patterns of Culture* by Ruth Benedict (New York: New American Library, 1934).

Michael Zaccaria brings out various views of specialists in child development on the appropriateness of formal history for the elementary school in "Development of Historical Thinking: Implications for the Teaching of History," *History Teacher*, 11 (May 1978), 323–340. The historian, George E. McCully, expresses doubts of history's appropriateness for children and proposes alternatives in "History Begins at Home" in *History Teacher*, 11 (August 1978), 497–507.

"Myths are an essential component in the study of cultures," writes Murry R. Nelson, who persuasively presents this view in "Clio, Calliope, Urania: Mythology in the Elementary Classroom," *Social Education*, 42 (February 1978), 132–135.

Four valuable articles on global education appear in *Social Education*, 41 (January 1977), 34–53. One of them, by Donald M. Morris, has explicit suggestions of what teachers in even the lower grades can do to further the concept of interdependence, of how the vocabulary may be handled and clarified, and of teaching-kits that will help.

Lists of curriculum materials for studies of global education are available from Center for Global Perspectives, 218 E. 18th Street, New York, NY 10003; Global Development Studies Institute, P.O. Box 522, 14 Main Street, Madison, NJ 07940; and Institute for Education in Peace and Justice, 3700 W. Oube Street, St. Louis, MO 63108. See also John J. Cogan's case study of global education as carried out in all the grades of a Chicago elementary school, in *Social Education*, 42 (October 1978), 503–505.

Probably the two best works on teaching ethnic studies are James A. Banks' *Teaching Strategies for Ethnic Studies* (Boston: Allyn and Bacon, 1975), with a chapter on each of eight ethnic groups; and Carlos E. Cortés' *Understanding You and Them: Tips for Teaching About Ethnicity* (Boulder, CO: Social Science Education Consortium, 1976).

> *We are caught in a major crisis of the human environment, and all other crises that may be described are related to it. . . . Our continuing pollution of the earth and our treatment of nature cannot continue.*
> **Raymond F. Dasmann**

For many years, the need to protect natural resources from wasteful exploitation and abuse has been recognized. But most people worried little about it. Units on "conservation" were taught in a few classrooms, but were seldom regarded as essential.

The situation has changed. Today, everyone has heard that many of the resources—chiefly fuels and minerals—upon which our civilization rests are not inexhaustible, and that others upon which our very life and health depend—air and water—are seriously polluted. Because of the burgeoning of population, coupled with increased demand in most underdeveloped countries of the world for industrialization and its products, it can no longer be taken for granted that the earth has an unlimited availability of land, fuel, clean water and air, and mineral resources.

A CONTROVERSIAL SUBJECT

The care of the environment has always been a controversial subject. Conservation-minded Americans throughout our history have had to battle for every protective measure.[1] Environmental problems have never been so acute as they are today. The public has been alerted to dangers unknown to their grandparents. These include risks to health from indiscriminate use of powerful insecticides, escape of radioactive materials from nuclear plants, poisonous smog caused by vastly increased accumulations of automobile exhaust, and gases from the increased burning of fuel in homes, commercial establishments, and industry. It was found that polluting chemicals are harmful not only to people, but also to wildlife. Ecologists explained that plants, animals, air, soil and water are all interrelated in the ecosystem or biotic community that is found everywhere in nature, where it has not been unwittingly upset by man's technology or by man's carelessness.

Alarm spread, and throughout the 1960s "ecology" became a watchword. "Stop pollution! Clean up the environment!" was the cry. Leaders of public opinion were in favor of taking steps to reduce the defilement of the environment, to minimize the dangers to the public health, and to lessen disturbance of nature's tightly knit web of life. Civic groups and college students across the land took up the cry, and many people became conservationists for the first time in their lives. New conservation organizations sprang up. Old ones, like the Audubon Society, the Wilderness Society, and the Sierra Club, acquired new members in droves and intensified their efforts to reduce these dangers, which they had been working on for years, largely ignored by the general public.

By 1973, public awareness of shortages was added to awareness of pollution. What conservationists had been pointing out for years finally became common knowledge, namely, that essential resources are limited. Estimates of global oil resources varied, but they all indicated that they are going fast. It is now generally recognized that we must not delay in finding alternative sources of energy. The supply of certain other nonrenewable resources (including gold, silver, zinc, copper, manganese, and chromium), too, is dwindling. Even certain renewable resources are in short supply: for example, the United States Forest Service predicts that between now and the year 2000 we can expect a decrease in forest acreage.

Concern over pollution and shortages led to governmental conservation measures. These were followed by a public backlash. For example, the National Highway Traffic Safety Administration's proposal to increase auto fuel efficiency by 30 percent was attacked by auto manufacturers who asserted that, if these standards went into effect, the manufacturers would be obliged to lay off thousands of workers. Community groups in Detroit and the United Auto Workers union were naturally worried by talk of potential job threats. Although consumer and environmental groups questioned the validity of the alleged necessity of such layoffs, the standards were

---

[1]Stewart L. Udall has provided a most readable history of these "battles" in *The Quiet Crisis* (New York: Holt, Rinehart and Winston, 1963).

lowered to increase fuel efficiency by much less—by not even 10 percent. Another illustration of backlash: Protests by environmentalists over the construction of nuclear facilities were counter-protested by local worker groups who saw opportunities for jobs in the building and operating of those plants, and by electric power companies that saw economic advantages in nuclear fission as a source of energy. Environmentalists were challenged in their opposition to a wide variety of projects that promised gains for industrial and labor groups—from offshore drilling for oil to the damming of wild rivers. The probability that in the long run conservation measures create more jobs than they eliminate is of little consolation to a worker who needs a job today, and a job near the location where he or she owns a home.

It is to be hoped that teachers will not flinch from the task of apprising their pupils of our grave environmental problems simply because they are controversial. Children can be introduced to some essentials such as the categories of resources and the sources of pollution. They can study their own natural environment first hand, pool their observations and seek solutions to the more obvious waste and pollution, and engage in simple conservation work. Suggestions for introducing children to conservation in these and other ways will be given later in the chapter.

SOME OF THE ISSUES

The Energy Shortage

The demand for energy throughout the world is enormous and is rapidly increasing. A major problem in the United States comes from our customary dependence upon vast quantities of petroleum. We consume one-third of the petroleum produced in the world, 40 percent of it for operating motor vehicles. We are obliged, therefore, to discover how to use petroleum more economically. More fundamental is the necessity of finding alternative energy resources. "Gasohol," a mixture of gasoline and alcohol, and steam-powered motors are among approaches being experimented with.

Our long dependence upon natural gas and coal for home and industrial use is well known. Nuclear energy (since about 1970) and water power are used increasingly. Geothermal energy was years ago put to work in volcanically active regions such as in Iceland and northern Italy. In varying stages of practical development are solar energy, wind energy, and tidal energy. These latter sources are to be prized, along with water power and geothermal power, because they are renewable and do not pollute (as does the sulfur dioxide from burning coal) or produce radioactive wastes (as does nuclear fission).

Hazards in Energy Production. Environmentalists emphasize the hazards to the environment that many current plans and practices entail. For example, they contend that the drilling for oil at the offshore tracts in the Gulf of Mexico will ruin the complex of marshes, estuaries, and barrier islands as habitats for wading birds, colony birds, fish, and fur animals that now inhabit them. Environmentalists are also worried about oil spills into the world's waters, estimated to be in the millions of tons annually.

Citizens in many communities oppose nuclear power plants in their vicinities. They fear a major accident similar to that which occurred at Three Mile Island, and worry about the radioactive waste which, because of its highly toxic nature, must be completely isolated from the environment for thousands of years. How such isolation can be guaranteed has still to be satisfactorily worked out.

Certain proposals for hydroelectric dams would inundate valuable and beautiful streams, farms, or other desirable terrain. Thus, with the flooding of Glen Canyon on the Colorado River in 1963, a unique and priceless section of wilderness was lost.

Environment versus Growth.   The developers and their champions say we cannot maintain our standard of living unless we continue to grow economically. This means we must increase our sources of energy. Conservationists reply that economic growth is a goal that, although once having served a beneficial purpose, now would lead to ecological deterioration and would therefore be suicidal unless significantly tempered.[2] Furthermore, they accuse energy-conscious officials and their supporters of having insufficient appreciation of the beauty and recreational value of unspoiled forests, mountains, swamps, deserts, and rivers, and of too often regarding these wilderness areas as expendable. The developers respond by stating that they are more interested in supplying the needs of people than in catering to the "sentimental" values of nature lovers. The environmentalists retort that the power developers fail to reckon with the biological and social consequences of ruthlessly disturbing the balance of nature.

Solutions.   Eventually, we must learn how to increase the supply of energy by processes that keep pollution to a minimum by continued research on utilizing tidal, solar, and other new forms of energy, and by experimenting further with fuels (such as manure and garbage) that are obtainable with a minimum of environmental disruption. Such research has been started, and improvements in the cleanliness of energy can be expected—hopefully before too much of the natural environment has been destroyed.

There is also the clear need of cutting down on energy consumption in order to save our fuels. This can be done, in part, by increasing the use of high energy-efficient systems and decreasing the use of low energy-efficient

---

[2]According to one group of M.I.T. researchers, the earth's resources probably cannot support present rates of economic and population growth much beyond the year 2100. They believe that recycling, pollution control, and contraception are "absolutely vital to the future of human society." Donella H. Meadows, et al., *The Limits of Growth*, rev. ed. (New York: Universe Books, 1974).

systems. By way of example, we could shift from using large automobiles to using smaller ones; reduce the use of private autos in urban areas by expanding mass public transportation, as has already been done in some cities; and transfer reliance upon airplanes and trucks to greater dependence upon railroads for both passenger and freight intercity transportation. Energy could also be economized by improving home and commercial insulation.

Pollution of the Environment

Air Pollution.   Air pollution, "the silent killer," is not a new danger. In 1948, in the small Pennsylvania city of Donora, a four-day smog caused thousands of people to become ill and 17 to die.

Since then, American cities, states, and the federal government have taken steps to reduce air pollution. Common measures involve mandatory installation of devices in autos and industrial plants to reduce the volume of poisonous gases they emit, limitation of burning of high-sulfur fuels for heating, and prohibition of outdoor burning of trash, leaves, and other refuse.

Water Pollution.   Rivers and ocean beaches are increasingly the outlets for sewage and industrial wastes of lumber mills, chemical plants, and other enterprises that use large quantities of water in their manufacturing processes. The runoff from fields containing pesticides and fertilizers adds to the pollution of water. Most creeks, rivers, lakes, and estuaries are polluted to some degree. Many appear oily, murky, or otherwise unnatural, become malodorous during warm weather, are of dubious safety for wading or swimming, and cause a decline of certain prized species of fish and waterfowl.

The United States now has a Clean Water Act providing an allocation of 11 billion dollars in matching grants for sewage treatment works. Enlightened factory owners have installed recirculating systems that separate out the chemicals for future use, and the cleansed water, also, for reuse. There is continued debate as to the degree of strictness the government should adopt in establishing and enforcing strong protective measures.

Radiation.   Radioactivity occurs in nature in elements such as uranium and in radioactive carbon. The testing of nuclear bombs and the construction of nuclear reactors to produce energy have increased radioactivity in the environment and have brought health hazards to the populations of the world. Radioactivity can cause certain forms of cancer. Unlike automobile and factory emissions, radioactive substances cannot be turned off. Nor can they be destroyed or converted to a harmless state. The radiation may continue for thousands of years. There is disagreement among scientists on tolerable limits and the best means for disposing of nuclear wastes. The Atomic Energy Commission is searching for improved and safer methods for their disposal. Certain citizen groups are actively calling for a halt to nuclear plants until undisputed safeguards have been fully tested. The government's regulatory commission has ordered the shutdown of several nuclear power plants, and a number of public figures view nuclear power as a risky energy supply.

Solid Wastes.   Every industrial society with a rapidly growing population sooner or later faces the problem of how to dispose of its non-biodegradable wastes, such as outworn cars and refrigerators, discarded bottles, plastic articles such as laundry baskets and trash containers, food containers, and broken plastic toys. Such trash is already piled high in junkyards and dumping grounds, is dumped into rivers, lakes, and the ocean, and litters our parks and highway edges. It mars the landscape and represents an economic waste.

Some of the waste items can be recycled. Creative imagination is needed to discover ways to conserve and reuse discarded items made of synthetic material that is incapable of being absorbed by soil and water.

Pesticides

Pesticides are another form of pollution. A pesticide is a poisonous chemical used by farmers, cattlemen, foresters, and gardeners to kill harmful insects, weeds, and other pests. People have used pesticides for hundreds of years, but always in small amounts until about 30 years ago. Also, the older pesticides were not so strong as those of today, which include powerful insecticides like DDT. These are often sprayed from airplanes—over swamps to kill mosquito larva, over forests to kill tree pests, and over farms to kill pests that damage fruit, potatoes, cabbage, and other crops. Dairy farmers use pesticides to keep down flies in their barns, and home owners spray insecticides in their gardens and in their houses to kill flies and cockroaches.

The federal government has now forbidden the use of DDT, except for a few specified crops. (DDT is the most widely known, but not the only, powerful pesticide.) Why does the government forbid unrestricted use of DDT?

Rachel Carson and *Silent Spring*.   A scientist named Rachel Carson wrote an important book called *Silent Spring*,[3] in which she told of the changes that might take place in a town which used pesticides too freely and carelessly—how springtime would be without the sounds of birds and bees because both birds and bees would be dead—i.e., of pesticide poisoning. Without bees to pollinate fruit trees, there would be no fruit. Streams would be without fish, also killed by DDT. The book pointed out how dangerous and poisonous modern pesticides are, having already destroyed bird life in

---

[3]Rachel Carson, *Silent Spring* (Boston: Houghton Mifflin, 1962). The pesticide story was brought up to 1970 by Frank Graham, Jr. in *Since Silent Spring* (Boston: Houghton Mifflin, 1970).

many communities, through poisoning insects which birds then ate. Eagles and robins laid eggs which did not hatch. Sprayed on the land, DDT was carried by rain into the soil and rivers, poisoning not only insects and earthworms, but also fish. She reported that every typical American meal sampled by the United States Health Service showed some DDT. She warned of possible dangers to man's health after years of eating small bits of pesticide, because the effects are cumulative.

Carson's book woke up hundreds of thousands of Americans. The dangers that she wrote about had been known to conservationists for some time, but not to the general public. The makers of pesticide sprays were upset. With a billion-dollar business at stake, they accused her of exaggerating the dangers, and declared that spraying was usually safe, and was also necessary.

They were partly right. Chemical pesticides have done much for man. Spraying with them has brought malaria, typhus, and other diseases under control in many parts of the world and has helped improve the amount and quality of our food. Other aids to food quality and quantity have been modern farm machines, improved fertilizers, and improved breeding of crops. Farmers can now get over twice as many bushels of corn and wheat per acre as the farmer of a hundred years ago. Another benefit is that famines are less common.

A group of scientists made a thorough study of the pesticide problem and wound up agreeing with Carson, praising her work and recommending less spraying of dangerous pesticides, and continued research in hopes of eventually doing away with them altogether.[4]

Conservation of Wildlife

Many forms of wildlife are declining; some are even in danger of dying out. Among these are certain large and beautiful birds, such as the California condor and the whooping crane; and certain picturesque mammals, such as certain species of rhinoceroses, lions, walruses, whales, zebras, and pandas. Environmentalists hold that it is in the interest of all of us to protect wildlife habitats, and that each endangered species is a resource potential for serving people's aesthetic and recreational enjoyment, scientific investigation, and in some cases, as food.

Environmental deterioration is cited by biologists as the chief cause of the decline of most of our endangered species. The deterioration comes about through habitat destruction, pesticide and other chemical pollution of water, and other contaminants. Ecologists point out that the presence of wildlife is a sensitive indicator of the health of the environment: where wildlife is abundant, the environment is in a condition that benefits people as well. Many people believe there is also an ethical consideration—that the

---

[4]*New York Times*, May 16, 1963, p. 1.

human species, as steward of the earth's resources, should show respect for the wildlife with whom it shares the earth, and display what Albert Schweitzer called "reverence for life." They find it hard to justify such permissiveness as allows polar bears and foxes to be hunted with airplanes, helicopters, and snowmobiles.

Steps Taken to Protect Wildlife.   Society has already taken steps to protect wildlife. For years, state game departments have protected wildlife by setting hunting seasons, restricting the number of animals a hunter may take, and propagating game and fish. To offset the loss of habitat, the government and conservation organizations have been acquiring land for game and for wildlife sanctuaries. Further progress was made when Congress passed the Endangered Species Act in 1969 (amended in 1978). Many states have laws protecting their own endangered species. Thus, Louisiana provides complete protection for the wolf, the cougar, and all birds of prey. In Oklahoma and Kansas, the swift fox (a small prairie fox believed to be wholly beneficial) is protected.

Land Use and Abuse

Planning for Land Use.   Land acquisition and even land zoning by the government are not always popular with property owners and real estate developers. Regional planning authorities, on the other hand, regard them as essential processes to provide orderly development of vacant land. The planners want attractive housing with adequate recreational areas and open space.

Probably no one would defend the unaesthetic appearance or ecological damage of urban sprawl—that haphazard, uncoordinated push of cities into suburban and rural area. Such sprawl usually results in a jumble of crowded subdivisions; towns springing up promiscuously along highways disfigured by ugly roadside stands and large signs and billboards of grotesque sizes, colors, and shapes; and ungainly shopping centers. To make room for the sprawl, attractive woodland is often uprooted, and streams quickly become polluted. Professional planners are likely to be called in too late, when the best they can advise is how to make the most of a bad situation. It is not easy to restore an area's one-time promise after blight has set in.

Taking Practical Measures.   Steps toward the goal of wise land use have been taken. The federal government now requires that, before federal projects are funded, environmental impact studies must be made to satisfy planning authorities that the impact will be only minimally detrimental. Conservation organizations such as the Nature Conservancy and the Audubon Society have for years been purchasing ecologically and environmentally significant land for preservation. They administer and patrol some of it themselves and turn other parcels over to governmental agencies for protection.

Conclusion

The foregoing are a few of the many issues being debated and discussed. In the main, the struggle is between environmentalists and commercial interests. Both sides have data and points of view which need to be weighed in each instance of conflict.

TEACHING SUGGESTIONS

Combining the Social Studies Appproach with the Natural Science Approach

Public policy considerations and scientific considerations of environmental problems are closely intertwined. For this reason, you may wish to plan a unit that merges the two. Some of the science topics that are appropriately included are food chains in nature, food pyramids and the role of predatory animals, the life histories of insects that damage forests, cloud-seeding, desalination of saltwater, and soil types.[5] One of the benefits of the science approach is its revelation of how little is known about many ecological processes and of our need for more scientific information.

Collecting and Discussing Pictures of Major Resources

A teaching goal with younger children is to promote their knowledge of the number and variety of resources that are required to supply our food, clothing, housing, and other needs. With your class's help, collect pictures from newspapers, organize them, and arrange them on charts. In discussing them, bring out such matters as our dependence upon animals, plants, minerals, fuels, and other resources for the products we use.

BOX 11.1   **KINDERGARTEN**

Environmental Education for Kindergarteners

A pioneer experiment offers evidence that many kindergarten children can form concepts concerning environmental issues and citizens' responsibility for their environment. A four-week unit was taught to two kindergarten classes. The first week familiarized the children with the vocabulary of environmental study through which they were exposed to the concept of "environment." The subsequent weeks were activity-oriented, dealing with air pollution (e.g., observing auto exhaust), noise pollution (e.g., discriminating between loud and quiet sounds), and solid

(Continued)

---

[5]Consult books such as Glenn O. Blough, *Elementary School Science and How to Teach It,* 5th ed. (New York: Holt, Rinehart and Winston, 1974); and William K. Elser, *Teaching Elementary Science,* 2nd ed. (Belmont, CA: Wadsworth, 1977).

waste problems (e.g., making bulletin board displays on littering). Following the unit, each child was tested by means of an individual interview. The questions asked were: "What new things have you learned in our study of the environment?" "With what part of the environment do we have problems?" "What do you think *you* should do about these problems?" "What do you think *other people* should do about the problems?"

The children's answers made it evident that they were able to acquire basic concepts of environmental problems and understand what responsibilities citizens might take to alleviate the problems.

The experiment is reported by Covey K. Bryant and Harold R. Hungerford, "An Analysis of Strategies for Teaching Environmental Concepts and Values Clarification in Kindergarten," *Journal of Environmental Education,* 9 (Fall 1977), 44–49. Plans are underway for possible publication of the unit. Meanwhile, Covey Bryant's masters thesis, which includes the unit, is available on interlibrary loan from Morris Library, Southern Illinois University, Carbondale, IL 62901.

Surveying the Immediate Environment

Observe the school grounds with your class before and after a rainstorm to see if erosion is taking place.

Have individuals report on energy uses they have observed (such as power tools, electric appliances, dams at hydroelectric plants, buses, and airplanes), and extravagances they are aware of, such as cars driven at excessive speed, with consumption of gasoline greater than if driven at moderate speed; street lights remaining lighted long after daybreak; and perhaps electric meat carvers and toothbrushes.

A few members of the class may test the cleanliness of the air by placing clean white handerchiefs in cake pans and putting each pan in a different place for a day, such as in the classroom, in the schoolyard, and by an active cookout fireplace. Have the children note the amount of dust and dirt that settles on each and make comparisons.

A more precise way of determining the amount of solid material accumulating in the air is as follows:

Punch a ¼-inch hole (standard paper punch) about one inch from the edge of a 3 × 5 card or any other piece of thin cardboard or even heavy paper. Cover the hole with a small piece of gummed transparent tape. Notice that some of the sticky stuff is exposed through the hole. Carefully fold the card in half so this sticky area is protected for transportation to the exposure site. Open and allow this to remain, tacked to a post, tree, house, and so on, for a period of time (eight hours seems adequate in most cases, but this is up to the observer). Analyze for the number of particles adhering to the exposed tape by using a small hand lens or a low-power (10 ×) microscope. An analysis can also be made by dividing the particles into different sizes or even different shapes or colors. Only count those that you can readily see, for there will be many, many more that you cannot see.

Again, make comparisons from place to place, to get a "feel" for the distribution of this larger size atmospheric dust.[6]

Take the class on a trip to a stream, creek, or river. Have the pupils observe the strength of its flow, its clarity or murkiness, its color, odor, and evidences of fish or other wildlife. Have them consider in what ways the stream is of importance to the community and to the larger region.

Have a committee of pupils form a "task force" to study the condition of a local park or stretch of woodland and submit a report of their findings to the class. You and the rest of the class may be able to offer guidelines on what to look for: the state of repair and appearance of any benches, plaques, statuary, or buildings; the cleanliness of any water that may flow through it; the condition of its trees and other vegetation; the extent of wildlife; the state of its lawns; evidences of erosion and litter; the presence of signs giving rules for use of the area.

Investigating the Litter Problem

Have the class locate a heavily littered area near the school for investigation such as a playground, a stretch of sidewalk, or a parking lot. Arrange for a committee of pupils to clean it up with a rake and work gloves, with a trash bag to contain the collected litter. One member of the committee may serve as record keeper, jotting down the types of litter deposited in the bag—the number and kinds of bottles, candy wrappers, gum wrappers, cigarette butts, etc. The next day, have a second committee clean up the area, adding to the previous day's record. Repeat on a third day with still another committee. Have the records displayed on the chalkboard or a poster and compare them. Discuss their implications with the class: Is our area probably worse or better than other littered areas we know of? In what ways is littering harmful? Is there a trash can nearby? If so, why don't more people use it? Does the town, city, or state provide a fine for littering? Why is it difficult to enforce anti-littering laws? How can littering be reduced?

Having Each Pupil Plan Improvement of His or Her Own Environment

Much as governmental agencies and industry can do to improve the environment, each individual citizen must do his or her part. A city can build a fine park, but its beauty and utility are easily lost through littering and vandalism. Have each pupil think of what he or she might be able to do to improve the environment of his or her home and neighborhood, and eventually make a plan which the pupil can tell or write about. It may include ways of saving electricity, refraining from littering, saving torn clothing and broken

---

[6]Alfred Hulstrunk, "You Can Sample the Air Around You," *Conservationist*, 25 (August-September 1970), 47–48.

toys to be repaired rather than discarded, saving string, plastic bags, paper bags, and other objects to be reused, giving newspapers to agencies for reuse, participating in other recycling programs, and speaking up when playmates needlessly destroy trees or other property, smash bottles, start playing with matches in unsafe places, or indulge in other destructive practices. Even in situations where families are careless about despoiling the environment, teachers have reported instances in which certain pupils have not only changed their own habits, but apparently have influenced siblings and parents to change theirs.

Encouraging Constructive Proposals for Environmental Improvement

Pupil surveys are worthwhile, but action should not end with reports. If some aspect of the environment is found to be in need of protection or repair, encourage the class to formulate possible solutions. If these are reasonable and based on fact, have the children send them to an appropriate agency. Some appeals are sometimes surprisingly effective. A fifth-grade class in Swarthmore, Pennsylvania, concluded that highway engineers were planning a new bridge that would pass too close to a creek dam, thus marring a beauty spot. The pupils sent letters of protest to the Commonwealth's Secretary of Transportation and enclosed drawings of the attractive dam. The Secretary replied, "I am pleased to tell you we will place the new bridge farther downstream from the dam."

Pleas for environmental causes do not always win, of course. But it is the essence of a democratic society that concerned, responsible citizens communicate their concerns to elected representatives. Active citizen support of a cause may influence future policy decisions, even if an immediate effort is unsuccessful.

Engaging Directly in Conservation Work

Conduct a class project, such as filling eroded gullies with brush or stones, restoring the fertility of a worn patch of soil, establishing a small sanctuary with facilities for attracting birds, or planting, on an eroding hillside, trees supplied by the government or interested local citizens. Through actual participation in such projects, the child will learn that even a few people, working directly and cooperatively, can be effective agents for improving the environment.

BOX 11.2   **GRADES 4–8**

Some Conservation Organizations

Knowledge of some of the numerous conservation organizations and governmental agencies should be one outcome of environmental study. A

(Continued)

few of the many membership organizations are listed below. For a complete listing, consult National Wildlife Federation's *Conservation Directory* (revised annually) which lists some 300 organizations as well as governmental agencies and people. Have the class send for brochures and compare the scope and purposes of the organizations.

Defenders of Wildlife, 1244 19th St., N.W., Washington, DC 20036.
Izaak Walton League of America, 1800 N. Kent St., Arlington, VA 22209.
National Audobon Society, 950 Third Ave., New York, NY 10022.
National Wildlife Federation, 1412 16th St. N.W., Washington, DC 20036.
Nature Conservancy, 1800 N. Kent St., Arlington, VA 22209.
Sierra Club, 530 Bush St., San Francisco, CA 94108.
Wilderness Society, 1901 Pennsylvania Ave., N.W., Washington, DC 20006.

For a description of what each organization focuses upon, see David F. Harrah and Barbara K. Harrah, *Conservation/Ecology: Resources for Environmental Education* (Metuchen, NJ: Scarecrow, 1975).

Learning About Reusing Solid Wastes

Throwing away solid waste (aluminum cans, bottles, paper, and the like) is an obvious drain on precious resources. Some of your pupils may be assigned to read Charter's *Let's Go to a Recycling Center*, and report on it to the class. Bring out that many things we dispose of as trash can be reused and recycled—that is, they can be remelted (in the case of inorganic substances) and reprocessed. The remelting of a metal is a procedure that consumes but a fraction of the power needed to extract it from the earth. Thus, recycling saves an exhaustible resource and also saves energy.

Another advantage of recycling is that it reduces the volume of potential litter. Every recycled beer or soda bottle means one less bottle to be left behind after a picnic or dropped elsewhere to blight the out-of-doors. Recycling of bottles is encouraged by laws that require a deposit on each bottle that is purchased. A bottle could be reused perhaps 10 times or more, thus reducing the cost of production. At this writing, seven states have laws that require refundable deposits on beer and soda bottles.

High school pupils who drive cars have contributed to the driving of solid wastes to recycling centers. Elementary pupils can participate by making posters that call the public's attention to the location of a center, and by passing on information concerning the value of such centers.

Classifying the Earth's Resources

Undertake with your class an inventory of the world's resources. Samples or small pictures of resources can be collected and placed in boxes, each bearing a label describing a different resource. Suggested labels and some of the objects that may be assigned to each are:

1. Cannot be used up (sunlight, air, ocean, rocks, sand).
2. Can be used up, but can be used only once (fuels such as coal and oil).
3. Can be used more than once (metals and most minerals).
4. Can be renewed (animals, vegetation, soil fertility).

Your pupils will see that, even though not all resources are in danger of disappearing, some of these, such as air and water, can be polluted. They will also learn that, although some resources can be renewed, it is still possible for a species of animal or plant to disappear. All classes of resources require vigilant protection.

Introducing Concepts Relating to Energy, Sources of Energy, and Wise Use of Energy Resources

Some concepts are best introduced through reading and discussion. Decide which energy sources are within the comprehension of your pupils. Write simple statements about them on a chart or chalkboard for reading. Follow up with leisurely discussion and frequent review. Examples of statements:

- We get our energy from eating. The food we eat is fuel that keeps our bodies alive and active. It makes it possible for us to do work.
- Energy is stored up in wood, coal, gasoline, and other things that we call fuel. When they are burned they produce energy.
- Nuclear energy is produced by an atom-splitting method. An atom of uranium is bombarded with a neutron. This gives off energy and sets off a chain reaction.
- Wind and water are forms of energy. Wind can be used to move sailboats and to turn windmills. The windmills then produce power to work machines.
- Energy can be used to make electricity.

Concepts are enriched by finding examples of energy at work. Look around the classroom and notice electric lights, sunlight coming through the windows, a movie projector. Find examples at home such as wind-up toys and clocks, electric toys and clocks, and stove.

A further step is to consider how energy sources can be wisely used and saved when possible. Examples: Turn off lights and air conditioners when they are not essential. Save bottles, scrap iron, aluminum cans, and newspapers for recycling.

Illustrating the Interdependence of Forests, Soil, and Water

Set up an erosion demonstration model to illustrate the close relationships among forest, soil, and water (see Box 11.3 and Fig. 11.1). This will depict vividly the role of vegetation in conserving water, preventing floods and dust storms, and holding precious topsoil in place.

BOX 11.3   **GRADES 3–8**

Directions for Constructing an Erosion Model

The erosion model illustrates the close relationship between forests and soil. It is appropriate at any grade level. It consists of two large mounds of earth (corresponding to two adjacent hills) placed outdoors on a slight ridge where the ground tends to slope gently in opposite directions. Make the piles of earth firm with the hands and, with hands or a stick, scoop out a stream bed on each slope, and continue it into the valley. The youngsters will enjoy constructing tiny bridges, houses, fences, and people to add a touch of realism. Press moss firmly to cover one of the mounds, including the banks of the stream bed. Evergreen twigs may be pushed into the moss to represent trees. Holding a filled sprinkling can or the nozzle of a hose (in spray position) about three feet above the forested hillside, pour the rain upon it. The full force of the rain's descent is broken by the trees, and much of the water is soaked up by the absorbent undercover. Consequently, the water flows down the stream bed in an orderly, leisurely manner. The water will be clear (during the second or third trial if not at first) and will do no damage (see Fig. 11.1).

When the water is sprayed upon the exposed hill, however, the water strikes the ground with an impact that forms gullies. The water rushes down the hill with great speed, is muddy, overflows the stream banks, and is apt to dislodge the bridges and flood the lower part of the houses.

This demonstration depicts vividly the role of vegetation in conserving water, preventing floods and dust storms, and holding topsoil in place. It can be repeated several times, with the barren mound needing continual reconstruction.

Follow up the demonstration by pointing out small-scale, close-at-hand evidences of rain-caused erosion. the hollowed-out faces of blocks of serpentine or other soft rock used in building are tokens of the work of rain upon an exposed soft material. The class may take trips before and after a heavy rain to observe how it has forced soil from a poorly seeded slope of lawn and deposited it as mud on the sidewalk below; or to note how the downpour has changed the earth in a garden, a neglected dirt tennis court, or a sloping dirt road or driveway.

Using Published Materials

On a table or magazine rack, make an inviting display of books and magazines that deal with the environment and conservation (see Boxes 11.4

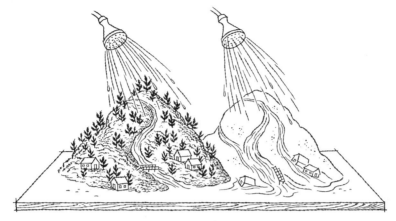

FIGURE 11.1.   An erosion model. See Box 11.3.

and 11.5). Not every child will read or even browse in every book, but periods for sharing what has been learned can be profitable. Most of the magazines in Box 11.5 are for adults, but each issue contains illustrations that are beautiful and arresting as well as instructive.

BOX 11.4   **VARIOUS GRADES**

Books for the Classroom Dealing with Environmental Issues

Grades 3–5

Berger, Gilda. *Mountain Worlds: What Lives There* (New York: Coward, 1978).
Blockson, Claudia. *It's Your World* (San Francisco: Troubador, 1979).
Boy Scouts of America. *Conservation Skill Book* (Dallas: Boy Scouts of America, 1979).
Elliot, Sarah M. *Our Dirty Land* (New York: Messner, 1976).
Purcell, Margaret S. *A Look at the Environment* (Minneapolis: Lerner, 1976).
Van Soelen, Philip. *A Cricket in the Grass* (New York: Scribner, 1979).

Grades 4–8

Adamson, Wendy W. *Who Owns a River? A Story of Environmental Action* (Minneapolis: Dillon Press, 1977).
Black, Hillie. *Dirt Cheap: Evolution of Renewable Resource Management* (New York: Morrow, 1979).
Branley, Franklyn M. *Energy for the Twenty First Century* (New York: Crowell, 1975).
Chester, Michael. *Let's Go to a Recycling Center* (New York: Putnam's, 1977).

(Continued)

Couffer, Jack and Mike Couffer. *Salt Marsh Summer* (New York: Putnam's, 1978).
Sigford, Ann. *Tall Grass and Trouble* (Minneapolis: Dillon Press, 1978).

BOX 11.5   **ALL GRADES**

Conservation Periodicals Adaptable for Use with Children, Often with Extraordinary Photographs

Audubon, 950 Third Ave., New York, NY 10022.
Defenders [of Wildlife], 1244 19th St., N.W., Washington, DC 20036.
Living Wilderness, 1901 Pennsylvania Ave., N.W., Washington, DC 20006.
National Wildlife, 1412 16th St., N.W., Washington, DC 20036.
Nature Conservancy News, 1800 N. Kent St., Arlington, VA 22209.
Ranger Rick's Nature Magazine [for children], 1412 16th St., N.W., Washington, DC 20036
The Conservationist, P.O. Box 1500, Latham, NY 12110.

TEACHING COMPETENCIES

This chapter has described how to perform the following tasks that are basic to teacher competency. The teacher should be able to:

1. Enrich environmental study by merging the content of social studies with the content of science.
2. Use pictures to help children understand our dependence upon the natural environment for the necessities of life.
3. Assist the class in surveying the school environment to discover energy uses and the quality of the air, water, and parkland.
4. Guide the class in an investigation of the litter problem in a selected area and, through discussion, to consider ways to check the littering habit.
5. Encourage each child to think through what he or she can do personally to improve the environment of home and neighborhood.
6. Involve the class in a real environmental problem, stimulating consideration of alternative solutions.
7. Direct the class in reading about the recycling of solid wastes and in examining the following relationships: (a) between recycling and conservation of energy and (b) between failure to recycle and the accumulation of litter.
8. Help the class set up a scheme for classifying resources and to distinguish between the various categories: resources that are exhaustible and not reusable; exhaustible and reusable; renewable; inexhaustible.

9. Clarify the concept of energy, its various sources, its utilization, and ways to conserve and wisely use it.
10. Set up a demonstration to illustrate the role of forests in flood prevention and soil conservation.
11. Select, display, and encourage the use of books and magazines that will broaden environmental study and will present selected environmental problems in depth.

TRYING OUT SOME OF YOUR COMPETENCIES

1. Plan a week's study of environmental vocabulary with kindergarten or first-grade children to parallel the first week of the unit described in Box 11.1. Try it out with a small group of children.
2. With either a class or with a smaller group, investigate the litter problem as represented by a badly littered area.
3. Make a display of publications suitable for a specified age or grade in a study of some aspect of the environment.

FOR STUDY AND EXPLORATION

1. Read up on a lively environmental issue of special interest to you (the hazards or safety of a nuclear power plant, the Endangered Species Act, or the like), and write about the pros and cons. Present what seems to you to be a reasonable resolution of the issue.
2. Make a survey of a school's immediate environment, recording processes such as erosion, instances of pollution, and conservation practices that would improve the environment.
3. Make an intensive study of one of the pioneer defenders of the environment, such as John Muir, John Burroughs, Theodore Roosevelt, Gifford Pinchot, or Rachel Carson. Write an account of his or her conservation work that would be suitable for children of a given age.

FURTHER READING

A readable, well-organized college textbook on the environment is Raymond F. Dasmann's *Environmental Conservation* (New York: Wiley, 1972). Dasmann has also written a more recent book in which he expresses a greater sense of urgency than in his textbook about saving the environment from further abuse: *The Conservation Alternative* (New York: Wiley, 1975).

The Environment Index (New York: Environment Information Center), published annually, overviews the year's events and legislation, lists conferences that are scheduled, and reviews books and films.

Books that take a critical view of the environmental movement should not be neglected: John Passmore's *Man's Responsibility for Nature* (New York: Scribner, 1974) challenges some of the doctrines of environmentalists and what he believes is their tendency to sentimentalize nature. Cy Adler's *Ecological Fantasies* (New York:

Green Eagle Press, 1973) takes the position that environmentalists are misinformed alarmists, that the crisis is exaggerated, and that science can be depended upon to deal with most environmental problems.

Ideas for curriculum and teaching will be found in Audean S. Allman and O. W. Kopp, *Environmental Education Activities for Children and Youth* (Columbus: Merrill, 1976); Larry Sale and Ernest W. Lee, *Environmental Education in the Elementary School* (New York: Holt, 1972); and King C. Kryger, "Some Guidelines for Energy Programs," *Today's Education*, 66 (September/October 1977), 60–62.

Research that provides evidence of children's readiness for studying the environment (in addition to that cited in Box 11.1) are:

Andrew Aird and Audrey Tomera, "The Effects of a Water Conservation Instructional Unit on the Values Held by Sixth Grade Students," *Journal of Environmental Education*, 9 (Fall 1977), 31–42.

Alan M. Voelker and Robert E. Horvat, "Elementary School Children's Views on Solving Environmental Problems," *Science Education*, 60 (July 1976), 353–361.

12 The World of Work

*What is it that keeps all these
millions of people busily hustling
about from morning to night?*
Fred Rogers Fairchild

This chapter suggests ways of helping children discover new meanings from their observations of the work-a-day world. Economic concepts form the structure of the chapter, but the emphasis is upon experiences that expand children's thinking and feeling about work, rather than upon economic principles.

EARLY CONCEPTS

Having Children Differentiate Goods from Services

Have your pupils identify various people's work that they know about and tell whether it results in the production of goods (furniture, toys, automobiles, and so on) or in the production of services (selling, teaching, policing, and so on).

Ask them to tell of their own jobs at home and those of other members of the family. Which of these jobs (such as baking cookies or building a model auto for little brother) produce goods, and which (such as washing dishes or running an errand) produce services?

Present a series of pictures of people at work. Have your pupils tell which pictures show producers of goods and which show producers of services.

Emphasize that both goods and service satisfy human wants and needs.

Helping Children Chart Relationships between the Community and the Outside World

Have your pupils make charts similar to that in Figure 12.1. They may work in committees, each choosing a single product or service. They may begin with any activity of their community, regardless of which band of the chart it falls within, and gather information that will enable them to trace it outward (or inward, or both outward and inward, as the case may be).

The four sections of Figure 12.1 correspond to four successive stages in the production of economic wealth. Starting at the hub and proceeding to the periphery, they are (a) sources of raw materials, (b) manufacturing plants, (c) stores and other distributing agencies, and (d) consumers. The stories of three products—electricity, bread, and shoes—have been simplified and plotted. Some children will know these products only at the

FIGURE 12.1.   Relationship between the community and the outside world.

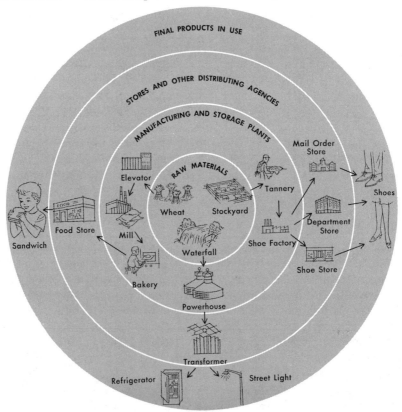

consumer end. Children in the wheat belt will know the bread story in at least two of its phases, and children in other specialized regions may know other phases of other processes. Their understanding of the complete chain of selected economic processes will contribute to their concept of inter-dependence that characterizes the world of work.

BUSINESS ENTERPRISE IN A MIXED ECONOMY[1]

Teaching the Role of the Entrepeneur

Although children have experience as workers at home and school, they are unlikely to see the world as the entrepeneur sees it. To understand that world, they need opportunities to occupy it.

Classroom Business Enterprises.   An account of how primary-grade classes produced and marketed a dictionary appears in Box 12.1 It provides evidence that the conducting of a business enterprise by elementary students is a feasible and valuable experience for them.

In one elementary school, a class operated the school supply store for a year. The pupils kept a record of the cost of the stock, and a bookkeeping charge (no payment of money) was made for rent and for the time pupils spent as clerks. Goods that did not move readily from the shelves and that were not returnable to the wholesaler were eventually sold below their cost. Profits at the end of the year were given to the library for the purchase of trade books.

Thorough-going pioneering in providing meaningful jobs for children was conducted by the City and Country School located in New York City.[2] "Jobs" were assigned to each class (there was only one class at each grade level) after finding a suitable match between the complexity of the job and the age of the children. The classes (designated by the age of the children rather than by school grade) eventually took over the following responsibilities:

8-year-olds. Purchasing office supplies wholesale and selling them to the school and its classrooms.

9-year-olds. Handling the school mail and maintaining a school post office.

10-year-olds. Providing lunchroom services and handling the monthly food bills.

---

[1]The economic system of modern noncommunist nations, popularly known as "free enterprise," is usually referred to by economists as a "mixed economy." Paul A. Samuelson writes: "Ours is a 'mixed economy' in which both public and private institutions exercise economic control . . . [in] a mixed system of government and private enterprise." *Economics* (New York: McGraw-Hill, 1976), pp. 41, 43.

[2]Caroline Pratt, *I Learn from Children: An Adventure in Progressive Education* (New York: Simon, 1948), chaps. 8 and 9.

11-year-olds. Running a foot press and an electric press for doing the school's printing, including production of a magazine of stories, poems, and linoleum-cuts.

12-year-olds. Running a toy-construction business for producing small figures for younger classes to use in block-building and to stock their shelves for a Christmas toy sale.

13-year-olds. Providing photographic services, including photographing, developing, enlarging, and printing for the school's personnel records and a file of school events.

The first requirement was that each job provide a useful service to the school. Each job involved selecting and purchasing goods, pricing and selling products, keeping goods and business records in order, and balancing the books at stated intervals—the latter with the teacher's help and with children taking turns as cashier.

Many teachers (including the senior author) who have taught in schools with classroom jobs created in the City and Country School tradition have expressed enthusiasm for their beneficial effects on children. It is probably the best, most direct way to provide what is currently called "career education."

BOX 12.1   **GRADES 1–3**

A Picture Dictionary Produced and Marketed by Children

By Janet Rogers

Three primary-grade teachers* planned a project that combined the teaching of concepts relating to free enterprise and careers, and that promoted learning of basic skills. Career education funds from the state (Florida) were made available to cover costs.

OBJECTIVES

The objectives were of two types: (1) Those that contributed to the social studies program (teaching basic concepts underlying our economic system, and exploring careers in the publications and advertising fields); (2) those that contributed to the reading program.

COMPILING WORD LISTS

The project of making and selling a dictionary was proposed and explained to the children. We compiled a listing of all the words from the Dolch Word List and the K–3 Reading Vocabulary of the Florida State Assessment Test.

(Continued)

PRODUCING THE DICTIONARY

Charts of the words were displayed around the rooms. The children drew pictures of various words. Every child contributed at least two drawings to the project.

PREPARATION OF THE PHOTO-READY COPY

The words (typed on a primary typewriter) and their illustrations were taped on large sheets of white paper. Activity pages of varying difficulty were constructed by the teachers. Pages were put in order and numbered. A cover, title page, credits, dedication, and table of contents were added. An alphabetical listing of all words comprised the final pages of the book. The children then proofread the photo-ready copy (Figure 12.2).

OBSERVING THE PRINTING

Each class visited the print shop to view the production of the book. We explained each step of the process to the classes, and a flow chart (see Figure 12.3) was distributed to each child for later review and coloring.

SALES CAMPAIGN AND DISTRIBUTION

Upon return to the school, a sales campaign was launched. Announcements of the sale were made by the children and displayed throughout the school.

When copies were available, children from each of the three classes visited the other classrooms in the school to display the finished book and to talk about it. The dictionaries went on sale the following morning at 8 o'clock in the three participating classrooms. By 8:30, all 300 books were sold! There were many disappointed prospective buyers and a reprinting was scheduled.

EVALUATION

The project was a financial success. The sale price of one dollar per book enabled repayment of the career education funds, a free copy of the picture dictionary for all the child-participants, and a free restaurant lunch for them.

The books met a community need. Many copies were purchased by adults in the community. Several teachers in other schools adopted the dictionary as a resource for their classrooms. Children could be seen reading the dictionaries at bus stops, in hallways, and on the playground.

Finally, the children learned essential steps of our economic system—the planning, construction, promotion, and marketing of a useful attractive, and interesting product.

*Carol Lyons, Lois Watts, and Janet Rogers, assisted by Jack Roberts, Supervisor of Media Center and Coordinator of Career Education, St. Lucie County (Florida) Public Schools.

FIGURE 12.2.   Proof reading the photo-ready copy. See Box 12.1. Courtesy of Janet Rogers, St. Lucie County Public Schools, Fort Pierce, Florida.

FIGURE 12.3.   Flow chart for study by primary-grade "publishers." See Box 12.1. Courtesy of Janet Rogers, St. Lucie County Public Schools, Fort Pierce, Florida.

Miniature Societies.   Various types of miniature societies have been introduced into classrooms.[3] While they differ in organization, each "society" operates as an economic system, with its own token money. Children may establish business enterprises such as the selling of used comic books, popcorn, a classroom newspaper, and other merchandise. Children may "invest" in any of the businesses of their classmates. A "bank" may be instituted to keep track of the "payroll" and to receive "deposits." Shelf space may be "rented" by an enterprise to hold merchandise and from which to conduct business. These "shops" may be be open for business two half-days per week. Enterprises that do not break even have to close. Some children become "rich," others "poor;" some may have to "go on welfare," paid for out of "taxes."

The miniature society has two objectives. One is to teach fundamental concepts of economics. The societies probably fulfill this objective. Kourilsky adapted such a society for kindergartens and made a careful study of pupil's learning. She found that economic concepts such as "scarcity," "opportunity cost," "specialization," and the like were learned even at that early level.[4]

The second objective is to improve academic performance and various behaviors through the reinforcement provided by the payment of token money. Whether or not pupils permanently learn promptness, how to apply themselves successfully to their studies, and other desirable behaviors through such a rewards system is hardly demonstrated. Poor study habits and unsatisfactory learning are often symptoms of underlying personality conditions which are generally not eliminated by reinforcement techniques focused upon the rewards system.

Many teachers will object to the contrived nature of the miniature society. More natural approaches are described in the preceding subsection, "Classroom Business Enterprises."

Teaching the Role of Banks

Many children think of banks merely as places in which to deposit savings for safekeeping and from which to withdraw them when needed. Role play often helps them to visualize the bank's more important job in granting credit.

Have one group of children play the part of entrepeneurs. Let us say they plan to open a hardware store. Perhaps they want to buy a building that was formerly occupied by a clothing store and that, to be converted for a different purpose, will require the hiring of a carpenter. They will need to lay in a stock of tools and other hardware. They go to another group of

---

[3]Stan Bennett, "Building Miniature Societies in Schools," *Education,* 97 (Winter 1976), 162–172. Describes four types of miniature societies.

[4]Marilyn Kourilsky, "The Kinder-Economy: A Case Study of Kindergarten Pupils' Acquisition of Economic Concepts," *Elementary School Journal,* 77 (January 1977), 182–191.

children who represent bank officials in order to try to borrow the money they need. The bankers will wish to know whether it is the only hardware store for miles around or whether it will have to compete with already established hardware stores in the same neighborhood. What experience in the hardware business have the owners had? What are their assests? Eventually, the banker may grant or deny the loan. The role play may be repeated with other groups. Each should decide on its business, its needs, and how to make a convincing case before the bankers.

Teaching About the Market and Prices

How a change in the supply and demand of a product can result in a change of the product's price may be illuminated through having a few children act out the situation. For example, Farmer Jones has an orange grove. Half of the crop is destroyed by frost. What is likely to happen to the price of oranges now that the supply is reduced, assuming that all of the farmer's customers continue to want to buy his crop? Most children, in talking this over, can see how a decrease in supply can result in higher prices.

Pupils in one class expressed the belief that the cost of a chair should be the same as the cost of the wood from which the chair was made. The class was stimulated by its alert teacher to analyze the cost of bringing a product to the market, beginning with the expense of renting or buying a factory, buying machinery, tools, and trucks, hiring workers, paying the electric bill, a profit for the owner for the risks involved—the class was able to add item after item of necessary expense.

Another class studied another type of market—the stock exchange, in which people buy and sell corporation stocks and bonds. Such a study, of course, requires prior familiarity on the part of the class with the operation of other types of markets and with the nature of a corporation.

Promoting Discovery of the Economy of Mass Production

Your pupils can learn of the greater economy of labor in mass production through first-hand experience. Senesh once told of how two teams of first-grade pupils produced gingerbread boys.[5] One team formed an assembly line, each child performing a separate function. One rolled the dough, another cut the forms, and so on. Each child on the second team, on the other hand, did all the jobs himself. Comparisons were then made in terms of waste of materials, duplication of equipment, and speed. The asembly-line team was ahead on all counts.

Keeping Your Class Abreast of Technological Change

Have your pupils gather information about automation and the introduction of the computer into industry from current newspapers and

---

[5]Instructions for setting up this demonstration are given in Lawrence Senesh, *Families: Teacher's Resource Guide* (Chicago: Science Research Associates, 1973) p. 136.

magazines. A random collection of clippings describes devices for unloading silos, feeding cattle, translating Russian into English, sorting mail, and operating a typewriter by voice. Make a bulletin-board display or a class scrapbook of the clippings your pupils bring in.

Challenge your pupils to explain the statement:"For the first time in 5,000 years the wheel is being displaced as the symbol of transportation progress." Have a committee of children do some library research on vertical-takeoff aircraft; pipeline transportation for gas, oil, and other products; and ground-effect (air cushion) vehicles, which are supported by air and may be amphibious. The committee may construct a poster reporting its findings.

Providing Experiences in Analyzing Costs

Most children are intrigued by simple analysis of costs and benefits. If a boy sets up a lemonade stand, he cannot decide how much he will need to charge until he knows the cost of doing business. It will probably occur to him that he must add up the cost of the required lemons, sugar, and other ingredients. Let us say that he paid for these with cash at a store. They were his *explicit costs*. (Children are able to handle that term.) There are other costs that may *not* have occurred to him, including the "rent" that his family is entitled to for his temporary use of a bucket, a ladle, and other equipment, and the cost of his labor in setting up the stand and dispensing the lemonade. These were his *implicit costs*.

There is another category of costs that even kindergarten children have been introduced to,[6] viz., *opportunity costs*. An example of an opportunity cost is the sacrifice made by the boy in having decided to operate the lemonade stand. He had to pass up the opportunity of going with a pal to the ballpark and buying a ticket to watch a baseball game. He decided, instead, to use that money for lemons and sugar and to use that time to manage his roadside business. He could not have his cake and eat it, too.

BOX 12.2   **VARIOUS GRADES**

Books on Economics for Children

Cavin, Ruth. *A Matter of Money: What Do You Do with a Dollar?* (New York: S. G. Phillips, 1978). Grades 3–7.
Chilton, Shirley et al. *Everybody Has Important Jobs to Do* (Chicago: Children's Press, 1970). Grades 2–4.
Cobb, Vicki. *Making Sense of Money* (Bergenfield, NJ: Parents Magazine Press, 1974). Grades 2–4.
Educational Research Council of America. *Choices and Decisions: Economics and Society* (Boston: Allyn, 1972). Grade 7.

(Continued)

---

[6]Kourilsky, "The Kinder-Economy."

Gay, Kathlyn. *Money Isn't Everything* (New York: Delacorte Press, 1967). Grades 4–6.

Senesh, Lawrence. *Our Working World* (series) (Chicago: Science Research Associates, 1974).

Shay, Arthur. *What Happens When You Spend Money* (Chicago: Contemporary Books, 1970). Grades 2–4.

CONSUMER EDUCATION

Helping Children Become Intelligent Consumers

Your pupils could do some comparative shopping by visiting stores, perusing advertisements in newspapers, sales catalogues, and flyers, and watch sales talks on television and radio. One class found a wide price range for television sets. They found that portable sets were the least expensive and color consoles were the most expensive; also, the larger the screen, the higher the price. They identified two different brands of a portable color set of identical size that were approximately similar in price. The teacher raised the question: "How can a person tell which of the two brands is better?" The advertisement for each made seductive guarantees and claims. The class discussed how one might insure making a wise choice in such a case and came up with the following suggestion: Visit stores and sample each model; ask friends who might have these sets for their experiences and opinions; consult *Consumer Reports*.

Giving Assignments in Advertisement Writing

One way to develop ability to read advertisements with discrimination and to diminish gullibility is to have children *write* advertisements. Discuss with them selected specimens of advertisements, pointing out various skills and approaches used by professionals. Then divide the class into committees to write some of each of the following types of advertisements:

1. Informative advertisements that stimulate a large sale, that make mass production feasible, and that, in turn, lower the unit cost of the product and, hence, raise the standard of living.
2. Informative advertisements that draw the consumer's attention to features of a commodity or service that he or she might not otherwise be aware of. Examples of these are a new safety feature of a car, extra space in a refrigerator, or a business school that teaches a new skill or process. Such advertisements contribute to better-informed decision making on the part of the consumer.
3. Advertisements that encourage "keeping up with the Joneses," snobbery, and extravagance.
4. Misleading, deceptive advertisements.

Pupils may write advertisements for goods or services actually on the market, products popular in years gone by, such as player pianos or high-button shoes, or goods and services of their imagination, such as a fountain pen that never runs dry.

CAREER EDUCATION

"Career education" is a movement launched by the United States Office of Education in 1971 to serve the needs, primarily, of the high school student in making wise choices—choices to fufill personal aptitudes and limitations, personal values, and personal outlook on life. Its other aims, not always clearly stated in promotional literature, have to do with decisions other than careers, over one's life span, and with preparation of the individual for the probable necessity to shift choices as technological and social conditions change. Millions of dollars in federal and state funds have been poured into "career education," and schools everywhere have been urged and encouraged to establish appropriate programs.

The particular emphasis of "career education" generally assigned to the elementary school is career awareness (career exploration to the junior high school and career preparation to the senior high school).[7] Through field trips, slides, bringing workers from various fields of work into the classroom, and displaying news items, charts, and pictures on bulletin boards, you can acquaint your pupils with a large number of careers, even if you as teacher had little background for vocational knowledge before the beginning of the study. Discussion following such exposure should focus on the role different workers play in society, some of the abilities required by each role, and the importance and dignity attending each career.[8] The specialists who visit the class can often tell about many careers that lie within their special fields, or can refer you to publications from which such information may be obtained. One example is a government publication describing each of the 114 careers in the environmental field, with a paragraph devoted to each.[9]

Acquainting Children with the Changing Status of Women in Careers

Women have not until recently entered business and the professions in large numbers as members of the paid work force. Certain beliefs about women (held by many women as well as by men) have retarded this movement. They include the notions that women who work lose their femininity, that they make petty administrators under whom men and some women do not happily work, that they are too emotional to deal with problems requiring logical decisions, that they are incapable of physical labor, and that they

---

[7]Henry M. Brickell, "National Perspectives on Career Education," in *Reading and Career Education*, Perspectives in Reading No. 19 (Newark, DE: International Reading Association, 1975), pp. 2–6.

[8]Marlow Ediger, "Careers in Our Community: A Suggested Unit of Study," *Education*, 97 (Summer 1977), 357–359.

[9]Olympus Research Corporation, *Career Education in the Environment: A Handbook* (Washington: U.S. Office of Education, 1971).

regard a job simply as a stopgap between school and marriage and hence cannot be counted on for deep commitment. These beliefs stem from special cases and are unwarranted generalizations. To some extent they have become self-fulfilling prophecies, causing otherwise qualified women to question their competence and to lose confidence in themselves.

Pupils may become familiarized with the work capabilities of women through biographical materials prepared for children such as are listed in Box 12.3. Children learn of the versatile skills and notable accomplishments of women as they read and discuss these books in class.

Children in the intermediate grades may extract statistics from standard library reference books such as *Historical Statistics of the United States: Colonial Times to 1970*, using the data to construct graphs and charts to show the steady increase in employment of women in the labor force. One possibility would be a graph to show how, for each decade from 1890 to 1970, the proportion of women who were employed rose steadily (from 19 percent in 1890 to 43 percent in 1970). To bring these statistics up to the current year, *Statistical Abstract of the United States* may be consulted; it records 48 percent for the year in which this is written. Another graph could show the increase in the proportion of *married* women who entered paid employment over those 80 years—from five percent in 1890 to 43 percent in 1970; the *Statistical Abstract* records 54 percent for the year in which this is written.

Discrimination that continues to curtail the employment of women should also be examined. Compared to the jobs of men, women's jobs tend to be less prestigious and lower paid at every educational level, and women tend to be directed into lower-paying occupations by parents, teachers, and counselors.

One elementary-school teacher enriched the topic by inviting a high school counselor into her classroom. The counselor, drawing upon her professional experience, related instances of sex inequality and discrimination— and, on the other hand, also cited cases of former high school female students who were later employed at wages comparable to those of men, others who were in prestigious positions, and still others who were enrolled in professional schools. The children learned thereby of the improved opportunities for women that are taking place, as well as of persistent inequalities.

The study of women's status proposed here could be combined with that dealing with the history of the status of women as proposed in Chapter 10.

BOX 12.3   **GRADES 4–8**

Biographies for Children Illustrating Capacities and Achievements of Women

Biddle, Marcia M. *Contributions of Women: Labor* (Minneapolis: Dillon Press, 1979).

(Continued)

Fowler, Carol. *Contribution of Women: Dance* (Minneapolis: Dillon Press, 1979).

French, Laura and Diana Stewart, *Women in Business* (Milwaukee, WI: Raintree, 1979).

Gutman, Bill. *Modern Women Superstars* (New York: Dodd, 1979).

Higgins, Ardis O. *Portraits of Courageous Women* (North Hollywood: Halls of Ivy, 1978).

Lengyel, Emil. *And All Her Paths Were Peace: The Life of Bertha Von Suttner* (New York: Elsevier-Nelson, 1975).

Matthew, Scott. *The First Woman of Medicine: The Story of Elizabeth Blackwell* (Morristown, NJ: Silver, 1978).

TEACHING COMPETENCIES

This chapter has described how to perform the following tasks that are basic to the social studies. The teacher should be able to:

1. Draw upon occupations known to the children, their own work at home, and pictorial work-scenes that will help children differentiate goods from services.
2. Direct children in charting relationships between their communities and the outside world to learn the successive stages of a manufactured product.
3. Help children organize a real business enterprise or a school job from which they will learn business procedures and responsibilities.
4. Employ role playing to teach primary functions of a bank.
5. Teach the determination of prices in a free market.
6. Introduce jobs of workers, with sufficient emphasis and depth to create "career awareness" in the class.
7. Stimulate inquiry into comparative prices, and introduce experiences in reading and writing advertisements, to sharpen children's sensitivity to their responsibilities as consumers.
8. Provide experiences that will promote discovery of the economy of mass production, the economy of the machine, and the history and consequences of technological change.
9. Teach children how to engage in simple analysis of costs and benefits.
10. Provide children with biographies that demonstrate women's abilities and accomplishments in the world of work; and with references that show the rapidly increasing participation of women in the working world.

TRYING OUT SOME OF YOUR COMPETENCIES

1. Using suggestions from this chapter, conduct a role playing experience for a group of children that will enable them to learn the

process of obtaining a bank loan. Two partners may be seeking the loan from a banker and his assistant. Encourage the would-be borrowers to select their own reasons for wanting a loan. Encourage the children to bring their own ideas and imagination to the play.

2. Have groups of first-graders test the efficiency of making gingerbread men by mass production, as proposed by Senesh. Consult his *Families* (cited in Footnote 5) for details, including a recipe.

3. Plan a series of lessons for a specified grade to expand "career awareness."

FOR STUDY AND EXPLORATION

1. Locate a unit on a culture region, and plan how it could incorporate basic concepts from the field of economics.
2. How would you explain to children the fact that a Coke costs more at a big-league ballpark than at a lunch counter or drugstore?
3. What activities other than those described in this chapter could be planned to teach children how to make wise choices as consumers?

FURTHER READING

Important research on children's ideas about economics and a statement of what it implies for teaching economics in the elementary school is summarized by Karen F. A. Fox in "What Children Bring to School: The Beginnings of Economic Education," *Social Education*, 42 (October 1978), 478–481.

Teachers with scant background in economics should find the following article helpful in preparing to teach about the world of work: "What Economics Should the Educator Know?" by William E. Becker, Jr. and Robert W. Reinke in *Social Studies*, 66 (September/October 1975), 195–204.

A teaching kit, "Economics for Young Americans," has been prepared for youth from Grade 7 and up. Its purpose is to clear up inaccurate ideas about profit, competition, productivity, and other economic concepts. It is available from the United States Chamber of Commerce, 1615 H Street, N.W., Washington, DC 20062.

An account of a highly educative and ingenious business enterprise carried out in an intermediate-grade classroom is given by David Kelton in "Economics in the Elementary School," *Social Studies*, 67 (July/August 1976), 163–164. The class formed a potato-chip selling agency and a bank, with half the class on the board of directors of the agency and the other half on the board of directors of the bank. (Note: A question might be raised about the choice of the product.)

Practical suggestions for career education in primary grades are given by Lawrence Senesh in *Families: Teacher's Resource Guide* (Chicago: Science Research Associates, 1973), chap. 19.

The "infusion approach" to career education will be popular with elementary school teachers who feel overburdened with subjects to teach. It is described by Judith E. Hedstrom in "Career Education in the Social Studies," *The Link*, 29 (March 1977),

2–4. "Career Education," she writes, supplying an example of infusion, "can be infused into a first-grade lesson on the seasons by simply asking the students, 'What jobs require different kinds of clothing in winter from the kind they require in summer?' or 'Can you think of any jobs which wouldn't be needed if there were no snow?'"

Hugh Rank offers ideas for teaching about consumer problems and the critical reading of advertisements in "Teaching About Public Persuasion: Rationale and a Scheme" in Dan Dietrich (Ed.), *Teaching About Doublespeak* (Urbana, IL: National Council of Teachers of English, 1976).

part IV
Special Teaching Strategies

Absorption without thinking can never get an individual very far. At best, it will lead to sterile erudition; never to investigation.
Lucy Sprague Mitchell

The promotion of critical thinking and problem solving is one of the teacher's more demanding tasks. It is an important task, not only as an end in itself, but also because it assures active student involvement in learning, giving added purpose and momentum to the student's acquisition of knowledge through reading and listening. Students learn the satisfactions that accrue from investigation carried out in collaboration with teacher and classmates, and from the use of their own minds and imaginations.

This chapter will suggest how critical thinking can be promoted through (1) a climate in the classroom that lends itself to probing and exploring, (2) productive discussion procedures, and (3) inquiry teaching procedures (i.e., teaching in which the student becomes an active investigator in problem solving and discovery learning).

CLASSROOM CONDITIONS THAT FACILITATE CRITICAL THINKING

Critical thinking flourishes best in classrooms in which:

1. Teachers frequently raise questions and encourage their pupils to raise questions, and pupils find their questions are treated with respect.

2. Teachers encourage their pupils to get in the habit of formulating hunches or guesses (hypotheses). One form of encouragement is spontaneous and hearty recognition by the teacher of imaginative hunches advanced by pupils.
3. Teachers rely more on their own personal resources to stimulate curiosity and thinking than upon textbook and workbook questions—which all too often do little more than ask pupils to recall what they have read and seldom to analyze, summarize, evaluate, or otherwise reflect critically upon what they have read.
4. Teachers give their pupils ample time to think about questions before attempting to discuss them. They avoid rushing into formal class discussions before having pupils, in pairs or small groups, play ideas off against one another, compare them, and synthesize them.

A classroom atmosphere, characterized by these conditions, nurtures productive discussion which, in turn, yields the questioning-exploring behavior that underlies critical thinking.

THE DISCUSSION AS A VEHICLE FOR CRITICAL THINKING

The teacher's ability to conduct discussions is the key element in the promotion of critical thinking. There is impressive evidence that class discussions cause learners to exercise thought processes different from those used in simply assimilating information; in discussion they spend significantly more time *manipulating ideas* than they do when merely recording mentally what they hear or read; they more often evaluate, synthesize, and apply ideas.[1]

Not all discussions are constructive learning experiences, however. If not carefully planned by the teacher, some can end up as talkfests in which uninformed pupils do little more than exchange their ignorance. While skill in leading discussion is achieved only through practice, certain rudiments can be learned second-hand, and it is the purpose of this section to cite some of the rules and to offer some suggestions.

Set a Purpose for the Discussion

The first requirement of a successful discussion is that it have an explicit purpose. The purpose should be implicit in the teacher's introduction to the subject to be considered. Some purposes are given below:

Purpose	*Example*
To solve a problem.	How can farmers in dry lands increase the size of their crops?

---

[1] B. Bloom, "The Thought Process in Discussion," in Sidney J. French (Ed.), *Accent on Teaching* (New York: Harper and Row, 1954), chap. 1.

Purpose	*Example*
To explore values.	What's the use of our learning about ancient times?
To air a controversial issue.	Was the bus drivers' strike necessary?
To review a complex operation, process, or idea.	How do the Panama Canal locks work?
To plan a class activity.	What do we want the scrapbook (or dramatization, or trip) to teach us?
To summarize and evaluate a group experience (e.g., an excursion or the viewing of a film).	Let's see if we can pull together the important things we have learned.

The purpose of some discussions may be to set standards of work. Here are some examples:

- Ways of organizing a social studies notebook.
- Giving an interesting oral report.
- Using an encyclopedia when writing a report.

When children participate in setting standards of work, they tend to work more painstakingly than if standards were set for them. By joining and guiding the discussion, teachers can help pupils set standards that are realistic (that is, achievable and appropriate to their years) and challenging.

See That Pupils Have an Information Base

The second requirement of meaningful discussion is that pupils have an information base for considering a subject. A discussion should be tied in with a presentation of information or ideas, or a completed reading assignment.

The teacher raises the question: "Why do some workers wear uniforms and others do not?" The teacher has seen to it that the class already has encountered the necessary data and ideas that hold the key to the question. They are able to identify certain jobs that call for the wearing of uniforms, and other jobs that do not require them. They can immediately begin forming hunches that might explain the situation.

In other instances, the class must first do some reading or listening, before answering the teacher's question, to get the necessary data to answer it. For example, the teacher may ask a sixth-grade class studying civil rights to consider the following: "Some people say that human attitudes can't be changed by laws, that such change must be made first in people's hearts. Does our country's experience with civil rights laws prove these people right or wrong?" This is asked *before* the class has learned about changes that have followed the civil rights acts of 1964 and 1968. The class, motivated by the teacher's question, starts to read about the effects of the acts and finds that these laws contributed to ending discrimination against many Negroes by hotels, restaurants, employers, and real estate dealers; that there is still a lot of resistance to the acts, and many violations; and, conversely, that there has also been a lot of voluntary cooperation in all parts of the country to help enforce them. After the pupils search out as much information as possible, the teacher restates the question and guides the class in sorting out the facts and coming to a rational answer. Members of the class then compare their conclusions against those of writers on the subject in newspapers and magazines.

See That Terms Are Defined

The class should take time at or near the beginning of a discussion to define essential terms, or else it will get nowhere. Even educated adults often wrangle pointlessly in a discussion because they do not first agree on the meaning of such terms as "law and order," "conservation," "profit," and the like.

Keep the Discussion Moving

One of the teacher's responsibilities is to keep the class headed toward a solution of the problem or a completion of the planning. At least a tentative conclusion should be reached before ending the discussion. Otherwise there will be frustration and a feeling of wasted time on the part of everyone. Whenever the class strays, as often occurs, it is up to the teacher to bring it back to the subject. This can be done through repeating the original question or statement, rephrasing it, or asking a member of the class to summarize what has been learned thus far. In the intermediate or middle grades, one pupil may serve as secretary and can be asked to read from his or her notes whenever the discussion wanders.

Seek Wide Participation

One of the difficulties encountered in class discussion is the likelihood that a few children will monopolize it. Furthermore, the most talkative children are by no means necessarily the best informed or the most thoughtful. Obviously, the teacher must take steps to establish as large a measure of equality of participation as possible. This may be accomplished through several avenues: through discussing with the class the need to have many take part; through asking the loquacious to listen more and give other children a chance to talk; through encouraging shy children by specifically calling upon them when their interest or knowledge is believed to be pertinent; and through dealing with extreme cases by trying to get at the causes of their overassertiveness or their shyness. Such efforts normally improve the situation. But rarely is there universal participation, and teachers should not make a fetish of trying to achieve it. B. Bloom found that "the teacher who judges the effectiveness of his (or her) class or of a particular student on the basis of overt participation in the dicussion is using an extremely inadequate and frequently erroneous criterion."[2] He found instances of students who did not participate overtly in discussions, but who had excellent recall of what took place during the discussion.

Arrange Small Discussion Groups

Some discusson may be carried on by children in small groups of five or six, which remain intact for weeks or months so that a sense of group identity and cohesiveness can be established. This has proved an effective way of increasing participation from children who are reluctant to speak up in the larger group, and to increase interaction. Each small group may discuss a question or problem from the social studies lesson and plan cooperatively something to read or tell the rest of the class; or its members may share ideas for a role play or other activity. As their ideas develop, some children contribute more freely than they do during teacher-conducted, entire-class discussions, in which they often feel "on the spot" and become self-conscious. Many a classroom visitor has expressed astonishment at the quality and sum total of ideas presented when the groups come together again as a class and a representative of each reports his or her group's conclusions.

James Moffett makes a strong case for such a scheme, pointing out that it encourages careful listening, a desire to keep to the subject, and a feeling of responsibility for learning through discussion.[3] Each group may have a scribe or secretary. At the conclusion of the discussion period these scribes pool their findings before the entire class.

Seek "Interaction" Rather Than "Coaction"

To understand the process of discussion it is helpful to distinguish between "coaction" and "interaction." Coaction is an exchange between two persons—often the teacher, who asks a question, and a pupil, who answers it. Too frequently, this pattern is repeated over and over again, with the result that usually the teacher talks more than half of the time. Interaction, on the other hand, is a child-centered discussion. Although it begins with the teacher throwing out a question, it very soon expands as pupils begin to respond to other pupil's ideas. Interaction not only encourages children to listen to one another; it also yields greater success with critical thinking.

When interaction occurs, children address one another or the entire group, instead of directing their remarks to the teacher. Having the class sit in a circle rather than in rows, with teacher up front, facilitates this mode of discussion, encouraging pupils to talk without raising their hands to be called on.

---

[2]Ibid., p. 45.

[3]James Moffett, *A Student-Centered Language Arts Curriculum, Grades K-13: A Handbook for Teachers* (Boston: Houghton Mifflin, 1973), chap. 4.

Participate in Discussions, but Avoid Dominating Them

Teachers are often tempted to short-circuit discussions by "selling" their own solution or plan to the class. This defeats the purpose of group thinking. On the other hand, they, as leaders of the group, should intervene to see that all available data and points of view are duly considered, and they should help the class think through the probable consequences of alternative conclusions and decisions.

Set a Framework for the Rational Discussion of Controversial Issues

It is impossible to encourage free inquiry and critical thinking without encountering conflicting, controversial views among pupils. If it looks as though these may flare up into heated arguments, you, as teacher, need to establish an atmosphere for calm, rational thought. The following sequence of activities has been proposed as a framework to guide discussions of controversial issues:[4]

1. State the issue.
2. Define terms.
3. Collect purported facts from varied sources.
4. Look for evidence that would test the accuracy of the purported facts.
5. Check the relevance of the facts that have survived the test of evidence.
6. Attempt to reach a conclusion.
7. Test the conclusion by thinking through the consequences. Box 13.1 gives an application of this procedure.[5]

BOX 13.1   **VARIOUS GRADES**

Example of Stages in One Discussion of a Controversial Issue

1. *The issue:* Why should not families who live in certain apartment houses be allowed to keep dogs as pets?
2. *Terms:* Landlord, tenants, etc.
3. *Purported facts:* It is good for children to have pets; landlords have too much power; dogs damage doors and floors; barking dogs annoy people in nearby apartments; etc.
4. *Evidence:* A landlord invited to the classroom tells about damage that

(Continued)

---

[4]Jerrold R. Coombs and Milton Meux, "Teaching Strategies for Value Analysis," in Lawrence E. Metcalf (Ed.), *Values Education,* 41st Yearbook of the National Council for the Social Studies (Washington, DC, 1971), chap. 2.

[5]For other applications, see Coombs and Meux, ibid.

dogs have done to his property; *Your Dog in the City,* a book, tells how dogs can be trained to be "good citizens"; a newspaper article by a physician tells how important a pet can be in the lives of lonely people; etc.

5. *Relevance:* Dogs can be trained, but can a landlord know ahead of time if his tenants *will* train them? etc.

6. *Conclusions:* Apartment tenants can keep animals other than dogs that will not annoy neighbors or damage property; landlords can ask higher rates from dog-lovers and then allow them to have dogs.

7. *Test of conclusions:* Are cats, canaries, etc., satisfying to every dog-lover? Is any landlord willing to change his no-dogs rule if the tenant agrees to pay higher rent?

Stimulate Critical Thinking Through Questions

Questions should lead pupils from data to generalizations. The late Hilda Taba and her associates have given us a procedure that will do this.[6] It offers superb guidance to teachers in formulating their questions. Taba's ideas, in revised form, are presented in the first three subsections that follow.

The First Questions in a Discussion Should Be Open Questions. An open question is one that a number of pupils can respond to appropriately in many different ways. Its effect, therefore, is to invite wide participation. An example of such a question to initiate a discussion is "What things did you notice in the museum that were made by the Indians of the Pacific Northwest?" This is a better question than an excessively open one ("What was the most interesting event of our trip to the museum?") or an excessively narrow, closed one ("What were their winter caps made of?").

BOX 13.2   **ANY GRADE**

Muriel Crosby's Guidelines for Using Open-Ended Questions

The chief device used in the Wilmington project in human relations (described in Chapter 9) was the open-ended question. Muriel Crosby, in her description of the project,* points out six rules to guide the teacher's use of this procedure:

1. Teachers should avoid prestructuring their pupils' responses. The activity is purposeless if pupils are encouraged to say things that are "nice" and "respectable." Rather, their honest responses should be fully accepted.

(Continued)

---

[6]Hilda Taba et al., *A Teacher's Handbook for Elementary Social Studies: An Inductive Approach* (Reading, MA: Addison, 1971).

2. The teacher should avoid using the procedure too frequently and should limit the number of open-ended questions that are used at one time. If children feel constantly prodded to react, their responses lose their spontaneity.
3. The open-ended questions should be used only when they tie in to something the class is studying.
4. Since not all open-ended questions are equally suitable for all grades and ability levels, the teacher should develop skill in formulating questions of genuine appropriateness.
5. Usually children are eager to discuss their responses. The teacher should be careful to keep the discussions centered on what *many* children do and think, rather than on what a few articulate children do and think.
6. Responses should be regarded as confidential. Children may volunteer to share their responses with classmates, but they should not be expected to.

*Muriel Crosby, *An Adventure in Human Relations* (Chicago: Follett, 1965), chap. 4.

The First Questions Should Also Be Formulated to Lead the Discussion toward the Unit's Objective.   If the teacher wishes the class to consider the division of the Indians' labor between men and women and to compare it with today's changing concept of men's and women's roles, the first question should be not only an open question but also one that will supply a natural transition toward that objective. The first question proposed above ("What things did you notice in the museum that were made by the Indians of the Pacific Northwest?") will enable the class to identify a number of objects they saw in the museum (or may have read about in a textbook). They learned, also, that some were made by men, others by women. The next question may lead the class to classify the artifacts in terms of the sex of the craftsmen. The responses may be summarized on the chalkboard.

Follow-Up Questions Should Encourage Pupils to Generalize.   In the follow-up questions, the teacher may have the class survey the information now brought together in their responses to the first questions. The teacher can ask the pupils to try to state what the data add up to: "What do you make of all this?" Thus, the class is invited to generalize. One child may say: "Men and women had different jobs." Another may venture: "Men did work like building canoes and fishing; women did work like weaving and cooking." Some of the generalizations may be faulty, such as: "The men did the hard work; the women did the easy work." The teacher may list them all on the chalkbord and help the class to decide which is the best of the generalizations—that is, the one that includes or accounts for most of the data.

The importance of a rich data base, as discussed earlier, is evident. Sometimes children are unable to generalize because they have too little information. In this case, further questioning should be deferred until the class has an opportunity to gather more facts from additional observing, reading, and listening.

The Preponderance of Questions Should Be High-Level. Studies show that teachers have tended to ask more questions of a factual nature ("What are two ways in which islands are formed?") than those that require thoughtful responses, demanding critical thinking ("What is good about living on an island and what is not so good?").[7] One way in which teachers can reduce their use of factual or low-level questions (questions that can be answered by simple recall) is to use categories of the *Taxonomy of Educational Objectives*[8] as a guide to selecting high-level questions:

- *Comprehension questions.* "What are the reasons for fire drills?" "How has automation changed everyday life?"
- *Application questions.* "If our population density were the same as India's, how would our way of life be changed?" "Why might the term 'welfare state' be applied to the empire of the Incas?"
- *Analysis questions.* "How can you tell a TV commercial from a TV news report?" "Why did many Frenchmen and Englishmen want their countries to side with the South against the North in the Civil War?"
- *Synthesis questions.* "How could traffic snarls at Eighth and Main Streets be avoided?" "In what ways is the president of Brazil more powerful in his country than the president of the United States is in his?"
- *Affective questions.* "What would you like to see changed in the neighborhood, and why?" "What beliefs would you stand up for, even if it meant you would be made fun of?"

There are, of course, occasions that justify the use of factual (low-level) questions, such as "Who invented the telephone?" and "How does a bill become law?" It should be borne in mind that the superiority of high-level questions upon student achievement has yet to be clearly demonstrated.[9]

CLASSIFICATION OF INFORMATION

Most social studies content cannot be well understood without a classification scheme. Hence, the ability to classify and to deal with content in

---

[7]Meredith D. Gall, "The Use of Questions in Teaching," *Review of Educational Research,* 40 (December 1970), 707–721.

[8]Benjamin S. Bloom (Ed.), *Taxonomy of Educational Objectives. Handbook I: Cognitive Domain* (New York: McKay, 1964). David R. Krathwohl et al., *Taxonomy of Educational Objectives. Handbook II: Affective Domain* (New York: McKay, 1964).

[9]Philip H. Winnie, "Experiments Relating Teachers' Use of Higher Cognitive Questions to Student Achievement," *Review of Educational Research,* 49 (Winter 1979), 13–49.

terms of categories is one of the more useful cognitive skills that children can acquire. Hilda Taba worked out a teaching strategy that has not since been improved upon, and that deserves to be used with all children who have learned to read and write.[10]

You, as teacher, begin by having the children (1) *list* items that have a common affiliation (such as the materials of which houses are built: shingles, plywood, pipes, and so on); (2) *group* those items that belong together according to selected criteria (such as "all the materials used on the outside of houses" and "all the materials used on the insides of houses"); and (3) *label* each group (such as "exterior building materials" and "interior building materials"). After these steps have been carried out a few times with the entire class and the teacher working together, pupils can apply them independently or in small groups. Other examples appear in Box. 13.3.

BOX 13.3   **GRADES 2-8**

Examples of Classification Strategy

I. Subject: Who are the workers in our school?
    Step 1. *Listing.* Teachers, aides, principal, custodian, etc.
    Step 2. *Grouping.* Those working in the classroom; those in the office; those who sweep and clean; those who serve lunch, etc.
    Step 3. *Labeling.* Teachers, administrators, custodians, food and health workers, etc.

II. Subject: What are our natural resources?
    Step 1. *Listing.* Air, rivers, timber, iron, coal, etc.
    Step 2. *Grouping.* Those not likely to be used up; those that can be brought back in abundance; those that can be used up but can be used more than once; those that can be used up and have only one use.
    Step 3. *Labeling.* Inexhaustible, renewable, exhaustible but renewable, etc.

TRAINING IN PROBLEM SOLVING

In a carefully designed research project, Lawrence F. McClure and his associates taught problem-solving procedures to fourth-grade students, dividing them into four groups.[11] One was a control group (it did not receive

---

[10]Hilda Taba et al., *Thinking in Elementary School Children*, USOE Cooperative Research Project 1574, San Francisco State College, 1964.

[11]Lawrence F. McClure et al., "Enhancing Social Problem-Solving Performance in an Elementary School Setting," *Journal of Educational Psychology*, 70 (August 1978), 504–513.

the instruction); the other three were taught the procedures, with a different strategy employed in each group, namely, role play, discussion, and TV.

Instruction continued for six weeks, one week being devoted to each of the following:

1. Problem-solving orientation, in which awareness of problem-solving situations and expectancy of success were established.
2. Identification of problems and setting of goals for problem resolution.
3. Generation of alternate solutions to problems.
4. Judgment of feasibility of solutions in terms of their consequences.
5. The necessity of concrete, step-by-step planning to implement a solution.
6. Integration of the foregoing five components in a unified set of strategies.

Each component was illustrated through a videotape, in which child actors of the same age as the students were used.

Following the training, the trained groups were able to generate more effective solutions than the controls. Students who had the role play experience were best equipped to apply their skills to a subsequent real-life problem-solving situation.

McClure's work has pioneered an area in social studies in need of further experiment and development. Meanwhile, it offers the best problem-solving curriculum currently available.

THE INQUIRY PROCESS

This chapter has thus far given illustrations of various forms of critical thinking: exploring values, dealing with controversial issues, planning activities, summarizing content, defining terms, generalizing, and creating. All these forms of thinking involve inquiry—i.e., the student looks into or investigates a situation.

Today, "the inquiry process" in education has a technical meaning of its own, denoting a distinct form of critical thinking (though it overlaps some of the foregoing forms). During the 1960s, "inquiry" was a label given by educators to describe a process called "discovery learning" by such distinguished contemporary psychologists as Bruner, Ausubel, and Gagné.

Nature and Purpose of the Inquiry Process

The inquiry process is a method of investigating and solving a problem so that the content of the learning is discovered by the learner rather than being presented to him or her ready-made, as in reception learning. The process consists essentially of six steps:

1. Recognizing and stating the problem.
2. Developing a hypothesis. A hypothesis is a hunch. It may be reasonable, it may be only plausible, or it may be no more than an intuitive guess. A brainstorming type of discussion usually leads to the formulation of alternative hypotheses.
3. Collecting data calculated to throw light on the problem.
4. Testing the validity of the hypothesis. In this step, the students draw upon the data they have collected and upon their background knowledge to determine the reasonableness or unreasonableness of the hypothesis.
5. Drawing conclusions. If the hypothesis is sustained, it often becomes a generalization.
6. Making applications of the generalization.

BOX 13.4   **PRIMARY GRADES**

Examples of Some Hypotheses Formulated by Second-Graders

The class was wrestling with the question: Why do some workers earn more income than other workers? Why does a doctor earn more than a shoemaker?
These hypotheses were offered:

- "If a doctor makes a mistake, the person he is fixing may die. A man repairing shoes may ruin a shoe, but people are more important than shoes."
- "People are willing to pay more to be fixed than to have their shoes fixed."
- "A doctor has more responsibility."
- "A doctor may have to work all day, and at night, too."
- "A person to be a doctor has to go to school more years than a shoemaker. You have to pay a lot to go to college."

The process's special contribution to social studies is to teach scientific method—that is, how problems are solved by scientists, and how the method can be used effectively by students. Furthermore, students' understanding of, and ability to apply concepts such as "hypothesis," "generalization," and "evidence" have widespread use in everyday life, putting them on guard against unwarranted generalizations and teaching them to look to evidence for proof.

Although research on the contribution of inquiry to learning is inconclusive, there are striking instances in which its use has increased the motivation of students, enabling some students to carry out this process independently while still in elementary school. As pointed out in Chapter 7, discovery learning is not, and is not likely to be, the major channel of classroom learning, but guiding children in the inquiry process should be a part of every teacher's repertory.

FIGURE 13.1.   During the inquiry process, the teacher assists children with problems occurring in the search for facts that sustain or reject hypotheses. Courtesy of Prince George's County Public Schools, Maryland.

Examples of Inquiry in the Primary Grades

Teachers may ask children in the primary grades to tackle a problem presented by a picture. One large photograph in the *People in Action* series of study prints depicts a child attempting to mail a letter, but the box is too high for her. The picture presents the problem dramatically. The teacher may ask the class to state the problem. The answers to the question, "What can she do?" are alternative hypotheses. "She could bring a chair," one child volunteers. Other responses are: "Why doesn't she wait for a passerby?" "She should return home and tell her parents someone else will have to mail the letter." These and other solutions would then be tested by thinking through the consequences of each. Then the class may decide which are the one or two more sensible things the child could do. Finally, the teacher may see if anyone can name some rules that can be made for solving this kind of problem. In what other situations would the rule decided on as the best one here be a good one?

In a third-grade class, the children learned that, within a given unit of time, it takes (1) fewer men to milk a given number of cows by machine than by hand, (2) fewer men to prepare a given quantity of hay with a power mower and a power baler than with hand tools, and (3) fewer men to weave a given amount of cloth on power looms than on hand looms. The teacher asked the class to think about what these three facts mean. One child replied: "Every new labor-saving machine seems to cut down the number of workers needed." This was a reasonably adequate generalization; the teacher repeated it and had other children restate it. (If a wrong generalization had been given, the class would have been asked to think further about the facts.) Children were then asked to find out if this was true in other industries.

Other problems that have been investigated by primary classes are:

- How can we stop the fighting on the playground?
- What is the reason for fire drills?
- How do the museum people know that Indians wore the turtle rattle on the leg and that they wore it for dancing?
- Why are tugboats rounded at the bow and not pointed?
- Why don't our mothers bake all the bread for their families the way mothers did 100 years ago?

Examples of Inquiry in the Upper Grades

In one classroom, the following question arose: Why are so many people moving away from this neighborhood? Following discussion, three hypotheses emerged:

1. Families move because they want to get away from bad housing. The houses need painting, many have leaking roofs, windows are broken, and rats live in the walls.
2. The Redevelopment Authority is tearing down many houses. People have to find other places to live.
3. Some families move when the father or mother gets a better job with more pay. That makes it possible for the family to move to the suburbs, where it is cleaner, quieter, and prettier.

The teacher wrote the hypotheses on the chalkboard. Ways of checking out each were considered. It was decided that hypotheses 1 and 3 could be tested by interviewing people who had already moved or who were planning to move. To test hypothesis 2, information could be obtained from the Redevelopment Authority and from members of the class who knew from observation how many houses had been torn down. After investigation, it was determined that hypotheses 1 and 2 supplied the best answers to the question.

In another example, we find a committee of children trying to answer the question: "How have the Swiss people been able to keep their small coun-

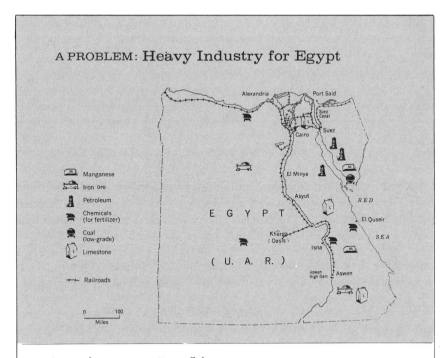

A PROBLEM: Heavy Industry for Egypt

Answer these questions. You will be planning where steel mills should be built.

1. Iron is a key resource. On the map, find places where iron could be mined.

2. Decide whether the mills should be right at the mines or on the river. Why?

3. Find a town near each iron ore deposit that might be a good place to build the new steel mills.

4. A nearby supply of electricity is very important. So what town is the best choice of all?

5. Of the seven resources needed, which are close to the town you have chosen? What one material will have to be transported from far away?

150

FIGURE 13.2.   Example of a problem-solving exercise.

try independent for so many years?" The following hypotheses were generated and served as starting points for their children's research activity:

Hypotheses	How to Check Out the Facts
1. Independence is a trait of people living in any small, mountainous country.	Check the record of independence of (a) other small, mountainous countries, and (b) small, nonmountainous countries.
2. Independence was a result of William Tell's bravery.	Check the history of Switzerland and the William Tell legend.

Hypotheses	*How to Check Out the Facts*

3. The more people do for themselves, the more independent they become.

Check to see how much the Swiss "do for themselves"—how self-sufficient they are.

4. Large, powerful countries find it useful to have a small, neutral country during wartime for mediation, exchange of prisoners, etc.

Check history of Switzerland during World War II.

A group of children were studying the geography of the North Central States. The children were given maps of the region that showed only rivers, lakes, and various natural resources. They were asked to show on their maps where the main cities, railroads, and highways would be located without looking up this information in books or maps. They were not starting from scratch, for they had previously studied the South Atlantic States, which gave them information about the location of cities and patterns of transpor-

FIGURE 13.3.   Another example of a problem-solving exercise.

A PROBLEM: Land and Water Use

1. Where could a small dam be built to make a reservoir and store monsoon water?
2. Where could ditches be dug so that gravity would carry water from the reservoir to the fields for more winter crops?
3. Where could the land be used if it were first smoothed and leveled?
4. Where should forests be replanted to hold the soil and slow the run-off of rainwater?
5. Where should grass be planted to hold soil in place and give good pasture for cattle?
6. Where could the land be terraced as the Swiss terrace their vineyards? (This would mean leveling off strips of cropland between steep drops.)
7. Where could wasteland be drained and made into fields for rice?

tation. Their reasoning was based on that information. A class discussion followed, in which individual children explained their reasons for situating cities in particular places and drawing arteries of transportation between various points. After an hour of intense discussion, the children excitedly compared their own maps with a wall map.[12]

A fifth-grade class learned that all the Piedmont cities, from New York City south to Columbus, Georgia, are at or near the Fall Line. The pupils were asked to hypothesize the probable reason for building the cities at these points. Once they understood the characteristics of the Fall Line, it was a short step to the conclusion that the Fall Line marks the limit of navigation for ocean-going ships and was, hence, a logical place for the early settlers to establish themselves. They also discovered the availability of water power at the falls and rapids along the Fall Line.

Figures 13.2 and 13.3 show inquiry problems as presented in a textbook. Each question states a problem to be pursued by the six steps of the inquiry process. Teachers can easily devise inquiry problems of their own.

Once a pupil learns the steps of the inquiry process, he has at his disposal a tool that can serve him usefully throughout his life. As in the case of other tools, mastery does not come about after merely one or two demonstrations or one or two practice sessions. The pupil becomes habituated to the process through repeatedly using it over many years.

TEACHING COMPETENCIES

This chapter has described how to perform the following tasks that are basic to teacher competency. The teacher should be able to:

1. Establish a classroom climate in which questioning, problem-solving, and offering of hypotheses are normal and frequent occurrences.
2. Hold frequent discussions that are purposeful and for which pupils have an information base.
3. See to it that essential terms are defined in class discussions.
4. Maintain wide participation in discussions, prevent monopoly of discussions by a few, stimulate interaction among children, and lead the discussions without dominating them.
5. Organize small-group discussions to increase interaction and productive thinking.
6. Organize discussions of controversial matters into rational rather than emotional consideration of issues.
7. Guide discussions through carefully planned open questions, questions that will lead to appropriate generalizations, and questions that will elicit divergent thinking.

---

[12]Richard C. Anderson and David P. Ausubel, *Readings in the Psychology of Cognition* (New York: Holt, Rinehart and Winston, 1965), pp. 80–81.

8. Give instruction in the classification of information that will enable pupils to clarify the problems under discussion.
9. Give instruction in scientific method through guiding pupils' thinking through the steps of the inquiry process.

TRYING OUT SOME OF YOUR COMPETENCIES

1. Conduct a discussion of a question or problem arising in a social studies unit (e.g., "What are the meanings of the many words used to show members of a family—sister-in-law, cousin, distant cousin, great-uncle, etc.?" "How does the owner of a coal mine decide whether to use open-pit mining instead of mining by shafts and tunnels?" "What are the arguments for and against open-pit mining?") Don't begin until you are sure your pupils have an ample information base.
2. Following discussion by the class as a whole, divide the class into small groups to discuss matters unresolved in the larger group. Have a representative from each group bring its conclusions before the entire class.
3. Use the Taba approach to draw up a classification scheme with the participation of the class. The scheme should be so organized that it will be useful for sorting out, labeling, and clarifying the content under consideration.
4. Plan a lesson for applying the inquiry process. Prepare some questions likely to evoke high-level thinking.

FOR STUDY AND EXPLORATION

1. Identify a teaching objective that could be achieved through a class discussion. Write a series of questions, beginning with open-ended questions that would both elicit wide participation and focus the discussion, and concluding with follow-up questions that would lead to formulation by the class of appropriate generalizations.
2. Observe a social studies discussion period in an elementary school. Make as complete a transcription as you can of what is said. Evaluate the discussion from the standpoint of its probable purpose, the effectiveness of the teacher's questions, and the extent to which it stimulated the pupils to engage in creative thinking.
3. What differences exist between pupils in the primary grades and pupils in the intermediate grades that call for corresponding modifications of strategy in the inquiry process?

FURTHER READING

To furnish a background for teaching critical thinking and problem solving, the following articles are recommended:

Roberta M. Milgram et al., "Quantity and Quality of Creative Thinking in Children and Adolescents," *Child Development*, 49 (June 1978), 385–388.

Beatryce T. Newton, "Theoretical Bases for Higher Cognitive Questioning," *Education*, 98 (March/April 1978), 286–291.

For books, consult Susan M. Stievater (compiler), "Bibliography of Recent Books on Creativity and Problem-Solving," *Journal of Creative Behavior*, 12 (no. 2, 1978), 146–149.

The research report on problem solving by McClure, cited in this chapter, also describes a six-week curriculum that proved highly effective with Grade 4 students. Lawrence F. McClure et al., "Enhancing Problem-Solving Performance in an Elementary School Setting," *Journal of Educational Psychology*, 70 (August 1978), 504–513.

For provocative suggestions for guiding class discussions, see Jimmie R. Applegate, "Why Pupils Don't Talk in Discussions," *Clearing House*, 44 (October 1969), 78–81; and Dana G. Kurfman (Ed.), *Developing Decision-Making Skills*, 47th Yearbook (Arlington, VA: National Council for the Social Studies, 1977).

Skills required by teachers in asking questions are treated by:

Norris M. Sanders, "A Second Look at Classroom Questions," in J. Michael Palardy (Ed.), *Teaching Today: Tasks and Challenges* (New York: Macmillan, 1975), pp. 158–168.

Francis P. Hunkins, *Questioning Strategies and Techniques* (Boston: Allyn and Bacon, 1971).

Roger T. Cunningham, "Developing Question-Asking Skills," in James Weigand (Ed.), *Developing Teacher Competencies* (Englewood Cliffs, NJ: Prentice-Hall, 1971), chap. 3.

14 Managing Committee Work

In any group every member, no matter
what his assigned role, can make
significant and unexpected contributions
to the success and well-being of the group.
Marcus A. Foster

The traditional practice of requiring children to work individually on nearly every assignment in the classroom has been supplanted by an allocation of time for both individual and committee work. Although organizing children in committees has long been employed by proficient elementary social studies teachers, this method of teaching has been avoided by those who are fearful of the behavior problems that can arise when groups of two or more children work together. It is administratively convenient for the teacher to have children work individually at their desks because the teacher can more easily control the situation and can spot and quickly correct any behavior infractions. This advantage, however, does not justify the neglect of grouping since numerous reasons support the frequent grouping of children in elementary school social studies.

Some teachers have reservations about allowing committees to meet for long periods of time, often because of their own guilt feelings when visitors happen to enter the classroom and find the committees engaged in construction, dramatic play, or painting a mural. The idea that children should always be engaged in intellectual tasks at their desks harks back to a time of formality and authoritarianism in our education.

Certain new teaching strategies—those involving children's participation in decision making, problem solving, critical thinking, and simulation, as well as in programs emphasizing creative activities like dramatic play, construction, dance, music, and art—lend themselves with striking aptness to small-group procedures. Some basic guidelines for managing small-group or committee work may help to promote successful teacher supervision and effective, enjoyable achievement by children.

THE FUNCTION OF A COMMITTEE

Although committees are formed for various purposes in the social studies, each committee has some kind of question or task to tackle.

Examples of Questions[1]

Questions That Elicit Listing.   These are especially appropriate for young or inexperienced committee members. They call for an elementary but important kind of thinking, "and we know that small children can do it and learn from it."[2]

- What are the uses of leather?
- In what ways is our air polluted?
- What kinds of crops are grown in this climate?
- What are some differences between cities and towns?

Questions That Elicit Comparisons.   Comparing is a more advanced type of thinking than listing.

- How is the work of a teacher like that of a parent?
- In what ways are air travel and bus travel different?
- In what ways are Christianity and Judaism alike?
- How are the Scandinavian countries alike, and how are they different?
- How is a governor's job like that of the President?

Questions That Elicit Chronology.   Chronological ordering includes composing a group story, planning sequential actions, or describing how something is made.

---

[1]The three categories of questions given here are adapted from ideas on procedures appearing in James Moffett, *A Student-Centered Language Arts Curriculum, Grades K-13: A Handbook for Teachers*, 2nd ed. (Boston: Houghton Mifflin, 1973), pp. 21-63. Chapter 4, "Speaking Up," is recommended for reading by teachers who are attempting small-group discussions with their classes.

[2]Ibid., p. 62.

- Make up a story telling how Sue solves her problem.
- How can we go about making adobe bricks?

There are advantages in having several committees tackle the same problem. When each has finished its assignment, the scribes, who have been taking notes, may form a panel. They report to the entire class how their committees have answered the question and are prepared to answer questions or reply to comments from the class.

Example of Tasks

The problems of other committees are task-oriented. Some examples of assignments for these committees include:

- Collect pictures for the bulletin board to illustrate an important aspect of the unit.
- Construct a poster to present key information.
- Make a graph on the chalkboard.
- Read and report on a phase of the unit that the class as a whole will not study.

The first need of task-performing committees is to list in proper sequence the jobs they must undertake; the second is to distribute responsibility to committee members who will carry out the jobs.

THE RATIONALE FOR HAVING COMMITTEES

Perhaps the greatest justification for committee work is that, in small groups, children learn the art of discussion by picking up ideas that are expressed, developing them, raising questions, trying to summarize, and so forth. James Moffett points out the probability that children who engage in such discussions internalize and gradually learn to use the processes of critical thinking, questioning, and summarizing when alone and faced with a problem.[3]

Another justification lies in the greater chance a child has in small groups to share responsibilities and decisions. The intimacy of the group encourages children to speak up, to confront one another, to seek ways to deal with disagreements, and to cooperate. These important skills cannot be learned in isolation; they are acquired when children are intimately engaged with each other in a cooperative enterprise.

Heber and Heber report that a committee's cooperative activities tend

---

[3] Ibid., p. 46.

to effect a rise in social maturity among children, especially if the group was successful in its endeavors.[4] Other research indicates that group work is effective in the formation and maintenance of a positive self-concept by the learner.[5]

Committees are essential if certain important learning activities are to be carried out. Painting a mural, making a large plastic relief map, and dramatizing a historical episode are examples of experiences that require small-group planning and cooperation.

Teachers have long realized that some children seem to learn better from their peers than from the teacher. The small group provides a setting in which each group member may excel in a way that can teach something to each other member. Zander goes further: "And by operating our elementary schools on the 'succeed on your own or not at all' motto, we may be depriving many of our children of the success experiences they need to develop individual initiative and to overcome fears of failure."[6]

Grouping often meets individual differences by providing tasks on various levels of difficulty, from which each child can choose; then he can proceed to work at his own pace. For example, for some problems committee members can divide the chores of reading, writing, selecting and pasting pictures, drawing and painting, and making oral presentations.

Through this kind of activity, children also learn the value of group work. The products are usually difficult, or perhaps even impossible, for any one child to bring about by himself. Each group member feels pride when he views the achieved result and recalls his special contribution to the total effort.

TEACHER QUALITIES THAT PROMOTE SUCCESSFUL COMMITTEES

The qualities required for conducting committee work differ little from those required for successful teaching. The teacher must be willing to accept a higher noise level than he or she would allow in the traditional classroom, for it is inevitable that when children are engaged cooperatively in an enterprise and must discuss matters among themselves, they will make more noise than when they are working individually.

---

[4]Rick F. Heber and Mary E. Heber, "The Effect of Group Failure and Success on Social Status," *Journal of Educational Psychology*, 48 (March 1957), 129–134.

[5]Rosanne J. Marek, "The Effects of Two Strategies of Teaching Social Studies on Fourth-Grade Pupils' Scholastic Achievement, Racial Attitudes, and Self-Concepts," *Dissertation Abstracts International*, 33 (April 1973), 5476–A.

[6]Alvin F. Zander, "Productivity and Group Success: Team Spirit vs. The Individual Achiever," *Psychology Today*, 8 (November 1974), 68.

BOX 14.1   **ANY GRADE**

Questions for Judging the Appropriateness of a Committee

1. Are the objectives for committee activity educationally significant in terms of the understanding, skills, and appreciations needed in the social studies unit?
2. Is this the most efficient use of time for accomplishing these objectives? What might be a more efficient means for accomplishing the same thing?
3. Is this committee activity consistent with what is known about the children's development and capabilities—intellectual, social, emotional, and physical?
4. Can individual differences be accommodated by the work of the committee?
5. Does the committee activity provide for variety in learning experiences?
6. Does the committee activity provide balance between creative opportunities and routine learning?

Teacher acceptance of individual differences is important. Disparities in abilities, such as reading, applying study skills, employing critical thinking, getting along with other children, mixing paints, cutting poster paper, hammering and sawing, and drawing become obvious as a teacher supervises each working group.

A teacher must be willing to have an orderly classroom disarranged at times in order to accommodate the demands of committee work. Sometimes the class must push desks together to provide more floor space, procure large work tables and set them up, and arrange special materials to preempt a library corner.

Another essential characteristic of the teacher is the ability to face the fact that children working together, instead of separately at their desks, usually take longer to complete a specified piece of work. It takes time for a committee to organize itself and to consider different points of view, delegate responsibilities, and carry out its mission. A practical rule of thumb for time allotments for committee work is 30 to 45 minutes.

ORGANIZING FOR COMMITTEE WORK

When and How to Begin

The second month of school is probably a good time to begin using committees. This allows the teacher enough time to accumulate helpful information about each child—his personal and school backgrounds, his special strengths, weaknesses, needs, capabilities, and peer relationships. By this time, too, the children will have begun to know each other.

Before the first committee meets—and periodically during the year—clarification and demonstration of small-group skills (see Box 14.2) is essential. Moreover, it is helpful to discuss behavior that blocks the progress of a committee, e.g., tangential ideas, arguing, long-windedness, clowning, bringing up personal problems, withdrawing.[7]

BOX 14.2   **GRADES 4-8**

Skills That Aid a Committee[8]

A Member:

1. Makes a contribution.
2. Listens and responds to other members' contributions.
3. Perceives similarities and differences in ideas.
4. Encourages the contributions of others.
5. Learns new roles: *initiator, clarifier, summarizer, evaluator, observer.*
6. Strives for consensus.

The first committee work in the school year, whether supervised by a neophyte or by an experienced teacher, should probably be just one project, carried out by one small group of children, to insure adequate teacher assistance for success. Moreover, this may be the first committee experience for some children. To get the work off to a good start, it is advisable for teachers to choose compatible pupils, representing a cross section of pupil characteristics. However, the most important ingredient is a specific function for the committee to perform—one that the children can accomplish.

Later, when the group has begun its work, the teacher can supervise unobtrusively, rendering assistance when difficulties are encountered with procedures, materials, and behavior. Brief, periodic reports by committee members will keep the remainder of the class informed about their progress and will provide them with information on the mechanics of group work in preparation for their turn to participate in similar activities.

After the first committee finishes its project, another can be formed, and so on, until all of the children have had a chance at this type of work. Then the teacher can allow two or more committees—and eventually the entire class—to function simultaneously. This progress of group work may take several months, depending on the success of each step. Even after children display success in this endeavor, some teachers stagger the beginning times of the committees by a few days to avoid the excessive noise and confusion that often attend the first meetings.

---

[7]Gordon Hart, "Preparing Students for Small Group Work in the Classroom," *Education*, 95 (Summer 1975), 351–353.
[8]Ibid.

Committee Work with Young Children

Committee work with primary age children needs to be approached with much patience and understanding since many of the children have experienced limited activities of a cooperative nature with other children. Nevertheless, with proper encouragement and support by the teacher, children enjoy being challenged to work in tandem and in small groups and display interest in acquiring group work skills to produce a product that is possible only by the interactive efforts of a small group.

The problems usually associated with committee work with young children pertain to developmental characteristics, personality traits, and limited social experience. Some teachers of intermediate children report that committee work in the upper grades is often plagued by the same factors, and often the cause can be traced to insufficient opportunity for committee work in the early levels of schooling.

Developmental Characteristics.   The stages of social development proceed from egocentric activity to parallel activity to cooperative activity. Because of delayed development or limited social experience some young children are simply not ready for group work; Huey suggests that young children "are more likely to work in parallel fashion than in a true cooperative manner."[9] Other developmental characteristics that need to be considered in conducting committee work with young children include their relatively short attention span, their need for motor activity, and their difficulty with making plans collectively. Also, since group work typically involves putting the parts done by various group members into meaningful relationships that produce a finished product, some young children are easily discouraged in the early phases of work because of their incapacity to comprehend the finished project.

Often the solution for the delayed development of some children is the passing of time. Other children's development will be assisted by observing their peers work on committees. For still other children who seem to respond well to new situations and challenges, the teacher may wish to gently nudge children along the path of development and new experience at a slow pace with extra encouragement and suggestion.

Personality Characteristics.   The personality traits of some young children interfere with successful relationships with other group members and restrict and sometimes shut down the productivity of a committee. Examples include those children who:

1. Are dependent on stronger group members and rarely initiate their own actions.

---

[9]J. Frances Huey, *Teaching Primary Children* (New York: Holt, Rinehart and Winston, 1965), p. 149.

2. Monopolize the work.
3. "Boss" group members.
4. Are inattentive.
5. Withdraw because of unfamiliarity with other group members.
6. Are inflexible in adapting to other members, fail to accept different ways of doing the same job, and are unable to change their mind on the basis of new evidence.
7. Are uncooperative after losing in a vote on a matter.
8. Are discourteous and always put themselves first.
9. Complain or criticize excessively.

Many of these characteristics are acquired through environmental influences, often in the family. Some teachers report that it is helpful from time to time to discuss personality attributes that enhance a committe's progress. Teachers as models of exemplary traits often influence children to replace unacceptable behavior with more desirable group behavior. Without embarrassing specific children in need of change, one teacher makes a practice of having a couple of "needy" children act as observers of a successful committee in action and report to the whole class a summary of their observations with particular attention to attitudes of children in various situations.

Limited Social Experience.   A variety of problems are possible when young children have sparse social experience. Some of these include children who are unaccustomed to doing a part of a job and sharing in the praise for the whole job; children who have difficulty in accepting leadership from a child stronger than themselves; children who fail to accept, respect, and endorse ideas better than their own; children who favor their friends' ideas over the superior ideas of nonfriends; children who always have to lead; children who are unable to criticize another child's idea or the majority's position; and children who are unable to work without the close supervision of the teacher.

From the authors' experience in the classroom, increased committee work and the emulation of more experienced children often provide the solutions to many of these problems. Nevertheless, some direct teaching often clarifies for children what is generally acceptable and unacceptable in interpersonal relationships. Some platitudes that have helped in this regard include: "Accept and respect all ideas;" "the whole project is always more than a part;" "judge the idea, not the person who made it;" "a group usually comes up with better ideas than individuals do;" and "you can disagree, but do it aggreeably."

Committee work with young children is especially rewarding when it is undertaken with the purpose of introducing and practicing interpersonal and group related social skills. As with other educational skills being taught to the young child, progress is often rapid, observable, and rewarding to children with patient and supportive teachers.

BOX 14.3   **GRADES K–3**

Guidelines for Committee Work with Young Children

1. Limit committees to three or four members.
2. Limit number of committees working at same time to one or two.
3. Provide adequate assistance and supervision, especially when the committee first begins to meet.
4. Avoid committee tasks that entail much reading or writing.
5. Plan simple tasks, e.g., arranging a picture display, dressing up and playing family roles, or taking care of pets, that require no more than one or two committee meetings for their completion.
6. Keep committees intact for a couple of months. This will allow children to become accustomed to each other.
7. Provide frequent opportunities for discussion of common problems.

Composition of Committees

One of the purposes of having committees is to insure that the positive qualities of each child can be discovered by all children in the class at some time or other throughout the school year. This suggests that the composition of committees should change occasionally throughout the school year.

Differences within a committee make a valuable, enriching experience for committee members. Moffett reminds us that "speech develops best when one has to talk to people *unlike* oneself, because overcoming differences requires more clarifying and explaining."[10] Thinking also develops best in such circumstances. Consequently, the teacher should probably select most committees in order to make sure there is a good distribution of traits with respect to such factors as ethnic background, sex, intelligence, personality, and socioeconomic status.

There are sound reasons, however, for occasionally using other methods in the formation of committees. Their use will give each child an opportunity to work with nearly all children in the class sometime during the year. These other methods are:

1. *Interest grouping.* Committees may be formed voluntarily by children, according to their preferred interest. The mode is popular since children work better when they enjoy their task.
2. *Ability grouping.* When a project requires expert skills, children possessing these skills may comprise the committee.
3. *Friendship grouping.* Sometimes committees may be formed on the basis of friendships. However, although friendships promote harmonious working relationships within a committee, this method should be used sparingly because it tends to encourage classroom cliques.

---

[10]Moffett, *A Student-Centered Language Arts Curriculum*, p. 55.

Size of Committees

Educators are fairly unanimous concerning what constitutes an optimum size for the problem-solving committee, in which discussion is the predominant activity. Moffett believes "the size of the group should probably not exceed six, simply because participation and interaction drop below a desirable level in groups of larger numbers."[11] Louise E. Hock believes the ideal number is from four to seven.[12] (It is of interest to note that with college

FIGURE 14.1.   Committee work for young children entails simple tasks. Courtesy of Center for Young Children, University of Maryland, College Park.

[11]Ibid.

[12]Louise E. Hock, *Using Committees in the Classroom* (New York: Holt, Rinehart and Winston, 1958), p. 23.

students, too, four to six in a group was found to be more satisfactory in terms of student satisfaction and problem solving than larger numbers.[13])

For committees concerned with specific tasks, the nature of the job determines the number. Some dramatizations (for example, the simulation of an Indian attack of Fort Boonesboro) call for many pupils. For this enactment, perhaps even the entire class could be divided between settlers and Indians. Herbert A. Thelen espouses the "least group," or optimal group, size. This is determined by selecting the smallest possible number of members (1) with the necessary skills to realize achievement goals and to accomplish the task in a well-executed manner, and (2) with the social skills needed to promote the healthy emotional climate and good morale factors that are needed to bring about group cohesiveness.[14] A task such as the construction of a poster might require no more than three children. With fewer than three, cross-fertilization of ideas is unduly limited; with more than six members, a committee is likely to have a surplus of ideas and to become so unwieldy that, in most cases, the committee leader will be unable to manage it. In addition, it will have a tendency to generate nonproductive members whose idleness may be disruptive.

Gifford G. Hale's report of an experience that a class had while making "minitexts" illustrates advantages of the "least group" theory.[15] The children decided to make minitexts by writing and illustrating booklets to show how to do dramatizations, make maps, and carry out several other social studies activities. Only those groups of two or three that chose both their own members and the project successfully finished their minitexts. When the teacher assigned the project, when he appointed the committee members, or when more than three worked together, the project was either aborted or dragged on beyond the time when the self-directed groups had accomplished their purposes.

Setting Standards and Procedures

General ground rules for committee work should be worked out by the entire class before the first group is selected. The teacher can initiate this by announcing that much of the work will be done by committees, that all children will serve on them sooner or later, and that rules for this type of work need to be made ahead of time. Box 14.4 contains questions drawn up by one class to guide committees.

---

[13]James A. Schellenberg, "Group Size as a Factor in Success of Academic Discussion Groups," *Journal of Educational Sociology*, 33 (October 1959), 73–79.

[14]Herbert A. Thelen, "Group Dynamics in Instruction: The Principle of the Least Group Size," *School Review*, 57 (March 1949), 139–148.

[15]Gifford G. Hale, Florida State University, personal communication.

BOX 14.4   **GRADES 4–8**

Questions Proposed by One Class to Guide Committee Work

1. Who will be our leader?
2. What is our main aim?
3. In what specific ways can our aim be reached?
4. Who would like to do these tasks? What methods can we use?
5. What materials will be needed? How do we use the materials?

Leaders of Committees

Group leaders are not always needed for a committee to function successfully. This is true of committees that have mature members who pitch in with about equal effort and who have considerable skill in personal relationships. Usually, when groups fail to elect a leader, one or two leaders evolve anyway. Normally, a leader facilitates the organization, implementation of objectives, and interpersonal interactions of the committee.

In any given classroom many potential leaders exist, but the highly verbal children who are school-achievement-oriented are often chosen by their peers as committee chairmen because academic success is often prized as a qualification for leadership. Naturally, when the goal is production of verbal materials, the best leader is likely to be a verbally proficient child. But social studies projects also include nonverbal activities such as painting, construction, dancing, interviewing, arranging exhibits, and experimenting, any of which can be managed by capable children who are often overlooked by their classmates as possible leaders.

Popularity is not, in itself, an important requisite for leadership. Knowledge of the issues involved in the job, temperament, flexibility, imagination, interpersonal skills, and persistence are more important than how well liked a person is.

Children do not always choose committee leaders wisely. One sound procedure is to maintain rotating committee chairmanships so that everyone in the class serves eventually. This permits a wider range of children to chair committees and develop leadership skills and simultaneously provides leaders an opportunity to participate in supportive roles. It is often advisable for the teacher to ask that one committee member become a temporary chairman until another is elected. A teacher's knowledge of a class helps greatly in getting things started.

Having Children Consider the Nature of Planning

Some task-producing committees are eager to get into the active part of the project before they have spent enough time in planning, only to find later that some unforeseen difficulty causes trouble. The cliché, "First we plan our work and next we work our plan," runs counter to some children's desire to stop the *talking* and get on with the *doing*. They want to tackle the objectives by the first or second method that occurs to them. The teacher

FIGURE 14.2.   Older children tackle complex tasks requiring both cooperative planning and division of responsibilities. Courtesy of Prince George's County Public Schools, Maryland.

must often remind them that the aims of a planning session are to be sure everybody understands the task or problem and to consider possible ways of solving it; to see how many real possibilities there are of performing the task or solving the problem; and to foresee the consequences of each acceptable possibility by asking questions ("How does this way affect our division of labor? our materials? our way of working? the quality of our product?" "What problems might we encounter?" "Does it insure reasonable success?").

The nature of planning, as here described, is not easily learned by children, and they can be inducted only gently into its use.

Informal Progress Reports

Brief progress reports given by each committee near the end of the social studies period is an effective way of organizing the following day's work: for example, problems concerned with needed supplies and tools, procedures, working space, productivity, morale, and interpersonal conflicts can be broached while they are fresh on everyone's mind; also, their resolution prevents a possible delay in the committee's work on the following day. It often happens that the problems of one committee are common ones with other groups.

A committee's report can have value for the class in the following ways:

1. It enables every child to know what other committees are doing. This promotes class unity.
2. It increases committee morale when it reveals that progress has been made.
3. It stimulates increased effort when it reveals that little has been accomplished.
4. Successful and unsuccessful procedures can aid other committees by showing what worked and what did not work.
5. Problems common to all committees are clarified and resolved through a consideration of alternatives.

Scheduling Committee Work

A question often asked is whether it is better to have committees meet daily until their tasks are finished or to intersperse total classwork every other day. Generally, once a committee begins work on a special job or project, it should be encouraged to complete the task in the shortest possible time. Otherwise, the motivation may be impaired. Some group projects have failed because the work was spread out over an excessive period of time.

SUPERVISION OF COMMITTEES

When committees are functioning, the overall role of the teacher is to supervise. But he must also, in an unobtrusive manner, pay close attention to what is going on, look out for children or groups needing assistance or encouragement, be alert for instances of positive and negative interpersonal relations that can be discussed objectively at a subsequent evaluative session, and recognize where improvements are required in teacher-planning that involve materials, procedures, and goals. The need for unobtrusiveness is emphasized here; indeed, the teacher will have to guard against giving suggestions and help with problems that children can resolve themselves. Ideally, the teacher should visit each committee during each work session.

The Stalled Committee

Committees usually become stalled because (1) they don't know what their goals are, or (2) they don't know how to reach their goals. When a group is in trouble, the teacher's objective should be to promote independence. Suitable comments would be in the form of questions: "What is your goal?" "What are possible ways to solve it?" "What would happen if you chose the first way?" "What steps will you need to take?" "In what order should the steps be taken?" It is better for the teacher to avoid solving the committee's problem.

The Discouraged Committee

Discouragement is a common malady that can cripple the production and morale of a committee. The cause can usually be traced to a few sources. First, discouragement can be caused because its members feel frustrated over an inability to accomplish some task of the committee. Specifically, this

FIGURE 14.3.   Until children acquire experience in group work, the teacher assists committees toward independence. Courtesy of Prince George's County Public Schools, Maryland.

frustration can be a result of the long time period required to complete a task, a task is too difficult for the committee members, or lack of success. Second, discouragement often occurs because of unhelpful behavior. This can take the form of some members provoking or making heavy demands on other members, weak leadership, lack of cooperation among members, lack of teacher guidance, or the recognition that other committees are accomplishing more. Last, a lack of purpose or commitment in the project by a committee frequently spawns discouragement.

Discussions are helpful in the treatment of discouragement. Often they reveal the underlying reasons which will suggest possible solutions, such as lowering unrealistic aspirations, listing accomplishments at the end of each work session, or importing skills from another committee. In a study of the Northwest lumbering industry, one of the co-author's elementary classes built a seven-foot square house with actual lumber used in home construction. During the following year another class formed committees to rebuild the house but the children became discouraged at the sub-floor stage. After discussion revealed little interest in the project, the construction was abandoned.

When it is difficult to pinpoint the reasons for discouragement, the teacher could introduce the idea that everybody gets discouraged at times, but that by "hanging in," feelings can and do often change. Also, it can be pointed out that perspective is required in any significant undertaking, that it is easy to see the bad in a situation and never to see the good. In such a case, realistic evaluation is needed to improve the morale of the committee.

Committee Members Waste Time

A certain amount of inefficiency characterizes all groups. Nevertheless, if the teacher ascertains that too much time is being wasted, the reasons will have to be determined in order to resolve the problem.

Some common reasons for low productivity include insufficient preparation of the pupils by the teacher for committee work (see Box 14.2); inadequate committee leadership, e.g., lack of supervision, little coordination of members' efforts, or failing to assign to each member a specific job and ensuring that he knows how to do it; poor planning; poor cooperation and morale among committee members; or too many in the group.

Children Visit Other Committees

The desire of children on one committee to observe another committee at work should be accepted as an indication of normal curiosity. Visits provide opportunities for children to learn about another committee's methods of attacking common problems or to seek assistance from more skilled peers. On large projects, such as a mural, a visit enables children to observe how their committee's part fits into the whole class endeavor which usually spurs them on. The purpose of some visits is to meet socialization needs, which may suggest that more consideration be given to sociometric data in the formation of committees. Other reasons could be that some children have little work assigned them by their leader or they have completed their tasks.

INTERPERSONAL PROBLEMS

Since one of the aims of committee work is to develop traits of independence, children should have considerable latitude to organize, manage, and evaluate their own committee efforts, while the teacher observes in the background. As any teacher who has used committees knows, the members are bound to have some interpersonal disputes and display aggressive behavior when they are working together so intimately. It is well to let the children themselves take the lead in resolving such personal problems. Their resolution of conflict, based on their own standards, is more influential in developing teamwork skills than is intervention by the teacher. Needless to say, some situations require teacher assistance. A few workable methods of assistance will be discussed in the succeeding sections.

Having Children Consider Ways to Settle Disagreements

Sometimes committees have difficulty getting started because members cannot agree among themselves on issues. In order to help them avoid such impasses, the teacher should discuss methods of decision making with the whole class during the planning stage, before children go into their committees. As a beginning, they can talk about the following three methods:

1. *Voting.* This method has a legitimate place but it is often misused. It is popular with many children, perhaps because of its clearcut character. (Of course, a motion to reconsider is always possible.) Since it magnifies differences between groups, it tends to divide members of a group into those for and those against a decision.
2. *Compromise.* Where division of opinion is sharp, compromise may be inevitable. This is not an ideal method, however, because it may leave the perspectives of conflicting groups unchanged. It can, however, serve as a stop-gap method in decision making until the participants are more fully in agreement. Rearrangement of plans can always advance a group beyond a compromise.
3. *Consensus.* Consensus is ideal for all problem-solving groups. Pupils identify, study, and discuss areas of conflict in an attempt to agree upon a common plan or decision. The smaller the group is, the better is the chance for consensus.

How can children learn such complex behavior as that involved in settling disagreements? Direct instruction of sets of rules or methods is likely to prove disappointing. A more promising approach is for teachers to set a model for settling disagreements. They can do this by demonstrating through their own behavior the preferred methods (see Box 14.5). They may also discuss, with the class or with a committee, alternative ways in which a concrete disagreement may be resolved.

BOX 14.5   **ANY GRADE**

Methods for Presenting Opposing Ideas

1. *Phrase your idea in the form of a question.*

Dubious: "I think Sue's idea won't work. What we need is water paints, not crayon."

Preferred: "Do you think water paints would show off our drawing better than crayons?"

2. *Word your suggestions positively instead of negatively.*

Dubious: "If we don't stop fooling around, we'll never get done in time."

Preferred: "If each of us does what we agreed to do, we'll get the whole job done before we know it."

3. *Use the "Yes-but" approach.*

Dubious: "Your idea would never work. My idea is . . ."

Preferred: "Yes, your idea to use crayons is a possibility, Sue, but water paints would show off our work better."

4. *Praise, instead of criticize, some part of the other person's idea and offer your idea.*

Dubious: "I think Sue's idea of using crayons is baby stuff. I think water paints are much better."

Preferred: "Crayons, as Sue suggested, is a good idea because we all have a box of them. I think water colors would show off better, though."

Hale reports an incident that occurred in a school of which he was principal.[16] A kindergarten class, in building a large cardboard-box model of an apartment house, became bogged down in an argument over the shape of the television antennas to be fashioned from wire coat-hangers and installed on the roof. Some said one shape was right; others said another was the real one. The teacher proposed that the children vote. She did this deliberately to teach a lesson. The vote was close between the two shapes proposed, but one shape received more votes than the other. The losers were dissatisfied with the vote outcome. The teacher asked whether people always get the right answer by voting. The children said, "No!" The teacher asked one child representing each of the contending views to go outside the building and look at real apartment houses near the school. The class accepted this as a

---

[16]Hale, personal communication.

possible compromise. The two children reported back within five minutes that both types of television antennas were on the roofs, so everyone agreed that their apartment house should have both. The children had moved from voting to compromise to consensus.

Complaining Committee Members

Complaining is a part of human nature, but an inordinate amount of it may indicate an underlying feeling of inferiority. By complaining about the weaknesses or faulty thinking of others, Jim may be concealing his own inadequacies. The way he thinks about others may be showing the way he thinks about himself.[17]

Even if the teacher feels limited in his or her ability to help Jim overcome feelings of inferiority, one way in which he or she can help improve the child's behavior is by setting a good example. Children do imitate adult behavior. As early as the second month of school, they begin to take on the behavior characteristics of their teachers. The teacher who rarely blames others is establishing a model which children often internalize. If, on the other hand, the teacher frequently finds fault and shouts criticism, this kind of behavior will permeate the classroom and eventually become the dominant pattern of behavior among the pupils.

Altercations

Billy was painting a section of a mural entitled "Major Characteristics of New England." Jim mischievously spattered some brown paint on an area that Billy had just painted red. Billy became irate and reciprocated by smearing Jim's section of the mural with strokes of red. In a second they were fighting.

Hostile, overly aggressive children usually have experienced rejection. Hostile acts shout, "I have been treated terribly. I haven't been allowed to satisfy my needs and wishes. Now I am going to pay you back." Both Billy and Jim may need assurance that they are important, that the teacher has a sincere concern for them as persons, that their efforts will be recognized, and that their peers will accept them and value their strong points.

Every individual has his worth and a contribution to make to the group. When other people show that they regard him or her as worthy, he or she will begin to think positively of him- or herself. This new-found self-esteem should help to improve social relationships.

Whatever action the teacher takes to end the fight, it should promote the social development of the children involved, as well as the social insight of the committee. Embarrassing the child before his peers, shaking him, or removing him from the committee may solve the immediate problem, but it

---

[17]Albert Bandura, *Principles of Behavior Modification* (New York: Holt, Rinehart and Winston, 1969), chap. 4.

will do little to foster the child's social adjustment. Nevertheless, if the misbehavior jeopardizes the welfare of the group, restrictive action by the teacher may be necessary.

When interpersonal difficulties occur with children, the teacher is placed in a judiciary role and is obligated to hear testimony from all participants. A strong temptation is to expedite a settlement, even if it means using incomplete evidence and punishing, willy nilly, all of the children involved. A wiser course is to seek the causes of the conflict and to consider what alternatives the teacher could take in similar incidents in the near future.

The Dependent Child

A child who frequently asks the teacher for help with tasks is usually the product of an autocratic, overprotective environment in which parents, older siblings, or teachers have stifled the child's development in self-reliance by doing too much for her. Consequently, confidence in her own abilities became subordinate to the confidence she placed in more able and usually older people. Moving children from dependent to independent behavior is one of the chief goals of instruction.

Children Want to Switch Committee Membership

Another interpersonal problem occurs when children want to leave their committee and join another one. In this instance an appreciation is needed of the nature of voluntary membership in classroom committees. A person accepts membership in a particular group because she agrees with the fundamental purpose or activity of its members; she withdraws membership for personal reasons such as having needs met or disagreeing with the aims of the group. On the other hand, members of a classroom committee have the authority to accept new members and to discharge delinquent members or those blocking the progress of the group.

Thus, a child who desires to leave Committee A in order to join Committee B must have the approval of the members of both committees. When the work of a committee is dependent on the skills of a pupil who wants to withdraw membership, the teacher can stress the importance of loyalty to the group, and encourage (not command!) the pupil to remain with his original committee.

In other cases involving disruptive and uncooperative pupil behavior, the teacher is obligated to describe to committees their responsibility to admit and discharge members. With young children, of course, the teacher will exercise considerably more guidance in managing committees than will teachers of intermediate-grade children.

A Committee Discriminates Against a Member

When members of a committee treat unfairly or unequally one of its members, the teacher is obligated to uphold the scales of justice. A general objective of the social studies is to provide opportunities for children to acquire the skills and attitudes of citizenship, and charity and fairness are essential earmarks of a democracy and of human relations per se.

Those who discriminate unfairly against another person may be attempting to cover up their own feelings of inferiority. They may do this by humiliating and setting apart unfairly another person; these people falsely assuage their own negative feelings about themselves in an attempt to build themselves up. Evidence must be taken from both sides in an attempt to reconcile the differences. With severe cases where remediation is unsuccessful, the child should have the option of joining another committee.

The Pupil Who Declines Committee Membership

Since membership on a committee is a voluntary act, a pupil has the right to work independently if he desires to do so. But because committees provide an important educational function, children should be encouraged to serve on them.

CONCLUDING COMMITTEE WORK

When Committees Finish at Different Times

There are many stretches of time when only one or two committees are at work during the social studies period, and when the remainder of the class is working with the teacher or at individualized tasks. Often, however, there will be many committees at work simultaneously, collectively involving all the children in the class. In the latter case, several days may elapse between the completion of work by the first group and by the last group. This situation is normal. Differences in the problem or task and in abilities, interest and procedures result in variances in the rate of completion. The teacher can plan with the class some enrichment activities for children finishing early. These activities can be listed on oak tag and posted in a conspicuous location for reference. See Box 14.6 for some ideas listed in one classroom.

BOX 14.6   **GRADES 4–8**

Suggestions for Committee Members Who Finish Early

1. Inspect your working site for cleanliness; make sure that books are shelved, tools and materials are put away, desks and chairs are returned to their places, etc.
2. Offer to help some other group.
3. Return to your desk and work on other assignments.
4. Return to your desk and read a library book.
5. Select a learning center and complete its tasks.

(Continued)

---

6. Do a housekeeping chore in the classroom.
7. Clean your desk.
8. Perform an experiment in the science corner.
9. Write a creative story.
10. Think of and list improvements needed in our classroom concerning routines, social studies projects, grouping, or anything else.
11. Read the daily newspaper.
12. Using one of the road maps, plan an imaginary automobile trip, paying attention to road routes, cities, towns, lakes, mountains, and special land features. Determine a scenic route to your destination and a direct route home.

Reports of Committees

At the conclusion of the project or assignment, committees should report their findings and accomplishments to the entire class.

The Teacher's Role in Helping with Reports. To avoid dull reports, the teacher must spend time with each group before the report is made, checking for accuracy and thoroughness and insuring an attractive format. Charts, maps, graphs, drawings, photos, dioramas, and demonstrations are all excellent means of capturing the attention and interest of the class.

The teacher should make sure that the report includes essential information and avoids giving so much that it becomes lengthy and boring. The report should also avoid giving insignificant details that obscure the important points.

The nature of each committee's task usually suggests alternative ways to present the finished product. For example, a group could report an interview with a resource person by replaying the tape of the conversation, if it has made one, or it could summarize the interview orally. Children can learn to make presentations in many forms. The teacher should set an example of variety in his daily instruction.

Committee Reports. Each committee may choose one or two members to present the report—perhaps the chairman or scribe. A report should be brief (not more than five minutes, if that long), and both class and teacher should have time to ask questions and add information or ideas. The reporting committee should never be made to feel that it is on the spot. The atmosphere should be friendly, and the predominant spirit or attitude of teacher and class should be that of *wanting to learn*, not of finding fault. When factual errors are reported, the teacher should correct them in the spirit of adding information. If the supervision has been adequate, in most cases factual errors and inappropriate procedures of work will have been caught and corrected before the report is made to the class.

A class may be divided into committees to consider some question such as, "What kind of law might reduce littering?" After meeting for two or three days, the scribes may meet before the class as a panel. Each reports on his committee's conclusions. Panel members may then interact with each other and with other class members who may wish to ask questions or offer comments.

The one or two members chosen from each committee to give the report should identify the other members by their names in order to make sure that they receive recognition. The others may be able to assist during the presentation by operating equipment or handling illustrative material.

Generalizing from Committee Reports

The problem of bringing the completed work of all committees into a meaningful whole exists when committees engage in dissimilar tasks or projects pertaining to a unit. After all committees have made their presentations, the various findings need to be discussed and related to each other, and finally, generalizations should be sought. For example, what is the relationship between the separate exhibits of (1) population density maps of Bolivia, (2) natural resources of the country, (3) clothes worn, (4) transportation used, (5) topography, (6) serious problems that the country faces, and (7) major occupations? Elementary children are able to identify cause and effect patterns, and after an examination of factual evidence, to formulate generalizations.

When major understandings or generalizations are summarized on a chart or the blackboard, children are able to see how the collected parts from each committee fit into the total picture to form order and unity. They also experience class esprit de corps since the work of each committee is synthesized into new and broader understandings; such a result they recognize is impossible for any one committee to accomplish by itself.

Evaluation of Committee Work

Through observation of committees at work, committee reports, class reaction to and discussion of the reports, and through any testing undertaken, the teacher is in a position to judge the value of committee experience. He or she must answer key questions: (1) Did the *product* improve children's understanding of the social studies content? (2) Did the *process* of acquiring the product improve children's skills in one or more of the following areas: human relationships, critical thinking, study, language arts, maps and globes, and so on?

Children benefit from receiving feedback concerning their performance on committees. General assessment of each committee's product by its members and by the teacher is needed.

TEACHING COMPETENCIES

This chapter has described how to perform the following tasks that are basic to teacher competency. The teacher should be able to:

1. Direct instruction to overcome committee problems associated with characteristics of development, personality, and limited social experiences.
2. Involve children in planning, setting standards, and devising procedures for committee work.
3. Supervise each committee during work, obtain informal progress reports from committees, and encourage members of committees to govern themselves.
4. Assist each committee in planning a cogent report to the entire class.
5. Bring the completed work of all committees into a meaningful whole, and aid children in seeing relationships among the findings and projects.

TRYING OUT SOME OF YOUR COMPETENCIES

1. Plan and conduct a discussion on a social studies topic with a small group of children. Before the discussion, cooperatively develop with the children some rules of discussion including the skills in Box 14.2.
2. Plan and conduct committee work with young children involving a simple task. Evaluate the proceedings.
3. Plan committee work with a small group of children. Discuss the need for rules, and cooperatively develop with children some rules needed in their work. Carry out the project.

FOR STUDY AND EXPLORATION

1. Why do some children enjoy working in committees while other children would rather work by themselves?
2. What are the attributes of leaders that influence whether or not their committees will be productive?
3. One of the goals of committee work is to encourage children to move from dependent to independent behavior. What are some different interpretations given by teachers of this goal? Why do teachers interpret this goal differently?

FURTHER READING

A book that has continued its popularity with many teachers is James Moffett, *A Student-Centered Language Arts Curriculum, Grades K–13: A Handbook for Teachers*, 2nd ed. (Boston: Houghton Mifflin, 1973). Chapter 4, "Speaking Up," is fresh in approach, inspirational, and practical. It focuses on how to get the most from small-group discussions. Moffett is interested in using small groups to stimulate language development, which, of course, is a correlate of the conceptual development sought in the social studies.

National Educational Association, Saw Mill Rd., West Haven, CT 06516 offers three overhead transparencies, *Group Processes in Elementary and Secondary Schools: What Research Says to the Teacher* (1973), *Independent and Group Learn-*

ing, and *Guidelines for Classroom Teachers: Understanding Intergroup Relations* (overhead transparencies).

Sometimes teachers tend to become discouraged after trying grouping in the classroom. The article by Harvard W. Mclean, "Models for Effective Groupwork," *Elementary School Journal*, 67 (February 1967), 271–275, provides progressively complex models for grouping in the social studies; these models start with one small classroom group and end with several committees.

The following articles offer useful information: Gordon Hart, "Preparing Students for Small Group Work in the Classroom," *Education*, 95 (Summer 1975), 351–353; Harry Johnson, "Committee Work—Tragedy or Triumph," *Education*, 97 (Summer 1977), 355–356; Frank Ryan and Ronald Wheeler, "The Effects of Cooperative and Competitive Background Experiences of Students on the Play of a Simulation Game," *Journal of Educational Research*, 70 (July/August 1977), 295–299; G. M. Schuncke, "Using Groups in Social Studies Classes," *Social Studies*, 70 (January/February 1979), 38–41.

15 Providing
Creative Experiences

. . . in all learners there is a creative spark which makes life exciting. To discover the spark is to discover reality; to overlook it is to overlook the central fact of human existence.
Frederick Mayer

Creativity will be viewed in this chapter as the process of the child's bringing into existence a product that is new to him or her, revealing new insights or a point of view. We shall not deal here with creative experiences involving the discovery of solutions to problems and the formulation of hypotheses. These were dealt with in Chapter 13. Here we shall confine ourselves to creative activities involving play, dramatics, construction music, dance, and the graphic, plastic, and industrial arts. Creative writing is dealt with in Chapter 20.

CONTRIBUTIONS OF CREATIVE EXPERIENCES TO SOCIAL STUDIES

The values of creative experiences are well known. They promote self-actualization—that is, they encourage children to try out and to develop their own capacities, and to accept themselves. Creative experiences support the goals of social studies instruction in the following ways:

1. They help children to consolidate and summarize what they have learned in social studies. The psychological, educational need for

such "output" exercises was succinctly dramatized by William James in his assertion that there can be no permanent impression on the mind without a motor expression to clinch it.[1] Expressive experiences are natural follow-ups to "input" activities (reading, listening, observing) and have the power of internalizing the child's learning—that is, incorporating it within the child's existing cognitive structure. For creativity is a form of review and self-recitation. What an uninformed classroom visitor might regard as merely "free expression" or "play" is actually a fact-fixing process.

2. Creating a product in social studies requires a certain amount of self-discipline in collecting data about the subject and organizing it. Moreover, the media used in the execution impose disciplines of their own.

3. Creativity often causes a unit to come alive. The printed word, the discussion, the film, and other input media are converted to children's own thoughts and imaginings; the creative products of children enable them to identify with the unit in a personal way.

4. Creative experiences also play a part in developing citizenship. Children learn respect for their own inventions and for the imagination and trailblazing of others. In certain creative activities, they learn how to cooperate—how to fit one's role in a dramatization in with that of others, for example, or how to harmonize one's contributions to the committee's mural with those of others.

5. Creative experiences help keep a balance between the cognitive and affective goals of education. As Douglas H. Heath points out, modern schools tend to concern themselves too one-sidedly with intellectual activities that "make brains arrogant," with the result that natural instincts, the imaginal side of children, and the performance of worthwhile tasks by hands are sacrificed.[2]

FACTORS CONTRIBUTING TO CREATIVITY

Creativity seldom occurs spontaneously in the classroom. It happens more often as a result of a number of favorable conditions, such as a special kind of teacher, an adequate reservoir of learning experiences, and the availability of materials, space, and time. The weakness or absence of any one factor can seriously impair the process and product of creativity.

---

[1]William James, *Talks to Teachers on Psychology* (New York: Holt, 1900), chap. 5. James overstated the case for overt responses. While they are not essential for all types of learning, they do offer positive advantages in acquiring new concepts and difficult concepts. See W. Howard Levie and Kenneth E. Dickie's summary of overt versus covert responses in Robert M. W. Travers (Ed.), *Second Handbook of Research on Teaching* (Skokie, IL: Rand McNally, 1973), p. 876.

[2]Douglas H. Heath, in a lecture at the Haverford (PA) State Hospital Annual Conference on Adolescence, November 1972.

Teacher Behavior

If teachers are to promote creative thinking, they need to respect children's ideas—to accept them, reward them, and urge the children to explore them.[3] Teacher behavior that is warm, patient, understanding, sympathetic, helpful, trustful, and accepting nurtures creativity, whereas the use of controls, threats, criticism, punishments, sarcasm, and ridicule curbs creativity.[4] Developing originality and fresh thinking in children requires that a classroom atmosphere of respect for individuality be established.

Research indicates that lessons designed to train the creative thinking abilities of children are effective.[5] Such skills as fluency, flexibility, originality, and elaboration have been significantly improved by carefully planned activities.

Before a class undertakes a creative activity, some "warm-up" may be necessary. But the "warm-up" should not consist of questions with predetermined answers.[6] Teachers who give too many examples or who evaluate too frequently freeze or unduly shape the creative process and product.[7] Thus, teachers who allow children to express their ideas and readily accept and support them during the "warm-up" period contribute to a classroom climate favorable to creativity.

To foster creativity, teachers also need some tolerance for surface confusion and noise. When children work together, they must be expected to talk to one another. The important question is whether a teacher's tolerance level is in the acceptable range that allows children to engage in creative activities in normal childlike ways, or whether his or her attitude restricts children to behaving like little adults.

Some creative activities require that a classroom appear disorganized for half a day, a week, or sometimes even longer. A classroom is a workshop. Too often the classroom is treated as a showroom, where children may engage only in activities that can be cleaned up when school ends. Such a standard seems unrealistic.

---

[3]E. Paul Torrance, *Creative Learning and Teaching* (New York: Dodd, Mead, 1970).

[4]Kenneth H. Wodtke and Norman E. Wallen, "The Effects of Teacher Control in the Classroom on Pupils' Creativity-Test Gains," *American Educational Research Journal*, 2 (March 1965), 75–82. Helen M. Branch, "A Study of the Relationship Between Selected Classroom Conditions and Growth in Creativity," *Dissertation Abstracts International*, 35 (February 1975), 4973-A.

[5]Jean H. Miller, "The Effectiveness of Training on Creative Thinking Abilities of Third Grade Children," *Dissertation Abstracts International*, 35 (May 1975), 7032-A. Joseph S. Renzulli and Carolyn M. Callahan, "Developing Creativity Training Activities," *Gifted Child Quarterly*, 19 (Spring 1975), 38–45.

[6]Charlotte Crabtree, "Effects of Structuring on the Productiveness of Children's Thinking," *Journal of Experimental Education*, 36 (Fall 1967), 1–13.

[7]E. Paul Torrance, *Creativity: What Research Says to the Teacher* (Washington, DC: National Education Association, April 1963).

Pupil Background

The prerequisite for pupil output is pupil input acquired through experience, either at first hand or vicariously. Many children in classrooms today have experiences that transcend those of children of only a decade ago. Travel, television, radio, mobility of the population, and availability of numerous reading materials increase their reservoir of experiences. For these children, the creative process has been adequately primed.

Nevertheless, there are also children in classrooms today whose life experiences are confined to the city block, the family farm, or in the case of the migrant worker's children, to the shack, the field, or the dilapidated bus. Although some children in these situations have had rich experiences, not all have. When creative activities are planned for children with limited experiences, the outcome can be improved through discussions, which clarify and extend the experiential concepts, and through the display and use of pictures, books, objects, artifacts, and other materials, which provide the necessary background.

It is revealing that certain studies relating creativity to social class indicate that disadvantaged children perform better on measures of nonverbal or figural creativity than advantaged children do; and that of the children who score in the upper 20 percent on a measure of creativity, 70 percent score below the 80th percentile on an intelligence test.[8] Many teachers report that opportunities for creative work provide strong incentives to economically and educationally deprived children for formal work in the social studies.

Availability of Materials

In the initial planning for a creative activity, teachers must make certain that sufficient appropriate materials will be on hand at the proper time. They can occasionally request children to bring materials from home. In general, however, if teachers provide the materials needed for the activity, no children will be disappointed because they forgot or did not have the necessary supplies. For individual creative activities, it is imperative that each child has adequate materials to work with.

Adequate supervision is essential when creative materials are being used. Teacher-pupil planning of appropriate work standards before the materials are distributed will head off numerous problems. Sending a note home to parents requesting children to wear old clothes or bring smocks or old shirts of their fathers on days when messy activities are scheduled is a good idea. It keeps parents informed of what is going on and minimizes the possibility of tearing or soiling good clothes.

---

[8]K. I. Gezi, "Analysis of Certain Measures of Creativity and Self-Concept and Their Relationship to Social Class," 1969 (ERIC: ED 031 533). Torrance, *Creativity: What Research Says to the Teacher*, pp. 8–9.

In a planning session, near the end of the period, teachers and pupils can decide what to do with:

1. Finished and unfinished products.
2. Excess paints, clay, leather, wood, or other materials.
3. Acquired materials and tools needed to complete a product at a future time.
4. Soiled floor, desks, or tables.

Availability of Space and Time

The amount of needed space depends on the kinds of media being used in the process of creativity. Large-scale wood construction, role playing in groups, and the use of paper-mâché in building life-size models require ample open areas of space. For creative writing and drawing, however, pupils can remain at their desks.

To have insufficient time to finish one's creative products is a frustrating experience. With some thoughtful planning, this condition can usually be avoided in the self-contained classroom, where there is ample opportunity for flexibility of time schedules. The problem is more difficult to solve in classrooms organized by departmentalization or team teaching, but careful planning over several sessions may enable pupils in such classrooms also to complete their products.

THE DISTINCTION BETWEEN FREE CREATIVITY AND CREATIVITY AS AN ASPECT OF SOCIAL STUDIES

To engage in free creativity is to express whatever one wishes to express. One does it for personal satisfaction and release, out of the desire to create. If the child carves an object in soap, writes a poem expressing his or her feelings, makes an abstract drawing, or performs an interpretive rhythmic dance without regard to the school's curriculum or other external restrictions, then his or her product is an example of free creativity.

The creative experiences discussed in this chapter serve a different purpose. They are the means for having children learn social studies. They must, therefore, bear a close relationship to the social studies curriculum. They may be dramatizations of a historical event or pictures drawn to illustrate a research report. In each case, they must reflect or interpret social studies content.

CREATIVE PLAY AND DRAMATICS

Play has an important function in the lives of children. It is exploratory. Some forms of play bring them into the adult world for a short time. Children can step into a role (farmer, housewife, pilot, cowboy, knight, or bulldozer operator), try it out, experiment with it awhile, and quit when they wish. Children identify with the exciting work of the world—past or present—and in the process come to a closer understanding of it. As Susanna Millar points out, make-believe play has many functions. "The child may be exploring his feelings, lessening his fears, increasing his excitement, trying to understand a puzzling event by graphic representation, seeking confirmation of a hazy memory, or altering an event to make it pleasant to himself in phantasy." She suggests that play may be a rehearsal of an observed event, which aids the child in assimilating what has occurred.[9]

Play as discussed in this section has the following common benefits for children.

1. It is enjoyable.
2. It meets the needs of the "whole child" simultaneously—intellectually, emotionally, physically, and socially.
3. It allows children to explore reality, to discover alternatives for action, to make choices.
4. It strengthens and extends language skills.
5. It promotes sensitivity to the feelings, ideas, and actions of other persons.
6. It aids children in gaining insight into and understanding of social studies information: vocabulary, concepts, generalizations, cause and effect, sequence of events, comparisons.
7. It leads to improvements in attitudes, appreciation, values, interests.
8. It meets the child's need to think and act creatively.
9. It reveals to the teacher those areas of child behavior that need correction, reinforcement, or further study.
10. It reveals to the teacher what content has been learned, what content requires reteaching, and what content would be appropriate as the next step in teaching.

Play proceeds from the free, spontaneous styles of young children to the more organized, sophisticated play forms of upper primary and middle-school boys and girls. Rate of progression to higher levels of play is often determined by experiences with other children, availability of toys in the home, and parental attitudes toward sharing and cooperation. From the independent play of early childhood, play proceeds to a level where one's peers contribute significantly to team effort in dramatic play or sociodrama.

Spontaneous Play of Early Childhood

Spontaneous play, involving one, two, or more children, is common in kindergarten and the early primary grades. An adequate assortment of "old"

---

[9]Susanna Millar, *The Psychology of Play* (Baltimore: Penguin, 1968), pp. 155–157.

clothes, large toys and blocks, and equipment such as children's stoves, refrigerators, and houses provide stimuli for play.

Teachers may influence play in three ways: (1) They may stimulate thinking about social studies topics (home and family life, people's preparation for the changing seasons, and so on) through discussion and field trips; (2) they may supply toys and costumes that lend themselves to play about the social studies topics; and (3) they may talk to the child about the toys not in a patronizing way but with adult vocabulary and concepts.[10]

The value of early, informal play is well known. It has positive effects on cognitive and social development, the promotion of imagination, subject achievement, and pupil behavior.

BOX 15.1   **GRADES K–3**

Developmental Levels of Play

Level 1. *Independent Play:* Tom plays with a large airplane by himself.
Level 2. *Parallel Play:* Tom spins the propellers of a large airplane while Andy (in the same vicinity) puts other airplanes in the hangar.
Level 3. *Cooperative Play:* Tom says, "I'll gas the plane while you load it with passengers, Andy."

Informal Dramatics

Few media offer greater possibilities for summarizing content than creative dramatics do. Dramatics helps children clinch knowledge and ideas following their study and discussion. For example, after a study of how opinion polls are planned and conducted, several pupils enacted a scene in a pollster's office; they decided on a question of current interest and importance, phrased the question so that it was easy to understand, decided on a sample (using the class as the population), then polled selected individuals and recorded and tabulated their replies. In another class, following a unit on the American Northwest Coast Indians, the pupils dramatized the ceremonial potlatch.

Other benefits of informal dramatics have been reported. A group of fifth-grade children grew in moral judgment through role playing, and the ninth grade students' growth in originality was attributable to their experience with creative dramatics.[11]

---

[10]Robert D. Strom, "Toy Talk: The New Conversation Between Generations," *Elementary School Journal*, 70 (May 1970), 418–428.

[11]O. P. Traviss, "The Growth of Moral Judgment of Fifth Grade Children Through Role-Playing," *Dissertation Abstracts International*, 35 (December 1974), 3581-A–3582-A; Shelby J. H. Ridel, "An Investigation of the Effects of Creative Dramatics on Ninth Grade Students," *Dissertation Abstracts International*, 36 (December 1975), 3551-A.

Creative dramatics needs no memorized lines. The play may be quite fragmentary. Small groups may act out stories or ideas discussed in class. An audience of classmates is sufficient. If costumes and properties are used at all, they should be of the kind that is improvised easily. For example, tables can serve as mountains; and strips of oilcloth or paper, as rivers. A rolled-up newspaper becomes a sword. A turban worn by a child makes him a Muslim. Children enjoy playing certain scenes over and over, taking turns in various roles. At the conclusion of the unit, a number of favorite scenes may be repeated as part of a final summary of the content.

The role of the teacher during creative dramatics is that of a consultant. Sometimes the class is divided into small groups; at such times, either all of them engage in a simultaneous play or each enacts a different episode. As the play evolves, the teacher becomes aware of which areas of content pupils clearly understand, as well as which areas they still have not learned. She can thus determine what teaching or reteaching is required to eliminate any remaining misconceptions, inaccuracies, or ignorance. She also discovers what new, relevant subject matter is needed to round out the class's perceptions of the content.

The dramatized story may be taken from actual experiences, such as

FIGURE 15.1.   Creative dramatics enhances an understanding of the House of Burgesses. Courtesy of Montgomery County Public Schools, Maryland.

their observations on a class visit to the post office or Marco Polo's adventures; or it may be taken from fiction, such as a story of village life in Mexico. The following account describes one possible procedure. Many other ways of developing creative dramatics are equally workable.

Mrs. Jones's class was studying a unit on Mexico. One day she asked the class if they would like to act out some of the stories about the Aztecs and Cortez. The children responded enthusiastically, suggesting the following topics, which they thought could be dramatized:

Topics are selected.

1. The Aztec custom of building islands (for homesites) in the marshes by fencing in areas and dumping dirt in the enclosures.
2. The Aztec religion, including human sacrifices.
3. Cortez and his conquest of the Aztec Empire.

Mrs. Jones divided her class into three groups, consisting of about 10 children each.

Groups are formed.

When Mrs. Jones asked the class how they might begin, Tom responded, "Well, we could take our textbooks, get in groups, elect a leader, and study the topics again so we know how to play each one." The teacher assigned a different classroom location to each of the three groups, which then spent the remainder of the social studies period studying and discussing their topics and planning appropriate action.

Plans are made.

Mrs. Jones took her class to the playground. Each group selected a different playground location appropriate to its topic.

The children acted out the roles suggested by the topics. The first group acted out cutting the timber, dragging it, and setting up fences around marshland. The second group carried a maiden to a seesaw for a sacrifice to the gods. Some of the children performed a sacrificial dance around the prone girl. The third group simulated forces of Cortez and Montezuma and engaged in hand-to-hand combat. Mrs. Jones moved from group to group, helping with some content problems when the children requested it and jotting down evaluative comments.

Play is executed.

Each group had a turn dramatizing each topic, and then they all returned to the classroom and evaluated the play. The discussion dealt with the

Play is evaluated.

accuracy of their portrayal of the content, the execution of the play, and general behavior. On
subsequent days, Mrs. Jones retaught content
about which the class had revealed significant inaccuracies in their play.

The Place of Published Plays

If a suitable published play is found, roles may be assigned to a group of
children, who may read the play through informally together. Such an activity can be an enjoyable experience and can provide a means of looking at
social studies content from a new perspective. More on the reading of plays
and sources of children's plays will be found in Chapter 19.

Planning a formal production of a published play, with children
memorizing lines and playing before an audience, is another matter. It can
probably not be justified, at least as a part of social studies instruction.
Skillful speaking of memorized lines and sensitive interpretation of a role are
part of a creative art of a high order, which few elementary school children
can execute, except in a stilted, unnatural manner. Furthermore, few if any
published children's plays with solid social studies content are sufficiently
distinguished to justify the expenditure of time required for thoroughgoing
rehearsals and coaching, during which the rest of the class must sit idly by
for hours watching a few children practice the same scenes again and again.
Most elementary school teachers lack training in dramatics coaching, and
final productions usually lack spontaneity.

Role Play or Sociodrama

Role play is an unrehearsed dramatic play, in which the participants
act out assigned roles for the purpose of understanding and remedying group
relationships. It grows out of problems occurring in the classroom as well as
out of social studies units.

Role play is effective at any level of the elementary school. It was used
with a sixth-grade class by a principal who had observed some boys picking
on and tormenting a classmate, Gertrude, during a game of kick-ball at
lunchtime. The principal related:

> I approached Gertrude's teacher and related
> what had happened. She had seen it, too. She
> said the boys had begun maltreating Gertrude
> the day before, for no valid reason. She had lec-
> tured the boys, but they had continued the abuse.
> I suggested the use of sociodrama.
>
> The offenders, about 10 of them, were asked to   **Describing the**
> come outside to the playground. When we were   **problem situation.**
> outside, I told them what I had observed and
> heard during the lunch hour, and asked if they

would like to play the same game of kick-ball over again, acting it out as the real game had gone. They thought the idea of playing kick-ball while class was going on was singular, and readily agreed. Two teachers and Gertrude were the special roles needed. Two boys volunteered to act the teachers' parts, but nobody would volunteer for the girl's role. "We can't play the game unless someone plays Gertrude," I said. "Why don't you play her role?" I asked Mike, the center and captain of the basketball team. He agreed. Two boys picked sides, and naturally "Gertrude" was selected last, amid comments that the boys wished she would play elsewhere.

Identifying and assigning the major and minor roles.

"Gertrude" played shortstop, and after a while a ball was kicked to "her." As Mike threw the ball to first base, the boys yelled, "Don't touch it! Dirty Gertie's touched it." The first baseman made no attempt to catch the ball, and the batter went on to second base. And so it went, exactly as it had at lunch time. The insults and abuse continued. Mike came up to bat and kicked an easy pop-up, but nobody would catch it. We had only played a few innings when I observed that Mike was feeling the effects of the maltreatment and had tears in his eyes.

Enacting the problem situation.

I stopped the game and said, "Now boys, let's talk about how you felt during the game." The boys who played the role of the watching teacher said he was very disappointed in the children's treatment of "Gertie." The other "teacher" wondered what other teachers would think of his class members and him as their teacher. "How do you think 'Gertie' felt?" I asked the rest of the boys. "Embarrassed," "Insulted," "Bad," "Awful," "Like crawling in a hole," "Like not coming to school anymore," came the answers.

Analyzing and evaluating the behavior.

Next, I asked Mike how he felt playing the role of Gertie. "In the beginning I didn't mind much," he replied, "but as the guys kept it up, calling me names and not touching the ball after I'd touched it or kicked it, I started to feel bad. I felt just like she probably felt at lunch hour. I don't want to play that part again," he concluded.

After more feelings and attitudes were explored, the boys played the game again, the "right" way, with the special roles played by

Reenacting the problem situation, using improved behavior.

other boys this time. After a few innings, we again discussed the participants' feelings. Positive feelings were expressed this time. I thanked the boys for reenacting the game, and they returned to their classroom.

Later, I learned they were very sober the rest of the afternoon. Significantly, each had voluntarily gone to Gertrude and apologized for what he had said. When their teacher asked them if acting out the game had helped them understand other people's feelings, they said, emphatically, it had. They added that they would not let anyone insult Gertrude in the future. They kept their word, and Gertrude was accepted in her classmates' games thereafter.[12]

Analyzing and evaluating the behavior.

It is thus evident that children, through role play, may gain insight into the feelings of another person by putting themselves in the other person's place. They may learn decent everyday treatment of their fellows. Role play is a powerful instrument for sensitizing children to the human and social implications of a wide range of situations, including cheating, breaking promises, and the practices of the bully. Insights thus gained may be used by the teacher to help children acquire a keener understanding of large-scale social, political, and economic situations encountered in the organized social studies program.

Other examples of role play are given in Chapters 9 and 12.

CONSTRUCTION

The construction by children of small-scale representations of objects they are studying has several values:

1. *Clinches learning.* As in all creative activities, impressions are clinched by expressive experiences that follow up the more passive learning.
2. *Provides realism.* Construction brings a touch of realism to the unit.
3. *Offers problem solving.* The construction process offers practical problem-solving opportunities: "How can we make the wheel turn?" "How can we cut the pieces so that they will fit more snugly?" "How can we make it sturdier to improve its appearance?" These are typical questions that arise and call for hard thinking.

---

[12]Wayne L. Herman, Jr., "Sociodrama . . . How It Works . . . How You Can Use It," *Grade Teacher*, 82 (September 1964), 84, 86, 153, Reprinted by permission of Macmillan Professional Magazines, Inc.

4. *Experiences with raw materials.* Children experience first-hand interaction with raw materials when they shape them or convert them to serve their purposes. This kind of activity fulfills a frequently overlooked need. Our society overflows with "instant," ready-mixed food packages and the processed products of chemical laboratories. Consequently children tend to have too little experience in handling raw materials.

5. *Experiences with adult tools.* Children learn to handle adult tools. As they saw, hammer, build, and paint, they acquire a sense of pride and experience much enjoyment merely from engaging in a creative process.

Construction for Active Play

Nursery and kindergarten children have built replicas of cars, airplanes, trains, and harbors—including bridges, freighters, tugboats, and truck depots—for floor play. Blocks are important elements in floor construction as brought out in Chapter 21 (see especially Figure 21.1). Children use the concrete objects symbolically as they rehearse or reclassify events of the adult world that they are still in the process of assimilating.[13]

BOX 15.2   **GRADES K-3**

Constructing a Play House

One class, after observing the construction of new homes in the neighborhood, undertook a house of its own, big enough for them to enter. The pupils drew and painted their plans for both the outside and inside of the house, including all details, from the design of the dormer windows to the doorknobs. They erected a wooden frame and covered it with cardboard, decorating the interior according to decisions reached during discussions of color harmony and color scheme. They made curtains and crude furniture, braided rugs, and pasted wallpaper made of newsprint with potato-print designs. They connected two battery-operated telephones and improvised a broom-handle floor lamp. Each pupil had a chance to "live" in the house with other members of his or her "family." This was more than a showpiece. It provided a springboard to the unit's intellectual content. Among the topics that such an enterprise may introduce are renting versus buying, blueprints, zoning, building permits, work of contractors, and the division and supervision of labor.

As children progress into the intermediate grades, construction projects continue to be appropriate. Older pupils become increasingly dissatisfied

---

[13]Millar, *The Psychology of Play*, chap. 10.

with crude representations and seek to construct objects that are true to life. Dissatisfied with the limitations of their craftsmanship, some may express a preference for playing with commercially produced models—planes, cars, boats, log cabins, and the like. These require merely fitting together parts that have already been shaped, then glueing and painting them. Although such pursuits rank low as creative activities they do possess some of the values of construction activities given above. Moreover, using prefabricated models may be a satisfactory way of meeting the needs of children whose standards of authenticity are high. Other children derive keen satisfaction from devoting much time and effort to constructing their own creative products. Particular motivation for construction is derived from the feeling of need for objects in dramatic play (see Figure 15.2).

Construction for Exhibit

Miniature representations of real objects aid learning if they accurately clarify details that are normally only hazily understood—such as how the logs are fitted and arranged in a pioneer's log cabin, how a suspension bridge is anchored, or how a canal lock works.

Another form of construction for exhibit is the diorama—a scene arranged in a shoe box on its side, the lid of which has been removed. It is constructed by a child who has done enough research on some phase of a unit to be able to portray it authentically and in detail; it might be a dairy farm, a

FIGURE 15.2.   Construction of a "prop" for a play.

dry dock, a colonial kitchen, a street in ancient Athens, or the like. Some teachers encourage all members of the class to take a subject for special study and to construct their own diorama. Each item (person, animal, tree, chair) is made separately and then anchored in the box with thumbtacks, tape, glue, clay, or some other device. Dioramas are fun to make, and the children who make them learn much through their preliminary research. By observing the finished dioramas of classmates, they learn of details not covered in their reading.

The construction of dioramas is difficult for nursery, kindergarten, and primary-grade children because it requires meticulous attention to detail and fine muscular coordination. These younger children can more successfully make larger models, which can be arranged as panoramas. Needless to say, pupils engaged in this work should be provided with photographs and books to insure authentic models.

BOX 15.3   **GRADES 4-8**

Constructing an Adobe House

The sixth-grade class was studying Mexico. During the warm weather in September one pupil's father, by prearrangement, dumped a load of dirt outside the classroom with his dumptruck. During the social studies period, small groups of children went outside, took their shoes and socks off, and, with their feet and a few sticks, mixed dirt, straw, and water. They then dumped the mixture into a one-foot-square form, constructed by a class member, to make an adobe brick. The form was lifted off the first brick and used repeatedly for 45 bricks. A couple of days later, when the sun had dried the bricks, they were carried into the classroom for construction of a three-by-four-foot adobe brick house. Two large poster boards were painted to resemble tile and to serve as the roof. Windows and a door were cut out of the walls. Later, the pupils decorated the interior of the house.

Teachers who feel uncertain about their competence to direct model making could consult a shop teacher or some of the excellent books on crafts written for teachers.

Teacher Responsibilities

Ideas for construction activities need to be screened in terms of (1) the likelihood of their teaching significant aspects of the unit, (2) the pupils' level of manual proficiency, and (3) the availability of materials and tools.

The teacher demonstrates the tools the class will use and guides the pupils as they hammer, saw, nail, and paste. He or she chiefly helps them use their tools efficiently and safely. Construction activities should give children a chance to try out their ingenuity, to make mistakes, and to figure out ways to correct them. The teacher should encourage them, but should be careful not to do for them what they can do for themselves.

Objects should be reasonably accurate representations, but strict adherence to authenticity is seldom practicable or necessary, provided the children understand in what respects their models differ from the real thing. For instance, since buffalo skins are unavailable, a blanket or sheet may be fashioned to serve as the outside of a tepee; and construction paper may be substituted for real feathers in making a headdress. All discrepancies between the children's creations and the real thing should be thoroughly discussed.

INDUSTRIAL ARTS

The term "industrial arts," as used here, refers to the reproduction of processes already worked out by others—for example, the making of paper, weaving, tanning a hide (see Figure 15.3), and the like. They are creative activities—although, on the surface, they may appear not to be—in that they enable children to discover the following:

1. The basic elements of a process that, in today's world of complex manufacture, became "lost" or at least "hidden."
2. The hard, muscular work, and often the tedium, required to carry out a process by hand.
3. The emotional gratification that accompanies any successful construction of a tangible object of utility or beauty.
4. The time-consuming nature of handcraft industry, which made leisure extremely rare and valuable before the industrial revolution;

FIGURE 15.3.   One step in tanning a hide.

the central economic role played by housewives and children in the days of handcraft; and the comparatively low standard of living.

The amount of *artistic* creativity called for varies from project to project. Sometimes children can give a personal touch to the created product. For example, they can weave something of their own design in connection with a study of the Indians of the Southwest—though the creation must be in keeping with the style and spirit of Pueblo blanket design, with which he can acquaint himself through books or museums. Tanning a hide on the other hand, is a chemical process that affords little or no opportunity for the child's creative impulses.

ART

Art is an important subject in the curriculum in its own right, deserving its own time allotment in the weekly schedule. Here it will be discussed, however, only insofar as it enriches the social studies. Its contributions in this respect are significant. The sketching, painting, or modelling of something being studied draws the pupil's attention to details otherwise overlooked. Moreover, this kind of activity is a form of recitation, aiding in the recall of things already studied but not yet fully learned or internalized. For instance, members of one second-grade class made pictures to summarize what they had learned in a study of fire prevention; pupils of a third-grade class painted pictures to illustrate activities of the American Indian; fourth-grade pupils, in a study of the colonial period, made crayon drawings showing "then" and "now"; and a sixth-grade class studying ancient Egypt modelled miniature temples out of clay and created designs on them in the Egyptian style.

It is apparent from these experiences that art in the social studies does not provide opportunities for *free* creativity. Nevertheless, in the examples just cited, some of the aims of art education were served. The children learned the use of art as a means of communication. Each child gave the art work his or her individual creative touch by expressing thoughts and feelings in his or her own way—although within an agreed-upon framework of content. Art became a means of enabling the creator to grow toward achieving his or her own identity.

Common Art Activities in Social Studies

There is no limit to the kinds of art experiences that can be provided in social studies. One art teacher, as a consultant to a classroom teacher, planned social studies projects involving batik, linoleum cuts, soap carving, applique, block printing, ceramics, mosaics, tile, wood burning, and stencils.

BOX 15.4   **GRADES K–8**

Some Popular Art Activities for Social Studies

Sketching (details of a process observed during a field trip to a paper mill; geographic features, such as streams and hills, in maps of the community; Victorian houses in the community; and so on).
Drawing (a flow chart of the steel-making process to illustrate a written report; figures on time lines as illustrated in the time lines shown in Chapter 22; and so on).
Modelling with clay or papier-mâché (the llama and other South American animals; the Arc de Triomphe; and so on).
Painting or crayoning (the cover of a booklet on East Africa; the decorative border of a map; and so on).

Murals

An instructive, colorful, and "fun" way to summarize a unit is through making a mural. The pupils may paint it on a long strip of sturdy wrapping paper and lay it on the floor of the hall or classroom while they are working on it. It may be either a unitary layout, depicting a harbor, a historical event, or a panorama of some aspect of a foreign culture—Swiss rural life for example (see Figures 15.4 and 15.5); or it may depict famous inventors, locomotive engines of the past 100 years, or aspects of medieval life. Poster paint, colored chalk, or pastels are commonly used. To prevent chalk from smudging, a colorless fixative may be sprayed over the completed mural.

Some details, such as the collars and cuffs of the figures represented, may be cut out of cloth and glued on the mural, as in collages. "Glitter" is a favorite addition also put on with glue.

The pupils in an entire class are normally too numerous to work on a mural all at once. A committee of six or eight children is about the right size. If the teacher plans several murals for the year, then every child can have the prized opportunity of working on one. A mural should be planned and executed cooperatively. Each child on the committee should have the opportunity to paint or draw some significant part of the study. Reasonably authentic, accurate representations usually require a good deal of research, and each child should be encouraged to visit libraries and museums with a sketchbook in preparation for the fulfillment of his or her part. The successful mural becomes a social project, requiring that children subordinate their private impulses to the larger purposes of the group.[14]

---

[14]For further suggestions see the pamphlet by Marjorie Kelley and Nicholas Ronkes, *Let's Make a Mural* (San Francisco: Fearon, n.d.). See also books on art listed at the end of this chapter under "Further Reading."

FIGURE 15.4.   Children working on a mural. Courtesy of the Merrick Union Free School Districts, New York.

Mural making is a delight to most children. They not only learn in various ways but also are thrilled with the work and the result. One class made a mural of Columbus' ships. Another made one of Civil War soldiers, for which committee members themselves served as patterns by lying on the wide brown paper, spread out on the floor of the corridor. The children in this school were so enthusiastic about mural making that they arrived before school at 8:00 A.M. to work on it. They also loved being able to take the murals home at the end of the school year, though perhaps their parents were a bit dismayed. One reported that her son's trophy reached twice around the large living room!

FIGURE 15.5.   A completed mural. Some of the figures are cutouts pinned to the mural. Courtesy of San Diego City Schools, California.

"Movies"

The misnamed "movie" is a well-known, popular device in primary or intermediate grades for presenting content, reviewing a social studies trip, or summarizing a unit or parts of a unit. A committee of children makes a series of pictures that eventually are mounted on a long strip of wrapping paper. Each end of the wrapping paper is fastened to a roller and placed in a box (see Figure 15.6). As the rollers are turned, the pictures slide past the open end of the box and tell the story, picture by picture.

MUSIC AND DANCE

The spirit of a people is often strikingly revealed by their music. Music teachers are able to supply suggestions for effective teaching procedures and for appropriate music for a particular unit. Books of folksongs and dances are listed in Chapter 10. They include songs of the American Indians, American blacks, Latin Americans, and other peoples throughout the world. There are work songs from the logging camp, the cattle range, the mine, the river, and the canal. Through singing folk songs and ballads and performing folk dances, children may acquire a feeling for other times and other places.

Teachers who lack sufficient confidence in their musical ability to conduct song and dance activities themselves, and who do not have access to a music teacher, may turn to the playing of records and tapes. There are hundreds of records of folk-dance music, folk songs, religious music and hymns, and instrumental music, authentically representing many cultures of the world. They are listed in the catalogues of major record companies, such as

FIGURE 15.6.   A "movie" device relates events in the life of George Washington.

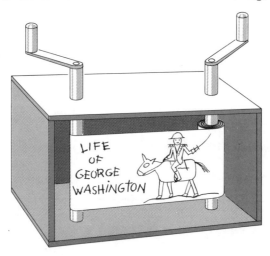

Decca and Columbia, and more specialized record companies, such as Folkway.

Music and dance, as used in social studies, afford children the opportunity to be creative through giving their own fresh interpretation to their reproductions of them. A wide variety of musical and dance activities are possible for any unit in the social studies. They provide the pupil a chance to discover and understand a new dimension of a people through this aspect of their culture.

TEACHING COMPETENCIES

This chapter has described how to perform the following tasks that are basic to teacher competency. The teacher should be able to:

1. "Warm up" a class for creative activity.
2. Convert the classroom into a workshop.
3. Guide children in informal dramatics.
4. Make beneficial uses of published plays.
5. Employ sociodrama to promote greater understanding of human relationships.
6. Plan construction and industrial arts activities.
7. Organize the creation of a mural.
8. Enrich selected social studies units with music and dance activities.

TRYING OUT SOME OF YOUR COMPETENCIES

1. Ask a small group of children to decide on a play based on the unit being studied. Plan, play, and evaluate the dramatics.
2. Plan a short-term construction project based on the unit being studied. Provide materials, instruction in tool safety, and sufficient time to complete the project.
3. Direct a social studies writing activity of a small group of children. With very young children, provide a means for recording their dictations, e.g., tape recorder, teacher-aide, older child.

FOR STUDY AND EXPLORATION

1. Why do some teachers neglect creative activities in the social studies?
2. Analyze the effect on children of teachers who have standards of perfection for creative products or of teachers who lack reasonable standards for creative products.
3. Why do you think the use of informal dramatic play has a solid positive research base for children of all ages and is beneficial in helping children with achievement, personality problems, social skills, moral development, etc.?

FURTHER READING

The many contributions of E. Paul Torrance to our knowledge of the creative process are brought together in three of his books: *Creative Learning and Teaching* (New York: Dodd, Mead, 1970), *Encouraging Creativity in the Classroom* (Dubuque, IA: William C. Brown, 1970), and *Is Creativity Teachable?* (Bloomington, IN: Phi Delta Kappa, 1973).

Helpful publications from National Education Association, Saw Mill Rd., West Haven, CT 06516 are: *What Research Says to the Teacher Series: Creativity; Creative Dramatics; Creative Teaching Tips; and How to Use Sociodrama.*

Many excellent ideas for guiding creative activities are contained in the following books:

Creative Dramatics

Joan E. Cass, *Helping Children Grow Through Play* (New York: Schocken, 1973).
Pauline Furness, *Role Play in the Elementary School: A Handbook for Teachers* (New York: Hart, 1976).
Nellie McCaslin, *Creative Dramatics in the Classroom*, 2nd ed. (New York: David McKay, 1974).

Art

Charles D. Gaitskell and Al Hurwitz, *Children and Their Art: Methods for the Elementary School*, 3rd ed. (New York: Harcourt, 1975).
Robert D. Hess, *An Activities Handbook for Teachers of Young Children* (Boston: Houghton Mifflin, 1972).
Norman Krinsky, *Art for City Children* (New York: Van Nostrand, 1970).
Viktor Lowenfeld and W. Lambert Brittain, *Creative and Mental Growth*, 6th ed. (New York: Macmillan, 1975).

Industrial Arts

Industrial Arts in the Middle School (Washington, DC: American Industrial Arts Association, n.d.).
Robert G. Thrower and Robert D. Weber (Eds.), *Industrial Arts for the Elementary School*, 23rd Yearbook of the American Council on Industrial Arts in Teacher Education (Bloomington, IL: McKnight, 1974).

Music and Dance

Dorothy Hickok and James A. Smith, *Creative Teaching of Music in the Elementary School* (Boston: Allyn and Bacon, 1974), chap. 8, "Music and the Social Studies."

Two practical articles on creativity are: A. M. Westcott, "Social Studies Smorgasbord," *Teacher*, 96 (November 1978), 102–104; and S. F. Heck, "Creative Classroom Environment: A Stage-Set Design," *Journal of Creative Behavior*, 12 (1978), 120–133.

*The kind of things which the children
observe on their trips and the kind
of use they make of their observations
is the most valid indication of their
maturity which the teacher has.*
Lucy Sprague Mitchell

FIELD TRIPS

First-hand experiences provide beneficial learning for pupils of all ages. Edith C. Forster found that fourth-grade children who went on field trips learned significantly more than a comparable group of fourth-graders who studied the same content without the benefit of field trips.[1] Merely reading about a bird sanctuary, Valley Forge, or assembly-line production is unlikely to clarify the elements that contribute to conceptual understanding as well as an on-site visit can. The visit fosters better comprehension of uncertain, nebulous terms and lends realism to the unit. Since such places and processes can obviously not be brought into the classroom, the class must go to them. When field trips take place at the beginning of a unit or at appropriate points during the main study of it, they supply motivation; when, on the other hand, they take place at the end of a unit, they serve as culminating activities.

---

[1] Edith C. Forster, "An Evaluation of the Field Trip in the Formation of Social Concepts and Generalizations," *Dissertation Abstracts*, 22 (July 1961), 181.

279

Placing Field Trips in Perspective

The fundamental objective of a field trip is to clarify or extend major concepts being studied. The community becomes a laboratory in which pupils become young social scientists. They explore and make observations; they look, listen, smell, taste, and touch; they collect information by taking notes, gathering live samples, taking snapshots, and interviewing appropriate people. After returning to the classroom, they reexamine their data. They compare, test, classify, and organize their material. Finally, they draw conclusions. Later they present their findings in the form of reports, exhibits, dramatic play, albums, or other creative products.

Caution is needed in choosing trips. The teacher should plan an excursion for his or her pupils only if it can clarify a lesson more adequately than other learning experiences can. Not all field trips offer instruction superior to classroom teaching. One of the authors took his class to a telephone exchange—an enormously complex organization. The trip was a waste of time. The guide had difficulty translating technical jargon into terms the children could understand. Moreover, he elaborated on nonessential details, which cluttered his explanation and confused the children. A couple of years later, the teacher found in a children's encyclopedia a lucid diagram of a telephone exchange, accompanied by a simply written description of its operation. In this case, the teacher himself, using an opaque projector and the information from the encyclopedia, would have served the class better than the useless trip did.

To avoid this kind of futile experience, teachers should, before taking a trip, compare its values with those of alternative experiences in order to decide which type of experience is superior. Films, filmstrips, lectures, books, models, and diagrams can also be highly effective—used alone, in various combinations, or as supplements to field trips.

Before the Trip

Detailed planning is necessary to insure the trip's success as a learning activity. Inadequate preparation may result in a slip-up that could cause the trip to fail in its aims and could subject the teacher to severe stress and worry. So, although planning may consume almost as much time as the excursion itself, it is worthwhile.

The Teacher Selects and Justifies the Trip.   The teacher should see that the trip satisfies several criteria before he or she decides definitely to make the journey. First, the children should be on a sufficiently high maturational level to benefit from the experience. For example, a trip to a hydroelectric dam or a large city newspaper plant entails a grasp of complex relationships that upper elementary or middle school pupils are more likely to have than are primary pupils.

Second, a majority of the class should demonstrate a need for the trip. If most of the children have already visited a farm with their parents and understand the concepts involved in operating one, a field trip to a farm obviously is unnecessary. If only a few members of the class display deficiencies in conceptual understandings about farm life, perhaps they could join in a trip with another class.

Third, there should be a close relationship between the trip and significant concepts being studied. For example, it would be germane for a class studying the fishing industry to visit Bonneville Dam to observe salmon working their way upstream over the fish ladders to their spawning grounds. On the other hand, a comparative study of human and nonhuman communal living that includes beaver communities would hardly justify a visit to the zoo to see beavers since most of the cages might contain too few specimens to exemplify community living.

Fourth, and finally, the trip must be justifiable in terms of distance, time, cost, and effort. Educational efficiency is an important consideration. A shocking example of disregard for this criteria is the transportation of one class to a chocolate factory about two driving hours away, where the children spent a half hour in the plant viewing assembly-line production, and then another two hours riding home.

The Teacher Requests Administrative Approval.   The teacher should obtain early endorsement for the trip from the principal or some other administrative official. Early approval will allow time for arranging necessary details.

The Teacher Previsits the Site.   There are three reasons why teachers should previsit the site (something, alas, they must normally do on their own time!). First, they must either sustain or reject their earlier justification of the trip. Second, they need to be sure the trip is a safe one on which to take children. Sometimes a trip, such as one to a steel mill, is fraught with hazards that may not be apparent to teachers until they visit the site on their own. Just the presence of high risk is sufficient reason to reject a trip. Third, teachers should familiarize themselves with the route and with the place to be visited and should talk with personnel who would serve as guides. Information collected on a previsit might concern:

- Road routes.
- Length of travel time.
- Safe intersection for crossing streets.
- Eating sites and facilities.
- Parking lots.
- Comfort stations.
- Opening and closing hours of site.
- Special regulations and rules.
- Features of interest to pupils.
- Cost and length of special presentations.

BOX 16.1   **ANY GRADE**

A Checklist of Conditions That Justify a Field Trip

1. The content of the trip is within the children's intellectual grasp.
2. The trip is a new, broadening experience for the pupils.
3. The subject matter of the trip clearly relates to the unit.
4. The trip offers distinctly superior opportunities to learn specific things not otherwise available.
5. The trip offers an opportunity for pupils to collect data that are new to them and that will enable them to discover generalizations they are not familiar with.
6. The guide is able to communicate effectively to children, and is willing to answer their questions.
7. The site can be reached without excessive expenditure of travel time. (If more than an hour is required to reach the site, the value of the trip should be reassessed.)
8. The trip, including the site, is safe.

BOX 16.2   **VARIOUS GRADES**

Examples of Field Trips

Shelter	Cross Cultural Differences	Transportation
Apartment house	Restaurants specializing in diverse national or cultural cuisines (see Figure 16.1)	Bus depot
Town house		Air terminal
Split-level house		Canal locks
Row house	Offices of organizations sponsoring diverse ethnic, cultural, or national purposes	Shipyard
Mobile-home park		Harbor
House boat		Dry dock
	Churches of diverse faith	

Government	Industry	Historical Sites
City Hall	Textile mill	Restorations and preservations (See Figures 16.2 and 16.3)
State or national capitol	Lumber mill	
	Coal mines	
Police station	Auto factory	Ghost towns
Courthouse	Food processing plant	Forts
Waterworks		Monuments

In addition, the teacher can collect brochures, on-site maps, pamphlets, pictures, and other printed materials for later personal study and for presentation to the class as background information. The teacher thus learns the lay of the land and can draw up a schedule for the events of the excursion.

The Teacher Obtains Written Approval of Parents.   The pupils' parents have a right to know about and to approve each trip away from the school. A typed request form signed by the parent or guardian is required *for each trip*. Teachers should file these forms for at least two months after an excursion is taken in order to protect themselves from any future charges of negligence arising from an injury or sickness suffered by a pupil during the trip.

A countersignature of the principal in addition to the teacher's signature assures parents of administrative approval. Some request forms include: "We (the parents) waive our right to hold the school responsible in any way for injuries occurring to our child during the trip." Even though parents may sign such a request form, the courts have ruled that a parent cannot legally sign away the rights of a child to collect damages caused by teacher negligence. Accidents do occur occasionally on trips, and teachers need to know about their own and the school's legal liability.

FIGURE 16.1.   Visiting a Chinese restaurant adds to an understanding of another culture. Courtesy of Prince George's County Public Schools, Maryland.

Elsbree, McNally, and Wynn describe legal liability this way:

> An important test of negligence is *foreseeability*. When in the judgment of the court a "reasonably prudent" person could have foreseen the harmful consequences of his act, the actor in disregarding the foreseeable consequences is liable for negligent conduct. . . . A second condition must also be present: his negligence must have been a proximate cause of whatever injury was suffered by the pupil or person involved. The injured party may have contributed to his own misfortune and if it can be demonstrated that the harm sustained was caused as much by the failure of the person suffering the injury to exercise reasonable cau-

FIGURE 16.2.   Visiting a restored historical site adds an impressive dimension to history. A field trip to Colonial Williamsburg, Virginia. Courtesy of Montgomery County Public Schools, Maryland.

tion as by the carelessness of the accused, then the courts will rule that recovery of damages is barred.

In determining whether or not the conduct of the injured party was below the standards to which he should conform for his own protection, the courts will take account of the age and maturity of the injured individual.[2]

It is much easier for a teacher to remain within the school's four walls than to take an excursion, and risk having to deal with sick, injured, misbehaved, or lost children. Nevertheless, if the guidelines in this section are followed and common sense is used, a teacher can be confident that an excursion will go smoothly. They almost always do.

FIGURE 16.3.   Examining equipment of an earlier historical period clarifies and broadens concepts. Courtesy of Prince George's County Public Schools, Maryland.

[2]Willard S. Elsbree, Harold J. McNally, and Richard Wynn, *Elementary School Administration and Supervision*, 3rd ed. (New York: American Book, 1967), pp. 24–25.

BOX 16.3   **ANY GRADE**

Necessary Information on the Request Form

1. Place to be visited.
2. Purpose of the trip.
3. Transportation to be used.
4. Departure and return dates, times, and places.
5. Arrangements for eating and housing.
6. Cost of the trip.
7. Proper dress for the trip.
8. Amount of supervision provided.

The Teacher Makes Reservations.   Reservations should be made well in advance. Leaders of groups of 10 or more persons normally need to give advance notification so that adequate accommodations and guide service can be arranged. It is prudent for the teacher to request an alternate date in case transportation is unavailable for his or her first choice.

The objectives of the tour should be discussed well beforehand with the guide, if possible, so that time can be distributed in accordance with the purposes of the trip. The teacher should mention the specific topics he or she would like covered, the age and maturity of the children, and the importance of simplicity in presenting information. Otherwise, the guide may overwhelm the children with information or may talk over their heads. Time should be allowed for the children to ask the guide questions and to comment on the presentation.

The teacher may reserve a bus or arrange for parents to provide transportation in their own cars. However, since management of a large group of children is facilitated if they are all in one vehicle, a bus is preferred. Moreover, bus companies employ skilled drivers and are adequately insured against legal liability.

Written confirmation is desirable for all reservations. A few days before the trip, the teacher should make final confirmation of reservations by telephone.

The Teacher Selects Chaperones.   The teacher should select chaperones with care, for the quality of supervision on the trip depends on the quality of persons selected. Parents are the usual choice for chaperones. While not every parent is qualified for this task, those who have had successful experiences as Sunday school teachers, recreation leaders, camp counselors, or athletic coaches of the age child they will supervise are normally excellent prospects. Help may be obtained from classroom "mothers" or "chairmen," who are often more familiar with the qualities of other parents than is the teacher. But the teacher should remain responsible for the final selection.

The number of parents required for supervision varies according to the age and general behavior of the children. Frequently, teachers of nursery school, kindergarten, and first grade recruit as many as one parent for every two or three children, whereas teachers of grades four through eight may find it sufficient to maintain a ratio of one parent for every 10 pupils. If upper elementary classes include children of unpredictable behavior, additional chaperoning may be required. As a protective measure, some preschool teachers take along a 40-foot length of rope for all the children to hold on to when walking from one place to another.

After the chaperones are selected, the teacher meets with them and prepares them for their duties. Each parent is given a list of the names of the children for whom he or she is responsible, annotated perhaps with a description of special traits of certain children. Placing name tags on children on the day of the trip is helpful if pupils are unknown to their chaperones. Teachers report that liberties are often taken by children who are placed in a group supervised by their own parent; consequently, these children are better assigned to another adult. The teacher is not assigned to a group; he or she needs to be free for general supervision of the trip.

The Teacher Plans the Trip in Detail.   Although the teacher is responsible for planning the excursion, children can assist with some tasks, such as scheduling the day and mapping out the trip. Some important planning activities include:

- Making provisions for children who for one reason or another cannot go on the trip.
- Making a route and time schedule of events for the entire itinerary.
- Deciding on locations for rest stops, lunch, intersections to cross, comfort stations, parking.
- Arranging a "buddy" system, consisting of paired children.
- Notifying art, music, and other special teachers who normally meet with the class that the pupils will be away on a trip.
- Planning activities for the pupils to engage in while en route, if that is deemed necessary.
- Assembling a first-aid kit to take along.
- Listing pupils' names and home telephone numbers, also school telephone number, in case of emergency and keeping the list in a billfold.

The Teacher Prepares the Children for the Trip.   The teacher should discuss some important matters with the class in order to prepare the children and give them necessary information. With older children, as already explained, some class members may assume this reponsibility, or at least part of it. The purposes of such a discussion include:

- Instilling motivation for the trip and establishing a serious attitude toward it.
- Presenting the purpose of the trip.
- Building a background of information by describing the specific features to be observed on the trip and by distributing or posting pamphlets, pictures, monographs, and maps.
- Enlisting the class's aid in jotting down important things to look for, questions to find answers to, and standards of behavior to observe.
- Assigning certain topics to small groups to investigate during the trip.
- Describing safety standards, unusual hazards of the trip, and emergency procedures, including rules for a lost child to follow.
- Discussing appropriate dress and money and other items needed.
- Describing a plan for follow-up of the trip.

During the Field Trip

The supervision of children is a full-time job, requiring balance between too much management, which regiments children and discourages their enthusiasm and inquiry, and too little direction which confuses pupils and results in disorganization. Maintaining a relaxed, unhurried, enthusiastic climate promotes an enjoyable trip for everyone. One of the chief jobs of the teacher is to count children frequently, especially after leaving one site and going to another and *always* when children board the bus.

Unexpected things are apt to happen, as both authors know from trips in their early teaching years. There was the boy who, on a class trip to a fish market, buried his shoes in the sand on a nearby beach and then couldn't find them. He had to go home in his stocking feet! Another time, the subway car doors closed with all the class safely in the car except one child, who somehow failed to get in and was left behind on the platform. One teacher reports having lost pupils at a world fair. Much about field trips can be learned only through experience. Children should be instructed in advance that in case they become lost they should stay where they are and seek out the nearest policeman or other official, or a store clerk.

Throughout the trip, all adults should be alert to the need for clarifying difficult concepts, pointing out important places, objects, or processes that are overlooked, and assisting children with special problems, such as loading or unloading a camera or purchasing souvenirs. Other duties entail maintaining appropriate noise levels on and off the bus, enforcing agreed-upon standards of conduct, and encouraging common courtesy. Naturally, a teacher should not allow pupils to engage in potentially dangerous activities such as climbing on the huge boulders of Devil's Den at Gettysburg National Battleground. Also, the collection of specimens at the site must be done under the supervision of the teacher with permission from authorities. The collection of specimens on land under Federal jurisdiction requires a permit.

When a bus breaks down or some other delay occurs, the school must be notified as soon as possible.

After the Field Trip

A Follow-Up Is Held after the Trip. Discussions conducted immediately following a trip often include pupils' reactions to incidents unrelated to the purpose of the trip; for instance, a child may remark, "We lost time when Peter got lost," or "Sally dropped her ice cream cone when Billy's arm struck her accidentally." If the follow-up is deferred until a few days after the excursion, most of these irrelevant events will seem less important.

The follow-up comprises (1) a discussion of the content gleaned, (2) enrichment of the subject matter, (3) an evaluation of the pupils' social behavior, (4) an assessment of the learning acquired, and (5) the writing of letters of appreciation to the hosts.

A discussion of the content is essential for promoting conceptual understanding and for correcting faulty impressions. Because young children often are attracted to the insignificant details of what they saw during their tour—a cat on the premises, a bright motorcycle, or the guide's uniform, for example, the teacher must continually focus on the purposes of the trip by stressing the new information that they gained. This can be done by directing their attention to the objectives or questions listed during the planning stage of the trip and by gently ignoring any irrelevancies.

The teacher should raise questions, such as: "What did we see?" "How did the process work?" "Why do they do it that way?" "What are some important things that we observed?" "What was the relationship between *this* and *that*?"

A summary of the trip should be undertaken to highlight significant understandings. Summaries can take many different forms—for instance, an outline, individual write-ups, an experience story, process charts, pictorial summaries, postcard and photographic displays, a time line of events, or an exhibit of memorabilia.

Enrichment activities should fulfill children's interest in a particular facet of the trip's subject matter and should probe questions that remain unanswered. These activities may include reference reading, interviews with experts, or creative expression through art, construction, dramatic play, and other outlets.

The pupils should also evaluate their social behavior during the trip. Their behavior should be matched against the standards set by the class before the trip was made. This may be done through group discussion or through individual self-evaluation. In the latter case, each pupil may respond in writing to the following items:

1. How well did I cooperate with my chaperone?
2. In what ways did I make the bus driver's job easier or harder?
3. I helped or hindered the guide in these ways: . . . .
4. My behavior as a member of the group could be described as . . . .

The quality of the pupils' learning, their acquisition of information, their appreciation of various aspects of the trip, and their attitudes and interests may be informally appraised by the teacher during all phases of the follow-up. The teacher can do this by administering teacher- or pupil-constructed informal tests, if appropriate, and by noting the ideas expressed, the kinds of questions raised, the thoroughness and accuracy of reports and the quality of work done in enrichment activities. For the pupil, the emphasis should be on such questions as "What did I learn?" "What do I still not understand?"

BOX 16.4   **GRADES K–3**

A Trip to a Firehouse

During a visit to a local firehouse, the kindergarten children tried on different parts of a fireman's protective clothing, were given a tour of the firehouse including the sleeping quarters, and driven for a short ride on a fire truck. On the way back to the school the teacher noticed that the children appeared disappointed. During a discussion of the trip later in the classroom, the children expressed dissatisfaction in not seeing a house on fire, which in their minds was the definition of *firehouse*.

BOX 16.5   **GRADES 4–8**

A Trip to a Textile Factory

By Sister M. Euphrosine

I brought a few cotton bolls into the classroom. Soon several youngsters, attracted by the downy softness of the bolls, began to investigate them. They touched the bolls and accidentally felt the little hard knobs-seeds. The questions came thick and fast. What are those hard things? How can thread be made from this fluffy thing? Is this made into cloth? This was just the proper motivation for a field trip.

We planned a trip to a textile factory which was located in the neighborhood. Preliminary preparations were made. The children discussed the purpose of the trip, collected information about cotton from available sources prior to the trip, and formulated the questions they were to ask at the plant. They also outlined the rules for proper and courteous conduct while on the trip. Arrangements were made with the personnel of the factory, and the specific aims of the trip were mutually agreed upon.

At the factory, under the direction of the guide, the children saw the large bales of raw cotton and followed the process until they saw the finished product. They were fascinated by the carding, roving, spinning, and weaving processes. Many of the questions were answered during the

(Continued)

tour; others remained to be answered during the discussion which would follow after they returned to school. Upon leaving, the pupils expressed their gratitude for the services rendered and returned to school with such souvenirs as samples of cotton, cotton thread, cloth, literature, etc.

From this lesson, the children had learned that their community was an important unit in their state and in their country. They learned that raw cotton came from the south and some came from Egypt and Asia, that our factory and other factories ship their products to clothing manufacturers, department stores, chain stores, auto builders, and manufacturers of furniture, and that some of it is stored in large warehouses and through the Exchange Markets finds its way to European, Asian, and other foreign outlets. The children made maps showing where cotton is grown, and showing important cotton markets and where most of the textile factories are located.

For the teacher, the important questions are, "What did the pupils really learn?" "Was it worth making the trip in order to obtain this learning, or could it have been achieved equally well through other means?" "Which procedures worked satisfactorily during the trip?" "Which procedures should be changed?" "What items did I overlook?" "Should the trip be modified in any way?"

A few days after the trip, it is only courteous to send letters of appreciation to chaperones, bus drivers, and hosts. At preschool and primary levels, several small groups of children may dictate thank-you letters to the teacher. In the upper grades, the task of writing letters to different persons may be assigned to various groups of children.

Trips by Fewer than the Entire Class

When it is impractical for an entire class to take a trip to a pertinent site, it may be possible for children to go either individually or in small groups. Sometimes parents are willing to escort their children to the point of interest outside school hours. This is a kind of "homework" that pupils and their parents can enjoy together. Or, the teacher may arrange to take a small group from the class on a Saturday. Or if the object to be studied is in the immediate neighborhood, pupils may be assigned to make the necessary observations independently, perhaps on their way home. In each of these cases, those involved can report their findings to the class.

BOX 16.6   **ANY GRADE**

Keep a File of Successful Field Trips

Here's a job for the entire faculty. Planning a trip is so time-consuming that a record of successful trips should be made as an aid and time-

(Continued)

saver in planning future trips. Some faculties, making generous use of the telephone book's yellow pages, have compiled the information into booklets. For each trip, record the following information:

1. Name and mailing address of the place to be visited.
2. Name, address, and telephone number of the person to contact for arrangements.
3. Road maps, hand-drawn or commercial, for each trip; round-trip mileage and time required for travel.
4. List of special presentations, with schedule and length of tours, admission rates, brochures, and special requirements.
5. Content information in brief: significant facts, concepts, and generalizations.
6. List of things to look for.
7. Hazards to watch out for and safety precautions needed.
8. Location of eating, parking, and rest room facilities at the site and along the route.
9. List of other places of interest nearby.
10. Follow-up questions, enrichment activities, and suggested evaluation procedures.

CONSULTANTS

The social studies consultant is a person in the community, but outside the school, with special experience, knowledge, or expertise in an appropriate area, who is invited to talk to the class. The consultant's specialty may be his or her vocation, talent, or travel experience.

A unit seems to come alive when an expert presents a first-hand account of experiences, a working document, a piece of equipment, or pictures. Generally, we all enjoy contact with a knowledgeable person who has had experiences different from our own. A consultant may be used in the beginning of a unit to stimulate children's interest in the topic or in any other phase of the unit.

Consultants and Aides in the Classroom

Consultants as Speakers. Although careful selection of speakers is needed to insure an appropriate presentation to the children, it is often impractical or impossible to appraise first-hand a consultant's ability to relate to children before inviting him or her to the classroom. If this is the case, it is advisable to seek a recommendation from a reliable person before the speaker is invited.

Special speakers would be used more often if teachers knew where to find them. This problem would disappear if each school would keep a central catalogue or file of experts who are willing to be called upon occasionally. Some principals send to all adult residents in the community printed forms explaining that the school is trying to find individuals willing to give their services as consultants. If the recipient is interested, he fills out the form, indicating his area of knowledge and stating the approximate grade level at which he would prefer to contribute. It is a good idea for a school to designate someone—the school librarian or an interested teacher or parent—to serve as curator of the catalogue and to see that it is kept up to date. The file may be arranged alphabetically by occupation (author, carpenter, engineer, librarian, musician, nurse, town official, and so forth) or by subject of special knowledge (conservation, France, medieval history, pottery, and so forth).

The teacher will, of course, discuss ahead of time with the speaker such matters as the allotted time for the presentation, the specific topics about which the class seeks information, the level of maturity of the class, and the desirability of allowing time for questions and discussion.

The children's reaction to the speaker is enhanced if they can participate in the planning session. They can help set up objectives, list questions to ask the speaker, assign certain responsibilities among themselves—such as the operation of projection equipment, if required—and review standards of behavior for meeting with the guest.

The value of a consultant increases when attendance is limited to the teacher's own class, when the classroom climate is friendly and hospitable, and when the proceedings are kept informal, relaxed, and unhurried. During the presentation the teacher should remain in the background, but be prepared to alert the consultant when children are missing the meaning of ideas or terms. Before the consultant leaves, children should have a chance to raise questions or to react in other ways.

BOX 16.7   **GRADES K–3**

The Custodian Tells a Class about His Job

Although several attempts by the teacher were made to persuade the members of her second-grade class to keep the classroom tidy and clean, the children continued to discard scraps of paper on the floor, to leave the sink messy with water paint smears, and to scatter personal possessions around the room.

The custodian was asked to speak to the class and describe his job at the school with particular emphasis on cleaning classrooms—what he did and some of his feelings about the different kinds of classroom conditions that confronted him (without identifying specific rooms) each day. The brief, low-key talk was descriptive and avoided critical remarks. Afterward the children asked the custodian questions.

The visit effectively established rapport between the custodian and the children. Tidiness increased from that day on! During the day and before school ended, pupils voluntarily displayed individual and general responsibility for a neat room. They spoke to the custodian when their paths crossed; and even invited him to participate in their recess kickball games, which he accepted.

FIGURE 16.4.   An expert on colonial homecrafts demonstrates spinning. Courtesy of Montgomery County Public Schools, Maryland.

Following the speaker's departure, the teacher and the pupils should evaluate the presentation by asking such questions as "What was gained from the presentation?" "What was unclear?" and so on, in this fashion. Reference reading, creative writing, and construction may be planned on the basis of what was learned. Thank-you letters are, of course, appropriate.

BOX 16.8   **GRADES 4–8**

Mountain-Climbing Consultant Enriches Unit

During a study of Switzerland, Mary told the class that her father was a mountain climber. The teacher invited him to visit the class and to bring appropriate mountaineering equipment. The children enjoyed his demonstration of varied materials and were permitted to handle the equipment. The father allowed the apparatus to be placed in two display cases in the foyer of the school: there were an ice ax, cleated boots, thermal underwear, mittens, windproof outer garment, snow glasses, first-aid kit, cooking gear, sleeping bag, tent, packsack, compass, waterproof matches, crampon, folding lantern, pitons, snap rings, and line.

Lay Aides.   The introduction of teacher-aides to the classroom scene seemed to spawn an acceptance of the notion that uncertified but capable persons in the community can contribute substantially to the learning process of children. A visitor to some elementary schools may observe several mothers working as volunteers with individual children or small groups in the classrooms, corridors, or small conference rooms. Many chores of the social studies are appropriate for such lay helpers, including taking dictation; discussing and building understanding of concepts; preparing instructional materials such as master copies, flannel board materials, displays, and apparatus for learning centers; previewing audiovisual materials; helping pupils who have been absent to catch up with the rest of the class in content, skills, and appreciation for particular aspects of a unit; tutoring; and supervising and assisting committees engaged in creative activities such as art, construction, dramatics, research, and experimentation.

Personal Interviews

One or two children may be asked to see if they can arrange a personal interview with a resource person who is unable to take the time for a school visit, but is willing to be seen in his or her work milieu. One advantage of the interview procedure is the personal responsibility that the one or two children must assume in arranging and conducting it. Over the course of a school year, every child in the classroom may have the experience of interviewing someone. It is easy to record interviews on cassettes and play them back in class.

The teacher should provide pupils with guidelines for conducting an interview, such as those in Box 16.9. Children should practice following the rule in advance through mock interviews with one another in the classroom.

Some teachers have reported success in having an entire class visit a consultant at his or her place of work, or elsewhere, for an interview. One or two children may still conduct the interview, but the entire class is in attendance, and, following the interview, others in the class may wish to raise questions.

BOX 16.9   **GRADES 4–8**

Guidelines for Conducting a Personal Interview

Children normally need some direct instruction in interview techniques. As needed, the following suggestions may be made:

1. Focus on a specific topic to be investigated.
2. Build up a background in the content.
3. Write down specific, open-ended questions that will treat the topic thoroughly.
4. Select an appropriate resource person.
5. Arrange an appointment by writing or by telephoning. Suggest alternate dates and times. Place the interviewee's convenience ahead of your own.
6. Send the resource person in advance a copy of your questions so that he or she will be prepared.
7. Plan ways to open and close an interview.
8. Learn to listen attentively. Ask for clarification of unclear ideas. Jot

(Continued)

down notes. Be alert to cues for drawing the interview to a close. Thank your host.

9. Follow up the interview with a personal letter of thanks.
10. Organize your notes for a clear, concise report that is illustrated by pictures, models, charts, diagrams, graphs, or audiovisual aids.

BOX 16.10   **GRADES K-3**

A Kindergarten Class Talks with a Pilot

One of the class member's fathers was a pilot with Northwest Orient Airlines. He visited the class in his uniform and described various parts of his job both on the ground and in the air. He brought airplane models, a water flotation apparatus for passengers, some large photographs of airplanes, and a short film of a flight showing what a take-off, clouds, ground, and landing look like from the pilot's seat. The children asked questions they had jotted down in anticipation of the visit. His visit clarified many concepts and ignited high interest.

BOX 16.11   **GRADES 4-8**

A Class Interviews an Old-Time Resident on Community History

By Sara N. Dalton

One class was interviewing a neighbor—an old-timer in the community. They stood beside a busy thoroughfare listening to the roar of the traffic. "This was an old Indian trail known as the Allegheny Trail," said the man. His words so impressed the class that during the ensuing weeks the children interviewed other residents and also searched the library for more information about the history and development of their community's roads and transportation.

MUSEUMS

The most effective field trips for elementary schools are to enterprises and operations which are currently functioning as active parts of community life. On the other hand, museums are storehouses of artifacts and art objects that often justify a field trip, especially in studies of the past. Teachers should explore the resources of museums within a 50-mile radius of their schools in search of exhibits that might bring a sharp touch of reality to the social studies unit. Among displays that teachers have found of value are:

- Horse-drawn coaches.
- Antique autos and airplanes.
- Tribal habitat groups.
- Early manned space-vehicle.
- Musical instruments and articles of dress of Native Americans.
- Rifle and saddle covers of the frontier.
- Working model of Whitney's cotton gin.
- Stages in the development of shipbuilding.
- Implements and machines of the days before steam power.
- Paintings of a particular period or region.

When the museum visit is identified with a specific unit of study, the museum can be used as a kind of laboratory to answer questions raised during the planning stage of the trip. Usually pupils list more questions than are answered, but the follow-up of the visit can lead the children to employ additional sources of information, such as encyclopedias, picture file, audio-visuals, interviews with experts, and both fiction and nonfiction books in children's literature.

The temptation to try to see all the displays in a large museum should be shunned, and the class's attention should be confined to the object of the visit. "Doing" a large museum is unprofitably fatiguing.

The role of the museum in society is changing. Early museums were designed for a smaller, less literate population. Now, contents of museums are pictured in books, colored slides, television, and films. The public is more sophisticated and expects—and deserves—more from a museum than merely a display of inert objects behind glass. As a result, the class with a single, specific purpose for a visit is well served in museums that have kept abreast of today's interests.

The response of leading museums to school needs has been to provide lessons to classes of children on designated subjects, such as Africa or the story of cotton. Relevant materials are taken from their cases for the children to touch, try on, examine, manipulate, and try out. A specialist on the museum staff tells what is known about their origin, function, and place in the total culture. One museum takes the position that its ancient musical instruments should not lie mute in display cases; it is rebuilding some three-thousand ancient instruments and is prepared to teach students to play them.

Not all "museum" objects are in museums. Some may be viewed in private homes or in libraries or other public buildings. Objects may range from furniture to farm implements. Some are heirlooms and collections from various historical periods and various parts of the earth. A Maryland schoolboy, with the help of classmates, brought a cannonball preserved from the War of 1812 from his cellar to the classroom.

Authentic objects that represent topics being studied help to vivify social studies units for pupils. Children in a first-grade class who had the opportunity to handle a fireman's coat gained better understanding of the concept "insulation." By seeing a spinning wheel operate, fourth-graders understood how animal or vegetable hairs can be twisted to make thread, and they appreciated the time-consuming nature of the task before the era of machine spinning.

TEACHING COMPETENCIES

This chapter tells how to perform the following tasks that are basic to teacher competency. The teacher should be able to:

1. Select and justify the trip.
2. Previsit the site and collect information that will be used in planning the trip with children.
3. Send to parents acceptable request forms for trips that provide necessary information.
4. Select and assign qualified chaperones.
5. Plan the trip in detail, with the children assisting in some phases of the planning.
6. Adequately prepare children for the trip.
7. Supervise a field trip in a responsible way.
8. Conduct a comprehensive follow-up after the trip.
9. Select and use consultants as speakers in the classroom; involve children in the activity: planning, reacting to the speaker, and evaluating the activity.
10. Effectively guide children in the use of the personal interview as a mode of collecting data on a given topic.

TRYING OUT SOME OF YOUR COMPETENCIES

1. Take a field trip to a site that is related to a social studies unit. Plan the trip thoroughly, provide adequate supervision, and after the trip, conduct a follow-up that includes thank-you letters, discussion of learnings, enrichment, and evaluation of pupils' conduct.
2. Invite a consultant to visit the classroom. In the entire activity, provide for student input and responsibility.
3. Give instruction to children on the procedures for conducting a personal interview. Have each child interview a person in the community on his or her opinions about a controversial topic in current affairs.

FOR STUDY AND EXPLORATION

1. Discuss with an experienced teacher his/her experiences—both positive and negative—in taking a class on a field trip.
2. React to the statement: "The field trip is the best activity a teacher can give children."
3. Why do some teachers welcome aides in the classroom while other teachers do not want them in their classrooms?

FURTHER READING

The How to Do It Series, edited by Jack W. Miller and published by the National Council for the Social Studies, 3615 Wisconsin Avenue, N.W., Washington, DC 20016, has several appropriate titles relating to some of the resources mentioned in this chapter. Among these, *How to Utilize Community Resources* (No. 13) by Miller R. Collings includes an extensive listing of places in the community that pupils can experience directly, as well as suggestions for bringing community resources into the classroom; and *How to Conduct a Field Trip* (No. 12) by Edgar C. Bye presents a rationale for trips and gives detailed information about liability and the necessary precautions to take.

One of the most comprehensive publications on field trips is by Shirley A. Brehm, *A Teacher's Handbook for Study Outside the Classroom* (Columbus, OH: Merrill, 1969). This paperback describes visiting trips, collecting trips, and field studies. Another helpful book is by Helen Ross Russell, *Ten Minute Field Trips. Using the School Grounds for Environmental Studies* (New York: Ferguson, 1973).

Although this section deals with reading resources, a departure is justified for a mention of the old but superior film *Near Home*, which is used in numerous courses in elementary and junior high social studies for preservice teachers. This splendid 25-minute film was produced by the British Ministry of Education in 1946 and exemplifies the use of the community in the unit method of teaching (available from most educational lending libraries).

The following publications can be purchased inexpensively from National Education Association Order Department, Saw Mill Road, West Haven, CT 06516: *Parents: Active Partners in Education: Parents Put Yourself in This Picture—Be a School Volunteer; Parent Involvement: A Key to Better Schools: Basic Guidelines for Parent Volunteers* (a transparency); *Teacher Aides at Work; and Library Service, Total Community*. Procuring, orienting, and using aides effectively is presented in Bryce Perkins, *Getting Better Results from Substitutes, Teacher Aides, and Volunteers* (Englewood Cliffs, NJ: Prentice-Hall, 1966).

An excellent description of some social action projects is offered in chap. 9 of R. Murray Thomas and Dale I. Brubaker, *Decision in Teaching: Elementary Social Studies* (Belmont, CA: Wadsworth, 1971). Included are some projects on enhancing the environment, welcoming newcomers, promoting social welfare, and exerting influence. A pertinent article is by C. Vitone, "Developing Language through Experiences," *Momentum*, 10 (February 1979), 27.

17 Using a Variety of Instructional Media

A discussion of teaching aids may seem like an unusual context in which to consider the teacher's role in teaching. Yet, withal, the teacher constitutes the principal aid in the teaching process as it is practiced in our schools.
Jerome S. Bruner

A conspicuous feature of today's elementary school classroom is the abundance of instructional aids that are there to carry out much of the teaching. Media that have particular relevance for the social studies will be discussed in this chapter, with the exception of those treated in detail elsewhere: reading materials (Chapter 19), maps and globes (Chapter 21), and tests (Chapter 18).

Because of the quantity and variety of instructional media purchased by school systems in the past decade, the central school library is a multimedia center containing books, records, tapes, filmstrips, fish, plants, small animals, and a host of other audiovisual materials. Some schools have media specialists whose function is to provide service to the curricular areas of the school. This service involves notifying teachers of available media, surveying teachers' needs, collecting and making available media and materials for social studies units being taught, scheduling the media center for pupil use, conducting an annual inventory, and evaluating the quality of services pro-

300

vided to teachers. Moldstad reports that the successful integration of media with the instructional program saves a significant amount of learning time; moreover, students react favorably to media instruction.[1]

GUIDELINES FOR THE PURCHASE, USE, AND EVALUATION OF LEARNING MEDIA

Involve Yourself in the Media Program

The teacher is the central figure in using instructional media and ought to be significantly involved in the decision-making process involving the selection, use, and evaluation of media.[2]

Select Learning Aids That Promote the Objectives of Instruction

Before ordering media, teachers should ask themselves questions such as "What specifically can I use the media for?" "To what degree will the media help me accomplish my instructional objectives?" Aspects of content must also be evaluated, such as accuracy, suitability for learners, and social acceptability of the information. These and related questions help teachers to avoid ordering showy but ineffective media that they will only infrequently use; they also make teachers wary of other items that they might be tempted to purchase out of a desire to keep up with the teacher next door or the school down the street.

Select Learning Aids That Emphasize Thinking

The teacher should locate materials that will promote thinking in order to counterbalance what is often an unjustifiable emphasis on the memorization of such facts as kinds of products grown, exports, imports, capitals, and dates. Some of the newer films, for example, raise questions for discussion and pose problems for solution; and social studies simulation games call for critical thinking and decision making.

Use Learning Aids to Meet Diverse Pupil Needs

To match the diverse abilities and learning styles of pupils, a reasonably wide assortment of instructional materials is needed. Types of materials that prove of special benefit to pupils of given abilities or cognitive styles are illustrated in Box 17.1. The teacher can also keep instruction fresh and invigorating for all by alternating the various media of learning.

---

[1]John A. Moldstad, "Selective Review of Research Studies Showing Media Effectiveness: A Primer for Media Directors," *AV Communications*, 22 (Winter 1974), 387–407.

[2]John J. Cogan, "A Rationale for the Selection of Instructional Materials," *Social Education*, 37 (October 1973), 548–550.

BOX 17.1   **VARIOUS GRADES**

Examples of Instructional Media

Example of Instructional Material	*Description*
A map with a legend including a symbol to denote firehouses.	Abstract.
A scale model of a firehouse.	Concrete.
A dramatization of the first Thanksgiving on audiotape.	Verbal.
A collection of pictures showing the first Thanksgiving.	Nonverbal.
A map showing the route of Lewis and Clark.	Permits passivity.
A blank map on which the route of Lewis and Clark must be reconstructed from data from their journals.	Requires activity.
A bulletin board with pictures of houses of contrasting design.	Lends itself to short attention span.
A 30-minute film showing variations in architecture.	Requires sustained attention.
An encyclopedia, to be used for a report on Mexican life.	Contains challenging reading.
A picture album on Mexico with captions made by pupils.	Contains easy reading.
A time line depicting the development of large-scale manufacturing.	Serves review purpose.
A television program entitled "Ralph Nader, Nemesis of Car Manufacturers."	Serves enrichment purpose.
A diagram of the circular flow of goods and services, to be studied.	Calls for memorization.
The simulation game, *Economy*, designed to promote understanding about the circular flow of goods and services in the economic system, to be played.	Calls for use of higher cognitive processes.

(Continued)

A learning center that instructs pupils to alphabetize certain topics, and, using the newspaper, to list the pages on which the topics can be found.	Maintains old skills.
A learning center that has a political cartoon on display for pupils to study and interpret.	Demands learning of new skills.
A film showing ways of using leisure time.	Simply requires viewing in order to be understood.
A filmstrip on leisure time whose final frame asks: "How can leisure be spent profitably?"	Requires thinking and discussion in order to be understood.
A standard classroom wall map.	Lends itself to large group use.
A programmed lesson on how to read a map.	Lends itself to individual use.

With Newer Learning Aids, Purchase
Only a Few Items for a Trial Run

It is wise for teachers to appraise a new item in terms of its fitness for the developmental level of their pupils, the degree of interest that the children have in using it, its durability, and its suitability in serving their teaching goals. This would apply to such newer media as simulation games and programmed materials.

Learn How to Use the Learning Aids Properly

Teachers cannot derive maximum benefit from learning aids unless they know how to use them properly and what all of their possibilities are. For instance, they should know that on most tape recorders they can use both edges of the tape. The machine has two speeds, one accommodating talk and another accommodating faster sounds such as music, and it also provides for a public address hookup. A teacher who does not know about the recorder's versatility restricts the benefits of the tape recorder to the learning process. Another aid about which teachers may lack sufficient knowledge is the filmstrip projector. It is quite possible that some teachers are unaware that a simple metal part, attached to the underside of many machines in an unobtrusive manner, makes the necessary adjustment for showing slides. Unfortunately, media like these often remain showpieces because few people know how to operate them. Some schools, aware of this, schedule in-service days for instruction and training in the proper use of educational media. In a study of randomly selected elementary and secondary teachers, Leader and Null reported that "teachers who had undergone in-service programs on media and teachers who are familiar with the operation of audiovisual equipment used significantly more films than . . . teachers who had no in-service training and who were unfamiliar with the equipment."[3]

Use Learning Aids During the Regular Social Studies Period

Some instructional materials, such as simulation games, learning kits, and manipulative devices, offer much enjoyment to children. Ironically, because of this, some teachers restrict their use to before and after school or during recess and lunch hour. It is advisable that those who subscribe to this policy consider incorporating such materials into the regular social studies period. There is nothing wrong with pleasurable learning, and furthermore, these materials require teacher supervision if pupils are to get the most out of them.

Conduct an Evaluation of the Effectiveness of the Learning Aids

The ultimate adoption and use of an instructional aid ought to be based on its effectiveness in promoting the goals of instruction. Teachers should ask themselves the following questions:

1. To what extent did this educational material accomplish what I thought it would? What did it fail to accomplish?
2. What is the most valuable outcome of using the aid?
3. How is what this aid accomplished different from what other aids have accomplished?
4. What are the specific limitations of the aid in terms of available classroom space, class size, and availability of required materials for the aid?
5. What improvements are needed in teacher-pupil planning for its use?
6. What problems arose that will have to be resolved before I use the aid again?

TYPES OF INSTRUCTIONAL MEDIA

Multimedia Kits

Some of the newer media comprise kits containing original source materials, films, filmstrips, audiotapes, records, charts, maps, photographs, games, transparencies, artifacts, and other items. Most of the filmstrips in multimedia kits are synchronized to records or audiotapes. The trend toward

---

[3]Harry O. Leader and Eldon J. Null, "What Kind of Teachers Use Instructional Films?" *Audiovisual Instruction*, 19 (February 1974).

multimedia programs accommodates both individual and group instruction. The materials cover isolated topics or are related to the year's curriculum. The rationale for multimedia is to produce a variety of learning materials that appeal to a cross section of learning styles. A list may be obtained from Social Science Education Consortium, Boulder, CO 80302.

Motion Pictures

Motion pictures give the viewer a front seat at the action, whether it be Apollo blasting off for a lunar landing, a sawmill making felled trees into finished lumber, or the incoming tide from the Bay of Fundy going up the Reversing Falls on the St. John's River. Cox found that more than 200 children in fourth and fifth grades liked best those films that depicted children in realistic settings.[4] Donald A. Ingli reported that films contribute substantially to students' factual learning, vocabulary growth, and critical thinking.[5]

An intriguing development is that of the 8 mm single-concept film.[6] The typical 16 mm instructional film runs from 20 to 30 minutes or more and tends to introduce many concepts at a rapid clip. The single-concept film, on the other hand, runs for less than five minutes and is designed to tie in with a specific lesson. Even the unique physical characteristic of the film recommends it: It is enclosed in a cartridge that fits easily into a lightweight, compact projector, thus eliminating the necessity of threading. The film can be stopped, reversed, and viewed at any point; a lighted room is satisfactory for viewing. Cartridges come with or without sound. These short film loops are designed for individual or small group viewing. As with 16 mm film, the 8 mm single-concept film is better than still projections when motion is an inherent part of the material.

Filmstrips and Slides

The chief advantage of the filmstrip and slide over the motion picture is that pupils can study and analyze the frame as long as necessary. It is possible to have a discussion when showing filmstrips and slides but not when showing a motion picture. Moreover, filmstrip and slide projectors are more easily operated than the film projector, and their expense and that of a filmstrip is relatively lower. For these reasons, filmstrips and slides are the most abundantly purchased forms of instructional media.

Numerous excellent filmstrips accompanied by sound discs are produced commercially. The setup allows the teacher the flexibility of showing

[4]Carole A. S. Cox, "Film Preference Patterns of Fourth and Fifth Grade Children," *Dissertation Abstracts International*, 36 (February 1976), 5017–5018A.

[5]Donald A. Ingli, "An Audiovisual Approach to the Intermediate-Grade Social Studies," *Dissertation Abstracts*, 21 (April 1961), 2967.

[6]Oakleigh Thorne, II, brings out the advantages of the 8 mm single-concept film in "The Case for the Silent Film," *Instructor*, 80 (February 1971), 112.

the filmstrips a second time without the sound so that the class may have the opportunity for discussion during the viewing.

BOX 17.2   **GRADES K–8**

Suggested Procedures for Using Motion Pictures and Filmstrips

1. Preview the film or filmstrip to determine its appropriateness for your class (in terms of content and the age and maturity of the class), its clarity, and the accuracy of its information.
2. Prepare the class for the viewing by clarifying your purpose in using it. Introduce unfamiliar terms and concepts used in the film or filmstrip.
3. Present the material a second time. If it is a film or filmstrip with sound, turn off the audio, and have a child provide the commentary. Review difficult parts. If possible, make it available for independent pupil use.
4. Follow up on the film or filmstrip. Encourage pupils to summarize what they learned from it and to evaluate it.

Cartoons

Cartoons are drawings that use symbols to satirize a situation. They are common and popular features of adult newspapers and magazines. Children look at them and read their captions, though they usually miss the subtle symbolic meanings. What experiences will enable children to understand cartoons?

The first experiences do not involve cartoons at all. The children are presented with simple pictorial symbols such as a jack-o'-lantern (Halloween), Uncle Sam (the U.S.A.), two extended fingers pointing upward (victory), a dove (peace), a mortar and pestle (pharmacy), caricatured profiles of well-known persons, and the symbols on maps. The meanings are quickly perceived.

The children may also be presented with uses of hyperbole—in tall tales, such as that of Paul Bunyan, the legendary American lumberjack; in Alice's strange encounters in Wonderland; and in lampooning drawings, such as one showing a congressman crossing the ocean on foot, and a proverbially tardy ballplayer at an airport catching onto the landing gear of a plane at take-off.

The first satirical cartoons to be examined by a class, probably not before fourth or fifth grade, should be based more on exaggeration rather than on symbolism. One such cartoon, containing a caustic comment on inflation, depicted a housewife paying the cashier at a food market a whole shopping bag full of money for groceries that were so few that they nearly fitted into her handbag. With cartoons of such relative simplicity, the teaching procedure may consist of having the pupils (1) describe the action, (2) explain the exaggeration, and (3) think of what the cartoonist is trying to say.

Not until children reach what Piaget calls the period of formal operational thought (see Chapter 6), usually at about 12 years of age, are they able to grasp the symbolism and analogy which characterize most political and other satirical cartoons. At that stage, cartoons become means for challenging children's growing intellectual power. They are able to extract the meaning of Low's cartoon, by way of example, in which a scientist is shown offering a tiny ball (nuclear energy) to a baby (tagged "Humanity") who is crawling over the surface of the globe. The scientists asks "Baby play with nice ball?" The man looks like a scientist only to those who recognize his laboratory jacket and the note projecting from his pocket, reading "atom." The hazardous nature of the offering could be understood only by those children who know about the destructive potential of nuclear bombs. Those who possess this information and can interpret the symbolism would be chilled (an effect intended by the cartoonist) by this reminder of mankind's awesome responsibility to find ways of protecting itself from this danger.

That children of elementary school age have difficulty with cartoons was shown by Laurence F. Shaffer, who presented 10 newspaper cartoons to children in Grades 4 to 12.[7] The children were directed to write what they thought each cartoon meant. Children in the elementary grades tended simply to describe the cartoon rather than to interpret it. Not until ages 11 to 12 was the average child able to write interpretations based on the symbolism of the cartoon.

Opaque and Overhead Projections

Teachers frequently wish to show the entire class a map, diagram, postcard, document, typed material, coins, or photographs. These may contain information or ideas that they would like the class as a whole to examine and ponder. If only one copy of the item is available, teachers can provide for its presentation by means of an opaque projector. The projector is ideal for enlarging a map, picture, or any item to be traced. Thus, its versatility makes it a valuable teaching device. Because of its heavy weight, however, a stand on rollers is imperative.

The overhead transparency projector, like the opaque projector, enlarges materials, but it enables teachers to face the class in a normally lighted classroom while conducting a discussion of the subject. They are able to call attention to various features of the projection by pointing to the corresponding feature on the transparency. The screen should be located as high as possible on the wall behind the teacher. When the stage of the projector is about desk height, the teacher can sit so as not to obscure the projected image for viewers. A principle in using a screen for any projection is to

---

[7]Laurence F. Shaffer, *Children's Interpretation of Cartoons* (New York: Teachers College, 1930). The hypothetic-deductive thinking presumably necessary for the interpretation of such cartoons continues, 50 years after Shaffer's study, to be rare even among high school students. See David P. Ausubel et al., *Educational Psychology: A Cognitive View*, 2nd ed. (New York: Holt, Rinehart and Winston, 1978), pp. 236–238.

place it where sunlight will not fall on it. In some classrooms the best place for the screen is in front of the classroom windows.

A transparency is always needed for projection; therefore, an infrared copying machine is used to convert the map, diagram, picture, or other opaque material into an acetate transparency that is projectable. With typed materials, the large characters of a primary typewriter are required for ease in viewing. Teachers may create their own acetate slides or transparencies of acetate for projection by writing or drawing with a china-marking pencil or felt pen upon the acetate.

Pictures

A valuable possession for teachers to have is a picture file for the units they will teach. The use of a large, varied collection of pictures on each unit significantly raises the level of understanding for all children. This is true not only in the case of children who have hazy or blank images of what they learn. Even children with relatively clear ideas about such concepts as "neighborhood," "poverty," "superstructure," and "tundra" receive needed verification or correction from graphic illustrations. Pictures may be used at any time throughout a unit. They may be used to arouse interest in a unit, to build vicarious experience and meaning before the study of a topic, or to clarify misconceptions that are detected in discussion and writing. Pictures on a bulletin board or wall keep before the class replicas of what they are studying—people, scenes, tools, occupations, and the like. Pictures of contrasting ways of life are particularly helpful. In one classroom, for example, a series of pictures compared the slow, backbreaking plowing operation of colonial times with today's efficient, mechanized plowing.

Pictures that portray important concepts deserve explicit teaching. "Reading" pictures begins with a description of what is seen to perceiving relationships and making interpretations. For example, a kindergarten or first-grade teacher displays a picture of a street scene. A thunderstorm has evidently come up unexpectedly. People are shown scurrying for shelter. An occupant of one house is closing a window. A stream of rainwater is rushing down the gutter and into a drain. The teacher may say: "What is happening in the picture? How can you tell that this storm came up suddenly? It is still daytime. Why is it necessary for houses and cars to have lights on? Where is the rainwater flowing?"

Picture books without words stimulate the language development of young children as they describe what is happening in a picture. With shy children and children with sparse backgrounds who seemingly have little to talk about, a picture draws them out as they forget self and tell a story about what they see.

Another teacher, in talking about a photograph taken in Brazil of Indians who continue to live primitively, says: "See the Indian chief in this picture leading a fishing trip like trips of 500 years ago. Look at their equipment. How is it like any fishing equipment you know about? How is it different? What do you think the lives of the Indians shown in this picture are like? Are you surprised that there are still people today who live so simply?"

And a teacher, directing the attention of a class to a picture of a mesa, comments: "These table-topped hills are called mesas. What borders them on all sides? Yes, cliffs. How can you tell that the mesas are in a dry region?"

Sometimes a much-needed picture may be hard to find. It may be a picture of a cross section of the *Mayflower*, of George Washington Carver, of Whitney's original cotton gin, or of Bombay Harbor. A picture index, available in reference libraries, can then be consulted profitably. Naturally, children should join in a search for pictures relevant to the unit. *World Traveler*, a periodical with readability on the early primary levels, contains numerous color pictures; subscriptions can be ordered from *World Traveler*, P.O. Box 1888, Salt Lake City, UT 84110.

After pictures are collected, they should be protected from wrinkles and tears. Mounting individual pictures on construction paper and using clear plastic covers are methods used extensively by teachers. The relatively new dry-mount procedure, in which one inserts specially treated paper between a picture and a poster-board backer and then presses, heats, and molds together the composite, offers an excellent preservative method.

Study Prints

Sets of sturdily mounted photographs specifically designed for study and discussion are called study prints. Those available cover a large assortment of topics and themes (see Box 17.3). A teacher's manual offering guidance in introducing the prints and conducting class discussion is usually included in the set.

Teacher's guides give suggestions for eliciting responses and having pupils act out possible solutions. Any study print is valuable insofar as it stimulates children to speculate, explain, and verbalize feelings, and to seek alternative ways to solve problems.

BOX 17.3   **GRADES K–3**

Selected Study Prints

Climates of the World and *Family Life Around the World*, Coronet, 65 E. South Water St., Chicago, IL 60601.

Discussion Pictures for Beginning Social Studies, Harper & Row, Publishers, 49 E. 33rd St., New York, NY 10017.

Families Around the World: Holidays and Special Occasions, Silver Burdett Co., 250 James St., Morristown, NJ 07960.

GRADES 4–8

America the Beautiful (set of 52 pictures), Superintendent of Documents, United States Government Printing Office, Washington, DC 20402.

(Continued)

> *Earning and Using Money; Learning About Human Relationships*, David C.
> Cook, 850 Grove Ave., Elgin, IL 60120.
> *Interaction of Man and His Resources, . . . Of Man and Man, . . . Of Man and
> His Environment, . . . Of Man and His Past*, Rand McNally, P.O. Box
> 7600, Chicago, IL 60680.
> *Life in the New Nation*, American Heritage, 1221 Avenue of the Americas,
> New York, NY 10020.
> *Visual Experience for Creative Youth*, Charles Merrill Publishing Company,
> 1300 Alum Creek Dr., Columbus, OH 43216.

Recordings

The possibilities of making dramatic, vivid presentation of social studies content through sound give special significance to available audio transcriptions, either on magnetic or audio-cassette tape, and on discs. The value of recordings in reproducing speeches, accounts of important historical events, and musical selections is well known.

Tape recorders and record players allow children to exercise to the fullest their listening comprehension, which until about the seventh grade is generally equal or superior to their reading comprehension. The cassette

FIGURE 17.1.   Experience with a record player and listening jack. Courtesy of Prince George's County Public Schools, Maryland.

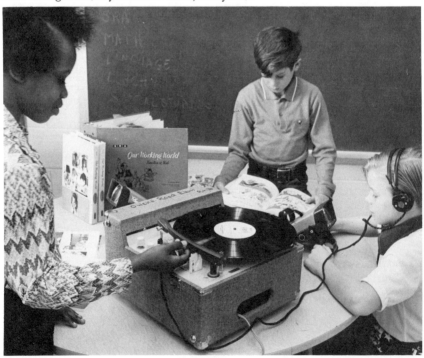

tape recorder's simplicity of operation, standardization of cassette size, low purchase cost, and light weight will no doubt increase the use of the tape recorder in the classroom. The cassette can be used by an individual child or by the entire class. Consult *Index to Educational Audio Tapes* and *Index to Educational Records*, National Information Center for Educational Media, University of Southern California, Los Angeles, CA 90007.

Radio

Most teachers have neglected to use the radio as a learning medium in the classroom. This is probably due to the problem of fitting the curriculum to scheduled radio programs. Yet children with their transistor radios listen avidly and appreciate the variety of station material beamed their way. Cultural programs such as concerts and operas, dramatic productions, special educational holiday programs, specific broadcasts of historic events, and especially news reports for building an interest and awareness in current events are some examples of how the radio can contribute to the social studies.[8]

Simulation Games

Social studies by their very nature fail to provide, in themselves, much opportunity for children to learn by doing—an opportunity present in science, for example, where children perform experiments in order to observe certain natural phenomena. But the pupil is unable even to "see" the operation of the market, corporate decision making by boards of directors, labor-management negotiations, and many other social processes. Simulation games are planned to fill, in part, this lack.

A simulation game is a scaled-down simplified model of an important process or institution. Its main characteristic is its ability to place the learner in a situation that simulates real life. For example, pupils may play the part of officials solving community problems, of congressmen enacting legislation, world leaders reacting to international conflicts, students making career choices, or environmentalists seeking to restore ecological balance.

The purpose of *Seal Hunt*, a simulation of *Man: A Course of Study* is to capture as many seals as possible so that the hunter's family might survive. The game's playing board which represents the ice is covered by a number of plastic corks. Each of these corks covers a recess in the board or a representative breathing hole for a seal. Players take turns pulling a plastic cork out (breaking the ice) and discovering if there is a seal in the recess. Each caught seal is worth five days of food for one person.

Indian Reservation: Life Today on the Northern Plains, a recent simulation by the Alabama Institute of Higher Education Research and Service,

---

[8]For information on obtaining audiotapes on educational radio programs, write National Publications Radio, 2025 M Street, N.W., Washington, DC 20036.

P.O. Box 6293, University, AL 35486, includes three phases of modern Indian life: Election of tribal chairman, activity period consisting of tribal activities and jobs; and family caucus. Role cards, time cards, play paper money, activity sheets, record sheet, and a teacher's manual compose the simulation.

Simulation games offer unique opportunities for decision making, negotiating, problem solving, reacting to opponents' strategies, and analytical reasoning. In the game situation the learner is required to react judiciously in order to protect his personal interests. Thus, children learn by experiencing the consequences of their own actions. After the game, a summarization of experiences occurs, knowledge is applied to new and related situations, and a linkage is made between gaming experiences and future learnings.[9]

The use of simulation materials and games has been a popular topic for regional and national meetings of social studies teachers, but at this writing only a few investigations have appraised the effectiveness of simulation in learning. Cherryholmes reported that high interest is generated by the materials.[10] On the whole, however, the results of experimental studies have been mixed. In a review of studies of simulation games, Janet Crist reported the following: No existing evidence proves that simulation is superior to other methods for promoting factual learning; but evidence does show that simulation increases comprehension and understanding of the intricacies and realities of various social systems and processes, and clearly engenders attitude changes among students.[11] After seven years of research with games, Coleman and others reported that the most consistent finding was that students prefer games to other classroom activities.[12] Additional findings by Coleman and his associates supported the results of Crist's investigation.

Unfortunately, relatively few games have been designed for use by young children. In its *Abbreviated Games and Simulations Guide*, 1977 Supplement, the Social Science Education Consortium (Boulder, CO 80302) lists five games for use below Grade 4. It recommends only seven games beginning with Grades 4 to 6, five games beginning with Grades 5 to 12, and eight

[9]Judith A. Gillespie, "Designing Simulation/Games in Social Studies—The Game Doesn't End with Winning," *Viewpoints*, 49 (November 1973), 9–21, 27.

[10]Cleo H. Cherryholmes, "Some Current Research on Effectiveness of Educational Simulations: Implications for Alternative Strategies," *American Behavioral Scientist*, 10 (October 1966), 5.

[11]Janet Crist, *Group Dynamics and the Teacher-Student Relationship: A Review of Recent Innovations*, Research and Development Memorandum No. 8, Stanford Center for Research and Development, Stanford University, January 1972. See also Joseph Decaroli, "What Research Says to the Classroom Teacher: Simulation Games," *Social Education*, 36 (May 1972), 541–543.

[12]James S. Coleman, et al., "The Hopkins Games Program: Conclusions from Seven Years of Research," *Educational Researcher*, 2 (August 1973), 3–7.

beginning with Grade 6. Of 64 games listed by William A. Nesbitt, only 13 are recommended for use in the elementary school.[13]

Programmed Materials

Programmed instruction is based on a "program" that is written either in the form of a book or for presentation by a teaching machine. The program contains information to be learned by the pupil. It is broken down into a series of short steps, each of which constitutes a "frame." (For an example of a frame, see Box 17.4.)

BOX 17.4   **GRADES 4–8**

Example of Format and Content of a Frame

You have already learned how to read a map's legend and how to find rivers on a map.

Did you know that rivers always flow down? They flow from high places, like mountains, to low places, like ocean shores.

You should be able to tell from a map in what direction a river is flowing.

Question: If you want to find out in what direction one of the rivers shown on Map 6 is flowing, how can the map's legend help you?

    a. It shows how colors are used to tell about elevation.

    b. It shows how to locate waterfalls.

    c. It shows how national boundaries are marked.

Compare your answer with the correct answer on page 5.

The pupils read one frame at a time and respond to it. It may call on them to answer a multiple-choice test question by pushing a key on a machine (a minority of available programs is presented by teaching machines) or by making their choice in a programmed textbook. Or they may be directed to construct an answer.

After the child responds, he or she is informed of the correctness or incorrectness of the response by a light or some other signal in a machine or by an answer appearing at a designated place in the programmed book. This information is known as "feedback." If the response is false, he or she is given either the correct information or information that can be advantageously utilized in making another choice. This feedback feature is a central element in programmed instruction: It informs the child of his or her progress and indicates the next step—whether to repeat an exercise, respond to a similar exercise, or go on to the next step. In any case, whatever, he or she is directed

---

[13]William A. Nesbitt, *Simulation Games for the Social Studies Classroom* (New York: The Foreign Policy Association, 1971).

to do next is designed to reinforce learning—to increase his or her chances of responding correctly to the question or task the next time it is encountered. It is evident that the program performs two functions that a busy teacher handling an entire class cannot accomplish: (1) It presents the subject matter to each child at a rate appropriate to his or her needs, and (2) each child responds overtly to each presentation and receives, without delay, reinforcement for every response he or she makes.

Educators are both pleased with and critical of the possibilities of programmed instruction.[14] Bone reports that the progress of underachievers and average achievers in arithmetic, reading, and language arts skills is positive with computer-assisted instruction. In a critique of programmed learning, Kneller and Hackbarth attack its claims, and question that it significantly provides reinforcement, genuine understanding, thinking, or individualization. They suggest that after programmed learning is used, time ought to be allotted for reacting to the learning by such activities as speaking, reading, writing, role playing, and debating.

Other questions have been raised about the claims made by promoters of programmed instruction. Do the programs discourage reflection because of their preoccupation with predigested ideas? Does the best quality of learning result from the fragmented goals of programmed instruction? Granted that programmed instruction individualizes instruction, is that more important than the personalization of instruction by a teacher? Can a program supply the motivation that matches the stimulation of a teacher who cares?

Doubts have also been raised regarding the adequacy of the motivating devices of programming. How effectively do the one-easy-step-at-a-time procedure and the feedback informing the pupil of a successful response, stimulate motivation? Wilbert McKeachie points out that ". . . for students with basic motivation for success, motivation is highest when chances of success are moderate." He expresses the view that learning should be paced ". . . so that each step offers some newness and a moderate risk of failure. One of the first steps may be to stimulate doubt about what has previously been taken for granted."[15]

Moreover, research on the comparative effectiveness of programmed instruction has not been impressive. Approximately as many studies show no

---

[14]For pro reports, see Jan Bone, "Turning On with CAI," *American Education,* 10 (November 1974), 33–37; Eugene Edgar, et al., "Progress Report of the Washington State Cooperative Curriculum Project," *Exceptional Children,* 42 (November 1975) 170–171; for con reports, see George F. Kneller and Steven L. Hackbarth, "An Analysis of Programmed Instruction," *Educational Forum,* 41 (January 1977), 180–188.

[15]Wilbert McKeachie, "Needed Research on Psychological Factors in Learning as Related to the Social Studies," in Roy A. Price (Ed.), *Needed Research in the Teaching of the Social Studies* (Washington, DC: National Council for the Social Studies, 1964), pp. 79–89.

difference between programmed instruction and conventional teaching as show superiority of programmed instruction.[16]

Despite all criticisms, however, one cannot ignore the unique advantages of programmed materials. They provide continuous verification. They are adaptable to the pace of the individual child and appear to contribute to the self-confidence of many children.[17]

Apart from its intrinsic merits, its limitations, and its prospects, the concepts of programming have had an impact on textbook writing and teaching practices. Today, social studies textbooks and teaching reflect greater attention—than they did before the advent of programming—to systematic introduction of facts and skills and to more frequent interspersion of questions, exercises, and tests to provide added opportunities for reinforcement of learning.

Educational Television

A large majority of American school children receive part of their instruction through television. The educational broadcasts carry prestige with both teachers and pupils. Edward A. Karns found that teachers and pupils rated television as a better authority source than text materials when there was conflict between the two media of instruction.[18]

In a national survey of instructional television which included about 6,000 superintendents, principals, and classroom teachers, Dirr and Pedone reported positive attitudes toward instructional television by about 50 percent of educators; 10 percent view it negatively and 40 percent have not formed strong opinions about it.[19] The researchers estimated that approximately one of every three school-aged children in the United States views instructional television on a regular basis. Lewis reports that the Ontario (Canada) Educational Communications Authority has grown from 170 programs without a station in 1965 to 1,899 programs and five stations in

---

[16]Phil C. Lange, "What's the Score on Programmed Instruction?" *Today's Education*, 61 (February 1972), 59.

[17]For indexes of programs, see the semiannual supplements of *Programmed Learning: A Bibliography of Programs and Presentation Devices* by Carl H. Hendershot (Bay City, MI: Hendershot Programmed Learning); and of *Programmed Instruction Materials* by Center for Programmed Instruction of the Institute of Educational Technology (New York: Teachers College).

[18]Edward A. Karns, "Teacher and Pupil Attitudes Toward Textbooks and Instructional Television as Authoritative Sources of Information in Sixth-Grade Social Studies," *Dissertation Abstracts*, 28 (August 1967), 393-A.

[19]Peter J. Dirr and Ronald J. Pedone, "A National Project on the Use of Instructional Television," *Audiovisual Instruction*, 23 (January 1978), 11–13.

1974–1975.[20] Although cable television has much potential for schools, it has been largely untapped.[21]

There are several ways in which instructional television may be used. Unfortunately, it is usually regarded only as a means for enabling children to assimilate information. That is but one of its roles. It also may be used to stimulate inquiry and discovery. Richard S. Craddock and Val Arnsdorf tell how it was used in this way in the state of Delaware.[22] A broadcast began by posing a problem; it then presented pertinent information. Following the broadcast, pupils attempted to solve the problem. First, the teacher encouraged them to set up hypotheses—that is, to propose possible ways in which they thought the problem might be handled. Then the pupils sorted out the information they had received from the broadcast. They analyzed it, they tested their hypotheses, drew inferences, and came to conclusions. Eight 15-minute programs were prepared, dealing with such topics as "Sections of a City," "People Make a Difference," and "The Idea of Location." Programs for each of the levels of the elementary school are described by Craddock and Arnsdorf.

The Appalachia Educational Laboratory has developed a home-oriented preschool education three-phase program for three-, four-, and five-year-old children.[23] In the first phase a trained paraprofessional goes to the home of each child in an assigned region and delivers weekly instructional materials. Each visit lasts about 30 minutes. In the second phase the child attends a two-hour group session once each week. Thirty-minute televised lessons which comprise the third phase introduce basic skills. These lessons are broadcast on regular commercial or educational channels into children's homes. Overall quality of the program was evaluated and the mean ratings for quality were at the above-average level.

The effectiveness of television as an instructional medium has been demonstrated in more than a hundred studies at every age level in a variety of subject areas.[24] Nevertheless, when compared with modes of traditional instruction, Roscoe C. Brown, Jr., reported: "The overwhelming majority (almost 90 percent) of gross comparisons between television and conventional communication conditions show no substantial difference in achievement."[25]

---

[20]Richard F. Lewis, "How to Improve a Television Series by Formative Evaluation," *Education Canada*, (Fall 1977), 42–47.

[21]Erling S. Jorgensen and William A. Anderson, "Low Traffic on Education's Highway," *Audiovisual Instruction*, 20 (May 1975), 34–37; John Maitland, "Use It Before You Lose It," *Audiovisual Instruction*, 19 (December 1974), 31–32.

[22]Richard S. Craddock and Val Arnsdorf, "Geographic Inquiry in the Elementary School via ETV," *Journal of Geography*, 70 (May 1971), 269–275.

[23]Joe E. Shivety, "Evaluation of the Technical Quality of Educational Television Programs," *Educational Technology*, 15 (November 1975), 49–52.

[24]G. C. Chu and W. Schramm, *Learning from Television: What the Research Says* (USOE Contract Z EFC 70894) (Stanford, CA: Stanford University, 1967).

[25]Roscoe C. Brown, Jr., "Evaluation of Instructional Television," in Robert M. Diamond (Ed.), *A Guide to Instructional Television* (New York: McGraw-Hill, 1964), p. 163.

The Carnegie Commission on Educational Television rated the potential of educational television high. "Properly used," its report stated, "television can bring a liveliness and an immediacy to education that no other medium can provide."[26] One program that accomplished such desirable results is *Sesame Street*. Started in November 1969 and carried nationally on about 130 noncommercial stations across the United States, the fast-paced hour-long program for three- to five-year-old children has been effective in teaching simple facts, reading-readiness skills, and cognitive skills.[27] Its successor program, *The Electric Company*, has had similar success.

Other television programs, some regional and others national, for children quickly followed *Sesame Street* and *Electric Company*. *Mister Roger's Neighborhood* aimed at humanizing preschoolers by raising such questions as why children get mad at their parents or fight with their brothers or sisters; *Captain Kangaroo* emphasized conceptual development; and *Zoom*, beamed at preteenagers, was written and performed by children for children for the purpose of developing the human side of preteens.[28]

FREE AND INEXPENSIVE MATERIALS

One of the early surprises to a neophyte teacher is the abundance of teaching materials that can be procured or rented for no more than the expenditure of a postage stamp, or for a small nominal charge. This profusion of aids consists of bulletins, pamphlets, monographs, graphs, transparencies, films, filmstrips, records, audiotapes, posters, maps, magazines, and books. One guide to free materials lists 2,252 free items.

The sources include industry, business, travel agencies, governmental agencies, educational councils, and offices of foreign countries. Their motivation for so freely distributing their materials presumably comprise (1) a bid to increase their sales or service, (2) a public relations effort to increase goodwill with people, (3) a desire to influence public opinion on pertinent issues, and (4) a sincere desire to keep the population informed on topics of general interest.

It is obvious that teachers must guard against using, for instructional purposes, material that is designed to manipulate opinion through such means as propaganda and misleading statistics. Among the materials of which teachers should be wary is extravagent promotional literature of all kinds. The only legitimate use for material of this sort in the classroom is to teach pupils how to analyze and detect propaganda and other slanted presentations.

---

[26]James R. Killiam, Jr., (Chmn.), *Public Television: A Program for Action*, Carnegie Commission on Educational Television (New York: Bantam, 1967), p. 81.

[27]Janet M. Rogers, "Summary of the Literature on Sesame Street," *Journal of Special Education*, 6 (Spring 1972), 43–50; Jim Warren, "Children's Television Workshop," *Educational Researcher*, 5 (September 1976), 6–8.

[28]For a free brochure describing the various guides to commercial programs, write: *Teachers Guides to Television*, P.O. Box 564, Lenox Hills, NY 10021.

BOX 17.5   **ALL GRADES**

Catalogs Listing Sources of Free and Inexpensive Materials

Catalog of Free Teaching Materials, Gordon Salisbury (Ed.), P. O. Box
    1075, Ventura, CA 93003.
*Educators' Guide to Free Social Studies Material; Educators' Guide to
    Free Tapes, Scripts, and Transcriptions; Educators' Guide to Free
    Films; Educators' Guide to Free Filmstrips*, Educator's Progress
    Service, Randolph, WI 53956.
Free and Inexpensive Learning Materials, J. W. Wiles (Ed.), Division of
    Surveys and Field Services, George Peabody College for Teachers,
    Nashville, TN 37205.
Selected Free Materials for Classroom Teachers, Lear Seigler, Inc.,
    Fearon Publishers, 6 Davis Dr., Belmont, CA 94002.
Sources of Free and Inexpensive Teaching Aids, Bruce Miller (Ed.), Box
    369, Riverside, CA 92502.

PUPIL-CONSTRUCTED MEDIA

Materials produced by pupils also promote learning. While pupils gain
much from such materials as finished products, they acquire their greatest
knowledge through the process of creating them. Excluded from the following discussion is the construction of maps, which is treated in Chapter 21,
and creation in writing and the arts, which is the subject of Chapters 15 and
20.

Graphs

Children can learn to construct and interpret graphs based on data they
are studying. One school conducted a campaign to reduce children's carelessness concerning their personal possessions. The principal appointed a
class to collect data on all articles that had been handed in to the lost and
found department during one week. The pupils constructed a circle graph to
summarize their findings (see Figure 17.2). Primary-grade teachers reported
that their pupils understood the graph and that it aroused interest and intelligent comment. Although circle graphs are easy to read and interpret,
they are the most difficult graphs to construct. The pupils must have considerable help from the teacher in using the protractor.

Bar graphs can also be constructed, to show, for example, the amount
of rainfall in various parts of the nation, the percentage of voting turnout in
recent elections in selected democracies, and the ratio of automobiles to
population in both advanced and underdeveloped nations.

A line graph is a more difficult form, but may be constructed by pupils
in the intermediate grades. The one appearing in Figure 17.4 shows what

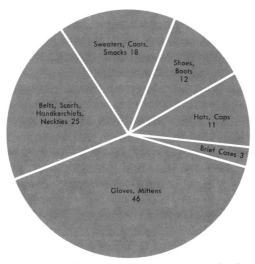

FIGURE 17.2.   A circle graph displayed in primary-grade classrooms, recording articles turned in to the lost-and-found department in one week.

numbers underlie the commonly used term "population explosion." Other line graphs of pertinence show major trends of the times—for example, the movement of women into outside-the-home employment over the past 50 years and the rise in real wages since 1900.

FIGURE 17.3.   Children use a bar graph to compare temperatures in different parts of the world. Courtesy of Montgomery County Public Schools, Maryland.

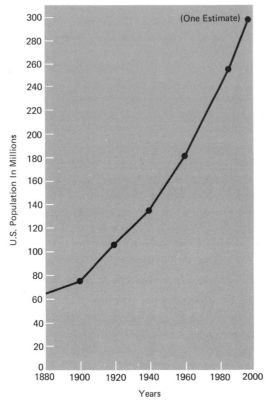

FIGURE 17.4.   A line graph explaining the term "population explosion."

In graph construction, pupils are faced with the necessity of making several decisions. For instance, if the time element is involved: "How far back should we go?" "What time intervals should we use?" The thinking they engage in while pursuing such questions is the most valuable exercise in graph making. They also gain worthwhile experience by browsing among almanacs, publications of the government, such as the *Statistical Abstract of the United States*, and other sources of needed data. When children's sole contact with graphs is confined to those that appear in textbooks, graphs take on a needlessly dry, forbidding appearance. After children begin constructing them, however, they will approach even prosaic ones in books with interest and understanding.

Diagrams

Diagrams are representations drawn to explain various organizations and relationships. Children are often intrigued by cross-sectional diagrams that show a volcano, the flow of water and heat through pipes from an outside source into and throughout a house, pneumatic caissons, canal locks, and other structures. After studying such diagrams in encyclopedias or textbooks, pupils may be encouraged to draw cross sections of structures about which they are learning or about which they have detailed knowledge through first-hand observation—perhaps the building in which they live, a mine, or an automobile engine.

A flow chart is a special type of diagram that shows a well-defined sequence of steps or alternative paths that lead to an identifiable end point, or series of end points. Some examples are the steps in the process of using raw material to make a woolen garment or the making of cheese. Squares □ , diamonds ◇ , or circles ○ can encircle and highlight the sequential steps on a chart. A flow chart clarifies a process, promotes an analysis of the process, and presents the process sequentially, as in Figure 12.3.

Older children enjoy drawing diagrams showing abstract relationships, such as those in a family tree or in the hierarchy of authority in the school or in a business organization.

DISPLAY OF MATERIALS

The educational value of certain media, such as maps, pictures, and time lines, is enhanced through their continuous display, more than two or three days or sometimes longer. The chalkboard is frequently neglected as display space. Teachers may set up opportunities for children to work at the chalkboard. A child may work alone, or small groups can cooperate in constructing graphs, time lines, or diagrams, or in creating the writing, drawing, and other products. There is another benefit in displaying various projects in this fashion. In most schools, children probably spend too much time at their seats. Their physical needs for motor activity can be met in numerous ways, as illustrated throughout this book. One way is by working at the chalkboard.

There are also opportunities for committees of children to arrange special displays on the bulletin board. The bulletin board does not need to be exclusively for the teacher's own use. Children are capable of making attractive displays that clarify ideas and raise provocative questions. If they are free to use their imaginations, a wide assortment of materials may adorn the bulletin board—posters, specimens, drawings, news clippings, flow charts and other diagrams, graphs, photographs, and so forth. Younger children may need teacher assistance, but even some first-grade teachers have prepared their pupils in the task so that before the end of the school year they could manage displays independently.

ORGANIZATION OF INSTRUCTIONAL MATERIALS

After teachers have collected many materials for each unit of study, it is vital that they store them in an orderly fashion so that they will be able to retrieve them readily whenever desired. A unit resource collection was proposed in Chapter 8—"an accumulation of newspaper clippings, mounted pictures, magazines, books, scale models, colored slides, and other potentially useful teaching aids." One plan entails the use of file cabinets in the classroom, with materials grouped according to units. Materials for a given unit may be kept in file folders and boxes within the cabinet according to subject or according to the order in which they will be used. The best plan of organization, of course, is the one that works best for the individual teacher.

TEACHING COMPETENCIES

This chapter tells how to perform the following tasks that are basic to teacher competency. The teacher should be able to:

1. Use a variety of learning media to support instruction.
2. Select an appropriate simulation game, build a background with children in the content that the game employs, prepare children for the game, and conduct a debriefing session after the game.
3. Use programmed instruction to introduce new learning or to reinforce learning.
4. Select a television program that relates to a unit of study, prepare children for the showing, and conduct a follow-up.
5. Collect and use a variety of free and inexpensive materials that support instruction.
6. Instruct children how to interpret graphs and how to construct their own.
7. Instruct children how to summarize and display data in the form of diagrams, cross-sectional drawings, and flow charts.
8. Accumulate a viable collection of materials, including numerous pictures, and use them in meeting individual differences, in clarifying difficult aspects of the unit, and for enrichment.

TRYING OUT SOME OF YOUR COMPETENCIES

1. Select a film, film loop, or filmstrip from one of the listed sources or other source. Preview it and develop a plan for its use with a small group or class of children: prepare the children for the showing, show the material, and follow up the presentation.
2. Select several pictures that help clarify a difficult concept—perhaps a concrete concept such as "soil" or "drainage," or an abstract concept such as "authority" or "religion." Teach the concept to a small group of children.
3. With a specific unit in mind, guide a small group of children in constructing a graph that explains the data they have collected.

FOR STUDY AND EXPLORATION

1. What are the advantages and disadvantages of using instructional media to support instruction?
2. Why should teachers have a picture file for each unit they teach?
3. What are some problems connected with collecting, storing, using, and retrieving materials that relate to the units a teacher is expected to teach?

FURTHER READING

Comprehensive textbooks of instructional resources are Edgar Dale's *Audiovisual Methods in Teaching* (Hinsdale, IL: Dryden Press, 1969); Jerrold E. Kemp, *Planning and Producing Audiovisual Materials*, 3rd ed. (New York: Crowell, 1975); John B. Haney, *Educational Communication and Technology: An Introduction for Teachers*, 2nd ed. (Dubuque, IA: William C. Brown, 1975); and Susan Rice and Rose Mukerji (Eds.), *Children Are Centers for Understanding Media* (Washington, DC: Association for Childhood Education International, 1973).

A variety of inexpensive pamphlets can be ordered from National Education Association Order Department, Saw Mill Road, West Haven, CT 06516:

- Elementary School Media Programs
- Cable Television: What's in It for Teachers
- Press, Radio, and TV Tips
- Learning from Pictures
- How to Use Your Bulletin Board
- Educational Games and Simulations
- Resource Guide to Free and Inexpensive Materials
- What Research Says to the Teacher Series: Educational Games and Simulations
- What Research Says to the Teacher Series: Educational Media

Simulation games are fully described and discussed in William A. Nesbitt, *Simulation Games for the Social Studies Classroom* (New York: Foreign Policy Association, 1971); Darrell R. Lewis and Donald Wentworth, *Games and Simulations for Teaching Economics* (New York: Joint Council on Economics Education, 1971); and Mark Heyman, *Simulation Games for the Classroom* (Bloomington, IN: Phi Delta Kappa, 1975). Social Science Education Consortium, Boulder, CO 80302 offers the monographs *Guidelines for Using a Social Simulation/Game, Simulation/Games in the Social Studies: What Do We Know*, and *The Use of Simulation Games in the Social Studies Classroom*.

Two thoughtful articles are: G. Kachaturoff, "Learning through Simulation," *Social Studies*, 69 (September/October 1978), 222–226; R. Cohen and R. Bradley, "Simulation Games, Learning, and Retention," *Elementary School Journal*, 78 (March 1978), 247–253.

The National Council for the Social Studies, Suite 101, 1515 Wilson Blvd., Arlington, VA 22209 has the inexpensive How to Do It Series that includes *How to Use a*

Motion Picture, How to Use a Bulletin Board, How to Use Recordings, and How to Use Simulations.

For a master listing of teaching materials, including what is treated in this chapter as "instructional media," see *Social Studies Curriculum Materials Data Book*, 4 volumes and annual supplements, published by Social Science Education Consortium, Boulder, CO 80302. It contains an analysis of more than a hundred new social studies curriculum packages, textbooks, and simulation games. Consult also Clearinghouse of Social Science Education (ERIC/ChESS), Boulder, CO 80302—a national information system that locates, selects, abstracts, and indexes current documents in the social studies; and Mary Sive, *Educators Guide to Media Lists* (Littleton, CO: Libraries Unlimited, n.d.).

18 Evaluating
Pupil Performance

> *While standardized measures are available and useful, only an unstandardized, flexible recording plan can hope to capture revealing samples of behavior from the life situations of the child.*
> **Willard C. Olson**

Performance in social studies, as in other areas, should be evaluated in terms of the teaching objectives. Since the objectives of social studies are comprehensive, the teacher's appraisal of progress must also be comprehensive. The main categories of objectives are *knowledge and understanding* (e.g., the facts, concepts, and generalizations of a unit), *skills* (e.g., cognitive, study, map and globe, social, language arts), and *attitudes and appreciations* (e.g., sense of justice, respect for evidence, interest in people of a different culture). It is evident that evaluation of children's progress toward such goals will require perceptive observation and a wide range of probing.

MENTAL HEALTH ASPECTS OF EVALUATION

"Of all aspects of school learning," write Laurel N. Tanner and Henry C. Lindgren, "evaluation exerts the most direct influence on the mental health of the learner."[1] When a child finds that the teacher is consistently

---

[1]Laurel N. Tanner and Henry C. Lindgren, *Classroom Teaching and Learning: A Mental Health Approach* (New York: Holt, Rinehart and Winston, 1971), p. 269.

satisfied with his or her performance, he or she takes a positive attitude toward life and usually turns out to be a well-motivated learner. On the other hand, when a child senses that the teacher, again and again, is disappointed with the child's best efforts, concept of self-worth suffers, and confidence is rapidly drained. The child tends to form a distaste for schools and teachers in general. Every assignment and every test may bring about intense anxiety.

The relationship between evaluation and mental health is not just another untested theory. John C. Glidewell and Lorene A. Stringer found a significant relationship between an overall estimate of mental health and the academic progress of elementary school children over a three-year period.[2] Their study revealed that test scores can contribute to a positive self-concept in those doing well on tests and to emotional disturbance in those doing poorly. Torshen also reported that teachers' evaluation of their pupils' achievement was significantly related to the pupils' self-concept.[3]

It is thus evident that evaluation is a process that can either promote mental health or impair it. In recent times an increasing disaffection and outright opposition exist with testing and grading practices in the schools. A strong trend is toward making evaluation more functional.[4] This can be accomplished by viewing evaluation as a normal, integral part of teaching and employing it as a means of finding out what was presumably not successfully taught and what the next period of instruction should provide. The next section will suggest how evaluation programs may be shaped to fit this concept.

SOME CHARACTERISTICS OF EVALUATION

Evaluation is much more than testing and grading. At its best, it takes on the following characteristics:

It Is Comprehensive.   The teacher as evaluator is as concerned with growth in a child's ability to work productively alone and with others as with his ability to master and apply major concepts.

It Is Continuous Throughout the Day and Throughout a Social Studies Unit.   It is not a process confined to testing only at the end of a lesson or unit.

It Is Related to Objectives.   Evaluation of children's progress is con-

---

[2]John C. Glidewell and Lorene A. Stringer, *Early Detection of Emotional Illness in School Children* (St. Louis: County Health Department, Division of Research and Development, 1967).

[3]K. Torshen, "The Relation of Classroom Evaluation to Students' Self-Concepts," reported by Marjorie C. Kirkland in "The Effects of Students and Schools," *Review of Educational Research*, 41 (October 1971), 303–350.

[4]See the entire issue of *Educational Leadership*, 32 (January 1975); John P. Joyce, "Humanistic Education Through an Analysis of Evaluation Practices," *Journal of Education*, 157 (August 1975), 39–53; and the entire issue of *Social Education*, 40 (November/December 1976).

nected to the broad goals, aims, and behavioral objectives set up prior to instruction.

It Involves Many Methods.   Evaluation includes the collection of information through informal means (observations, interviews, examination of samples of pupils' work) and formal means (teacher-constructed and standardized tests).

It Is Pupil-Centered.   While test norms have a place, the more useful forms of evaluation are based on what the pupil knew before instruction began (not on what the teacher might think the pupil should have known), on the pace of learning, and on the peculiarities of the pupil's learning style.

It Determines the Next Steps in a Pupil's or a Class's Learning.   It enables the teacher to discover (1) evidence of growth in knowledge, understanding, insight, and skills; (2) signs of readiness for the next concept, problem, or topic; and (3) weaknesses or gaps (in other words, evaluation is in part diagnostic)—and what experiences are best calculated to deal with them.

It Produces Information for the Teacher.   Evaluation helps teachers determine which teaching strategies work and which do not work; it also reveals with which pupils a particular strategy works or does not work.

It Produces Information That Can Be Shared with Children and Parents.   The purpose is to review assets and indicate needed steps in learning.

INFORMAL EVALUATIONS

Checklists and Rating Scales

Checklists are frequently used to record pupils' attainment of behavioral objectives. The following partial list, in chart form, is for use in the teaching of map skills (pupil A has attained the first objective, so a check mark has been placed in the appropriate cell):

OBJECTIVE	PUPIL A	PUPIL B	PUPIL C	ETC.
Can draw a rough map of school neighborhood.	✓			
Can show on the map where school bus is parked during school hours.				
Can show accurately on the map shortest way from school to bank.				
Etc.				

The following partial list was constructed to record pupils' achievement of the ability to interpret a picture of a Mexican village:

OBJECTIVE	PUPIL A	PUPIL B	PUPIL C	ETC.
Can tell what is taking place in the village.				
Can give accurate information about time of day and weather.				
Can suggest an appropriate title for the picture.				
Etc.				

If the teacher is interested in recording the degree of attainment of an objective, a rating scale may be constructed along the following lines:

OBJECTIVE	PUPIL A	PUPIL B	PUPIL C	ETC.
Takes active part in discussions				
Most of the time				
About half the time				
Rarely				
Keeps to the point during discussions				
Most of the time				
About half the time				
Rarely				
Is an attentive listener during discussions				
Most of the time				
About half the time				
Rarely				
Etc.				

Another form of the rating scale is the continuum in which the rater places a mark anywhere along the scale to indicate his or her judgment. Instead of using such vague terms as "excellent," "fair," or "poor" on the scale, the rater should use descriptive categories to categorize the response. These help raters to comprehend the meaning of their ratings and what aspects of performance need further practice and improvement. "Accepts ideas" could be rated as follows:

```
:           :          :           :           : X          :            :            :
```

| Rarely accepts ideas that differ from own ideas. | Accepts ideas that differ from own ideas about half the time. | Accepts ideas that differ from own ideas nearly all the time. |

Up to a point, usually about five to seven categories, reliability increases. The important consideration is that differences between categories should represent observable differences in performance.

It is desirable to provide each child with a copy of the checklist or scale so that the child may keep personal records. Also, the checklist or scale serves as a training aid to specify the important steps in a process.

Dividing learning into it component parts can be a helpful procedure for evaluation, but we should not be misled into thinking that it necessarily suggests a useful teaching sequence. Furthermore, in most social studies learning, these separate parts are rarely self-contained subdivisions. They are useless unless the learner integrates them with other components. Just as one can learn all the arm and leg motions of the swimmer without being able to swim, so can one learn separate components of map reading, picture interpretation, or discussion without necessarily being successful in performing the larger activity. When using checklists and scales, teachers should recognize that most social studies learning is not acquired in a simplistic, additive manner. Instruction should begin by having pupils undertake the activity (such as map reading) *in its entirety*, then concentrate on the more difficult subskills, then return again to the total activity.

Interviews

A method of obtaining information not easily accessible by other means is the personal interview. Interviews may be the only practical way of obtaining certain beneficial information from young children or from older children who have difficulty in reading and writing skills. The personal interview can be used with all children in ascertaining causes of pupil misbehavior, pupil feelings and interests, and in the collection of data on a wide array of topics that impinge on the teaching-learning process.

To have a successful interview, rapport between the teacher and the pupil is imperative. Without a feeling of trust and affection for the teacher, a child will probably say very little, might say what he thinks the teacher wants to hear, and may even distort or fabricate certain pieces of information. When rapport exists between the teacher and pupil, the interview can be considered one of the best methods of reaping valuable and often useful data.

Interviews with children are usually limited to a few key questions. The teacher encourages the pupil to expand on his or her answers, and may probe some areas in great depth to uncover the reasoning behind the answers. The skillful interviewer guards against posing a threat to the child by verbal or nonverbal expressions of disapproval of the child's responses. The skillful interview seems like a conversation.

Home Visits

A home visit provides information to the teacher in another but most important dimension of a child's life. Some teachers who visit the homes of their children early in the school year report that information thus obtained enables them to understand, appreciate, and be sympathetic with individual children with special problems during the rest of the school year.

One of the authors regularly visited the homes of all his children during September and October. *All* parents and guardians seemed to appreciate the visits! One visit revealed why Johnny seldom had his homework completed: he lived in a small bungalow with four siblings, including year-old twins, all under the age of five. Another visit revealed the reason why Eileen requested the teacher's help with insignificant tasks numerous times throughout the day: over coffee the mother indicated that she and her husband were estranged.

Home visits take time. Nevertheless, they afford opportunities to form a parent-teacher team for the instruction of children, to explain the instructional program, to assess home conditions and parental attitudes toward education, and to acquire special information about children for use in the instructional program. The value of the home visit may be inestimable in the instruction and evaluation of children.

TESTING PUPIL PERFORMANCE

Three kinds of tests are appropriate for evaluating pupil performance in the social studies: (1) the criterion-referenced test, (2) the "home-made" test, prepared by the teacher, and (3) the familiar norm-referenced (standardized) achievement test.

Criterion-Referenced Tests

Criterion-referenced tests (sometimes called mastery tests or prescriptive tests) are not new, but they have been given a new emphasis in recent years. Their purpose is to evaluate a pupil's progress toward explicit objectives without comparing it to that of other pupils (as in norm-referenced tests). They measure degree of mastery, which may be computed as the percentage of correct items. The incorrect items indicate what additional instruction is needed to bring about complete mastery.

By way of illustration, let us consider the general objective "To have the pupils acquire the knowledge that in modern democracies the people do not make all the decisions of government, but lend part of their power to law makers, officials, and judges."

The teacher, curriculum agency, or publisher undertaking to construct a criterion-referenced test or item to cover this objective has two alternatives. One is to formulate a question (either essay or multiple choice) for the objective. The second is to convert this general objective to a behavioral objective and test for the performance of it. For example, the objective might be converted to a behavioral objective, such as "the ability to give examples of commonly delegated powers (e.g., the power to make rules for parking cars and to set fines for those who do not follow those rules)."[5]

If the teacher gives a series of criterion-referenced tests in the course of teaching each unit, at the conclusion of the school year pupils will have "comprehensive, explicit records that . . . indicate what they set out to learn, what they had learned, and the point at which learning should begin in the next school year."[6] Most test publishers have prepared criterion-referenced tests (primarily in the fields of reading and mathematics). State and local school districts have also begun constructing them to fit their particular curriculum objectives. One pitfall in their use is their tendency to freeze the curriculum. Curriculums require frequent review and revision, and that is not likely to occur when teachers realize that a change in the curriculum calls for a change in the test.

Informal Teacher-Constructed Tests

There is no reason why teachers should not construct their own criterion-referenced tests. They may be of either the objective or the essay form. To conform to the critical feature of criterion-testing, each question or item should relate in a significant way to the basic generalizations and skills that constitute the objectives of the unit. This will avoid cluttering the test with questions about trivial, inconsequential information.

Two important factors in any test are validity and reliability. Validity answers the question, "Am I asking what I want to find out?" One teacher wanted to give a test on the pupils' *understanding* of the forces resulting in the westward movement. Her test was not valid for it included mostly *factual* items about the westward movement—about dates, personalities,

---

[5]This example illustrates one of the dangers lurking in the use of both behavioral objectives and criterion-referenced tests. They can result in much sterile memorizing and parroting by children of information or ideas.

[6]William F. Brazziel, "Criterion-Referenced Tests: Some Trends and Prospects," *Today's Education*, 61 (November 1972), 52–53.

equipment, and dangers—not about the movement's motivation. Knowing facts, of course, is not equivalent to having understanding.

Reliability answers the question, "If I tested the same population tomorrow with the same test I administered to them today, would I get about the same results?" The most important way to insure reliability is to write unambiguous test items. An ambiguous item can be interpreted in more than one way. To determine the degree of ambiguity of an item, the teacher can, following the administration and scoring, return the tests to the class for discussion. Children are normally quick to explain why they marked certain items as they did, and what they thought the items meant. Teachers discover through such discussion which items to discount, and they also learn something about how to write an unambiguous item.

Some teachers use their constructed tests as both pretests (the results inform the teacher of known and unknown areas of information which aid in instruction) and posttests (the results of which are used for assessment of teaching and learning, purposes of diagnosis, and to indicate progress in learning to children when they compare pretest results with posttest results).

True-False Tests.   The true-false item is a statement which examinees must decide is either true or false. True-false items are excellent for young children and older children alike. Ebel states that highly reliable test scores can be obtained from true-false tests and . . . "that good true-false tests are not vitiated by guessing."[7] Oosterhof and Glasnapp report that between three and five times as many true-false items as multiple-choice items are necessary in order to produce equivalent reliabilities.[8]

An example of a true-false item: T   F   The farmer works longer hours than the fireman.

BOX 18.1

Guidelines for Constructing and Administering True-False Items

1. Arrange the items in a sequence that has no discernible pattern with respect to the order of true and false items.
2. Keep all statements about the same length. Avoid the long statement as it is usually true.
3. Avoid negative words as they confuse the sense of the statement. If a negative word such as *no* or *not* is used, underline it so it stands out for the examinee.

(Continued)

---

[7]Robert L. Ebel, "The Case for True-False Items," *School Review*, 78 (May 1970), 373–389.
[8]Albert C. Oosterhof and Douglas R. Glasnapp, "Comparative Reliabilities and Difficulties of the Multiple-Choice and True-False Formats," *Journal of Experimental Education*, 42 (Spring 1974), 62–64.

4. Avoid the use of *all, none, always, never,* and such terms as items containing them are usually false. Avoid the use of *usually, generally, should, may* and such terms as items containing them are usually true.
5. Reduce ambiguity by using specific rather than general terms wherever possible. For instance, instead of saying " a long period of time," say "for 50 years."

Completion Tests.   These tests measure simple associations related to knowledge of names, dates, and terms. In one form of the test, words are supplied and the pupil selects the word that best completes the sentence correctly. This is a form of the multiple-choice test, and also of the matching test.

    a. proprietor   b. mechanic   c. engineer   d. clerk

1. Fixing cars is done by a _____(b)_____.
2. Placing items on shelves in a supermarket is done by a _____(d)_____.
3. The owner of a business is the same as a _____(a)_____.

Another type of completion simply has the pupils fill in the blanks.

A place where coins are made is a _____(mint)_____.

BOX 18.2

Guidelines for Constructing Completion Tests

1. Above the sentences (or paragraph) give the words that go in the blanks. Otherwise the examiner has to accept all reasonable answers, and deciding which answers to accept or reject becomes a problem for the teacher.
2. Help the examinee by placing the blank near the end of the main thought.
3. To avoid clues, keep all the blanks the same length.

Multiple-Choice Test.   A multiple-choice item is composed of a stem in the form of a question or incomplete sentence followed by a series of possible alternatives, one of which is correct or clearly a better response than the other options. Items can measure almost any kind of achievement including knowledge, application of principles, and understanding of concepts. Items are made up of a stem, a correct answer, and distractors (incorrect responses.)

(1) What percent of the work force is unemployed?

   a. 2.5 percent

   b. 7.9 percent

   c. 12.3 percent

   d. 17.1 percent

BOX 18.3

Guidelines for Constructing a Multiple-Choice Test

1. Use positive statement in the stem. Negative statements tend to confuse the examinee.
2. Use randomness to decide the placement of the answer. This avoids the overuse of some positions and the underuse of others.
3. Each alternative should be reasonable and plausible.
4. Keep the length of alternatives about the same.

Matching Test.   Matching items include terms, phrases, principles and applications, or definitions in the left-hand column of the page which are matched to responses on the right-hand side of the page.

	Sources of Energy	*How Obtained*
(E)	Petroleum	A. Mining
(B)	Rivers	B. Damming
(A)	Coal	C. Pushing
(D)	Uranium	D. Atom-splitting
		E. Drilling

Essay Test.   An essay test requires that the child recall appropriate information, organize it, and present a clearly written answer. It is perhaps superfluous to add that the scope of the question should depend upon the pupils' experience in writing and the ease and fluency with which they write. Thus, for a typical second-grade class, an appropriate question should probably require only a single-sentence (or even single-phrase) answer (e.g., "What is the quickest way to send a package from where you live to a town 100 miles away?"). A question for a fourth- or fifth-grade class, on the other hand, can reasonably require a paragraph or more (e.g., "How can farmers and other land owners prevent soil erosion?").

Norm-Referenced (Standardized) Tests

Norm-referenced tests have been standardized by administration to thousands of pupils, whose scores become the basis of "norms." By referring to a table of appropriate norms, furnished by the test publisher, the teacher may convert a pupil's raw score to a figure that tells how he or she stands in relation to the performance of others. The conversion may be in terms of percentile ranks (if a pupil has a percentile score of 62, his or her performance is better than that of 62 percent of those upon whom the test was standardized); or in terms of grade-equivalent scores (if a pupil has a grade-equivalent score of 4.2, his or her performance is equal to that of the average child who is in the second month of Grade 4).

Cautions.   Teachers should exercise certain precautions in interpreting the results of standardized tests: (1) They should discount social studies achievement scores of poor readers. The chances are that the test is more a gauge of their reading ability than of their social studies achievement. (2) Before teachers take test results too seriously, they should study the test to see how closely it measures content that corresponds to the content of the school's curriculum. There is wide variation in social studies programs. No matter how diligently a test author may attempt to construct an instrument that will conform to the central tendencies of curriculum practice, the instrument is certain to contain items of information that pupils in a particular school never had an opportunity to learn.

Limitations.   Makers of standardized tests aim to measure broad understandings related to widely accepted social studies objectives . They try to avoid details that are likely to be products of rote learning. But they fail to achieve their aims fully or convincingly. (See Fig. 18.1)

The explanation is fairly simple. An understanding does not exist in a vacuum. Suppose test makers wish to test pupils' acquisition of the broad understanding that "climate affects how people live." They would not learn much about the pupils' achievement by asking a question such as "How does climate make a difference in the way people dress?" In the usual multiple-choice form, a pupil would merely need to recall and recognize a platitude such as "In warm climates people wear fewer clothes than in cold climates." Test makers conclude, therefore, that it is better to ask questions about particular climates and particular peoples. They might ask: "In what way does a Laplander above the Arctic Circle live differently from a Congolese living at the Equator?" and list four or five alternatives.

Immediately we are plunged into a difficulty. For while some curriculums may provide for a study of Laplanders and Congolese, others will sample other peoples to illustrate the same understanding. The test will be centering on facts instead of a broad understanding. Thus, the absence of a nationally standardized social studies curriculum points up a severe limitation of the practical value, for most schools, of nationally standardized social studies tests.

These Pictures Tell The Story Of Bread.
They Are Not In The Right Order.

Bread On A Store Shelf

Grain Elevator

Flour Mill

Bakery

Slice Of Bread Being Buttered

Shocks Of Wheat

20 Which picture should come first?
   E The grain elevator
   F The flour mill
   G The bakery
   H The shocks of wheat

21 Which picture should come next after the
   grain elevator?
   A The bread on a store shelf
   B The flour mill
   C The bakery
   D The slice of bread being buttered

22 Which picture does NOT show a step in
   the making of bread?
   E The bakery
   F The flour mill
   G The grain elevator
   H The bread on a store shelf

23 In which of the following states would you
   be most likely to see wheat growing?
   A Vermont   B Florida
   C Kansas   D Utah

24 Which picture shows something which
   would have looked most nearly the same
   in George Washington's time as it does
   today?
   E The bakery
   F The flour mill
   G The shocks of wheat
   H The grain elevator

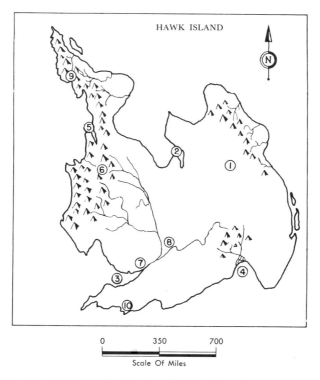

HAWK ISLAND

0   350   700

Scale Of Miles

29 About how far is it across Hawk Island
    from place 1 to the mouth of the river
    directly south of it?
    A   200 miles
    B   700 miles
    C   1400 miles
    D   2200 miles

30 Which of these places is on a peninsula?
    E 4   F 6   G 7   H 9

31 If explorers came by ship to Hawk Island,
    at what place would they find the safest
    harbor?
    A 2   B 4   C 9   D 10

FIGURE 18.1.   (left and right.) Items from a standardized test designed to measure ability to read and interpret maps. Sequential Tests of Educational Progress (STEP): Social Studies. Educational Testing Service, Princeton, NJ. Published by Addison-Wesley Publishing Company, Menlo Park, CA. A third edition of STEP tests (STEP III) is now available.

BOX 18.4

Examples of Standardized Social Studies Tests[9]

Kindergarten-Primary-Intermediate Grades

Iowa Tests of Basic Skills (Grades 3–9), Houghton Mifflin, 110 Tremont St.,
    Boston, MA 02107.

(Continued)

---

[9]For a comprehensive listing of tests, accompanied by critical reviews, consult *Social Studies Tests and Reviews* edited by Oscar K. Buros (Highland Park, NJ: Gryphon Press, 1975).

Primary Test of Economic Understanding (Grades 2–3), Joint Council on Economic Education, 1212 Avenue of the Americas, New York, NY 10036.

Tests of Basic Experiences: Social Studies (Prekindergarten-kindergarten, kindergarten-Grade 1), CTB/McGraw Hill, Del Monte Research Park, Monterey, CA 93940.

Intermediate to Junior High School Grades

Cooperative Sequential Tests of Educational Progress (STEP): *Social Studies* (Grades 4–6, 7–9), Educational Testing Service, Princeton, NJ 08540

Hollingsworth-Sanders Geography Test (Grades 5–7), also *Intermediate History Test* (Grades 5–6), Bureau of Educational Measurement, Kansas State Teachers College, 1200 Commercial, Emporia, KS 66802.

Metropolitan Achievement Tests: Social Studies (Grades 4–9), Harcourt, 757 Third Avenue, New York, NY 10017.

Social Studies: Minnesota High School Achievement Examinations (Grades 7–8), American Guidance Service, Inc., Publishers Building, Circle Pines, MN 55014.

SRA Achievement Series: Social Studies and Work Skills Supplement (Grades 4–9), Science Research Assovaites, 259 Erie Street, Chicago, IL 60611.

Stanford Achievement Test: Social Studies Tests (Grades 5–7, 7–9), Harcourt (address above).

Test of Elementary Economics, Revised Experimental Edition (Grades 4–6), Joint Council on Economic Education (address above).

RECORDS OF EVALUATIONS

Informal evaluations consist of reading the cumulative records, home visits, teacher observations, checklists, rating scales, interviews, and questionnaires. These methods are usually nonsystematic but represent important and reliable methods of gathering information and making evaluations.

Cumulative Records

Cumulative records are usually kept in folders, one for each child, and are passed on by the teacher to the children's successive teachers. They contain a variety of information acquired about children during their school years, including health, family, behavior, attendance, standardized test results, course marks or grades, and teacher comments about progress in academic skills and performance, and in affective and psychomotor domains.

These records may be read by the teacher early in the school year not only to acquire general information about the children but also to learn special circumstances that affect children during the teaching-learning process. For example, a child with a hearing or visual loss may be placed near the front of the classroom; another may have a history of a weak heart or a bladder problem which requires extra attention by the teacher. Whenever a signficant problem occurs with a child, the cumulative record ought to be perused as soon as possible.

Cumulative records need to be read with considerable care. Personal comments by previous teachers often represent subjective interpretations of behavior as well as a teacher's personal preference, bias, and interest. Even objective information in the record has its limitations because of errors in measurement, changing future conditions, or accelerated developmental changes in the child.

Discretion needs to be exercised at the conclusion of the school year when teachers write personal comments in the records. A single overgeneralization, tactless remark, or harsh judgment about a child's performance may work to his or her detriment throughout the school years. A comment describing specific observed behavior provides a more useful record than a loose generalization. Thus, rather than writing that a boy is selfish, a better statement would be that "he needs help in learning to share his possessions with others."

Anecdotal Records

One of the most frequently used sources of information—many people would say the most reliable source—on pupils' achievement is informal daily observation of them at work. Because children are engaged in a vast array of learning experiences in the social studies, the use of observation during social studies periods produces a lot of different kinds of useful data. This information is derived from episodes such as a child's giving an oral report, behavior on a committee, creative products, comment or question during a discussion, the accuracy and completeness of written assignments, the items voluntarily brought to class to enrich the unit, and the like. The teacher, of course, ought to guard against giving too much weight to any one episode and to guard against the teacher's own preferences and biases. Nevertheless, taken collectively these observations provide general impressions that aid evaluation.

Many teachers keep individual records of children's significant behavior. These records are extremely useful when the time comes for the teacher to prepare for an individual conference with a parent or pupil, to record comments on report cards or cumulative record forms, or to help children with problems that are recorded.

The teacher can conveniently keep such records on cards (five by eight inches), one for each child in the class, with the child's name entered at the top. At the end of the day, the teacher goes through the stack of cards and enters the date and an objective report about any significant achievement or behavior occurring that day. It is desirable to record only the behavior and not the teacher's feelings about it. It is unlikely that the teacher will have something to write for more than a quarter of the class on any one day. As the school year advances, the cards begin to fill up, and second cards for each child are required. Needless to say, events relating to the child's entire school program, not just social studies, are recorded on these cards; it would be unduly laborious and pointless to keep a separate card for each subject.

An example of cumulative information about a child (confined here to social studies performance) on one of these cards follows:

- *April 8:* Showed organizational ability as chairman of committee to prepare poster on the work of the city council. Kept discussion to the subject. Proposed a useful classification scheme for poster.
- *April 11:* One of the references is really difficult for her. I suggested that another child might read it aloud to her. She thought that would be too embarrassing. She asked to take it home, where her mother could help her with it.
- *April 16:* Presented her committee's poster to class. Was generous in giving credit to fellow committee members. Her explanation was clear, as were her answers to questions from the class.
- *April 25:* I looked through her notebook today. Her spelling is poor, but the pages are neat and the content is solid. It shows that she looks for causes behind conditions of poverty and poor housing.

A limitation of observations is that some important behaviors may occur quite rarely in the natural setting, and when they do occur the teacher may not be present to notice them. A more formal situation—such as a test situation—may be necessary so the pupil can demonstrate his or her abilities. Checklists and rating scales, described above, are other systematic ways to collect evaluative information.

Another limitation of direct observation is misinterpretion when the teacher misses part of the sequence of a child's behavior, fails to assess correctly the context of the episode, employs personal bias or preference in interpretations of behavior, or seeks a single cause for behavior rather than recognizing that behavior usually is accounted for by multiple causes.

File of Pupils' Paper Work

Some of the best evidence of pupils' growth and level of achievement is provided by their logs, reports, records, and drawings. Many teachers find that keeping a file of pupils' folders containing this kind of work is indispensable in evaluation. Each folder keeps the materials in chronological order, so that by going through them sequentially from time to time the teacher can discover changes in such matters as the following:

- Substantiveness of content.
- Clarity in expressing ideas.
- Interest level.
- Social sensitivity.
- Intellectual curiosity.
- Organizational ability.
- Neatness.

The teacher may rate the materials periodically and enter an appropriate note in the anecdotal records, or keep a record on a checklist of qualities such as those listed above.

Examples of pupils' products that teachers have found worth filing in their folders include a log of social studies reading or of committee work; drawings or paintings that summarize social studies experiences or illustrate ideas; social studies glossary of troublesome terms; a list of pictures and their sources on a specified subject; reactions to an experience in industrial arts, music, folklore, art, or role playing; a graph summarizing a collection of data; and numerous other paper products based on activities.

Many teachers make these pupil folders available to parents at conferences or on visitation nights at the school. At various times of the school year they are sent home with the pupils to show their parents. An important use of the materials is to have the pupil occasionally review them to note progress. Since considerable effort has been expended by the pupils in producing the materials, after the purpose of the collections has been served the materials may be appropriately returned to the children.

HELPING CHILDREN SET STANDARDS FOR EVALUATING THEIR OWN PERFORMANCE

As already pointed out, tests tend to be overemphasized as instruments of evaluation. Children need to learn how to evaluate their own performance. They develop a feeling for excellence and learn to appraise themselves when their teachers discuss standards with them and help them use these standards in evaluating their work. The entire class can profitably explore such questions as:

- What are good ways of organizing a social studies notebook?
- Why is it important not to make unnecessary disturbances during study periods and testing periods?

- How can Jane's committee improve its plan for painting the mural on "Japan Today"?
- How often should the bulletin board be changed, and how can its appearance be improved?
- How detailed should Jim make the drawing of the map of our state on the chalkboard in order to insure that it will be useful to those who have oral reports to give?
- How can the lines in our play about Indians be spoken so that they will sound natural?

When children participate in setting goals in such a fashion, they tend to work more painstakingly than if standards are set for them, or are not explicitly developed. By joining the discussion and guiding it, teachers can help their pupils set standards that are realistic and challenging—that is, achievable and appropriate to their years.

Standards imposed by the teacher may give an external appearance of being effective, but the results may be superficial and fleeting. Forced standards may yield work that possesses a surface, stilted "finish" but does not represent actual growth—often at the cost of the integrity of the pupil's expression. Standards that children help to create, that they understand and accept, and that they can meet are often naive; yet, they represent the only sound base from which true growth can occur. The teacher's role is to provide the questions that children should explore, to guide their discussion and decisions, and to demonstrate how to judge their work against their standards.

THE PLACE OF TESTING IN ELEMENTARY SCHOOL SOCIAL STUDIES

The space in this chapter devoted to testing and tests may exaggerate their importance. We suggest that at this point the reader return to the section at the beginning of the chapter entitled "Mental Health Aspects of Evaluation" and review it. As stated there, "an increasing disaffection and outright opposition exist with testing and grading practices in the schools." While we need to identify children's abilities and gauge their progress, heavy reliance upon testing results would be a mistake.

Let us first look at teacher-made tests. Teachers lack the time and technical facilities to construct tests that can compete in terms of validity, reliability, and polished items with published standardized tests. (One test publisher spends well over one hundred dollars for each test item that is eventually used.) We have provided a few pointers in this chapter on how teachers may construct tenable tests, but the best of the tests will be technically deficient. Crude as teachers' tests tend to be as measuring instruments, *they have the possibility of becoming first-rate instructional tools.* They serve valuable educational ends when they are used for discussion by which children may confirm and review what has been learned in social studies and that will clear up misconceptions.

The current reliance by schools on standardized testing and the technical sophistication of current tests blinds us to their limitations.[10] As Ralph Tyler has pointed out, the testing movement provided a "basis for the practice of schools and colleges in sorting students rather than educating them . . . Furthermore, the testing movement promoted the simplistic notion that important outcomes of schooling could be adequately appraised by achievement tests."[11]

The teacher's main evaluative efforts at the present time and in the absense of suitable alternatives should be directed to the informal evaluations described in the first half of this chapter. If that were done, teachers would be evaluating almost continuously while teaching.

REPORTING PUPIL PERFORMANCE TO PARENTS

Parents are entitled to frank information concerning their children's schoolwork. In filling out a report card, teachers discharge part of their obligation to them. However, they should be aware that parents may read more into a report card than is actually there and attach greater importance to it than is justified.

This points up how necessary it is for the teacher to schedule face-to-face individual conferences with parents of all pupils. During these conferences mutually useful information and suggestions may be shared. The parent is as likely to have information and suggestions that will aid the teacher as the teacher is, for the parent. The report card and test results can be discussed and interpreted, and data from the teacher's anecdotal records and the pupil's individual folder can be used to add to the sum total of evidence of progress or problems, or to illustrate them.

The parents may also be told how the child's progress is being judged. The teacher may want to point out that the report card not only tells something about children's academic achievement, but also reflects things not tested, such as how well they organize and keep a useful notebook, how well they can tell fact from opinion, how effectively they stand up before classmates and explain concepts from a picture or graph, or how much they have broadened their understanding of foreign peoples.

Another way to supplement the report card is for the teacher to invite all the parents to an evening meeting in the classroom. It is important to give them a description of the units that have been planned for the year. The

---

[10]Paul L. Houts (Ed.), *The Myth of Measurability* (New York: Hart, 1977).
[11]Quoted by Houts in introduction to *The Myth of Measurability.*

teacher may suggest ways in which parents can help their children with the units—trips they might take; books they can read together; and clippings, pictures, and objects they can search for together. The teacher may also present personal views and methods regarding evaluation.

No matter how well the teacher handles such conferences and meetings, however, some parents will continue to regard the report card as the most important indicator of their child's progress. It is highly desirable, therefore, that the teacher increase the reliability of the rating on the card by basing it on as many types of evidence as possible—for example, observation of the child, teacher-made tests, and pupil's daily work with maps and reference work, and written and oral reports on individual and group projects. Teachers who are systematic about keeping records of such evidence of performance will be in a position to report a defensible grade.

One limitation of a report card is its failure to indicate at what point a child may need help. It may report a low level of performance, but not a statement of factors that may be contributing to it. Many parents are frustrated by their inability to deal with such a reported difficulty. This fact merely reinforces the importance of parent conferences. Conferences can help such parents, as can also a periodic letter from the teacher, which some schools send out to parents, in which the teacher analyzes the children's performance, diagnoses their needs, and suggests how parents may help in meeting these needs.

DELAYED EFFECTS OF INSTRUCTION

Accountability too often implies the use of test scores to determine teacher success. One limitation of such a narrow procedure is its failure to take account of the long-term and often delayed effects of instruction.

Almost every class includes pupils who seem to gain very few ideas from a unit, whose social concepts do not seem to expand, and who seem to retain little information and few generalizations of a tangible nature. Intellectual confusion or indifference may be revealed in their contributions to class discussions, their participation in dramatics, their notebooks, their drawings, and their maps.

Yet, it is not always correct to conclude that the unit has been a total loss for them. Inner development often takes place without its immediate disclosure. Perhaps not until similar materials are encountered by the child at a later period of his life will the full value of the unit be manifested. An ardent conservationist recalls having his enthusiasm for the out-of-doors, not realized until he became an adult, first kindled by a study of conservation in elementary school. An acquaintance traces her ability to listen with an open mind to a teacher who stressed the need for it, often with seeming futility at the time.

Teachers never positively know *which* stroke of effort has the profoundest influence and *which* of their pupils have been the most deeply affected. But this should not disturb them. They are on safe ground if they consistently praise and encourage pupils; accept their feelings, whether positive or negative; accept their ideas; and raise questions for discussion. Ned A. Flanders found that pupils' achievement in social studies was significantly higher in classes in which teachers frequently employed these practices than in classes in which teachers exercised the commanding, critical, authoritarian type of behavior.[12] Teachers can normally rest assured that if they pour enthusiasm into their teaching, if they consistently express their respect for their pupils, and if they hold the class to high standards, every child will gain something of value and will make progress. The teacher's productivity or success cannot always be fairly judged by this year's test scores, but by the results over the long haul.

TEACHING COMPETENCIES

This chapter has described how to perform the following tasks that are basic to teacher competency. The teacher should be able to:

1. Evaluate children's progress on the basis of the teaching objectives.
2. Make evaluation humanitarian, and reduce anxiety over test-taking.
3. Evaluate pupil performance through personal observation, home visits, anecdotal records, checklists, rating scales, teacher-made tests, standardized tests, etc.
4. Write objective anecdotes concerning significant behavior.
5. Construct criterion-referenced tests that relate to objectives of instruction.
6. Assist children in setting standards for the evaluation of their work.
7. Guide children in keeping individual folders of their work.
8. Confer with parents to exchange information and suggestions concerning the progress of the child.

TRYING OUT SOME OF YOUR COMPETENCIES

1. Review the cumulative records of a class and list beside children's names important facts that a teacher should be aware of early in the school year.
2. Plan and execute a few home visits of school children. Write a brief summary of (1) "new" information you gleaned from the visits, and (2) a brief description of how you plan to use the information in your teaching.

---

[12]Ned A. Flanders, *Teacher Influence, Pupil Attitudes, and Achievement* (Washington, DC: Superintendent of Documents, 1965).

3. Observe a social studies class, and make a list of occurrences that appear of sufficient significance to be noted in an anecdotal record.

FOR STUDY AND EXPLORATION

1. How can pupil evaluations be a positive experience for children?
2. Have a discussion with another teacher and make recommendations for improving the use of standardized tests with children.
3. Analyze reasons why parents might need to talk to their child's teacher.
4. Explain the statement: "When a teacher visits a pupil's home, her/his thinking about the child might be appreciably altered."

FURTHER READING

The Association for Supervision and Curriculum Development, 1201 16th St., N.W., Washington, DC 20036 offers the following publications on evaluation:

Sidney B. Simon and James A. Bellanca, *Degrading the Grading Myths: A Primer of Alternatives to Grades and marks* (1976).
Fred T. Wilhelms, *Evaluation as Feedback and Guide* (1976 Yearbook).

National Education Association, Saw Mill Rd., West Haven, CT 06515 offers the following monographs: *Evaluation, Choosing Evaluation, Teacher Save My Writings, Parent-Teacher Conferences, Parent-Teacher Relationships, What Research Says to the Teacher Series: Evaluation and Reporting of Student Achievement, Reporting to Parent, Evaluation* and *Reporting of Student Achievement.*

Specialized treatment of evaluation in elementary social studies will be found in the following:

Janet Hanley Whitla and Dean K. Whitla, "Social Studies Tests," *National Elementary Principal*, 54 (July/August 1975).
The entire issue of *Social Education*, 40 (November/December 1976).
Dan B. Fleming, "Social Studies Standardized Achievement Tests: Are They Worth It?" *Peabody Journal of Education*, 54 (July 1977), 292–295.
Arthur Ellis and Janet Alleman-Brooks, "How to Evaluate Problem-Solving Oriented Social Studies," *Social Studies*, 68 (May/June 1977).
M. T. Herlihy and J. Herlihy, "Social Studies and the Elementary Teacher: Informal Assessment of Social Studies Learning," *Social Education*, (November 1976), 567–581.

The all-important mental health aspects of evaluation are discussed in the following publications:

John P. Joyce, "Humanistic Education Through an Analysis of Evaluation Practices," *Journal of Education*, 157 (August 1975), 39–53.
James B. MacDonald and H. Millard Clements, "Moral Concerns in Assessing Pupil Growth," *National Elementary Principal*, 45 (May 1966), 29–33.
William W. Purkey, *Self Concept and School Achievement* (Englewood Cliffs, NJ: Prentice-Hall, 1970).

Laurel N. Tanner and Henry C. Lindgren, *Classroom Teaching and Learning: A Mental Health Approach* (New York: Holt, Rinehart and Winston, 1971), chap. 10.

The merits and limitations of both criterion-referenced and norm-referenced tests are clearly presented by William P. Brazziel in "Criterion-Referenced Tests: Some Trends and Prospects," *Today's Education*, 61 (November 1972), 52–53.

A critical evaluation of all published assessment, diagnostic, and prognostic instruments for elementary school children is *CSE Elementary School Test Evaluation* (Los Angeles: Center for the Study of Evaluation, University of California at Los Angeles Graduate School of Education, n.d.). Also published tests and critical appraisals are included in Oscar K. Buros, *Social Studies Tests and Reviews* (Highland Park, NJ: Gryphon Press, 1975).

part V **Academic Skills through Social Studies**

19 Improving Reading Comprehension in the Social Studies

*What message the reader produces
is partly dependent on what the writer
intended, but also very much
dependent on what the reader brings
to the particular text.*
Kenneth S. Goodman

Social studies textbooks are used in all grades, beginning with kindergarten. Children are frequently expected to make use also of encyclopedias, almanacs, and other reference books. Many teachers encourage their pupils to read juvenile books, including biography, poetry, historical fiction, and even some easy-to-read adult trade books (i.e., nontechnical books of interest to most people) that relate to the subject of the current unit.

WHY TEACHING READING COMPREHENSION SHOULD BE PART OF SOCIAL STUDIES INSTRUCTION

We cannot assume that children's ability to handle all these reading materials in social studies has been developed in previous grades or in periods set aside for reading instruction. Children are faced with special difficulties in their social studies reading. In the first place, social studies materials have an element of unreality for children—textbooks, especially—for they deal much of the time with historical periods, places, and conditions unfamiliar to them. That obstacle is compounded by the fact that textbook

351

readability scores tend to be high—that is, the textbooks tend to be hard for children to understand.[1] This comes about largely because of the appearance of many words and terms essential to social studies that are new to the children, and because of the density of concepts. Because of space limitations, textbook authors face the necessity of crowding a great deal of content onto each page and omitting the kind of concrete detail that makes for interesting reading. The more detail that is dropped, the higher the proportion of abstract generalization, and the harder the reading.

NEGLECT OF TEACHING READING COMPREHENSION IN SOCIAL STUDIES CLASSES

Dolores Durkin conducted the most intensive study probably ever made of how much teaching of reading conprehension actually takes place in reading and social studies classes.[2] She visited each classroom approximately every three weeks on three successive days, from September to May. She found virtually no occurrence at all of teachers directly helping a class understand word meanings, sentence meanings, and paragraph meanings. The most frequent forms of comprehension instruction in social studies classes (each involving 8 percent or less of the total time in which social studies classes were observed) were: (1) Asking a question but doing nothing with children's answers except, perhaps, saying they were right or wrong; (2) helping one or more children with a written comprehension assignment; and (3) preparing children for reading a selection, as by identifying new words and their meanings. In summarizing her social studies observations, Durkin reported: "None of the observed teachers saw the social studies period as a time to improve children's comprehension abilities. Instead, all were concerned about covering content and with having children master facts."[3]

TECHNIQUES OF TEACHING READING COMPREHENSION

Most of the techniques discussed here are applied to textbook reading, simply because that is the most prevalent form of social studies reading matter found in the schools. The techniques can, of course, be applied equally to

---

[1]An examination of 56 elementary school social studies textbooks published in the 1970s revealed a modest trend toward lower readability scores than those of the preceding decade. Roger E. Johnson, "The Reading Level of Elementary Social Studies Textbooks Is Going Down," *Reading Teacher*, 30 (May 1977), 901-906. But readability, of course, consists of more than the factors normally measured by readabilty scores.

[2]Dolores Durkin, "What Classroom Observations Reveal About Reading Comprehension Instruction," *Reading Research Quarterly*, 14 (no. 4, 1978-1979), 481-533.

[3]Ibid., p. 521.

the reading of encyclopedias, newspapers, pamphlets, and other printed sources of social studies content.

Use Dictated Materials and Reading Charts in the Beginning School Years

By dictating their own social studies records and reports, primary-grade children can compile materials that will afford them practice in basic reading and study skills. For example, one class visited a museum to see American Indian artifacts. Upon returning to the classroom, the pupils co-operatively dictated their own account of the experience to the teacher. The teacher wrote it as dictated on the chalkboard, and later transferred it to a chart (often called an "experience chart"), to which the children referred frequently on subsequent days. It read:

> We saw the Lenape exhibit.
> The guide showed us clay pots, axes, and bows and arrows.
> We saw moccasins, leggings, robes, and other clothes.
> We were allowed to feel them and try them on.
> The guide told us how the Lenapes made all these things.
> He also told us how they used them.

The pupils learned that a personal experience can be written down and referred to later to recall details.

FIGURE 19.1.   A reading chart constructed by children provides built-in motivation to read. Courtesy of Prince Georges County Public Schools, Maryland.

The teacher discovered (1) that children can easily learn certain words that are connected with an experience. "Lenape," for example, was learned, even though its pronunciation differed from phonic rules learned in reading class; and (2) that the children created, without at first recognizing it, a set of notes—a record.

Select a Textbook

Ideally, a textbook should be readable for every child; the child should be able to read accurately about 95 percent of running words of typical passages, and able to give evidence of getting the gist of these passages. If the child reads fewer than 90 percent of running words, the book is probably too difficult for him or her. Using these percentage figures as rough guides, teachers can estimate the appropriateness of any textbook as far as its readability is concerned. Rather than have every pupil make a test reading, some teachers judge a book's readability by calling upon one good reader, one average reader, and one poor reader to read selected passages.

But teachers often find that the selected book is too difficult for a substantial minority of a class. They may be unable to find an easier alternate textbook for those pupils that parallels the content, and furthermore, they may like the book's organization, treatment of topics, glossary, maps, and photographs. These features, too, are important aspects of appropriateness. Consequently, the teachers may decide to use it. But can the pupils benefit from it if they can read only 50 to 90 percent of its running words?

They can, to a considerable degree. They usually can learn to read its table of contents, even if they have to memorize certain of its words. If they can master the table of contents through this means, they have achieved a valuable learning. The table of contents will acquaint them with the organization of the subject and with the relationship of the major topics to each other. Similarly, they can learn the captions of important pictures, charts, tables, and maps as necessary aids in interpreting such graphic material. The book can be used by them in an even more productive way through "team learning," described later in this chapter.

Explain How to Preview Books and Chapters

When a textbook is first presented to the class, its various parts should be explored as a regular class activity. Start with the front matter. Who are the authors? How recent is the book? Why may the date be important? What information does the table of contents contain, and how might it be used? The index? What is the purpose of other parts, such as the glossary, questions at end of chapters, and appendix?

Just before a chapter is read, it, too, may be similarly explored. In many chapters, if the first and last paragraphs and the main headings are read, and the pictorial aids examined, a great deal of information about the contents of the chapter is learned before actual reading begins. Previewing either a book or a chapter leads to better understanding and faster reading.

Have a Flexible Teaching Arrangement

For some activities, such as finding how a book or a chapter is organized, the entire class may be taught as a unit. At other times, as when teaching how to locate the main idea of a paragraph or how to learn a new word through the use of context, it is usually better to work with small groups based on homogeneity with respect to degree of mastery of decoding skills, length of experience in independent reading, or customary volume of voluntary reading.

Certain reading may be assigned as homework. For example, in a second-grade unit on "Keeping Safe," one section of a textbook is headed "About Fire." The teacher would first want to prepare the class for the reading (see the following section for what this involves), and then ask the children to read the section at home, writing or drawing pictures of the "three things" the book says a fire must have in order to start. Because of the wide spread in reading ability of most classes, the advanced readers might be asked to read about rules for preventing fires in a science book and to report in written or oral form about their reading the next day.

Prepare Pupils for Reading Assignments

The more difficult the reading selection, the greater the need of the class for preparation. Children who have not attained independent reading status need preparation for every assignment.

The teacher's role is an important one. If the class, or a small group, is about to read a selection, the teacher may ask one or more questions that will build a bridge between the child's background of experience and the passage. The question may be an utterly simple one. "Have you ever passed by a field stacked with new-mown hay?" Such a question may evoke recollections of such an experience—the workers, machinery or other equipment, appearance of the stacks, fragrance of the hay, and so forth.

New words should be identified and written on the chalkboard, and their pronunciation and meaning discussed. The teacher may also ask questions that can be answered by the selection. In the case of a particularly difficult assignment (occasioned by a high degree of concept density, an exceptional number of new terms and ideas, or a heavy concentration of abstractions), the teacher may read it aloud to the class and, with the class, find ways of penetrating the puzzling language or ideas. The pupils then read the selection to themselves, silently.

Introduce the Usefulness of Intonation

Intonation is the melody of speech—the rise and fall of the voice, its emphases, its pauses, and its rhythms. The ability to discern intonation in the written page is one of the keys to effective reading. Good readers have this ability. Others can acquire it.

The degree to which we gain an author's intended intonation depends upon the extent of our involvement with the selection and upon our ability to draw inferences concerning intonation from the content that has gone before and the direction in which the events or ideas seem to be moving.

The teacher begins by reading a passage. Then volunteers from the class are called upon to read the same passage, urged to watch for commas, italics, and other signals, and to give their reading as much expression as possible. To provide contrast, the teacher my read the passage without intonation, droning the words throughout. The immediate purpose of this repeated oral reading of a single passage is to improve its comprehension; its ultimate purpose is to alert children to the desirability of looking for intonation when reading silently, even in the often prosaic description and narrative of social studies textbooks.

Provide Practice in Using Clues That Suggest Word Meanings

Before children have learned to decode with reasonable dependability, the most efficient way of building vocabulary is through social studies experiences and science experiences (observing, collecting, sorting, visiting unfamiliar places and operations, following TV travelogues, and the like) that bring them in contact with new ways of doing things, new phenomena, new personalities, and new ideas. Each enriching experience, and the new vocabulary associated with it, can be consolidated by recording the experiences on reading charts as recommended earlier in this chapter.

Once children have learned to "break the code," they are ready to benefit from more sophisticated methods. They can learn to get the meanings of new words by using available clues, such as the examples in the paragraphs below.

Structural Analysis.   Before giving a reading assignment, locate difficult words in the textbook that have smaller units that your pupils already know and that can be used in getting meanings. Have your pupils try out this strategy.[4]

Examples of such words are *roughland* (an area that is not level or smooth, and that has hills, mountains, steep slopes, ravines, and gullies); *switchback trail* (a trail made to switch back and forth up a slope so that the climb will be less steep); and *water power* (use of the force of flowing or falling water to turn a wheel or other device). Structural analysis does not always work so clearly, as in *watershed* (the area drained by a river), yet it is one of the more reliable aids.

Context.   The context almost always narrows the possibilities of what a new word might mean. "They put big nets in the water to catch hundreds

---

[4]It is presumed that words which appear in the following paragraphs in italics can be more-or-less correctly pronounced; it is only their meaning that is puzzling.

of small fish called *sardines*." The sentence states that a sardine is a fish. For the purpose of immediate comprehension, that is sufficient knowledge. When the child later sees *sardines*, as in the sentence "Sardine canning is an important industry in Maine," he or she will know that the author is writing about the canning of fish. "Inside the ship is its most expensive part, the part that supplies the power. It is a huge, complicated *diesel*." "Diesel," concludes the child, "must be a kind of engine."

Prediction.   Teachers should frequently point out how words with unknown meanings may be understood by means of prediction of their meaning, and provide practice with sentences from the textbook, placing them on the chalkboard for analysis. This meets a particularly vital need for literalminded pupils who may have been mistakenly taught that they are not reading unless they can read every single word with precise meaning.

An account of automation in a modernized post office appears in a juvenile news weekly. One sentence reads: "If an envelope is smaller than postal *regulations* permit, the machine *automatically rejects* it." Children who have learned that reading is, in part, a guessing game, and who have closely involved themselves in the news weekly's report of postal automation procedures, will be in a position to predict the meaning of the three unknown words. They already know the word "permit," let us assume; it suggests that the sentence must have something to do with a rule, and that *regulations* may have something to do with permission; permission implies rules or laws. The article has already introduced the word "automation," so it is not difficult to decipher the probable meaning of *automatically*. The meaning of *reject* may not be guessed, but the meaning of the total sentence can be approximated without it. If they were well instructed in their reading classes, they will rely on the total context for meanings that will make some sense of the sentence. The children's guess will likely be confirmed by the next sentence: "Letters that have been thrown out by the machine drop into a special box."[5]

Affixes.   Give each pupil a list of common affixes to keep for reference (see Box 19.1). The meaning of *intratribal dispute* becomes clear through locating the affix "intra"; an account of a ship's captain who was *pitiless* is similarly clarified through knowing that "less" often means "lacking."

---

[5]Those not familiar with guessing and predicting procedures are referred to Yetta M. Goodman's description of reading-strategy lessons in "Strategies for Comprehension" in P. David Allen and Dorothy J. Watson, *Findings of Research in Miscue Analysis: Classroom Implications* (Urbana, IL: National Council of Teachers of English, 1976), pp. 94–107.

BOX 19.1   **GRADES 4-8**

Some Common Affixes

Prefixes	Chief Meanings
circum-	around, about, on all sides
equi-	equal
intra-	within
mis-	wrong, wrongly
non-	not
syn-	with, together

Suffixes	Chief Meanings
-able	able
-ful	full of
-graph	something recorded
-less	lacking, not able to
-meter	instrument for measuring
-ology	a branch of knowledge

Base Words.   In preparing the class for a textbook asignment, point out some difficult words whose meaning may emerge from a known base word—a word familiar to children. In the sentence, "The revolution was *suppressed*," have the class look at "press." Most children know that "press" means pushing down upon something.

Flexibility.   Several strategies in the use of clues have been described. Flexibility in the use of these strategies is essential. Because the pupils' ability to shift from one strategy to another is so important, teachers should plan frequent practice in using all of them, illustrating instances in which a given clue fails, as well as instances in which it helps to supply the needed word meaning. If none of the clues yields help, resort must be made to a dictionary, which presupposes that the class has had prior instruction in alphabetization and how to handle multiple definitions of a word.

Suggest Ways to Improve Grasp of Paragraphs

Suggest various practices of good adult readers in reading long, involved paragraphs, and have the class try them out under your supervision.

Main Ideas.   Have your class read the first sentence of a long paragraph of high-concept density. Does it give a hint of the paragraph's topic? Sometimes the first sentence does not suggest the topic. See if your class can locate a good topic sentence elsewhere in the paragraph. Once found, turn it into a question and, while reading the paragraph, look for an answer to the question. (Example of topic sentence: "The first man to lead a party all the way to the North Pole was Robert Peary." Examples of questions it may evoke: "How long ago did he do that?" "How large was the party?" "How did they travel to the North Pole?" "How did they keep warm?") Naturally, not all pupils will formulate the same question; that is inconsequential. The significance of asking a question and looking for an answer is that this process maintains active thinking and looking, keeps the mind from wandering, and prevents the reader from becoming mired in detail.

Mental Pictures. Encourage your pupils to form mental pictures as they read. Ask them to close their eyes following a reading and tell what they see. This can be an enjoyable small-group experience, successive children adding to the "picture" described by the first child.

Their images often disclose fuzzy understandings and misconceptions. It is a good practice to ask children what mental pictures have been created by certain sentences. One child, upon being asked what he "saw" after reading the phrase "hacking a highway through the jungle," said he "saw" men with picks and drills in the process of destroying a concrete highway. Other statements causing misconception include:

Most of Greenland is covered by an ice cap.
It took people a long time to travel from Philadelphia to Boston by stagecoach.
One type of machine is the lever.
The breaking waves dashed high.

The frequency of wrong images shows the desirability of having pupils describe their mental pictures. The habit of forming mental pictures enhances reading comprehension.

Inferences. In the upper grades of the elementary school and beyond, we can help children learn to go beyond what is written, in search of facts or ideas that are implied. One textbook describes the logging industry. Nothing is said explicitly about the danger of some of the work, but in reading about the felling of trees, the operation of chain saws, and the floating of logs, the reader infers that it is dangerous work and that those who engage in these operations will probably have to be paid more than those who have relatively safe jobs in the industry, like bookkeepers and typists.

Many pupils have developed the habit of going from page to page without stopping to reflect. In teaching inferential reading, we start by emphasizing, through demonstrations drawn from specific examples, that we may have to spend as much time thinking as reading. The teacher, usually, must go through the process slowly and repeatedly, with children asked to offer inferences which they draw from a given passage.

Recitation. The key to paragraph mastery is self-recitation. Any reproduction of material may be called recitational: summarizing to oneself the contents of a passage just read; taking notes on a passage; telling someone about it; summarizing it to himself or herself; memorizing the main points of the passage. Some teachers introduce children to the value of recitation by having them recite an important passage, or even a whole chapter, to one another in pairs.

Develop Skills for Reference Reading

Reference books for children are of two kinds: (1) those that expand, illustrate, and explain a subject in greater detail than is possible in a textbook; and (2) those that systematically catalogue information, as encyclopedias and almanacs do. No textbook satisfies these requirements, and increasing the number of different textbooks does not provide reference or depth.

The role of books in providing information is important even at the kindergarten and first-grade levels. "Where is China?" and "How many kings are in the world?" are typical of young children's questions that can be answered through books. Teachers, with children in tow, may locate a reference that will supply the answer—by studying pertinent pictures with the children and reading explanatory passages to them. The children gradually learn the usefulness of books and may acquire considerable independence in using them to track down information. One four-year-old received a trumpet for Christmas. He was confused when an older sister referred to it as a horn. He went to a book with pictures of musical instruments on his bookshelf, looked up the picture of the instrument most closely resembling his own, asked an adult to read the names, and found it was closer to a trumpet than to a horn. Thus he settled the question in his mind and demonstrated how books can be used for reference even by the very young.

After children start reading, it is only a small step further to teach them how a reference book is organized. For example, in dictionaries and encyclopedias, entries are arranged alphabetically; in an almanac, they are arranged topically throughout the text, and alphabetically only in the index. Practice in looking up information on suitable subjects, such as "Australia" or "myths," will teach children something about what they can and cannot expect to find in a given reference book.

Work with reference books requires some knowledge of alphabetization, of course. In the early grades children can learn that they will find pictures of, say, ants, in the encyclopedia volume marked "A to CEL" on its cover. In the intermediate grades, they can learn why "ant" occurs after "Andes" and before "anvil." Finally, when still in the intermediate grades, youngsters, upon finding the entry, can learn how to scan the article for the pertinent information they want, looking for headings in order to locate sections that will probably contain the desired information.

Children in Grades 4 to 8 are often asked to make written reports from information gleaned from reference books. They should be instructed to enclose by quotation marks, and give full credit for, those portions of an article that are quoted. Teachers should discourage children from copying whole sentences or passages, even when credit is given, as a substitute for taking notes in their own words and writing a report from the notes. How to take such notes needs to be demonstrated by teachers and practiced by the pupils, with the entire class observing and given opportunity to raise questions and offer suggestions.

Guide Pupils in the Use of Difficult Textbooks: Team Learning

In many classrooms the textbook is too difficult for as many as one-third of the pupils. As already pointed out, the teacher may wish to use the book despite its difficulty, if it is exemplary with respect to organization, treatment of topics, and has excellent maps and other desired features. What kind of guidance will help those pupils who cannot read it independently?

One tried-and-tested procedure for using a difficult textbook with poor readers was developed by Donald D. Durrell, who called it "team learning." It consists of dividing the class into teams of from three to five pupils each. Each team includes one good reader who serves as its captain. Each pupil is given a study guide—a teacher-prepared list of questions covering that day's lesson. (See the illustration of a guide in Box 19.2.) Each captain reads the

FIGURE 19.2.   Some children require special teacher help with the social studies textbook. Courtesy of Prince George's County Public Schools, Maryland.

first question aloud to his or her team. The pupils look for the answers in their textbooks and give them orally. When in doubt, members of a team discuss the question together. They then consult an answer sheet. The other questions are read and answered similarly. This procedure allows pupils to work together. The scheme assures success and security for the children because it enables them to check the accuracy of their knowledge im-mediately. Every child responds to every question. This prepares each for whatever discussions and tests the teacher may have planned. As its name implies, a study guide is a *guide*, not a test. It poses questions, provides alter-native answers, and allows for discussion of best answers. It takes pupils through the mental procedures required for understanding the textbook.

BOX 19.2   **GRADES 4–8**

Example of Study Guide for Practice in Literal Interpretation*

1. What two types of boundary divide the United States and Canada?

    _____ a. A river boundary.
    _____ b. A mountain boundary.
    _____ c. A mathematical boundary.
    _____ d. A cultural boundary.

2. Before the airplane was invented, which type of boundary made a na-tion feel safest from an unfriendly neighbor?

    _____ a. A river boundary.
    _____ b. A mountain boundary.
    _____ c. A mathematical boundary.
    _____ d. A cultural boundary.

3. A country would like to trade with its neighbor. Which kind (or kinds) of boundary would be best?

    _____ a. A river boundary.
    _____ b. A mountain boundary.
    _____ c. A mathematical boundary.
    _____ d. A cultural boundary.

*Based on a chapter on boundaries.

It is not necessary to use the team plan every day. Some teachers call the teams together only on the days when they intend to discuss what, in their judgment, are essential pages.

Stimulate Love of Reading and the Habit of Reading

The reading skills and habits discussed thus far are unlikely to become permanently established in children unless, along the way, they have found interest and value in the reading experience. If teachers create the *desire* to read, their pupils will read books in ever-increasing quantity, and their comprehension will improve as a by-product.

Reading to Children.   The keystone of a program designed to build in children a love of, and respect for, books and reading is the practice of reading to children.[6] Our concern in this chapter is with books that will add fresh perspective to social studies units.

Individualized Reading.   Every classroom should be well-stocked with a miniature rotating library of titles relating to the unit, from which children can make choices. From four to six books per child are ideal. Once the unit catches the pupils' imagination, they need little encouragement to browse through these books and to take some from the shelf for reading.

Many volumes in the classroom collection should be specialized informational books. A story is not necessary to hold their attention; in fact, children sometimes state they prefer to read for information without having to keep up with a story line (so often introduced artificially by an author to add "interest"). Examples of straightforward informational books are Sam Epstein's *European Folk Festivals*, M. Sasek's *This Is the United Nations*, and C. B. Colby's *Astronauts in Training*.

Biographies are also popular. Children like to know more about the personalities, temperaments, and adventures of real people. They gain enthusiasm by vicariously visiting Thomas Edison in his laboratory, traveling the underground railway with Harriet Tubman, trudging along the trail with Lewis and Clark, establishing an enlightened new colony with William Penn, or entering outer space with a team of astronauts.

Fiction, of course, is another important category for inclusion. Much of children's fiction has a historical setting; other fiction may be laid in a particular region of the contemporary world. Both kinds have the power to add authentic color to a topic. The value of such works of quality fiction as Carol R. Brink's *Caddie Woodlawn* (a girl in early Wisconsin), Edward Eggleston's *Hoosier Schoolboy* (backwoods Indiana of 1850), Patricia Beatty's *Hail Columbia* (rights-of-women theme), and Elizabeth Coatsworth's *Jon, the Unlucky* (Danish setting) is their successful transmission of the spirit and culture of the time and place of each setting.

Reading Plays Together.   Children enjoy dividing roles and informally reading aloud together. Plays are available dealing with historical events, personalities, fire prevention, work of the Red Cross, family life in other lands, and numerous other social studies subjects. Plays have been compiled by A. S. Burack (*One Hundred Plays for Children*), by Claire Boiko (*Plays*

---

[6]For a spirited defense of reading aloud, even to older children, see Harryette B. Ehrhardt, "Let Them Listen," in Sam L. Sebesta (Ed.), *Ivory, Apes, and Peacocks: The Literature Point of View*, proceedings of the Twelfth Annual Convention, International Reading Association (Newark, DE, 1968), pp. 55–63.

and Programs for Boys and Girls), and by Donald D. Durrell and Alice Crossley (*Favorite Plays for Classroom Reading*); and others are published in a drama magazine for children, *Plays*. Still other plays may be found in the standard library reference, *Plays Index*.

Sustained Silent Reading.   To maximize the benefits of individualized independent reading, some teachers set time aside each day for silent reading. They have found it beneficial to make a ritual of the silent reading period by placing a "Do not disturb" sign on the classroom door, by reading silently to themselves during the set time, and by setting a kitchen timer to signalize the period's beginning and conclusion. A five-minute session may be long enough for younger children unaccustomed to the practice, with its extension to 15 minutes after a month or so. Teachers of older children may wish to schedule from 20 to 30 minutes for uninterrupted reading.

TEACHING COMPETENCIES

This chapter has described how to perform the following tasks that are basic to teacher competency. The teacher should be able to:

1. Take children's dictation and construct experience charts.
2. Select an appropriate textbook.
3. Explain how to preview books and chapters.
4. Prepare the class for reading assignments.
5. Introduce the usefulness of intonation and provide practice in improving it.
6. Provide practice in using five categories of clues that reveal word meanings.
7. Suggest ways to improve grasp of paragraphs.
8. Develop skills for reference reading.
9. Guide pupils in the use of difficult textbooks by means of team learning.
10. Stimulate love of reading and the habit of reading through reading to children, individualized reading, and sustained silent reading.

TRYING OUT SOME OF YOUR COMPETENCIES

1. Provide a group of children in Grades K to 3 with a new experience, such as a tour of a nearby point of interest. Have them dictate an account of what they saw, did, and learned, and prepare an experience chart for their subsequent reading.
2. Find a published play for children, with obvious social studies content. With a small group of children (as many children as there are parts in the play), have them select parts and read the play together. Before and after the reading, use ways suggested in the chapter to bring about their "involvement" with related reading materials.

3. Plan and teach a lesson to help a class see how a difficult passage of a textbook may be made more readily understood through use of context and prediction.

FOR STUDY AND EXPLORATION

1. What are the purposes of having a teacher read to a class in which the pupils are able to read themselves?
2. Make a selection of three biographies that would be suitable for a fifth-grade study of United States history, and write a composite review.
3. Tell how Goodman's "Strategies for Comprehension" would operate in the teaching of a social studies passage of your choice. Her strategies are described in *Findings of Research in Miscue Analysis: Classroom Implications* (cited in footnote 5).
4. Locate a typical social studies reading selection and prepare a study guide for it as described in this chapter.

FURTHER READING

For a detailed description of the procedure for using dictated material by school beginners, see Russell G. Stauffer, *The Language-Experience Approach to the Teaching of Reading* (New York: Harper, 1970), chap. 2, "Dictated Experience Stories."

The important role of children's literature in the social studies is brought out by a number of authors. Alan H. Wheeler ["Individualizing Instruction in Social Studies," *Social Studies*, 62 (April 1971), 166–171] takes the position that trade books are not just "supplementary" but are, in fact, the foundation of the curriculum. A doctoral dissertation concludes that informational trade books for children are a much more adequate and logical source of content for elementary school social studies instruction than are most textbooks. [Robert W. Dalke, "Non-Fiction Writing for Children," *Dissertation Abstracts International*, 34 (December 1973), 3016–3017-A.]

Solid treatment of reading comprehension (though not applied to social studies) is to be found in the following splendid texts:

Dolores Durkin, *Teaching Young Children to Read* (Boston: Allyn and Bacon, 1976), chap. 8, "Comprehension: What Reading Is All About."
Albert J. Harris and Edward R. Sipay, *How to Teach Reading* (New York: Longman, 1979), unit 8, "Helping Children Improve Comprehension."

Those wishing to pursue the subject further will find much of value in Pennsylvania's forward-looking state reading curriculum prepared by Morton Botel in *A Comprehensive Reading-Communication Arts Plan* (Harrisburg: Pennsylvania Department of Education, 1978).

Most controlled investigations of individualized reading have shown distinct benefits as judged by children's improvement in reading. See Richard Thompson, "Individualized Reading: A Summary of Research," *Educational Leadership*, 33 (October 1975), 57–63. How individualized reading may be introduced into social studies is discussed by Ruth K. J. Cline and Bob L. Taylor, "Integrating Literature and 'Free Reading' into the Social Studies Program," *Social Education*, 42 (January 1978),

27–31. Though written with high school classes chiefly in mind, it has clear implications for elementary schools.

Help in locating trade books is provided by "Notable Children's Trade Books in the Field of Social Studies," *Social Education*, 42 (April 1978), 318–321.

More on sustained silent reading appears in Richard Allington, "Sustained Approaches to Reading and Writing," *Language Arts*, 52 (September 1975), 813–815.

20 Providing Writing Experiences

> *. . . fine writing is, next to fine doing,*
> *the top thing in the world.*
> **John Keats**

Social studies offer exciting opportunities for creative writing. The full possibilities of writing projects have still to be explored by many teachers. In one survey of fifth-grade social studies classes, less than 5 percent of the time was observed to be devoted to writing activities.[1] While that survey was conducted more than 10 years ago, current informal observation of social studies lessons lead us to conclude that writing experiences continue to be slighted. Such neglect of writing is difficult to understand in view of the ever-present appropriateness of reports, summaries, and imaginative writing. Writing can play an important role in helping children review, recite, explore, and fix the content they have learned.

Kinds of Writing

Reportorial Writing. In reportorial writing, the child gives a literal account of an event or a faithful description of a personality, social custom, or practice. Possible topics include:

- My Town
- What I Learned on Our Trip to the Airport

---

[1]Wayne L. Herman, Jr., "The Use of Language Arts in Social Studies Lessons," *American Educational Research Journal*, 4 (March 1967), 117–124.

- How Work Is Divided at My Home
- The Strike Leader's Opinion of the Company's Latest Offer
- How the Mayor Spends a Typical Day
- My Father's Job
- What the Bank Does with My Savings
- Games Played by Japanese Children
- Eskimo Folklore
- How Friendly Behavior Is Different from Unfriendly Behavior
- The Writing of "The Star-Spangled Banner"

As reporters, children learn to stick to verified fact. On the other hand, they are free to write as forcefully, colorfully, and dramatically as they wish and are able to. Their reports are usually in prose, but they may also be in verse. One 10-year-old composed a ballad of the Civil War, uneven in meter, but faultless in chronology and geography. It began:

The North and the South were in fierce combat,
    They battled back and forth.
Most of the battles had been won by the rebels,
    Only one had gone to the North.

It is evident that reportorial writing has creative aspects. As Ernest Horn pointed out years ago:

> Actually, a paper that deals directly with a straightforward historical or geo-graphical problem is just as creative and just as much an act of the imagination as any of the exercises listed above (imaginary letters, and so on). For example, writing a description of how the Plains Indians hunted buffalo is just as real a challenge to creative imagination as composing an imaginary letter about it.[2]

Imaginative Writing. Imaginary letters, diaries, autobiographies, and editorials are exercises in which the pupil puts himself in the place of another person or situation and writes in the first person. In another form of imaginative writing, the pupil expresses his feelings or opinions about a social studies topic. For example, one girl, in a study of community services, wrote on "Why I Would Like to Be a Nurse." Following a year of study of world cultures, one class wrote about "The Foreign Country I Would Like to Visit Most."

In a unit on governmental service, a committee prepared a report on "How I Think the Postal Service Could Be Improved." Pupils have written imaginary editorials—on civil rights, on legislation adverse to billboard advertising, and on other current issues. One pupil wrote a story of the Rip

---

[2]Ernest Horn, *Methods of Instruction in the Social Studies* (New York: Scribner, 1937), p. 459.

Van Winkle genre in which a person who has just awakened from a long sleep makes comparisons between 1920 and today and comments on the astonishing changes that had occurred. Another type of imaginative writing consists of trying to account for a baffling situation or problem, such as the low percentage of voting turnout in the United States.

Still another type of imaginative writing deals with "imaginary worlds." It may be suggested by the teacher that children invent their own utopias, or ways of preventing war, or a different kind of school than the one they are familiar with.[3] A variation of this has been proposed by Kantor and Perron who see value in presenting children with a challenge such as: "Children someday may go to school all year long. Do you think it is a good idea? Why or why not?" Kantor and Perron believe that the exposition and argument that are required have a beneficial stretching effect on the linguistic and cognitive powers of elementary school children.[4]

Imaginative writing in the social studies should, of course, have a factual base. It should avoid anachronisms, such as the one that a pupil unwittingly wrote when he had Benjamin Franklin state, in an imaginary page of his diary, that his fountain pen was running dry. Also to be avoided are flights of phantasy that depart from "the disciplined use of the imagination."[5] An example of a piece that successfully avoids such pitfalls was written by a third-grader in connection with the study of the Plains Indians:

If I Were an Indian Long Ago

If I were an Indian I would have to work hard. I would have to feed the horses. I would have to eat different things if I were an Indian. I would have to learn how to shoot a bow and arrow. I would have to go hunting for buffalo. I would have to be quiet while I was hunting so I could sneak up without the animal hearing me. My mother would have to cook our meals over a fire. We would have to make our house with skins. We would hunt deer too. We would have to travel many places if the buffalo herd wasn't near us. Many Indians in the tribes are dying because they have no food.

Magnificent historical novels, such as those by A. B. Guthrie, Jr., and ballads about unassuming heroes, such as those of Sara Cleghorn, attest to the congeniality of creative writing and authenticity.

Practical Writing.   There are numerous occasions for pupils to write letters for specific practical ends. The class has to order materials (maps,

---

[3]Richard Murphy, *Imaginary Worlds: Notes on a New Curriculum* (New York: Teachers and Writers Collaborative, 1974). May be obtained from ERIC Document Reproduction Service, P. O. Box 190, Arlington, VA 22210.

[4]Ken Kantor and Jack Perron, "Thinking and Writing: Creativity in the Modes of Discourse," *Language Arts*, 54 (October 1977), 742–749.

[5]Horn, *Methods of Instruction in the Social Studies*, p. 459.

books, folders, and so forth), seek information (from embassies, governmental bureaus, authorities, and others), make arrangements (for visiting a museum, inviting a guest consultant, and so forth), and send thanks to guides at the site of a field trip and to parents or others who have provided a service in connection with a unit.

Letters are not the only kind of practical writing. For example, frequently the teacher can display pictures of places, events, and personalities and ask the children to write captions for them that are apt and clear. Before the school year is over, there are normally enough needs of these kinds to permit every pupil to have the experience of undertaking at least one of the writing responsibilities.

Dictated Compositions in the Primary Grades

In kindergarten and first grade, before children can write with any degree of fluency, the children may dictate their thoughts to the teacher, as illustrated in Chapter 19. Even in third grade much of children's creative composition may be accepted in oral form. For those children at this age who find handwriting laborious, any writing assignment requires a heavy investment of time, out of proportion to the meager product. (Some third-graders, of course, are productive writers.) In seeing their dictated accounts written, first on the chalkboard and then transferred to a chart, pupils in the beginning years learn that their recollections and ideas can be written down. Soon they will want to do the writing themselves.

Although some teachers encourage the entire class to "write" an account in this manner, a few children tend to monopolize the dictation, and retiring children do not contribute. A better plan is to have individuals or small groups (three to five pupils) do the dictation. Teachers sometimes "borrow" pupils from the upper grades in order to enlist their help in taking down the dictated reports, ideas, and stories.

BOX 20.1   **GRADES 3–8**

Types of Possible Writing Experiences in Social Studies

Reportorial Writing: descriptions, summaries, narratives, and poetry about—

Events	Processes	Discoveries
Games	Jobs	Inventions
Folklore	Products	Conflicts
Behavior	Problems	Personalities
Experiments	Services	Social Customs

(Continued)

Imaginative Writing: Writing about the past, present, or future—

If I were . . .	Logs	Descriptions of
Personal letters	Poetry	events, sports,
Diaries	Pantomimes	family life
Editorials	Character sketches	Secret thoughts of a
Newspapers	Skits	major or minor
Advertisements	Solutions to problems	character
Historical or	Radio and TV	
regional stories	commercials	

Practical Writing: Writing for practical purposes—

Ordering material	Corresponding with
Extending and	pen pals, relatives,
responding to	friends
invitations	Requests for reser-
Thank you notes	vations
Captions for pictures	Daily or project plans
Requests for	
information	

Ways of Stimulating Writing

Provide a Secure Environment.   A protective and secure environment and a supportive atmosphere will promote children's writing. "The spontaneity of a child's use of language is an indication of his sense of security."[6]

Prepare Children for Writing Experiences through Exposure to the Writing of Others.   The best stimulation that children can have for writing is exposure to what others have written either through having it read by others or reading it themselves.[7] The younger the child the greater the advantage of having the exposure occur in listening to the teacher read, but the benefits of listening continue throughout the elementary school years. This places upon the teacher an obligation to seek out published materials containing suitable, arresting content. The selection may consist of a description of a place, an imaginative or literal account of an event, an interesting idea, a moving poem, or the scene of a play. The selection should relate, of course,

---

[6]Ruth Strickland, *The Language Arts in the Elementary School* (Lexington, MA: D. C. Heath, 1969), p. 90.

[7]Leah M. Wilcox, "Literature: The Child's Guide to Creative Writing," *Language Arts*, 54 (May 1977), 549–554.

to the social studies unit and should serve to enrich and extend it. Through inviting the class to comment on the selection ("Was the author telling us what really happened or was it make-believe?" "What problem was the girl in the story trying to solve?" "Was the author trying to get you to agree with him about how to save money?" and similar questions), the teacher discovers that many children become eager to produce accounts of their own.

BOX 20.2   **GRADES K-3**

Children Learn to Write by Listening to Literature

Joy F. Moss, teacher of six- and seven-year-olds, knew that "creative writing does not evolve spontaneously out of a vacuum." [See Joy F. Moss, "Learning to Write by Listening to Literature," *Language Arts,* 54 (May 1977), 537–542.] By becoming immersed in the world of literature, her pupils developed a "theory of narrative." After exposure to stories with a common theme (toy animals), the pupils were asked to compare those stories with respect to such story elements as setting (winter versus summer), form (verse or prose), position on a reality-fantasy continuum, and how each of the authors was trying to make the reader feel. The children then brought favorite animal toys to school. Before writing about them, they were asked to decide on viewpoint (who will do the talking, you or the animal?), events (what will happen?), problems (how will they be solved?), etc. Production of stories by the children was found to be a natural extension of their prior exposure to published stories and discussion and comparison of them. Applications of this approach to social studies stories immediately suggest themselves in studies of littering, beautifying the school grounds, the work of moving men, and so forth.

Have Children Exchange Ideas Preceding the Writing. A discussion of ideas or topics for writing serves to motivate children's desire to write. Sufficient time is needed to entertain numerous ideas.

Try Team Writing. There are some children in almost every class who find the task of writing physically and intellectually overwhelming and personally threatening. Tway, observing in English schools years ago, found that a procedure called by the British "team writing" offered an ideal solution which she verified later by her work with children in the United States. A small group of children collaborated on a report or a story, exchanging among themselves sources of information, ideas, and writing techniques. This created a low-risk situation for the reluctant writers who found it almost impossible to know how to get started independently. The support which the insecure writers received from their classmates proved invaluable, and eventually they branched out on their own.[8] Some children achieve independence and fluency in their writing *only* after collaborative experiences.

BOX 20.3   **GRADES 4-8**

Pictures for Warm-Up

Many teachers have discovered that pictures provide fruitful starting points for children who find writing a chore. Chapter 17 lists sources of pictures, and librarians are resourceful aids in helping teachers find illustrations of specialized subjects that vividly stir the imagination. Dramatic pictures, pictures showing fine detail, and pictures that take the viewer behind the scenes will often stimulate children who otherwise find it hard to find a subject or who feel they have nothing to say.

Have Children Choose Their Own Topics.   While there are occasions when teachers may legitimately challenge a class with an assigned topic, as has already been illustrated, self-selected topics are usually much to be preferred. Unfortunately, a great deal of children's writing today is prescribed by teachers. According to one report, more than half of one group of seventh-graders never had the opportunity to choose their own subjects. Children tend to write more, with more substantial content, when they are encouraged to select their own topics.

Have Children Share Their Writing with One Another.   Children enjoy writing for their classmates. Times can be set aside for them to read their written works to the class or to small groups. Occasionally, the teacher can help them share their work with one another by dittoing their writing and passing it out.

The rationale for having children share their writing is based on more substantial considerations than simply their enjoyment of it. No one has presented the rationale more fully and persuasively than James Moffett.[9] Moffett points out that, under ideal conditions, children would write because they have something to say and because they want to have certain effects on an audience. Classmates are a natural audience and their feedback is important to the child writer. Moffett has observed that children write much better when they write for each other than when they write for the teacher.

---

[8]Eileen Tway, "Writing: An Interpersonal Process," *Language Arts*, 53 (May 1976), 594–596.
[9]James Moffett, *Teaching the Universe of Discourse* (Boston: Houghton Mifflin, 1973.)

Furthermore, he discovered that peers are likely to be more candid than is the teacher. The chief role of the teacher, then, is to teach the children how to teach each other.

Moffett's procedure is to break the class into groups of four or five and to have the pupils exchange their reports or stories. This should be done *during* the writing instead of only afterwards, for what is learned during the feedback can be incorporated in the final draft. Older pupils can write comments on the papers. (It seems logical to believe that it would be better for most elementary school children simply to discuss them.) The small size of the group, Moffett points out, makes the comments responsible and helpful; no one speaks to impress the teacher or to show off before the class. After the group meetings, the papers are revised. (The teacher does not give grades on individual papers, but eventually, if the papers go into a pupil's folder, they may be evaluated as a group by the teacher when reports are due.)[10]

The teacher plays an active role during these small-group sessions by circulating among the groups and sitting in on them in rotation, serving as a consultant. Thus, the teacher becomes a member of each small audience in turn. Moffett has found that while children as young as age nine "can spot the writing of their peers, they often do not have enough understanding of the cause of a problem to know how to solve it." For example, children may correctly report that they find someone's report boring and that it repeats certain words too often. "But the real reason for the monotony and for the repetition of the words," writes Moffett, "is that there are too many simple sentences, some of which should be joined."[11] The teacher's knowledge of such technical elements of composition enables him or her to offer a most important kind of instruction. Not only does the child whose writing is under scrutiny receive direct aid, but all those in the group learn a writing technique that they can apply in their own future compositions.

Some teachers feel it is beneficial to have the sharing of writing include the teacher's writing. Teachers, too, on occasion, may prepare a social studies report. They may read it to the class and tell of the writing problems they met (the choice of a word, what to leave out, how to end it, etc.) and how they solved them. Children thereby gain a new perspective on the pleasures and discipline of writing.

Assist Children in Finding Ways to Preserve Their Writing.   One means for having children develop pride in their writing is to encourage them to keep it. They may need help in acquiring techniques for organizing it in a notebook, filing it in personal folders, or binding it in handmade booklets. As the school year advances, they like to reread their earlier work and note their progress as writers.

---

[10]Ibid.
[11]Ibid.

Place Emphasis on Content Rather than on Mechanical Features of Writing.   Writing for social studies should focus upon social studies content. The teacher's first objective should be to arouse the child's desire to write with spontaneity and freshness. This goal is not achieved when teachers go through every composition with a colored pencil, marking errors of punctuation, syntax, and spelling. As children widen their reading, they become increasingly aware of the mechanical conventions of writing and their functional purposes. When this occurs, they may be appropriately helped to use these conventions in their writing. Gebhardt makes a good case for "balancing discipline and creativity in writing classes." Children, he states, need to learn the various stages of composition, including revision. Thus, writing "begins in creativity and playfulness and moves toward discipline and craftsmanship."[12] Finally, they should be taught how to proofread their compositions for errors and encouraged to make a habit of it.

Teacher Praise and Teacher Criticism

We have already said that children are believed to write better when they write for each other than when they write for the teacher, and that they probably benefit more from their peer's praise and criticism than from their teachers. But teachers, too, should provide feedback. What is the proper balance between teacher praise and teacher criticism?

John Holt expresses the view that children do not need the amount of praise they often get; that the child who struggles with a task and finally completes it does not need to be told by the teacher that he has done well.[13] Elaine H. Wagner deplores the practice of student teachers who, through the commendable desire to offer reinforcement, are too glib with their praise: " 'That's good, Johhny;' 'That's good, Mary;' 'Good, Billy;' 'Good, good, good.' Unfortunately, children realize that no real feelings or thoughts are being communicated thereby and that they cannot trust this style of 'praise.' "[14]

She recommends that teachers give their affirmative statements a concrete basis. For example, teachers may speak favorably about a child's use of picturesque language, or effective repetition, or a vivid word picture, or an unusual idea. From such explicit praise, Wagner believes, children are helped to grow both in self-esteem and in their use of language.

What about teacher criticism? Groff, in reviewing the research on effects of criticism, found that negative criticism as well as positive criticism may have a positive effect on the quality of children's written

---

[12]Richard Gebhardt, "The Timely Teeter-Totter: Balancing Discipline and Creativity in Writing Classes," *Language Arts*, 54 (September 1977), 673–678.

[13]John Holt, *How Children Fail* (Belmont, CA: Pitman, 1974).

[14]Elaine H. Wagner, "Affirmation and Children's Writing," *Childhood Education*, 53 (February 1977), 195–198.

compositions.[15] We do not interpret that to mean that *any* criticism is permissible. If criticism threatens the secure environment described earlier in this chapter as the first essential, it will lead to reduced writing productivity, to avoidance of writing, and to diminished quality. Constructive criticism is always offered with encouragement, support, and specific direction for improvement.

TEACHING COMPETENCIES

This chapter describes how to perform the following tasks that are basic to teacher competency. The teacher should be able to:

1. Stimulate writing experiences related to the social studies unit by providing a secure environment, by reading what others have written, by conducting discussion of ideas before writing, and by allowing children to choose their topics.
2. Encourage various kinds of writing: reportorial, imaginative, and practical.
3. Have young children dictate compositions to him or her.
4. Evaluate pupils' writing by employing a balance of specific praise and constructive criticism.
5. Organize team writing, and have children share their writing with one another.
6. Teach children how to proofread and revise their writing.

TRYING OUT SOME OF YOUR COMPETENCIES

1. Have a small group of kindergarten or primary children dictate to you a common class experience. Write it on the chalkboard and later rewrite it on experience chart paper.
2. Have intermediate children compose one of the following kinds of writing: reportorial, imaginative, practical. Allow them to share their writing with one another.
3. Discuss with a child the strengths and weaknesses of his or her writing. Give constructive criticism accompanied with specific instructional ideas to improve the writing, and be supportive in your advice.

FOR STUDY AND EXPLORATION

1. Why are writing skills—as compared with listening, speaking, and reading skills—generally the least developed with pupils of all ages?

---

[15]Patrick Groff, "Does Negative Criticism Discourage Children's Compositions?" *Language Arts*, 52 (October 1975), 1032–1034.

2. As a teacher, how would you respond to a child who says, "I can't think of anything to write."

FURTHER READING

How to develop writing readiness is discussed in a highly practical way by Charles K. Stallard in "Writing Readiness: A Developmental View," *Language Arts*, 54 (October 1977), 775–779; and by Joy F. Moss in "Learning to Write by Listening to Literature," *Language Arts*, 54 (May 1977), 537–542.

Ronald I. Cramer tells how to teach writing in "The Nature and Nurture of Creative Writing," *Elementary School Journal*, 75 (May 1975), 507–512. He suggests how to develop sensitivity to good writing, how children's written work may be shared and displayed, and how the teacher may function as a catalyst.

The March 1979 issue of *Social Education* was devoted to "Writing to Learn in Social Studies," and included six insightful articles edited by Barry K. Beyer and Anita Brostoff. Some of them are: "Writing and the Generation of Knowledge" by A. D. Nostrand; "Developmental Writing: Social Studies Assignments," by Raymond Ventre; Henry A. Giroux wrote "Teaching Content and Thinking Through Writing"; and the editors dealt with "The Time It Takes: Managing/Evaluating Writing and Social Studies."

*Journey all over the universe
in a map, without all the expense
and fatigue of traveling.*
Miguel de Cervantes

Maps are graphic drawings of the earth's surface or portions of it. Globes are scaled-down models of the earth. Both maps and globes give definiteness to geographical ideas. Maps and globes aid children in a number of ways. (1) Children learn a region's shape, size and boundaries; (2) they learn the meaning of various geographical terms (such as "island," "isthmus," "earth"); (3) they perceive relationships, such as the role of the Suez Canal in shortening shipping routes, or the advantage to early settlers of establishing themselves by the mouths of rivers that afford snug harbors; and (4) they discover correlated phenomena, such as vegetation and rainfall, through side-by-side comparison of maps (or map overlays), each of which shows the distribution of a different phenomenon.

Not everything on a map is self-evident, however. Children using maps and globes have revealed erroneous conceptions: that rivers flow in from the sea; that islands are somehow anchored to the bottom of the sea; and that state boundaries are barriers through which a river must cut a channel in order to traverse them. It is not enough, therefore, merely to expose children to maps and globes; instruction is also needed.

378

MAPS AND GLOBES IN THE PRIMARY GRADES

Just as reading is a part of every unit, so are maps. But we must remember that many children in the primary grades have difficulty grasping the spatial relationships required for understanding maps. Perhaps the best-known study showing this was conducted by Piaget and Inhelder.[1] They placed three cardboard mountains on a rectangular table and a chair at each of the four sides of the table. A child was asked to sit in one of the chairs. Then the investigators moved a doll from one of the empty chairs to the others and asked the child in each instance how the mountains looked to *the doll*. The child could answer in one of several ways, for example, by selecting one drawing from a set—a drawing best matching the scene that the doll "saw." Children in the preoperational stage (up to about seven years of age) were unable to perform this task, and the performance of children at the stage of concrete operations (from seven to 11 years of age) was spotty.

John Eliot cites 11 studies that have tested Piaget and Inhelder's conclusions, and states that, "generally speaking, these studies have supported Piaget's contention that children experience a sequential development of concepts of space, and that the ability to conceptualize space is a relatively late developmental product."[2] Eliot points out, however, how little uniformity there has been in these experiments and how much more we need to know.

It is well for teachers to be aware of children's limitations in learning spatial relations. But it is also important for them to know that even kindergarten children and beginning first-graders have a partial understanding of the earth.[3] Furthermore, it is known that steady progress can be made by most children through a carefully planned, unhurried sequence of learning activities.[4] We now turn to a description of experiences that will promote map understanding.

---

[1]Piaget and Inhelder worked with Swiss children. Similar limitations have been found among children in the United States. See Joseph P. Stoltman, "Children's Conceptions of Space and Territorial Relationships," *Social Education* (February 1977), 96–104.

[2]John Eliot, "Children's Spatial Visualization," in Phillip Bacon (Ed.), *Focus on Geography: Key Concepts and Teaching Strategies*, 40th Yearbook of the National Council for the Social Studies (Washington, DC, 1970). John Towler found the same developmental sequence as did Piaget, but he found some children as young as five who were capable of performing the task correctly; see his "Egocentrism: A Key to Map-Reading Ability?" *Social Education*, 35 (December 1971), 893–898.

[3]Dora Portugaly, "A Study of the Development of Disadvantaged Kindergarten Children's Understanding of the Earth as a Globe," *Dissertation Abstracts*, 28 (April 1968), 4056-A. Jack M. Sheridan, "Children's Awareness of Physical Geography," *Journal of Geography*, 67 (February 1968), 82–86.

[4]Haig A. Rushdoony, "The Geography, the Teacher, and a Child's Perception of Maps and Mapping," *Journal of Geography*, 70 (October 1971), 429–433. George F. Howe, "Teaching Directions in Space," *Journal of Geography*, 31 (May 1932), 209–210.

Making Layouts with Blocks

Children *make* maps before they *read* them. They make them as pre-schoolers and kindergarteners when with blocks, boxes, and other construction play materials they arrange farm layouts, neighborhoods, skyscrapers, rows of stores on a street, harbors, or roads connecting home and airport or other known points. The crudity of these portrayals should not blind us to their significance: They are symbolic resemblances on a reduced scale to some spatial arrangement children have seen or heard about. In essence, this is what every map is. Blocks should be standard equipment for kindergarten and first-grade children, both large blocks for the playground and smaller ones for the classroom.[5]

By the way children build their bridges, locate their bodies of water, and arrange their buildings, the teacher can tell wherein their experience and observation are lacking. He can aid them by taking the class on walks in the community, calling attention to arrangements as they actually exist, and suggesting after the walks that they use blocks to show what they saw. Pictures showing how the community is laid out will also help. Children who show insight into spatial arrangements may be asked to explain their block layouts to their classmates.

FIGURE 21.1.   Young children's first "maps" are constructed with blocks. Courtesy of Childcraft Education Corporation, Edison, NJ, manufacturer and distributor of early educational materials.

[5]Lucy Sprague Mitchell, *Young Geographers* (New York: Basic Books, 1963), pp. 27, 88–89.

Acquiring a Bird's-Eye-View Perspective

One of the authors was asked to help a group of third-grade children learn how to read maps. They had spent several fruitless weeks working with maps of the United States. One reason they were making no headway was that many of them lacked the bird's-eye-view concept. They were unable to draw, for example, a bird's-eye view of a book lying on the floor. It was necessary for some of the children to mount a chair and look down upon the book, and also to compare several sketches of books drawn from different positions, before the concept became intelligible to them. In order to increase their spatial concepts, these children required trips to points at various elevations in order to view the neighborhood from different perspectives. They also needed to do some informal sketching, construction of floor plans, and construction of diagrams and models showing the routes that members of the class took to get to school each day. The emphasis of their social studies book on maps—among the more difficult tools a child must come to understand—was obviously premature.

Another way to develop the bird's-eye-view concept is to present a sequence of photographs of something—say, the school and schoolyard. The first photograph should show the school as seen horizontally—from across the street or from an extreme corner of the playground; the second, the school as seen from an oblique angle—from a tall building nearby; and the third, the school as seen from an airplane directly above—a truly vertical bird's-eye view.

Using and Making Community Maps

At some point in the first grade most children are ready to use a teacher-made map of the community (see Figure 21.2). This should be based on a local street map from a real estate office, or a vertical aerial photograph, and be large enough to show each block.

BOX 21.1   **GRADES K–3**

Introducing Map Symbols in Primary Grades

1. Place a large community map on the floor, oriented according to true directions, with only streets shown.
2. With the children gathered around, draw a picture of a school on the map.
3. Have children suggest nearby landmarks and locate their positions on the map. Have them draw the landmarks on the map.
4. Post the map on a wall, and refer to it frequently.
5. Some time later, post beside this map a similar one (same dimensions, same streets shown, etc.), but with abstract symbols in place of pictorial symbols. Show rectangles for the school and other buildings,

(Continued)

perhaps with further symbols to identify certain landmarks—for example, make a religious symbol for a house of worship; make green-colored patches for parks and playgrounds; draw cross-hatching for a construction site. Discuss the new map with the pupils.

6. Leave both maps posted for several weeks to give pupils an opportunity to make comparisons and to become accustomed to the symbols.

Such a map is useful in many ways: Each child can locate her own house and those of her friends and note their distance from and directional relationships to the school; the class can orient itself before and after each trip; relatively safe walking and bicycling routes can be worked out; and places being studied can be located. These maps are drawn on large sheets of paper. Part of the time they should be spread out on the floor, properly oriented with respect to directions. Such maps provide a good opportunity to introduce children to map symbols, such as the conventional blue coloring of bodies of water, and lines with crossbars to represent railroad tracks. The children may themselves originate symbols, such as swings drawn on a space

FIGURE 21.2   Portion of community map prepared by the teacher for the first grade.

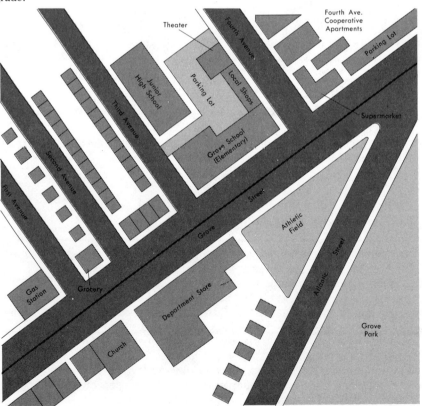

to represent a playground. If, at first, only those features they have seen at first hand are symbolized, the utility of these markings will be obvious. Pupils should be encouraged, when using a map, to be conscious of ways in which it departs from reality, so that the symbolic nature of its coloring, marking, and size is understood. Use of teacher-made maps of the community should continue throughout the primary grades.

Children should have the experience of making their own maps, too. Their first maps generally spring from direct observation. As already suggested, they can be constructed from blocks, or they may be drawn, painted, or modeled in clay. The teacher's map is a standard against which children can check their own for accuracy. They can verify relative distances by counting their steps while walking between various points represented on their maps.

Learning the Cardinal Directions

Children in our present culture, with its abundant signs and guideposts, appear to have no pressing practical need to become direction-conscious, and many of them, indeed, do not develop this awareness.[6] Yet the ability to orient oneself and to acquire a sense of direction is essential in making and using maps.

Children's ignorance of directions cannot be attributed solely to the absence of practical demands upon them for directional knowledge, however. One factor to be reckoned with is the failure of many teachers to provide them with experiences that make the language of direction meaningful. Several procedures have proven their worth:

1. Place the maps on the floor occasionally, giving the children a chance to orient them with the aid of a compass.
2. Before the class takes trips, diagram the route with chalk on the floor, surfaced playground, or sidewalk, and identify the cardinal directions.
3. Call attention to directions by painting a north-pointing arrow on the classroom floor and on the playground, and also by displaying a sundial and a weather vane.
4. Have the members of the class face north. Their backs will be toward the south; their right hands, east; and their left, west. They can remember this because the right hand is usually the more important one, and the sun rises in the east—the most important event of the day!

---

[6]John R. Lee and Lee Stampfer, "Two Studies in Learning Geography," *Social Education,* 30 (December 1966), 627-628. Ralph C. Preston, "A Comparison of Knowledge of Directions in German and in American Children," in Wayne L. Herman, Jr., (Ed.), *Current Research in Elementary-School Social Studies* (New York: Crowell-Collier-Macmillan, 1969), pp. 424-427.

5. Give formal instruction. Take the class outside to observe the position of the sun and identify the cardinal directions. Hold a stick
erect, one end on the ground, and observe the relation of the stick's
shadow to the position of the sun. Tell about its similarity to sun-
dials.

Initiating Informal Experiences with Globes

The kindergarten child's view of the earth is likely to be a limited one,
circumscribed by the horizon of the child's environment. However, the
kindergarten year is not too early to introduce the concept of the earth as a
sphere. The teacher need do no more at this level than keep a large globe in
the classroom and make occasional reference to it. Later, in the primary
grades, children can learn regions that are mentioned in discussion, such as
the United States, the Pacific Ocean, Africa, Virginia, the North Pole, or the
equator. The approximate site of the community in which the school is
located can be marked with a paper arrow affixed to the globe with rubber
cement.

MAPS AND GLOBES IN THE INTERMEDIATE GRADES

Maps are not only for units that are largely geographic. They are essential in *every* unit. The skills underlying their use must, of course, be taught,
for studies have shown that many concepts basic to map interpretation are
poorly developed in intermediate-grade children.[7] This is due in part to inadequate teaching. Several investigators have found that children can be
taught certain fairly sophisticated map skills.[8] There is little question that
children's potential for map learning has been underestimated.

Conditions Favorable to Map Learning

Instruction That Promotes Inquiry and Discovery.   A study by Val
Arnsdorf points to the advantages of the "go-slow" discovery method in
teaching map concepts.[9]

Arnsdorf's subjects were fifth-grade children who discovered geo-

[7]Lee and Stampfer, "Two Studies in Learning Geography." Daniel H. Brown,
"Knowledge of Important Principles of Physical Geography Possessed by Selected
Sixth-Grade Children," *Dissertation Abstracts*, 24 (June 1964), 5072.

[8]O. L. Davis, Jr., "Learning about Time Zones in Grades Four, Five, and Six," in
Wayne L. Herman, Jr., (Ed.), *Current Research in Elementary-School Social Studies* (New
York: Crowell-Collier-Macmillan, 1969), pp. 80–87. Val Arnsdorf, "Teaching Social
Studies with Map-Overlays," *California Journal of Educational Research*, 16 (March
1965), 65–74. O. L. Davis, Jr., "Children Can Learn Complex Concepts," *Educational
Leadership*, 17 (December 1959), 170–175.

[9]Val Arnsdorf, "Teaching Social Studies"; and "Teaching Map Reading and
Geographic Understanding with Projectuals," in Wayne L. Herman, Jr., (Ed.), *Current
Research in Elementary-School Social Studies* (New York: Crowell-Collier-Macmillan,
1969), pp. 413–431.

graphical relationships through the use of color-sensitized transparent map overlays.[10] Each overlay depicted a different geographic feature (population density, land use, mineral resources, and so on). Lessons were conducted twice weekly.

During each lesson, the teacher attempted to develop an understanding of how the feature was distributed throughout the United States. To do this, he had each child cover the map grid with a transparency that revealed, say, the population density, and plot the information on an outline map. During each lesson, the teacher also attempted to develop an understanding of the relationship that might exist between one feature and another. In this connection, the children attempted predictions—for example, concerning what role precipitation might play in the distribution of vegetation and land use. Following the study of related overlays, the children read up on the subject from various authoritative sources in order to test the accuracy of their predictions. This pattern of instruction was continued for 12 lessons.

Before and after the experiment, the children were tested on the work-study skills section of the Iowa Tests of Basic Skills, which contain tests of map reading, interpretation of graphs and tables, and reference skills. Arnsdorf's data showed that the children made substantial progress following the instruction.

Instruction That Is Intensive.   The typical daily time allotment for the teaching of map skills is undoubtedly insufficient, and the teaching is often lackadaisical. In the Arnsdorf study, instruction was intensive. His subjects devoted one hour for each of 12 lessons to their maps. O. L. Davis, Jr., demonstrated that intermediate-grade pupils can learn such concepts as time zone, rotation of earth, and International Date Line when they devote 30 minutes a day to it for 14 days.[11] Haig A. Rushdoony's third-grade subjects, who clearly benefited from map instruction, were taught 90 minutes weekly for 15 weeks.[12]

Instruction That Is Varied.   There is no need for children to groan, "Oh, we had map work again today!" Map work need not and should not connote a single type of exercise or activity. A map is a tool, which, like a pocket knife, hammer, or other versatile tool, can be used to achieve a variety of purposes. The remainder of this chapter will indicate the wide range of instructional techniques at the teacher's disposal.

---

[10]Map overlays are provided by many map manufacturers (see list in Box 21.11). Allyn and Bacon, Rockleigh, NJ, has three or four base maps for each of several regions—Europe, South Asia, and others—with 29 or 30 overlays illustrating natural resources, climate, land use, transportation routes, industry, etc. Sunburst Communications, Pound Ridge, NY 10576, has 14 overlays for the United States and 10 for Africa.

[11]Davis, "Learning about Time Zones."

[12]Haig A. Rushdoony, "An Achievement in Map Reading: An Experimental Study," in Wayne L. Herman, Jr., (Ed.), *Current Research in Elementary-School Social Studies* (New York: Crowell-Collier-Macmillan, 1969), pp. 407–413.

Continuing Work with Directions

The five types of activities given on pages 383–384 for teaching directions in the primary grades should be repeated in the intermediate grades, and the underlying principles should be reviewed. Direction-consciousness may then be further extended.

1. When hanging maps that show north at the top, the teacher should use the north wall of the classroom, so that the maps continue to be as nearly correct, in relation to the earth's directions, as possible. Then, when the children face the map and the north, the right side of the body is always toward the east of the earth and the map, and the left side of the body is toward the west. This practice has one obvious drawback: It causes some children to adopt a fixed notion of north as up and south as down. Ways of preventing this are suggested in Box 21.2.

BOX 21.2   **GRADES 4–8**

How to Offset the Notion That North Is Up and South Is Down

1. Post polar azimuthal projections of the earth in which "up north" and "down south" do not apply (see Figure 21.9F). Most modern atlases and geography books have at least one such projection.
2. Occasionally invert maps and globes, pointing out that their position does not make them wrong. (Drawing maps with north at the top is just a convention.)
3. Plan a drill in which children point to a river on a wall map. Then make such statements as "the Po flows down and east" and "the Nile flows down and north." (Rivers *always* flow down, from higher elevations to lower elevations.)
4. Plan a drill in which children point sequentially to the cardinal directions (north, east, south, west), naming each; then have them point up (directly overhead), saying "up!", and point down (toward the center of the earth), saying "down!"

---

2. The compass can help in developing direction-consciousness. Because the compass needle points to the magnetic North Pole and not in the direction of the geographic (true) North Pole, except in a few places, a correction must be made to determine true north. Box 21.3 shows how this is done. The magnetic North Pole is located in the Northwest Territories of Canada. Periodically it shifts its position. The geographic North Pole is the point at which the meridians (the north-south lines shown on a globe) meet. It is not necessary to know the deviation between the poles (called declination) when reading maps in the classroom, but it is essential when finding one's way out-of-doors with a map and compass.

BOX 21.3   **GRADES 4-8**

Finding Magnetic North and True North

1. Consult a recent almanac under "magnetic declinations" or write to Solid Earth Data Services, National Geophysical and Solar-Terrestrial Data Center, Boulder, CO 80302 for copy of table of declinations for your state. Find the declination for the city nearest you. (The declination-changes shift, so obtain a recent table.) For example, the recent declination for Minneapolis is 5° E.
2. Place the compass so that its needle comes to rest pointing at 5° east of north, for example, or to the declination for the city nearest you.

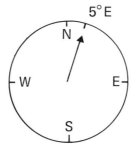

3. Note the direction of the north mark (not the needle); it lines up in the direction of geographic (true) north.

---

3. Discuss nature's guideposts as indicators of direction. Children are fascinated by this topic. The direction of shadows is an indicator that is easy for children to study, and makes a logical starting place. The sun is always south of the United States, so shadows are always pointed in a northerly direction (but due north only at noon). The sun always rises in the east and sets in the west, so morning shadows point in a northwesterly direction and afternoon ones in a northeasterly direction. Children can make these and other observations of the sun and its shadows as rough indicators of direction and can bring records of their observations to class for discussion.

Other signs are more mysterious and are not infallible. Woodsmen who use them report that they make several observations and determine the central tendencies of signs by "averaging" them. According to one well-known woodsman, the late Horace Kephart, the tip of a large pine or hemlock usually points toward the rising sun—somewhat south of east. Exceptions do occur (trees in deep valleys or on wind-swept crests are among the exceptions), but Kephart believes that the tips of three-fourths of the trees he has examined do point southeastward. Similarly, if the stumps of fallen trees are examined, the annual rings are said to be larger typically on

BOX 21.4   **GRADES 4–8**

Test Your Pupils' Directional Sense

Give the following test to your class before you teach about directions. Collect the tests and file them away, neither discussing them nor reporting the results. Following a week of teaching about directions, give the test a second time, and now report to your pupils the results of both testings. Both you and your pupils will probably be pleased at the gains they have made.

The items are arranged according to difficulty, as determined by the performance of American and German elementary school children. Without instruction, only the first question was answered correctly by a majority of the children.

Directions: Put an X in front of each correct answer.

1. I was going toward the east and turned left into a street. I was now going toward what direction?

   _____ north

   _____ east

   _____ south

   _____ west

2. I am lying in bed on my stomach with my head toward the south. Which wall of the room is to my left?

   _____ north wall

   _____ east wall

   _____ south wall

   _____ west wall

3. A boy stood on a beach and looked out toward the setting sun. Then he turned sharply to the right. In which direction did he turn??

   _____ north

   _____ east

   _____ south

   _____ west

4. When I arise in the morning, the sun shines through my bedroom window upon a closet in the middle of the opposite wall. When I stand in

                                                                 (Continued)

the middle of the room facing the door, the closet is to my right. In which wall is the door?

_____ north wall

_____ east wall

_____ south wall

_____ west wall

KEY: (1) north,   (2) east wall,   (3) north,   (4) south wall.

the north side, frequently on the northeast or east side, but very seldom on the south, southwest, or west side. Moss, not to be confused with lichen, is reported to favor the north and northwest sides of trees if the trees are straight, rough-barked, and exposed to direct sunlight. Because of the southern direction of the sun, the moisture is retained longer on the northern side of the tree, and moisture is a condition that is conducive to the growth of moss. All of these signs are probably the result of the direction of the sun and its effect upon living things. Such signs are used by woodsmen as rules of thumb. They are no substitute for the compass, or for direct guidance from sun, shadows, and stars.

Making and Using Special-Purpose Maps

A special-purpose map is designed to explain an explicit feature, condition, or event. Geographers sometimes call it a "thematic" map. Most maps appearing in newspapers are of this type. For example, the map in Figure 21.3 shows how cotton-growing has spread westward in recent years. Figure 21.4, drawn for school use, explains why the interior of Africa was difficult for explorers to enter. It emphasizes (1) the falls and rapids that render the great rivers of the interior unnavigable and (2) the extensive Sahara, which cuts off the Mediterranean countries of Europe from Africa's interior. Note that this map contains no marks to indicate political boundaries, mountains, lakes, cities, oceans, or other irrelevancies; every mark on the outline is designed to contribute to one objective: an understanding of the historical inaccessibility of interior Africa to explorers.

Because of the continual need for such representations, schools should keep on hand a quantity of printed outline maps that can be used in this manner as work sheets by both teachers and pupils;[13] they should also obtain slate-surfaced globes that can be marked with chalk; transparent globes (see Figure 21.5) that can be drawn on with china-marking pencils; and trans-

---

[13]Outline maps are available from most map manufacturers (see list in Box 21.11). Outline map masters for spirit duplicating may be obtained from McKinley Publishing Co., Brooklawn, NJ.

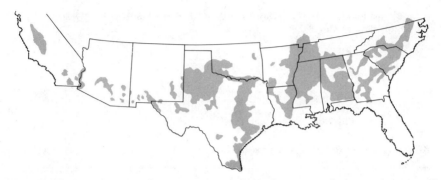

FIGURE 21.3.   A special-purpose map showing how cotton has spread westward.

FIGURE 21.4.   A special-purpose map showing two reasons why Africa was a difficult continent to explore: (1) falls and rapids along great rivers; and (2) the Sahara Desert.

FIGURE 21.5.   A transparent globe. Courtesy of Farquhar Transparent Globes, Inc., Philadelphia, PA.

parencies, for use in overhead projectors, that teacher or pupils can shade, label, or mark in some other way.

Aside from using special-purpose maps in connection with social studies units, pupils should make some of these maps to serve their own personal interests. A class may make a map showing the home of each of its members or depicting plans for a class excursion.

Finally, it is worthwhile for teachers and children to collect a number of different kinds of special-purpose maps: maps showing zip codes, local real estate maps, topographical maps (from the Geological Survey), harbor maps (from the Coast and Geodetic Survey), weather maps, and news maps (from newspapers and magazines). Such a collection can be made into an attractive, informative exhibit.

Road maps are perhaps the most commonly used special-purpose maps. They can be purchased from service stations. Each pupil can have his own and should learn to read it, in order to determine distances and to discover the diversity and usefulness of its symbols.

Using Standard Maps and Globes

Standard maps include classroom wall maps and maps found in atlases and textbooks. They are storehouses of miscellaneous information and are consulted for information, as are dictionaries or encyclopedias. Most of these maps emphasize political information (boundaries, cities, and the like) or relief information (contours of the land), or combine these types of information. They may be used by pupils to obtain locations, distances between locations, proximity of areas, direction of one point with reference to another, and similar information.

BOX 21.5   **ANY GRADE**

Making a Special-Purpose Wall Map*

1. Obtain a piece of oilcloth of the desired size of the map.
2. On the back of the oilcloth, draw the outline of the map with a felt pen. (You can do this by hanging the oilcloth on a wall, projecting a small map on it with an opaque projector, and then tracing the outline.)
3. Staple a sheet of heavy, clear acetate (having the same dimensions as the oilcloth) to the back of the oilcloth.
4. Cut two or three holes at the top of the map so that you can hang it. The acetate sheet over the map may be written on, shaded, or otherwise marked with a china-marking pencil or a washable felt pen. Marks are easily wiped off with a damp cloth.

*Adapted from Margaret Lawrence, "Make a Reusable Wall Map," *The Instructor*, 80 (October 1970), 135–137.

BOX 21.6   **VARYING GRADES**

Some Uses of Special-Purpose Maps

1. To show the locations of particular places in the community: dangerous intersections, play areas, bus routes, etc.
2. To show the distribution of resources, conditions, and population: filling stations in the community, rainfall throughout a country, nonproductive land, population density, dry-farming areas, etc.
3. To show historically significant places: the original locations of the American Indian tribes, colonial settlements, the "seven wonders" of the ancient world, etc.
4. To show important historical routes: Marco Polo's journey, the Santa Fe Trail, the 'round-the-world voyage of Magellan's *Vittoria*, etc.

Doing Reference Work.   Some reference work may be of a casual nature. For instance, if a prominent person is visiting town, pupils may list the points he or she is scheduled to pass or visit and locate them on a map of the city with relation to the position of the school. They can then decide where to assemble to see him or her. But most pupil reference work is in connection with preparing reports, verifying hunches and discoveries, visualizing the location of places encountered in reading, and checking the accuracy of performance on map exercises.

Finding Information Needed in Making Special-Purpose Maps.   Let us suppose that a group of pupils is constructing a special-purpose map to show the route of the Lewis and Clark Expedition. They list the following itinerary: St. Louis, Council Bluffs, intersection of the Yellowstone and Missouri rivers, Great Falls, Three Forks, Columbia River, and the mouth of the Columbia at the Pacific Ocean. They then locate these places on a wall map or in an atlas and draw the route on individual outline maps of the United States.

Illustrating Oral Reports.   When pupils make oral reports to their classmates, encourage them to use a pointer and a wall map, where appropriate.

Extending Knowledge of Map Symbols.   Have the children learn to use a map's legend and to match map symbols with pictures of the features that the symbols portray. On a certain map, we find:

EXAMPLE OF SYMBOL	FEATURE DEPICTED
Blue	Water
Green	Elevation from sea level to 500 feet
⌒	Bend in river
⬡	Mountain
—·—·—	National boundary

Of course, not all lines on a map are symbols of natural features. A national boundary, for example, may be arbitrary and not coincide with physical features. Such boundaries are common in the desert lands of Africa and elsewhere and are found along stretches of the United States–Canada boundary, as well as along numerous other boundaries throughout the world. This is a point to emphasize, since boundaries are so prominently marked on maps that show political divisions. Relief maps (discussed subsequently), especially when used in conjunction with photographs of the areas represented, are extremely useful in teaching map symbols. The teacher's objective is to have each symbol call vividly to the pupil's mind the feature for which it stands.

Learning Place Locations and Geographical Relationships.   Maps help fix in mind names of places and their locations, shapes, approximate distances from one another, and the like. Globes help in this way, too.

BOX 21.7   **GRADES 4–8**

Further Suggestions for Teaching Map Symbols

1. Show the practical importance of being able to read symbols. (Display and discuss road maps, airline maps, etc.)
2. Relate familiar symbols to new symbols. (Familiar symbols: lines, which denote streets; new feature: degree of thickness of lines, which denotes breadth of streets. Familiar symbol: circles, which denote towns and cities; new feature: dots within circles, which denote large cities, etc.)
3. Connect selected symbols on a wall map by strings to posted photographs of each (e.g., hills, railroad tracks, swamp, and city).
4. Have pupils make a map, or use blank outline maps, on which to apply newly learned symbols.
5. Raise questions to stimulate inquiry. ("Here is a map with tiny circles of different sizes to show where the cities are; what might the size of a circle tell us about that place?" "Why are similar colors used on almost all maps to show elevation, water, and so on?")

Children should learn the names and locations of the continents and the oceans; through use of the globe, they discern the relationship of these areas to each other and note that there is more than twice as much water area as land area.

BOX 21.8   **GRADES 4–8**

Making an Outdoor Map

One sixth-grade class made a large map (90 x 45 feet) of Europe on the school's hard-surfaced playground. It took the class two months to plan it. Each degree of latitude and longitude was converted to five inches on paper and later to five feet on the playground. Members of the class drew the outlines, parallels, and meridians with chalk on the playground's surface, using the preliminary paper drawing as a guide. Gallons of paint were used to mark the countries and selected cities. The project is described in an illustrated article, "Our Giant Map," by James Monk, the teacher, in *The Instructor*, 80 (August-September 1970), 98.

Exploring Latitude and Longitude

At an early age, children observe the parallels and meridians that appear on globes and maps. The possibility of using these lines for establishing locations can be introduced in the primary grades. It is not until later, however, that most children will fully understand this concept. It needs to be taught and reviewed systematically throughout the intermediate grades.

Learning about Grids.   The need for locating a particular cell of a grid (a network of horizontal and vertical lines) is not unfamiliar to children. Examples of gridlike arrangements that children encounter are the partitioned bookshelves in many libraries, the library's card-file cabinet, bins for holding tools, toys, and the like, lockers at bus stations and air terminals, crossword puzzles, checkerboards, boxes in post office lobbies, calendars, and street maps of communities that have rectangularly arranged streets. Classrooms where seats are set in rows also provide a gridlike arrangement. With a minimum of instruction, children can learn to locate a particular cell of a grid by naming the two coordinate numbers that indicate the horizontal and perpendicular rows, respectively. For example, scissors are kept in the classroom in the second bin of the top row; Johnny sits in the third seat of the fourth row; and the fifth of March falls in the sixth column of the top row of the calendar (or on Friday of the first week).

Once children are familiar with such elementary ideas, they can be introduced to globe and map grids. They can at this time readily learn that a north-south line is called a "meridian," and an east-west line is called a "parallel." The problem has now shifted. We are no longer concerned with locating a cell; we now wish to describe the location of a point on the earth with considerable exactness. It might be a city, a lonely island, or the spot where a plane made a forced landing. When this problem is presented to a class, some children are likely to suggest that the spot be measured from the North Pole. For a start, this is satisfactory; as a result of the spinning of the earth on its axis, the two poles are indeed the natural points from which to measure—and the only such points.

However, the children next need to learn that the equator, midway between the poles, is the line from which measurements are conventionally made. The equator is $0°$ latitude; the latitude at the poles is $90°$. Children with an adequate background in mathematics can work out the reasoning of this: that there are $360°$ in a circle (such as that represented by the circumference of the earth), that the distance from the equator to a pole is one-fourth the circumference, and that, hence, the distance is $90°$ ($360 \div 4$). Moreover, since the earth is approximately 25,000 miles in circumference, children can figure out that each degree is approximately 70 miles in length ($25,000 \div 360$).

Locating Points on the Earth.   After the children have understood the foregoing and have practiced using latitude in numerous map exercises, the teacher should pursue the subject further. He can now have them fix the latitude of a shipwreck (see Figure 21.6). But they are apt to be stumped when faced with the necessity of determining the east-west location of the spot. After discussing the matter, however, they will probably realize that one of the meridians of the grid must be chosen as the basis for this measurement. Which one? This is the time for the children to learn that the arbitrary, conventional choice for this purpose is the "meridian of Greenwich" (designated as 0° longitude) near London and that the longitude of any point on earth is measured east or west from this meridian.

Working with latitude and longitude will be easy for children who have received instruction in the new mathematics. They will perceive that the grid and the problem of describing the location of a point, such as is shown in Figure 21.6, is similar to the grids and "ordered pairs of numbers" worked over in fifth-grade math class (see Figure 21.7).[14] Describing the location of the point shown in Figure 21.6 will therefore entail only a simple extension of their knowledge. They will describe the location of the shipwreck as longitude 15°W., latitude 30°S.

FIGURE 21.6.   The position of the "shipwreck" (designated by black dot) in the South Atlantic Ocean is described as longitude 15° west, latitude 30° south.

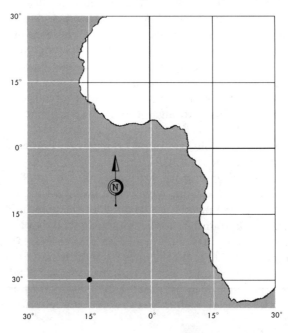

---

[14]*Growth in Mathematics*, Purple Book (Grade 5) (New York: Harcourt, 1978), "Finding Points," pp. 98–103. This math book is particularly apt in that it devotes a page to the application of ordered pairs to longitude and latitude.

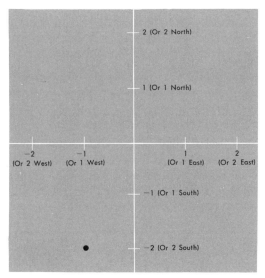

FIGURE 21.7.   The dot corresponds to the ordered pair of numbers (–1, –2).

BOX 21.9   **GRADES 5-8**

Parallels, Meridians, Latitude, Longitude

Parallels: Circular lines parallel to the equator; true east-west lines.

Meridians: Circular lines that pass through the North Pole. True north-south lines.

Latitude: The number of degrees between a place and the equator. (Latitude may range from 0° at the equator to 90° at the North or South Pole. Lat. 41°N. is read "latitude 41 degrees north.")

Longitude: The number of degrees between a place and the meridian of Greenwich (see text). (Longitude may range from 0° at Greenwich to 180° either east or west. Long. 15°E. is read "longitude 15 degrees east.")

Example of use: The archeologist set up his camp at lat. 32°S., long. 122°W.

Judging Distances

Children probably do not develop an accurate or dependable concept of map scale before age 10 or 11.[15] At this age, however, they may study and

---

[15]John O. Towler and L. D. Nelson, "The Elementary-School Child's Concept of Scale," in Wayne L. Herman, Jr., (Ed.), *Current Research in Elementary-School Social Studies* (New York: Crowell-Collier-Macmillan, 1969), pp. 428–433. A summary of their interesting and instructive findings appears in Chapter 6 of this textbook.

use the graphic scales on maps in estimating and computing distances and areas. Frequent exercises of this type will prevent children's misconceptions of distances. Many an easterner, through casual map examination, thinks of Los Angeles and San Francisco as being more or less "twin cities," much like St. Paul and Minneapolis. By noting the graphic scale in Figure 21.8, however, they can easily see, even without measuring, that Los Angeles is about 350 miles from San Francisco—a good day's auto ride away, as far as Chicago is from Minneapolis, or Munich from Budapest!

Globes are useful for finding and measuring the shortest route between places. Since the shortest distance between any two points on the earth lies along a *great-circle* route, the problem is to find the great circle that passes through two given points on the globe (see Box 21.10). This can be done by means of a ring cut out of cardboard, with an inside circumference just barely larger than the circumference of the globe. For this purpose the globe should be of the kind that can be detached from its base. One slips the ring over the globe, then turns it to connect any two points; at the same time, the ring divides the globe into equal halves. The routes thus indicated, if drawn on a Mercator map, will be curved lines and will not look like the shortest distances at all. For instance, the shortest route from Tokyo to the Panama Canal will be found by the cardboard ring to pass near Pike's Peak—a fact that would never be suggested by drawing a straight line between these two places on a Mercator map.

Understanding Map Projections

The task of map projection is to transfer the system of parallels and meridians (the "grid") from the spherical globe to a flat surface. It is

FIGURE 21.8.   Illustration of graphic scale for estimating the distance between two points.

BOX 21.10   **GRADES 4-8**

About Great Circles

1. A great circle divides a sphere (such as a globe) or a spheroid (such as the earth) into two equal halves.
2. A great circle is the largest possible circle that can be drawn on the surface of a sphere or spheroid.
3. On a globe, all meridians are halves of great circles.
4. On a globe, the equator is the only parallel that is a great circle.
5. An infinite number of great circles could be drawn on a globe.
6. The shortest distance between two points on the globe lies along a great circle.

---

desirable for a class to understand why this necessity arises at all—why is the globe not sufficient? By asking the question and directing the discussion, the teacher will usually enable the class to make a few interesting discoveries: (1) There are occasions when we wish to see the earth as a whole; with a globe, we can never see more than a part of it at one time. (2) There are occasions when we wish to see a portion of the earth in great detail; a globe would have to be inordinately large to show the significant details of a state or a small nation. (3) There are occasions when we wish to carry a representation of part of the earth with us—for instance, when we hike or go on a car trip; for this purpose, a globe would scarcely be convenient.

Children's contact with maps that appear in newspapers, atlases, and textbooks leads them to raise questions about the diversity in appearance of the earth and certain portions of the earth. They express wonder at the differing shape and size of a continent on different maps, as they would if the familiar profile of Abraham Lincoln were to vary markedly from picture to picture. When such questions arise, it is time to introduce children to the problem of rendering a spherical surface upon a flat surface.

The concepts inherent in map projection are complex, and it is not to be expected that children of elementary school age will acquire more than a nodding acquaintance with them. The presentation should be unhurried and repeated as often as necessary. However, although there are more than 200 kinds of projections, and many of the intricacies are beyond a child's grasp, he can understand the reasonableness and utility of a few common types of projection. The following exercises cover (1) an azimuthal type, (2) a cylindrical type (the Mercator), (3) an individual type (an interrupted equal-area form), and (4) a conic type. The class will learn through the exercises that all maps are, necessarily, distortions of the earth, that none shows everything accurately, and that each has its peculair utility.

A preliminary exercise for a child to perform—one that will bring him face-to-face with the problem of projection—consists of cutting an orange in half, removing the pulp from one of the halves, and placing the empty hull, face down, on a flat surface (Figure 21.9A). He then pushes it down in an attempt to flatten it out. The result is depicted in Figure 21.9B. The difficulty of transferring a sphere to a flat surface in this manner becomes evident.

FIGURE 21.9.   Introduction to map projection. (A) Half an orange represents hemisphere of earth. (B) Attempt to flatten orange reveals difficulty of flattening spherical surface. (C) Paper cut to fit neatly around globe. (D) Same paper, wrapped around globe, with outline of continents sketched upon it. (E) Same paper flattened out again. (F) Azimuthal projection made by tracing *E* and connecting broken lines and dispersed points. (G) Same gores as in *E* arranged side by side. (H) Tracing of *G* and connecting broken lines and dispersed points. (I) Approximation of Mercator's projection made by revising *H* so that outlines are stretched north-south to compensate for previous east-west stretching. (J) Equal-area projection made by new arrangements of gores. (K) Conic projection made by tracing small area directly from globe upon transparent cone of paper.

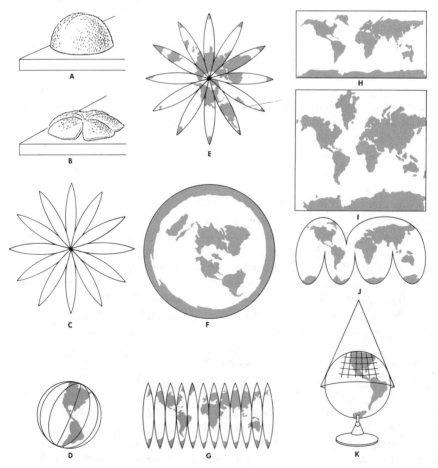

Constructing an Azimuthal Projection.   To help children understand the azimuthal equidistant projection, select a ball and a circular piece of paper with a diameter equal to the circumference of the ball. Then cut the paper as shown in Figure 21.9C. Place a thumbtack or chalk mark on the ball to represent the South Pole, and wrap the paper around the ball so that the points converge at the South Pole. Fasten them with masking tape, and, using a globe as a model, sketch the outline of the continents roughly on the paper (Figure 21.9D). Then, open the paper (Figure 21.9E); the class will see that the continents and the South Pole are now split. Place a sheet of tracing paper on this circular map, trace the outlines, and draw the lines to connect the split portions of the continents. The result will be an approximation of one form of azimuthal projection (Figure 21.9F). The advantage of this projection is that a straight line connecting the center of the map with any other point on the map is along a great circle and gives the exact distance to that point—a significant advantage in an age of air navigation because great-circle routes can be travelled by air.

Constructing a Mercator Projection.   Tear apart the gores used in the preceding projection and arrange them as in Figure 21.9G. Again, trace the outlines and connect separated lines. The result will be similar to Figure 21.9H. Note the east-west distortions, which increase as one advances from the equator to either pole, and attempt a freehand sketch that will stretch the distorted landforms as much in a north-south direction as they have been stretched east-west. The result is an approximation of the Mercator projection (Figure 21.9I). Despite distortions in distances, directions are accurate. A straight line drawn anywhere on the map is a line of constant compass-bearing, a *rhumb* line. For the ship navigator who likes to keep his ship on a constant course, even when this means a longer voyage, this has always been the favorite projection.

BOX 21.11   **GRADES 4–8**

Sources of Maps and Globes

Aero Service, 4219 Van Kirk St., Philadelphia, PA 19135

Allyn and Bacon, Rockleigh, NJ 07647 (map transparencies)

American Map, 4926 Broadway, New York, NY 10023

Denoyer-Geppert, 5235 Ravenswood Ave., Chicago, IL 60640

Farquhar Transparent Globes, 5007 Warrington Ave., Philadelphia, PA 19143

George F. Cram, 301 S. LaSalle St., Indianapolis, IN 46206

Hammond, 515 Valley St., Maplewood, NJ 07040

Hubbard Scientific Co., 1946 Raymond Drive, P.O. Box 104, Northbrook, IL 60062

National Geographic Society, 17th and M St., N.W., Washington, DC 20036

(Continued)

News Map of the Week, 7300 N. Linder Ave., Skokie, IL 60076 (a current-
events map)
Nystrom Division of Carnation Company, 3333 Elston Ave., Chicago, IL
60618
Panoramic Studios, 2243 W. Allegheny Ave., Philadelphia, PA 19132
("earth-curved" relief maps)
Rand McNally, 8255 Central Park Ave., Skokie, IL 60076
Sunburst Communications, Pound Ridge, NY 10576 (map transparencies)
Weber-Costello, 1900 N. Narragansett St., Chicago, IL 60639

Many geographers do not advocate the Mercator projection for use in
the elementary school for several reasons. It is based on sophisticated
geometry; its shapes are good only for small areas; its distortions of scale are
great, except in areas near the equator; and its great circles do not appear to
have the characteristics of great circles (see Box 21.10) and hence cause confusion. These complexities justify only limited use of the Mercator projection
with children.

Constructing an Interrupted Equal-Area Projection. Arrange the
same gores referred to above so that all contiguous land areas actually fit
together without separation (Figure 21.9J). Because land areas, except in the
polar regions, are intact, this projection is useful for showing the distribution
and relative density of population, natural resources, and the like.

Constructing a Conic Projection.   Improvise a cone from a sheet of
tracing paper, and invert it over a globe. Then trace the outline, meridians,
and parallels of any regions not too close to the equator. In Figure 21.9K, the
United States has been thus drawn. It shows converging, straight meridians;
curved, concentric parallels; and minor distortion of shapes, distances, and
directions for areas in temperate zones.

Other Procedures for Teaching Map Projections.   A number of commercial aids that are ingenious and intriguing are available to teach map
projection.[16] It is recommended that teachers try them out in combination
with the more informal procedures described above.

Studying the Physical Environment through Relief Maps

Although study of how to protect our physical environment has been increasing in recent years, physical geography as a descriptive study has been
declining. One reason for its decline has been a strong reaction against "environmental determinism"—the belief that cultural features of a region can

---

[16]*Impossible Map* is a film obtainable from National Film Board of Canada, New
York. *The Map Projection Device* (Farquhar Transparent Globes, Philadelphia) and *A
Map Projection Model* (Hubbard Scientific Co., Northbrook, IL 60062) include globe and
projection accessories.

be accounted for by its physical features. As pointed out in Box 2.3, a given environment may mean one thing to one cultural group and be used accordingly; it may mean something quite different to another cultural group.

On the other hand, given the presence of a certain culture, that culture's physical environment will determine to a large extent the kinds of work its members undertake, and its prosperity. Certainly we cannot ignore the physical environment. Yet in teaching physical geography, two generalizations should be kept in mind. First, physical features make less difference to people now than they did formerly. Second, we have made intelligent adjustments to unfavorable physical features. Each of these generalizations deserves a close look.

Physical Features Make Less Difference to Us Now than They Did Formerly.   It is important when using the relief map as a teaching instrument to emphasize how we have grown into steadily increasing command of our physical environment, learning to overcome some of its disadvantages and to make the most of its advantages. People ". . . play more and more the part of cause, not of effect."[17] Modern facilities for bridge building, tunneling under rivers and through mountains, cutting through hills, and foretelling the presence of obstacles in travel reduce the omnipotence of the physical environment. The airplane, in particular, has revolutionized geography. It overcomes the barrier formed by the impenetrable jungles of South America, for example, even providing the transportation of heavy logs and cattle. The North Pole and the South Pole are no longer the inaccessible regions of a generation ago. We can also now hop over high mountain ranges. Continued development of the airplane is creating a world in which ocean, mountain, swamp, desert, jungle, and frozen waste are ceasing to be important barriers to the world's people. In consequence, physical geography is increasingly a subject that does more to explain the past behavior of the world's people than their present behavior.

This means that when we use relief maps to illustrate the following sub-generalizations, we tend to deal to a considerable extent with history.

Some physical features invite settlement. Waterfalls were factors in the location of numerous cities such as Minneapolis, Rochester, and the fall-line cities fron Trenton to Macon.

Many rivers have served to attract settlement, not only because of assured access to water, but also because of excellent soil built up during floods by the deposit of fertile river sediment. The soils of the valleys of the Nile, the Ganges, and the Mississippi are examples of this process.

Mouths of rivers along ocean and lake shores, large enough to offer good harbor facilities, have been important points of settlement. The deep waters

---

[17]Lucien Febvre, *A Geographic Introduction to History* (New York: Knopf, 1925), p. 351.

and generous expanse of drowned river mouths that characterize the Hudson, Delaware, Sacramento, Thames, Seine, and other rivers have proved especially attractive to settlement.

Some physical features discourage settlement. The inaccessibility, eroded soil, and low temperatures of high mountains have been deterrents to settlement.

Glaciated, rocky coasts, with their poor soil, such as those of New England and Norway, have proved forbidding to all but very rugged settlers.

A smooth coastline like Australia's offers few good harbors and has consequently discouraged settlement.

Some physical features invite movement. Rivers have been historic arteries of exploration. LaSalle used the Mississippi, Lewis and Clark used the Missouri, and Livingstone used the Zambesi—all attesting to this fact.

Wide plains with their distant horizons have had a beckoning effect, as shown in Hamlin Garland's autobiographical writing describing the restlessness of pioneer farmers in the Middle West.

Mountain passes have played an important role in the movements of people, as seen in the historical use of the Cumberland Gap in Tennessee—the "wilderness road" of pioneer days.

Some physical features discourage movement. Oceans have been isolaters. They have had the effect of rendering islands—for example Madagascar and Australia—socially and biologically unique. And they have given persecuted peoples with strong motivation, such as the Puritans and Quakers, a huge barrier to help protect their refuge.

High mountains have tended to isolate regions by forming an enclosure, as in Switzerland and Tibet; mountains in conjunction with a peninsula—Italy and Spain are prime examples—have had similarly isolating effects.

Intelligent Adjustments to Unfavorable Physical Features.   Engineers have constructed artificial harbors, as in Madras, India; lock systems along rivers and canals; great bridges across abysses in mountainous regions; and tunnels through mountains, including six along the Pennsylvania Turnpike and more than 60 in the Swiss Alps.

Poor agricultural prospects in mountainous regions have been overcome through terracing, by which the Incas of Peru maintained their civilization in the Andes, and through herding.

People along rocky coasts, such as Norway's, have turned to fishing and merchant sailing to supplement their scant livelihood from meager soil resources.

In isolated areas of limited natural resources such as Tibet, Ecuador, and Iceland, the people have developed advanced forms of democratic government, made possible in part by the lack of opportunity to exploit the environment—the chief means of creating wealth and, hence, class distinctions, which in turn make democracy difficult to practice.

The Place of Three-Dimensional Relief Maps.   A three-dimensional relief map has a raised surface that shows the physical features of the mapped area. In light of the preceding section, teachers may wonder if they should spend much time on them.

BOX 21.12

Other Physical Factors That Influence Settlement, Movement, and Climate

1. Abundance and accessibility of natural resources.
2. Temperature.
3. Rainfall.
4. Factors that influence temperature and rainfall:
    a. Latitude (distance from equator and poles).
    b. Direction of prevailing winds.
    c. Elevation.
    d. Patterns of air-mass movements.

Relief maps are important for young children because they help build the imagery essential to understanding those problems that the world's people still face as a result of the earth's uneven surface. For older children, they help in explaining climatic conditions and in building an understanding of the problems of historical movement and settlement. A variety of three-dimensional maps are available from map and specialty companies (see Box 21.11).

Construction of Relief Maps in the Classroom.   The commercially manufactured relief maps are a boon to the teacher, but they have certain limitations. They do not cover local community areas. They may not show, emphatically enough, a selected relief feature (such as the Cumberland Gap, Mount Kosciusko, or Cotopazi) to which the teacher might have reason to call attention. Furthermore, children gain superior understanding of an area by mapping it themselves. The activity demands that they give attention to detail and acquire a knowledge of landforms and position that can hardly be acquired by merely looking at a map made by someone else. Map making improves a child's ability to read published maps and interpret their symbols.

The first plastic maps should be of areas children are acquainted with at first hand. Primary-grade children can map their communities with clay or Plasticine on a cardboard base, modelling not only natural relief but man-made landmarks as well. If the map is modelled from putty in a waterproof container (a cake pan is suitable), water may be poured to fill the hollows that represent ponds, lakes, and so on. Pupils should model the relief partly from memory and partly from special field trips to gather map data. The maps will, of course, be quite crude, but their rough approximations are important beginning lessons in the nature and purpose of maps.

Common errors in young children's beginning maps include these:

1. Omissions—for example, of terraces or bridges.
2. Distortion of shapes—for example, of the schoolyard or parks.
3. Disregard of directional relationships—for example, in placing a factory on the wrong side of a river or in drawing parallel streets at right angles to each other.
4. Separation of contiguous areas—for example, in building rivers as separate entities not in contact with the shore.
5. Disregarding of natural law—for example, in having streams run a gravitation-defying course or in allowing vigorous streams to peter out before reaching a larger body of water or the edge of the map.

Such geographic misconceptions thus indicate what "repairs" are required and offer clues on what to emphasize on subsequent field trips, during discussion periods, and in future map making.

The plastic maps of intermediate-grade children are more elaborate (see Box 21.13). Teachers inexperienced in this task may want to make some maps themselves in order to be prepared to supervise pupils in their construc-

FIGURE 21.10.   Commercially available three-dimensional map. Courtesy of Nystrom, Chicago, manufacturer and distributor of maps including raised relief maps of various nations and world regions.

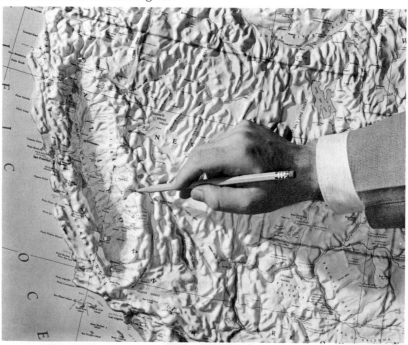

tion. A map may possess a certain amount of amateurish crudity and naïveté without having its utility impaired. Yet, fundamentally, a map should be regarded by teachers and children as a scientific tool.

Before beginning construction, pupils should become familiar with the territory to be modelled and avoid inaccuracies that easily occur when working too literally from the purely topographical data shown on a flat map.

BOX 21.13   **ANY GRADE**

Modeling Three-Dimensional Maps

Papier-mâché is probably the cheapest of plastic materials and the most generally satisfactory. However, it requries considerable work to prepare. White tissue paper (or newspaper if you are satisfied with a fairly course medium) is cut into squares of 1 or 2 inches, soaked in water overnight, and boiled for several hours. A quicker and equally satisfactory method is to soak the paper and then put it into an electric blender, beating it to a fine pulp. Pour off the water, and add a cup of flour and water (the consistency of heavy cream, into which stir two tablespoons of powdered glue). Work this mixture into the paper with your fingers.

Wood putty requires no preparation, is easier to model with than papier-mâché, and produces a smoother surface. However, it is much more expensive.

Putty is easy to model with and is cheap. It is good for use in the primary grades and for making small maps.

Plasticine handles well in modelling, but it is expensive.

Molding sand, mixed with water, hardens in about 12 hours. You can use it repeatedly after it has set by breaking it up into small pieces with a mallet and again mixing it with water.

Sawdust when screened and mixed with wallpaper paste powder in a four to one proportion makes a strong, light map and lends itself to delicate molding.

It is best to avoid clay (which cracks easily), salt-and-flour mixtures (which are moisture collectors), and plaster of paris (which hardens too quickly and makes a heavy map).

In applying the plastic mixture to the board, build the relief one layer at a time. Build with an eye to the brads that have been driven in as guides and with frequent reference to the map that you drew on the large paper sheet. Show the drainage systems accurately, with rivers flowing continually downhill until they reach the lowest level. Cracks and holes usually appear in papier-mâché upon drying, and these can be filled by painting a thick glue over the entire modelled portion of the map; or, if an electric blender was used in making the pulp, by filling the cracks and holes with the fuzz that forms in the blender. Varnish the map when it is dry, or apply two coats of some waterproof paint. Finally, paint the rivers and lakes with blue oil paint, applied with a fine paintbrush.

Pictures from books, periodicals, and library picture collections may be used to convey a feeling for the character of a region. If the pupils are mapping the United States, for instance, they will need pictures in order to depict the contrast of the high, jagged western mountains and the low, rounded eastern mountains; the differing landscapes of the coastal plains on the Pacific, the Gulf, and the Atlantic; the appearance of the Mississippi and its valley; the Ozark Mountains; the plains; the fall line. They are not likely to be satisfied with their translation of the features on the plastic map, but their creation will be considerably closer to realistic representation if they study the pictures carefully and keep them in mind as they work. Posting the pictures in the classroom during the period of map making will promote familiarity with the features depicted.

TEACHING COMPETENCIES

This chapter tells how to perform the following tasks that are basic to teacher competency. The teacher should be able to:

1. Use children's block arrangements diagnostically in order to plan experiences and opportunities for observations to sharpen the pupils' insights into spatial arrangements.
2. Provide instruction to develop the bird's-eye-view perspective.
3. Make a map of the school community or other familiar places to provide initial experiences in map reading and interpretation.
4. Teach map symbols through a variety of procedures, moving step by step from pictorial devices to abstract symbols.
5. Teach cardinal directions by means of a variety of materials and procedures.
6. Promote understanding of maps and globes by helping children discover relationships through map overlays.
7. Teach the use of special-purpose maps as well as standard maps, and have children apply each type for the purpose for which each map is best suited.
8. Teach the use of grids and have children apply the learning in describing specific locations by citing longitude and latitude.
9. Direct the use of map scales and great circles as aids in determining distances.
10. Lead advanced classes to discover nonmathematical reasons for several common map projections and to understand the relationship of each to the globe.
11. Help children discover how physical relief features have historically resulted in many decisions about travel and settlement, and how modern technology has reduced the significance of many formerly decisive relief features for travel and for selecting sites for settlement.

12. Direct construction of three-dimensional maps that will contribute to children's map thinking.

TRYING OUT SOME OF YOUR COMPETENCIES

1. Over a two-month period, introduce map symbols to a group of primary-grade children, as suggested by the six steps shown in Box 21.1.
2. Take a few children outdoors; test their knowledge of the cardinal directions; then teach them what they still don't know about directions by having them observe the time of day, the position of the sun, and the direction of shadows.
3. Experiment with demonstrating map projections through the informal procedures described in this chapter and through one of the commercially available devices, such as Farquhar's *Map Projection Device*, cited in Footnote 16.

FOR STUDY AND EXPLORATION

1. Compare the map and the globe as teaching instruments.
2. Read, in a textbook on physical geography, such as Strahler's (given under "Further Reading") about the declination of the compass needle from true north, and plan an explanation of this phenomenon to children.
3. Obtain a set of the *Where and Why* map and globe skills program produced by Nystrom (see Box 21.11). It provides a model for teaching with 23 cassette lessons. Study it carefully and write a review that would be useful to a faculty.

FURTHER READING

More about teaching of maps and globes will be found in the following:

Charlotte C. Anderson and Barbara J. Winston, "Using Maps," in Dana G. Kurfman (Ed.), *Developing Decision-Making Skills*, 47th Yearbook, National Council for the Social Studies (Arlington, VA, 1977), pp. 82–90. Focuses on map symbols, directions, and scale.

M. L. Hawkins, *Skill Development—Maps and Globes*, Proficiency Model #8 (Athens, GA: Department of Social Science Education, University of Georgia, 1972). A case study of the development of seven basic map skills.

Lucy Sprague Mitchell, *Young Geographers: How They Explore the World and How They Map the World* (New York: Basic Books, 1963). This classic by a master teacher was first published in 1934. An early exponent of pupil discovery, Mitchell viewed geography as a laboratory subject in which children made and used maps as a means of consolidating their observations and discoveries.

Teachers wishing to master the technical intricacies of maps and globes will find them clearly and interestingly explained by Arthur N. Strahler in *Physical Geography*, 4th ed. (New York: Wiley, 1975).

Skill deficiencies in the use of maps by sixth-graders are considerable and provide clues for teachers of what to emphasize. They are reported by Donald O. Schneider in "The Performance of Elementary Teachers and Students on a Test of Map and Globe Skills," *Journal of Geography*, 75 (September 1976), 326–332.

22 Guiding the Development of Time Concepts

Being able to recall a series of happenings in a chronological sequence is not enough for a proper study of history . . . [The student] must be able to visualize duration, a passage of time, a stream of time flowing on, and within it a series of connected episodes.
Carl G. Gustavson

A grasp of time concepts is as important for understanding the past as a grasp of spatial concepts is for understanding geography. Yet the fact must be faced that time concepts are abstractions which develop in the child much more slowly than do the more concrete concepts of space. The difficulty this causes children in their efforts to learn history has been discussed in Chapters 2 and 10. The reader will recall that it has led many thoughtful educators and historians to recommend postponing formal study of history until Grade 8 or an even later period.

The abstraction of a former era not experienced is an elusive one even for many an adult. It is known that children who are plunged into the study of history, or even the reading of historical biography before having become "time conscious," tend to think of an episode of the past as cut off from the present, assuming fairy-tale qualities. They become absorbed in the color and uniqueness of the period—the costuming, language, architecture, and quaint ways of living; but they do not see how the lives of these men,

411

women, and children may have influenced their own lives, how certain of the old problems are also the new problems in a different setting, and how the approach of a former generation to life can be a warning or an inspiration to us in our approach to life today.

Words alone will not fully convey to children the impact of the past upon the present. This abstraction, the past, must be given flesh, and its relationship to us must be expressed in graphic terms. Time must be based on a spatial metaphor, such as the time line. Techniques for doing this will be discussed together with a description of ways in which the elementary school can assist its pupils in the development of time concepts.

TEACHING TIME CONCEPTS

In the area of time relationships, the elementary school has fourfold responsibility: it must help children (1) form an understanding of terms that designate temporal units; (2) think of an event as part of a series of events; (3) think of the separation of an event from the present in measured units; and (4) form an understanding of the differences in duration of various historical periods. The teaching of these concepts should be tied into every unit in which historical content is prominent.

Forming an Understanding of Terms That Designate Temporal Units

Primary-grade teachers can take advantage of daily opportunities to help children build mental images of time units. Children may take turns each morning writing the day's schedule and the day or the date on the chalkboard, and marking the weather each day on the calendar. Teachers may consciously use and emphasize conventional symbols and abbreviations, both orally and on the board, that denote hours, days, and other units: a.m., p.m., min., hr., wk., mo., yr., Mon., dst., Feb., and the like.

In the intermediate grades "generation," "decade," "century," and other such temporal terms are encountered. A class can furnish data to illustrate "generation" as follows: Each member supplies the date of his or her own birth and the birth of father and grandfather. These dates are then arranged along a line, as shown in Figure 22.1, with the average date of birth for each generation prominently marked. Finding the differences between these average dates will reveal that a generation is about 33 years and that there are about three generations in a century.

Thinking of an Event as Part of a Series of Events

Since history is a continuum from ancient times to the present, the correct concept of chronology is important. It can be introduced early in the school life of a child. Countless opportunities present themselves in the typical classroom, even in kindergarten. For example, when a caterpillar

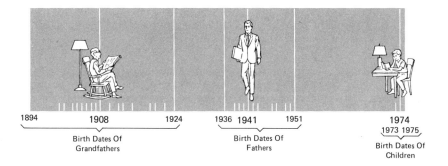

1894   1908   1924   1936 1941   1951   1974
                                              1973 1975

Birth Dates Of   Birth Dates Of   Birth Dates Of
Grandfathers   Fathers   Children

FIGURE 22.1.   Time line: Concept of "generation."

that has been brought to school, later enters the chrysalis stage and eventually emerges as a butterfly, the teacher may prepare a strip of pictures to show this sequence of development, giving to each stage a proportional share of the strip. This is one kind of time line. Children are usually stimulated by graphic and systematic reviews of this sort, concerning experiences that they are otherwise inclined to recall only in loose fragments. Teachers have found a host of experiences that, when similarly summarized, help the child to grasp the flow of events. Typical time lines for use in the early school years include the following:

1. A series of pictures of children of various ages to show their progression, at intervals, from birth to their present age (see Figure 22.2).
2. A series of pictures to show the child's daily routine, each picture depicting an event such as eating breakfast or arriving at school.
3. A line drawn along a lengthy stretch of chalkboard, divided to show the weeks and months of the school year; it provides the opportunity to enter words or sketches to record significant school events as they occur.
4. Rearrangement of a calendar by clipping it to make the days of a month run in a continuous horizontal line.

FIGURE 22.2.   Time line: Development of a child, birth to age 6.

Just Born   One   Two   Three   Four   Five   Six

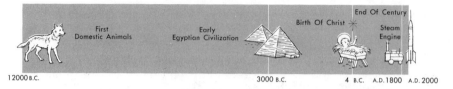

FIGURE 22.3.   Time Line: Points in the development of civilization.

Later on, time relationships more directly related to the content of social studies will need clarification. At that point, a chronology of certain significant developments in the history of the human race may be presented, as in Figure 22.3.

Apt verbal descriptions of a relationship often help to make it more apparent that time is all of one piece. One of the authors, when a boy, heard a speaker make the statement that he once met a man who had seen George Washington. As a consequence, for the first time, the father of his country seemed within reach! This seemed incredible and yet brought the formerly remote, unreal great man infinitely nearer, timewise. In addition to the verbal approach, however, graphic techniques should be employed. For example, in connection with a study of inventors and inventions, the overlapping of historical figures and generations and their closeness to each other and to contemporary times may be shown in chart form, as in Figure 22.4.

Thinking of the Separation of an Event from the Present in Measured Units

The capacity to measure the distance of a past event from the present can also grow, early in school life. Before a child tells time, clocks with hands appropriately arranged may be drawn in the background of each sec-

FIGURE 22.4.   Time chart: Overlapping life spans of some importrant inventors.

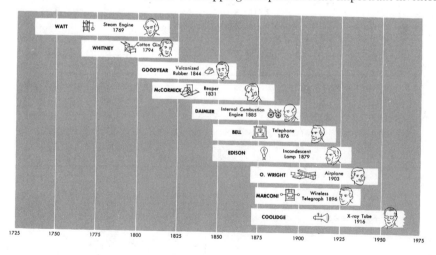

tion of a time line to summarize the order of events in a school day. Cardboard clocks can be used in various ways. For example, just before the class is dismissed for lunch, one second-grade teacher sets the hands of two cardboard clocks and says, "We leave for lunch at twelve," pointing to the hands of the first clock, "and we come back to the classroom at one," pointing to the hands of the second clock.

Other examples of measured time that the child can learn in elementary school include these: (1) The calendar shows there are 30 days between the beginning and ending of September. (2) Today is Arbor Day—365 days since last Arbor Day. (3) Your little brother was born in the 1980s—almost 2,000 years since the birth of Christ. If teachers encourage their pupils to think of the separation of events in measured units, the units soon become familiar, convenient devices.

Forming an Understanding of the Differences in Duration of Various Historical Periods

In the upper intermediate grades, some children are capable of understanding the vastness of time and the differences in length between various historical periods. Such understanding, however, is inclined to be inaccurate and vague unless, again, graphic foundations for thinking are provided. A grasp of the concept that recorded history covers a relatively brief period (about 6,000 years) of the estimated total tenure of human beings upon earth (about one million years) requires tangible representation upon a time line. Contrasting shorter periods—for example, the duration of the government of the United States with that of the government of England—requires time lines, too. Where very prolonged periods are to be compared with very brief periods, temporary outdoor time lines are often advisable. Points in time may be indicated by driving stakes into the ground or making chalk marks on the pavement. Space may be measured off in steps. For example, the contrast between the period of prehistory and that of history may be illustrated by allowing 167 steps to represent prehistory and one step to represent history (the ratio of one million years to 6,000 years).

CONSTRUCTION OF TIME LINES: PRACTICAL CONSIDERATIONS

A time line is a device used to give concrete quality to the abstraction of time. A line, divided into time units, is drawn on a long, usually horizontal, strip of paper. Pictures are drawn or mounted at appropriate points along the line to represent episodes associated with particular time periods.

Time lines should approach precision, and pupils may require teacher assistance in planning and constructing them. An inaccurate time line distorts time relationships and is worthless.

Develop a Single Theme for Each Time Line

As a rule, it is wise for children to depict the chronology of only one subject at a time. For example, transportation through the ages is a sufficient theme for one time line and is better than putting transportation, shelter, and architecture through the ages all on one line.

Adopt a Scale Appropriate to the Purpose of the Time Line

A line drawn to too generous a scale may not fit on the walls of the classroom. A more usual error is to make the scale too small. To be a visual display that can be read from any point in the classroom, a time line should be 15 or 20 feet long. The time lines shown in this chapter were scaled small to fit the dimensions of this book and are not intended to suggest the scale for classroom use. Those covering vast periods of time may appropriately extend unbroken along an entire wall of a classroom and even continue around corners or along an unbroken hallway wall. There would be many feet of blank paper if Figure 22.3 were to be so enlarged, but these open spaces would aid in building a concept of the magnitude of time and would not be wasted. It would be a mistake to shorten these long intervals by telescoping the time line.

The time line should be scaled accurately with a ruler. If one inch is chosen to represent one hour (or one week or one century), it should represent that unit of time consistently.

Bring the Time Line Up to Date

Children who are studying the Colonial period might think it necessary to end the time period with 1776. It would be better to extend the line to the present so they could see the Colonial personalities and events in relation to those of today. They should be able to find their own birth dates on the line. This helps tie the past in a meaningful way to the present.

Keep the Time Line Simple and Make it Attractive

The amount of writing or printing should be kept to a minimum. A time line need not convey more information than is necessary to show change and development of the selected subject. It should lend itself to interpretation by a child at a glance and should not require figuring out.

Attractiveness adds to effectiveness. Each time line should be well arranged, colorful, simple, and clear. A little thought, imagination, and care in execution are the requisites.

BOX 22.1   **GRADES 6-8**

The Use of Time Lines with Sixth-Grade Pupils

By Barbara E. Smith

To clarify the meaning of dates and time relationships, I started a class of sixth-graders working on personal time lines of their own lives. We set up a skeleton scale on the blackboard, starting with the present and blocking out each year with its 12 months. These were copied by the children, and then filled in with birthdays, schools attended, summer vacations, trips, and any other events which were important to them. Most of the children used pictures to represent the various events. One boy drew a birthday cake, increasing the number of candles for each succeeding year. Many interesting reactions came from the discussion of these charts. The most common comment concerned the percentage of time spent in school. One child had thought that the year was divided in two equal parts—half for school and half for summer vacation; he thought the summer just went faster because he was having a good time. These charts were valuable to me as a graphic expression of the children's experiences and backgrounds.

The next step was to change our scale from one year to five years, and make family time lines. These went back to the birth of the parents (in some cases, to the grandparents) and included important family events. On these time lines the child's own life became much more insignificant in the total picture, and a clearer concept of 20 or 30 years ago was developed.

Then came the question of dates, what they meant, and what would happen if we kept on going back in time. So we set up still another scale on the blackboard, of 100-year intervals, and marked the time back till we came to zero. One child knew that this point represented approximately the birth of Christ, and that it was from this point that we count our years. We discussed the meaning of B.C. and A.D. A discussion of centuries followed. Most of the children thought that we lived in the nineteenth century. It was easy to correct this misconception on our B.C.—A.D. chart.

The children become so interested in this graphic representation of time relationships that we made a long paper chart, and as we studied history, they marked important events by pinning pictures on it. They started with dates with which they were already familiar, such as 1492 and 1620, and these became more meaningful seen in relation to a whole time picture. This was one of the most interesting and valuable projects of the year.

SUPPLEMENTARY WAYS OF STIMULATING THE GROWTH OF TIME CONCEPTS

Using Primary Sources

One way to develop in the child an understanding of an important aspect of historical method and also a feeling of intimacy with the past is to provide contact with primary sources: autobiographies, diaries, letters, photographs, newspapers, family stories, oral or written testimony of eyewitnesses, films, church or court records, and tangible remains (tools, clothing, buildings, and so on). Many written reports of eyewitnesses have been copied, compiled, and published (see Box 22.2).

BOX 22.2   **GRADES 4–8**

Compilations of Primary Sources

Angle, Paul M. *The American Reader: From Columbus to Today* (Skokie, IL: Rand McNally, 1958).

Boorstin, Daniel J. *An American Primer* (Chicago: University of Chicago Press, 1966), 2 vols.

Commager, Henry S. and Allan Nevins. *The Heritage of America* (Boston: Little, Brown, 1949).

Commager, Henry S. *The Blue and the Gray: The Story of the Civil War as Told by Participants* (Indianapolis: Bobbs-Merrill, 1954).

Commager, Henry S. *Documents of American History,* 7th ed. (New York: Appleton, 1963), 2 vols.

De Voto, Bernard (Ed.), *The Journals of Lewis and Clark* (Boston: Houghton Mifflin, 1953).

Downs, Morton. *Medieval Pageant* (Princeton, NJ: Van Nostrand, 1964).

Driggs, Howard R. *The Pony Express Goes Through: An American Saga Told by Its Heroes* (Philadelphia: Lippincott, 1936).

Eisenschiml, Otto and Ralph Newman. *Eyewitness: The Civil War as We Lived it* (New York: Grosset & Dunlap, 1960).

Neider, Charles. *The Great West* (New York: Bonanza, 1958).

O'Neill, Edward. *A History of American Biography, 1800–1935* (New York: Barnes & Noble, 1961).

Stefansson, Vilhjalmur. *Great Adventures and Explorations* (New York: Dial, 1947).

Founding Fathers series (lives of six told in their own words) (New York: Harper, 1975), 6 vols, well illustrated.

Discuss with your pupils the difference between primary and secondary sources. First explain that a primary source is any report by an eyewitness (one that appears, say, in a letter or a newspaper), or any surviving object (such as an article of clothing); and that a history textbook or a biography is a secondary source. It was written by someone who consulted, or at least knew about, the contents of the primary sources.

When possible, have your class evaluate a primary source (such as a grandmother's account of her girlhood, a newspaper reporter's account of an inauguration of a Governor or President, a section of Benjamin Franklin's autobiography, or the passage from chap. 1 of Malcolm X's autobiography in which he describes his family's experience when two white men set fire to their home and compare it with a secondary source that describes the same event.

Finding Local Traces of the Past

History can be brought "home" by exploring reminders of local history—dates on buildings, examples of early architecture, and the recollections of "old timers." Some communities have obelisk-shaped memorials (for example, the Washington Monument), a distinctive form derived from ancient Egypt. Many churches reveal the medieval invention of the Gothic style in their pointed arches and flying buttresses.

Written records are also reminders of earlier times. The inscriptions on tombstones may reveal not only routine information (such as names, dates, achievements of the deceased, and occasion of death), but also attitudes (for example, moral edification during the seventeenth and eighteenth centuries when Puritan influences were strong, and sentimentality during the ensuing romantic period).

Don't overlook nearby roadside historical markers. For example, a sign near Southampton, Pennsylvania, marks the place where John Fitch tested his model steamboat in 1785. "What would Street Road have looked like then?" the teacher could ask. "What traffic noises would we have heard?" "What comments might John Fitch's neighbors have made about his model boat?"

See what your pupils can turn up in the way of heirlooms, old photographs, old newspapers, and the like, that relate to the unit. A corner of the classroom may be reserved for a miniature museum in which such articles can be exhibited.

Relating the Past to the Present

One defect in the traditional teaching of history was its isolation of the past from the present. How can history be used to illuminate the present? A few reminders and questions from the teacher can be highly productive. Here are some examples:

> You have learned how the colonial family raised its own food, baked its own bread, churned its own butter, and made its own clothing. Most of today's families in the United States do not do these things. What does today's family do with its time? Do you think it was more fun to be a child then, or now? Is an easier life necessarily a happier and better life?

You have learned about religious customs of the Roman Empire. Which of these customs have remained? Which ones have changed?

You have learned that the Mississippi River was named by the Indians. What other Indian names are still with us?

You have learned that the early automobile was unreliable and that many predicted it could never take the place of the horse. Is there any invention today about which many people feel the same way? Do all inventions succeed?

Teaching about the Past Through Pictures

Photographs and paintings are important teaching media because they give needed vividness to the dim past. You and your class will find many splendid reproductions in textbooks, reference books, and trade books. Project these on a screen, if possible, so that the class can examine and discuss them together.

Trips to art museums are also productive. Young children usually need to be reminded that the artist has rendered *his* interpretation of an event or a personality. This adds interest to the study of the past. "How would you have painted the scene?" the teacher may ask.

Sometimes a much-needed picture is hard to find. The subject may be a horn book, Robert Fulton, a portion of the Chinese Wall, or the Baltic entrance to the Kiel Canal. Your librarian can then lead you to a picture index, such as *Illustration Index, Travel through Pictures*, or *General Index to Illustrations*. Teachers who maintain their own picture files have incalculable assets and timesavers.

TEACHING COMPETENCIES

This chapter has described how to perform the following tasks basic to teacher competency. The teacher should be able to:

1. Take advantage of daily opportunities to help children build mental images of terms that designate temporal units.
2. Teach children to think of an event as part of a series of events.
3. Make a practice of having children think of the separation of an event from the present in terms of measured units.
4. Stimulate older children to compare the varying duration of different historical periods.
5. Guide the construction of time lines that are uncluttered, that are scaled appropriately, and that convey meaning.
6. Promote a feeling of intimacy with the past through introducing primary sources, finding local traces of the past, relating the past to the present, and through showing pictures.

TRYING OUT SOME OF YOUR COMPETENCIES

1. Have a group of primary-grade children make a series of observations over a period of time, such as the development of a butterfly from the caterpillar stage, or weather changes over a week. Prepare a strip of drawings to show the sequence of changes. Ask the class to talk about the changes, drawing by drawing, with the aid of the picture record.
2. Plan and conduct a lesson for teaching the terms "generation," "decade," and "century" to children aged 10 or older.
3. With a specific unit topic in mind, construct a time line that will effectively summarize the development of a significant institution or process.

FOR STUDY AND EXPLORATION

1. Review the sections in Chapters 2 and 10 on children's time concepts and relate them to the content of this chapter.
2. Locate a social studies textbook prepared for the elementary school that consists at least in part of historical material. Evaluate the way in which the book presents the concepts.
3. Give an example of each of the approaches to time concepts (in the section, "Supplementary Way of Stimulating the Growth of Time Concepts" in this book), indicating the age or grade of children you have in mind.

FURTHER READING

Activities to help children deal with continuity and order of events in time are described by James V. Bruni and Helene J. Silverman in "Developing Intuitive Ideas about Time" in *Arithmetic Teacher*, 23 (October 1976), 582–591.

Suggestions that encourage children to become aware of time as it relates to familiar, everyday experiences will be found in "Learning Set-Ups" by Polly Behrmann and Joan Millman in *Day Care and Early Education*, 5 (Spring 1978), 48–49.

Procedures for teaching chronology to older children are presented by Kenneth Hilton, "Some Practical Classroom Remedies for Parochialism of the Present," *Social Studies*, (July/August 1978), 163–170.

Roy N. Smith reports the novel approach he took in studying children's facility in handling time concepts and history in "The Development of Children's Construction of Historical Duration: A New Approach and Some Findings," *Educational Research*, 19 (June 1977), 163–170. His subjects were British children aged 10 to 15. American teachers are urged to try his approach in assessing the amount of historical knowledge their pupils possess, and their judgments of duration.

Name Index

Abbey, Edward, 98
Allen, P. David, 36n, 357n
Almy, Millie, 96
Anderson, Richard C., 101n, 227n
Anderson, William A., 316n
Anticaglia, Elizabeth, 171
Arasteh, A. Reza, 74n
Arasteh, Josephine D., 74n
Arnoff, Melvin, 24
Arnsdorf, Val E., 31n, 316, 384n–385
Ausubel, David P., 13, 33n, 40, 88n–89, 94, 97, 99n, 100n, 101–102, 223, 227n, 307n

Bacon, Phillip, 379n
Bandura, Albert, 12, 109, 250n
Banks, James A., 170n
Barr, Robert D., 4
Barzun, Jacques, 107n
Batinich, Mary Ellen, 92
Beard, Charles, 6
Beatty, Patricia, 363
Beck, Clive M., 139n
Bee, Helen, 89
Benedict, Ruth, 171
Bennett, Stan, 201n
Berenberg, S. R., 42n
Berger, Evelyn, 46n
Berlyne, Daniel E., 98n
Bernstein, Charlotte Werner, 147n
Beyer, Barry K., 141n
Bioko, Claire, 363
Blanshard, Brand, 59–60n
Bloom, Benjamin S., 214n, 216n, 221n
Blough, Glenn O., 184n
Boggs, S. Whittemore, 152n
Bone, Jan, 314
Bono, Stephen F., 39n
Boynick, David K., 171
Branch, Helen M., 259n
Brazziel, William F., 331n
Breen, Michael J., 81n
Brickell, Henry M., 205n
Briden, Renate, 171n
Brink, Carol R., 363
Brooks, Van Wyck, 171n
Brown, Daniel H., 384n
Brown, Roscoe C., 316n
Brown, Sterling, 168
Bruner, Jerome S., 91, 99n, 223
Bryant, Covey K., 185

Burack, A. S., 363
Buros, Oscar K., 337n
Burroughs, John, 193
Burt, Olive W., 169
Busch, Jackie S., 144n

Callahan, Carolyn M., 259n
Capps, Lelon R., 80n
Carlson, Natalie S., 169
Carson, Rachel 181–182, 193
Carter, Jamie L., 37n
Carter, Sylvia M., 74
Carver, George Washington, 169
Chase, W. Linwood, 82n
Cherryholmes, Cleo H., 312
Chu, G. C., 316n
Cleghorn, Sara, 369
Clemenceau, Georges, 52
Coatsworth, Elizabeth, 363
Cobia, Jacqueline, 20n
Cogan, John J., 48, 301n
Cohen, Miriam, 169
Colby, C. B., 363
Coleman, James S., 312
Coleson, Edward, 160n
Conte, Anthony E., 40n
Coombs, Jerrold R., 218n
Cox, Carole A. S., 305
Cox, Linda S., 80n
Crabtree, Charlotte, 259n
Craddock, Richard S., 316
Crist, Janet, 312
Crosby, Muriel, 135n, 219–220n
Crossley, Alice, 364
Curry, Robert L., 80n

Dale, Edgar, 63
Davis, Arthur, 168
Davis, O. L., Jr., 31n, 384n–385
Decaroli, Joseph, 312n
Dengler, Clyde, 149
Dennis, Jack, 23n
Dewey, Evelyn, 120n
Dewey, John, 101, 120n
Dickie, Kenneth E., 258n
Dirr, Peter J., 315
Dodds, Edith L., 31n
Douglass, Frederick, 168
DuBois, W. E. B., 168

Durham, Philip, 169
Durkin, Dolores, 352
Durrell, Donald D., 361, 364

Earhart, Amelia, 170
Easton, David, 23n
Ebel, Robert L., 332
Edel, May, 163, 171
Edgar, Eugene, 314n
Ediger, Marlow, 205n
Edison, Thomas, 363
Egan, A. L., 81
Eggleston, Edward, 363
Ehrhardt, Harryette B., 363n
Eliot, John, 379
Elkind, David, 141n
Ellison, Ralph, 168
Elsbree, Willard S., 284–285n
Elser, William K., 184n
Emmons, Frances, 20n
English, Betty L., 170
Epstein, Edna, 152, 363
Euphrosine, Sister M., 290

Fantini, Mario D., 48n, 135n, 137
Featherstone, Joseph, 62
Febvre, Lucien, 403
Fenton, Edwin, 141n
Ferguson, Miriam (Ma), 171
Fiedler, Robert E., 40n, 42n
Fiedler, William R., 57
Fitch, John, 419
Flanders, Ned A., 345
Flexner, Eleanor, 171n
Forster, Edith C., 279
Fox, Karen F. A., 33n
Fraenkel, Jack R., 141n
Fraisse, Paul, 30n, 168n
Franklin, Benjamin, 369, 419
French, Sidney J., 214n
Friedman, K. C., 30n
Friedman, William J., 30
Fulks, Bryan, 169
Fulton, Robert, 420

Gadin, André, 167–168n
Gagné, Robert M., 102n, 105n, 223
Gall, Meredith D., 221n
Galloway, Jane, 149
Gates, Arthur I., 79n
Gearing, Frederick O., 172–173
Gebhardt, Richard, 375n
George, Paul S., 40n, 42n, 46n
Gesell, Arnold, 88, 168n
Gezi, K. I., 260n
Gillespie, Judith A., 312n
Glasnapp, Douglas R., 332
Glidewell, John C., 326

Goldreich, Esther, 170
Goldreich, Gloria, 170
Goodlad, John I., 43
Goodman, Yetta M., 357n, 365
Graham, Frank, Jr., 181n
Graham, Katherine, 171
Gray, Roland F., 46n
Green, Frederick E., 74n
Greenblatt, E. L., 80n
Greenstein, Fred I., 23n–24
Groff, Patrick, 375–376n
Gross, Richard E., 68n
Guthrie, A. B., Jr., 369
Guzzetta, Charles, 31

Hackbarth, Steven L., 314
Hale, Gifford G., 15, 242, 249
Hallam, Roy N., 30–31n
Harlan, Louis R., 168n
Harrah, Barbara K., 188
Harrah, David F., 188
Hart, Gordon, 237n
Havighurst, Robert J., 75
Hays, H. R., 163n
Heath, Douglas H., 258
Heber, Mary E., 234
Heber, Rick F., 234
Herdershot, Carl H., 315n
Herman, Wayne L., Jr., 31n, 80n, 268n,
    367n, 383n–384n, 397n
Hock, Louise E., 241
Hoffman, Lois Wladis, 26n, 170n
Hoffman, Martin L., 26n
Holmes, Ethel E., 80n
Holt, John, 375
Horn, Ernest, 368–369n
Hornik, Robert C., 92
Houts, Paul L., 343n
Howe, Julia Ward, 171
Huey, J. Frances, 238n
Hulstrunk, Alfred, 186n
Hungerford, Harold R., 185

Ingli, Donald A., 305

Jackson, Florence, 169
Jackson, Philip W., 13
James, William, 258n
Jersild, Arthur T., 19, 80n, 131n
Johnson, James Weldon, 168
Johnson, Roger E., 352n
Jones, Everett L., 169
Jorgensen, Erling S., 316n
Joyce, John P., 326

Kantor, Ken, 369
Karns, Edward A., 315
Kavanagh, Ellen, 37n

Kelley, Marjorie, 274n
Kennedy, John F., 24
Kephart, Horace, 387
Kepler, Karen, 40, 53n
Killiam, James R., Jr., 317n
Kirsch, Dorothy, 74
Kirst, Nancy, 37n
Kliman, Gilbert, 23n
Kneller, George F., 314
Kohl, Herbert R., 108
Kohlberg, Lawrence, 10, 26, 139, 141
Koonz, Claudia, 171n
Kourilsky, Marilyn, 33n, 201, 203n
Krathwohl, David R., 221n
Krause, Merton S., 23n
Krumboltz, John D., 98n
Krutch, Joseph Wood, 98

Lange, Phil C., 315n
Larkins, A. Guy, 34n, 93n
Lavatelli, Celia Stendler, 95
Lawrence, Margaret, 392n
Lawrence, T. E., 98
Leader, Harry O., 304n
Lee, John R., 383n–384n
Lee, Ulysses, 168
Leiner, Katherine, 170
Levie, W. Howard, 258n
Lewis, Douglas R., 60
Lewis, Richard F., 315–316n
Lexau, Joan, 169
Lincoln, Abraham, 171, 399
Lindgren, Henry C., 325
Lippitt, Ronald, 61
Locke, Alain, 168
Lockwood, Alan L., 48n
Lowrey, George H., 42n
Lukasevich, Ann, 46n
Lyons, Carol, 199

McAulay, John D., 40n
McBride, Angus, 163n
McClure, Lawrence F., 222–223
Maccoby, Eleanor E., 92
McCully, George E., 31n
McKeachie, Wilbert, 314
McMillan, James H., 79, 81
McNally, Harold J., 284–285n
McNaughton, A. H., 89
Macy, Daniel J., 37n
Mager, Robert, 12
Mairieu, Philip, 168n
Maitland, John, 316n
Malcolm X (Malcolm Little), 168
Marek, Rosanne J., 235n
Marshall, Thurgood, 169
Martin, Lyn S., 43n, 47n
Maury, Inez, 170
Mead, Margaret, 163n, 171

Meadows, Donella H., 179n
Meir, Golda, 170
Meltzer, Ida S., 171
Metz, Kathleen E., 90
Meux, Milton, 218n
Millar, Susanna, 262, 269n
Miller, Jean H., 259
Minor, Marz, 166n
Minor, Nono, 166n
Mitchell, Lucy Sprague, 101
Moffett, James, 217, 233n–234, 240–241,
    373–374
Moldstad, John A., 301n
Monk, James, 394
Moore, Helen Cornfield, 144n
Morrow, Suzanne, 163n
Mosher, Howard H., 80n
Moss, Joy F., 372
Mugge, Dorothy J., 28n, 92–93, 95
Muir, John, 123, 193
Muller, Phillipe, 74n
Murphy, Richard, 369n

Nelson, L. D., 28, 93, 397n
Nesbitt, William A., 313
Nolte, Karl F., 36n
Norbeck, Oscar E., 166n
Null, Eldon J., 304n

Oakden, E. C., 30n
Oettinger, Anthony G., 14
Ojemann, Ralph H., 19–20n, 58–59,
    138–139, 154
Oosterhof, Albert C., 332

Parker, Arthur C., 166n
Paulson, Wayne, 48
Pavan, Barbara N., 43n, 47n
Peattie, Roderick, 152n
Pedone, Ronald J., 315
Penn, William, 363
Pennacchio, Olga C., 146n
Perron, Jack, 369
Phillips, John L., 76n
Piaget, Jean, 84–85, 87–88, 90, 93–95, 168n,
    307, 379
Pinchot, Gifford, 193
Pistor, Frederick, 30, 131n
Portugaly, Dora, 94n, 379n
Powell, Meredith, 170
Pratt, Caroline, 197
Preston, Kathleen, 171n
Preston, Ralph C., 383n
Price, Roy A., 314n
Pritchard, Miriam C., 79n

Randall, Jill W., 40, 53n
Rasmussen, Knud, 163

Raths, Louis, 47
Renzulli, Joseph S., 259n
Rice, Joseph P., Jr., 80n
Rice, Marion J., 58
Ridel, J. H., 263n
Roberts, Jack, 199
Rogers, Janet M., 198–199, 317n
Ronkes, Nicholas, 274n
Roosevelt, Theodore, 193
Ross, Nellie, 171
Roth, Heinrich, 168n
Rousseau, Jean-Jacques, 101
Rushdoony, Haig A., 379n, 385
Russell, Diana E. H., 170n

Salomon, Julian H., 166n
Santaro, Wendy, 135n
Santayana, George, 8
Sasek, M., 363
Schellenberg, James A., 242n
Schramm, W., 316n
Schwartz, Marilyn S. 48n
Schweitzer, Albert, 183
Sebesta, Sam L., 363n
Sellers, Charles G., 31n
Senesh, Lawrence, 61, 202n, 208
Sewell, Edward G., 33n
Shaffer, Lawrence F., 307
Shaver, James P. 34n, 93n
Sheridan, Jack M., 379n
Shively, Joe E., 316n
Smart, Mollie S., 74n
Smart, Russell C., 74n
Smith, Barbara E., 417
Spears, Sol, 34n
Spencer, Herbert, 101
Spiller, Robert E., 171n
Stall, Edith, 169
Stampfer, Lee, 383n–384n
Stedman, Mark E., 81n
Steinem, Gloria, 171
Stephens, J. M., 13
Steptoe, John, 169
Stoltman, Joseph P., 379n
Stowe, Harriet Beecher, 171
Strickland, Ruth, 371n
Stringer, Lorene A., 326
Strom, Robert D., 263n
Sturt, M., 30n

Taba, Hilda, 57, 62, 219, 222, 230
Tanner, Laurel N., 325
Tasch, Ruth T., 80n
Tax, Sol, 163n
Thelen, Herbert A., 242
Thomason, Julia, 42n

Thorne, Oakleigh II, 305n
Torrance, E. Paul, 259n
Torshen, K., 326
Towler, John O., 28, 93, 379n, 397n,
Travers, Robert M. W., 258
Traviss, O. P., 263n
Tubman, Harriet, 363
Turner, Marion E., 108n
Tway, Eileen, 372–373n
Tyler, Ralph, 343

Udall, Stewart L., 177n

Vacc, Nicholas, A., 37n
Van Camp, Sarah S., 144n
Van de Ven, Nicole, 170n

Wagner, Elaine H., 375
Wallen, Norman E., 259n
Wann, Kenneth D., 74
Warren, Jim, 317n
Washington, Booker T., 168
Washington, George, 414
Watson, Dorothy J., 36n, 357n
Watson, Ernest H., 42n
Watts, Lois, 199
Weinstein, Gerald, 48n, 135n, 137
Weinstein, Joshua, 48n
Werner, Thomas J., 39n
Wesley, Edgar B., 31n
Wheeler, Jesse H., 29n, 160n
Whitehead, Alfred North, 63
Wilcox, Leah M., 371n,
Wiles, Jon W., 42n
Willens, Joan, 125, 137
Williams, A. M., 36n
Williams, Selma R., 171n
Wilson, Gilbert M., 81n–82n
Winnie, Philip H., 221n
Winters, Bonnie A., 46n
Witty, Paul A., 92
Wodtke, Kenneth H., 259n
Wolfenstein, Martha, 23n
Wood, Robert W., 80n
Wright, Richard, 168
Wrightstone, J. Wayne, 131n
Wynn, Richard, 284n–285n

Yokubina, Gail, 170
Young, Andrew, 169

Zaccaria, Michael A., 30
Zander, Alvin F., 235

Advance organizers, in children's learning, 100
Adventure in Human Relations, curriculum
    program, 79
Advertising writing, assignments in, 204–205
Affective education:
    and curriculum topics, 135
    definition and purpose, 134
    fantasy trips, 137–138
    improving self-concept, 136–137
    introducing, 134–138
    probing prejudice, 137
    teaching about individual differences,
      135–136
    and values clarification, 48–49
Air pollution in environmental studies, 180
American Indians, stereotyped notions of, 98
    See also Native Americans
Anglo-America, culture region, 160
Anthropology:
    anthropologist's method, 163
    curriculum programs, 20-21, 57–58
Anthropology Curriculum Project,
    curriculum program, 20, 57–58
Art as creative activity, 273–276

Back to basics, public pressure for, 35–37
Background information in children's
    learning, 97
Balance of curriculum content, scope and
    sequence, 62
    charts, 64–67
Behavioral objectives, 11–14
    advantages, 11–12
    limitations, 12–14
Behavioral sciences, 5–6, 17–21
    conceptual structure, 18
    curriculum programs, 57–61
    defined, 5–6
Black studies:
    black contributions, 168–169
    curriculum framework, 169
    objectives, 168
Business enterprise in a mixed economy, 197

Captain Kangaroo, educational television, 317
Career education, emphasis in schools, 205
Careers, changing status of women, 205–206
Carnegie Commission on Educational
    Television, 317

Cartoons, instructional media, 306–307
Children:
    altercations in committee work, 250–251
    attitudes toward learning, 9
    attitudes toward social studies, 79–82
    benefits of creative play, 261–262
    characteristics, 73–95
    complaints in committee work, 250
    consumer education, 204
    the dependent child, 251
    development of motivation, 97–99
    developmental characteristics, 238
    disadvantaged (*see* Disadvantaged children)
    as doers, 75
    economic concepts for, 33
    evaluating performance, 325–347
    geographical concepts for, 28
    imaginative life, 76
    individualized instruction, 38–40
    interest in detail, 75–76
    interests, 73–74
    introduction to government, 146–151
    as investigators, 74
    knowledge of political world, 23–24
    learning cardinal directions, 383–384,
      386–389
    learning citizenship, 141–146
    learning about government, 146–151
    learning social studies, 96–103
    learning about work, 195–209
    limited social experience, 239
    moral character, 10
    need for information background, 97
    personality characteristics, 238
    political socialization, 24
    readiness for time concepts, 30
    settling disagreements, 248–250
    skills, 10
    social values, 9–10
    spontaneous play, 262–263
    switching committee membership, 251
    understanding planning, 243–245
Children's characteristics, implications for
    social studies, 73–95
Children's learning:
    advance organizers, 100
    citizenship, 134–146
    classroom management, 107–111
    generalizations, 99–100
    practice and review, 102–103
    principles, 96–103

Children's learning (*continued*)
  psychology of, 96–111
  reception and inquiry, 101–102
  reinforcement, 102
  topic structure, 99–100
  self-discipline, 110
Citizenship, 134–146
  community service projects, 143–144
  and emotional health, 134–141
  promoting in the classroom, 141
  providing opportunities for practicing,
    141–146
  school service projects, 142–143
Civil rights, discussion of, 151–152
Classroom, open (*see* Open classroom)
Classroom activity:
  analyzing economic costs, 203
  automation and technological change,
    202–203
  career education, 205
  economy of mass production, 202
  market and prices, 202
  personal interviews, 295–296
Classroom management:
  making rules, 108
  rewards and punishment, 109–110
  teacher planning, 109
  teacher's responsibility, 107–111
  in teaching social studies, 107–111
Classroom projects:
  business enterprise, 197–198
  entrepreneurs and bankers, 201–202
  miniature societies, 201
  picture dictionary, 198–200
  production of goods, 196–197
Committee reports, 253–254
  generalizing from, 254
  teacher's role, 253
Committee work:
  concluding, 252–254
  evaluation, 254
  interpersonal problems, 248–252
  managing, 232–256
  organizing for, 236–245
  scheduling, 245
  settling disagreements, 249–250
  with young children, 238
Committees:
  altercations, 250–251
  children in planning, 243–245
  complaining members, 250
  completing work, 252
  composition, 240
  the dependent child, 251
  discouraged, 246–247
  discrimination against a member, 251–252
  functions, 233–234
  informal progress reports, 245
  leaders, 243
  observing other committees, 247–248

  pupils declining membership, 252
  rationale for, 234–235
  reports of, 253
  size of, 241–242
  stalled, 246
  standards and procedures, 242
  supervision of, 245–248
  task-oriented, 234
  teacher qualities, 235–236
  wasting time, 247
Community planning, introducing to children,
    147–148
Competency of teachers (*see* Teaching
    competencies)
Concepts:
  definition and examples, 103–104
  importance of, 104
  related to facts and generalizations, 106–107
  suggestions for teaching, 104–106
  teaching of, 103–107
Concepts and Inquiry, curriculum program,
    20, 55–56
Constitution, learning about the, 150–151
Consultants:
  defined, 292
  examples of use, 293–294
  lay aides, 294–295
  sources for, 292
  as speakers, 292–293
Consumer education for children, 204
"Covering ground," curriculum content, 63, 67
Creative construction, 268–272
  for active play, 269–270
  for exhibit, 270–271
  teacher responsibilities, 271–272
Creative experiences:
  contributions to social studies, 257–258
  free creativity, 261
  providing, 257–278
Creative play and dramatics, 261–268
Creativity:
  art, 273–276
  as aspect of social studies, 261
  availability of materials, 260–261
  availability of space and time, 261
  creative play and dramatics, 261–268
  factors contributing to, 258–261
  industrial arts, 272–273
  making "movies," 276
  murals, 274
  music and dance, 276–277
Critical thinking:
  classroom conditions, 213–214
  inquiry process, 223–228
  promoting, 213–231
  role of discussion, 214–222
  stimulating through questions, 219
  teaching strategies, 213–231
  See also Problem solving
Cultural anthropology, 156

Culture regions:
   geographic methods of inquiry, 158
   study of, 160
Culture studies:
   avoiding stereotypes, 162–163
   black history, 168–169
   building global understanding, 172–173
   conceptual conflicts, 162
   emphasizing objective investigation, 162
   framework for history, 167–171
   interpreting cultural differences, 172–173
   minority group backgrounds, 169–170
   "pen pals," 172
   using folklore, 163–164
   using music and art, 164–165
   women's rights, 170–171
Cultures:
   choosing for study, 157
   study of, 156–175
   ways of life and beliefs, 162
"Curriculum of Affect," 48–49
Curriculum development, teacher's role, 69
Curriculum-less classrooms, 67–68
Curriculum programs:
   Adventure in Human Relations, 79
   in anthropology, 20–21
   balance of content, 62
      charts, 64–67
   criteria for judging, 61–67
   depth of content, 62–67
   *Human Behavior and Potential—
      Behavior Science*, 79
   maturity levels of children, 61–62
   Our Working World, 34
   readability of textbooks, 62
   recycling of ideas, 62
   scope and sequence charts, 64–67
Curriculums:
   commercially produced, 52–61
   components of published programs, 53
   comprehensive social studies, 55–57
   goals of published programs, 53
   inquiry learning, 53–54
   pressure for "back to basics," 35–36
   prevailing practices, 52–55
   published, 52–61
   social studies, 52–70
   study of cultures, 156–157
   values clarification, 47–49

Diagrams, as pupil-constructed instructional
   media, 320–321
Dictated materials, in teaching reading
   comprehension, 353–354
Disadvantaged children:
   Adventure in Human Relations program
     for, 79
   background, 77
   definition, 77

*Human Behavior and Potential—Behavior
   Science* program for, 79
   social studies program for, 78–79
   teaching approaches, 77–78
Discussion:
   of controversial issues, 218–219
   defining terms, 216
   follow-up questions, 220–221
   formulating questions, 220
   high-level questions, 221
   information base for, 215–216
   "interaction" versus "coaction," 217
   participation, 216–217
   in promoting critical thinking, 214
   purpose for, 214–215
   teacher participation, 218
Dramatics:
   in creative experiences, 263–268
   informal, 263–266
   published plays, 266
   role play for sociodrama, 266

Economics, 6, 32–34
   conceptual structure, 32–33
   curriculum program, 61
   curriculum trends, 33–34
   as social science, 6
Educational television, instructional media,
   315–317
Electric Company, The, educational
   television, 317
Elementary education, trends in 35–51
Elementary school, 35–40
   individualized instruction, 38–40
   mainstreaming, 37–38
Elementary school classroom, using
   instructional media, 300–324
Elementary School Teaching Project,
   curriculum program, 136
Emotional health in developing citizenship,
   134–141
Energy in environmental studies, 189–190
Environment, 176–194
   controversial subject, 176–178
   energy shortage, 178–180
   pollution of, 180–182
Environmental studies, 178–184
   conservation work, 187–188
   energy concepts, 189
   energy sources, 189
   erosion, 189–190
   pupil improvement of environment,
     186–187
   resources, 184
   reusing solid wastes, 188
   surveying immediate environment, 185–186
   teaching suggestions, 184–192
   use of energy, 189
Erosion in environmental studies, 189–190

Evaluating pupil performance:
  characteristics of, 326–327
  checklists and rating scales, 327–329
  home visits, 330
  informal evaluations, 327–338
  interviews, 329–330
  mental health aspects, 325–326
  pupils' self-evaluation, 341–342
  records of evaluations, 338
  reporting to parents, 343–344
  See also Pupil evaluation records;
    Testing pupil performance

Family of Man, curriculum program, 20, 56
Fantasy trips in affective education, 137–138
Federal agencies, teaching about, 149
Federal government, teaching structure and
    functions of, 149–151
Field trips, 279–292
  administrative approval, 281
  benefits for pupils, 279
  examples, 282–285, 290–291
  follow-up, 289–292
  justifying conditions, 282
  making reservations, 286–288
  museums, 296–298
  parents' approval, 283
  placing in perspective, 280
  precautions, 284–285
  preparations, 280
  selecting chaperones, 286–287
  supervision, 287–288
  teacher's previsit, 281
  teacher's role, 280–288
Filmstrips and slides, instructional media,
    305–306
Folklore in culture studies, 163–164
Foreign cultures, curriculum programs, 21

Games (*see* Simulation games)
General Index to Illustration, 165
Generalization:
  in children's learning, 99–100
  related to concepts and facts, 106–107
Geographic areas, modelling, 159
Geographic location, using maps and globes,
    161–162
Geography, 6, 28–29
  children's concepts, 28
  curriculum trends, 28–29
  as social science, 6
  study of culture areas, 156
  using home life, 158–159
Globes:
  informal experiences, 384
  teaching place-location, 160
Government, 146–155
  curriculum trends, 25–26
  introducing childen to, 146–151
    of the school system, 146–147
    See also Political science
Graphs as pupil-constructed instructional
    media, 318–320

History, 6, 29–32
  children's time concepts, 30–31
  conceptual structure, 29–30
  curriculum trends, 31–32
  as part of social studies, 6
  study of cultures, 156
Holt Databank System, curriculum program,
    56–57
Human behavior:
  approach through moral education, 139, 141
  causal orientation to, 138–139
  children's concepts of, 19–20
  in social studies, 138–139
*Human Behavior and Potential—Behavior
    Science*, curriculum program, 58–59, 79
Humanities related to social studies, 8
Hypotheses:
  formulated by second-graders, 224
  in inquiry process, 223–224

Identity education, curriculum programs, 21
Illustration Index, 165
Imaginative writing, 368–369
Indian (*see* American Indians; Native
    Americans)
Individualized instruction, 38–40
  limitations, 40
  technique, 38–40
Individualized reading, stimulating reading,
    363
Industrial arts as creative activity, 272–273
Inquiry learning, 53–54
Inquiry process:
  in critical thinking, 223–228
  nature and purpose, 223–224
  in primary grades, 225–226
  in upper grades, 226–228
Instruction:
  delayed effects of, 344–345
  individualized (*see* Individualized
    instruction)
Instructional aids (*see* Instructional media;
    Learning aids)
Instructional media:
  display of materials, 321
  examples, 302–303
  free and inexpensive materials, 317–318
  organization of materials, 321–322
  pupil-constructed, 318–321
  types, 304–317
  See also Learning aids
Interdisciplinary studies:
  controversy over, 7–8
  in social sciences, 7

International law and order, teaching about, 152–153
Interpersonal problems in committee work, 248–252
Intonation in teaching reading comprehension, 355–356

Land use and abuse in environmental studies, 183
Law and order, international (*see* International law and order)
Learning aids:
  abundance of, 300
  emphasizing learning, 301
  guidelines for, 301
  meeting diverse pupil needs, 301
  promoting instructional objectives, 301
  selection and purchase, 303
  types, 304–317
  using properly, 303–304
  when to use, 304
  See also Instructional media
Learning experiences organized as teaching unit, 115
Learning unit topic structure in children's learning, 99–100
Litter problem in environmental studies, 186
Local government, acquainting children with, 147–148

Mainstreaming:
  defined, 37
  research on, 37–38
  social studies under, 38
Man: A Course of Study, curriculum program, 59–60, 118, 163
Maps:
  bird's-eye-view concept, 381
  community, 381–383
  conditions favorable to learning, 384–385
  making layouts, 380
  special-purpose, 389–391
  teaching place-location, 160
Maps and globes:
  constructing azimuth projections, 401
  constructing a conic projection, 402
  constructing an interrupted equal-area, projection, 402
  constructing Mercator projections, 401–402
  defined, 378
  exploring latitude and longitude, 395–397
  in intermediate grades, 384–408
  judging distances, 397–398
  learning cardinal directions, 383–384
  in primary grades, 379–384
  promoting understanding of, 378–410
  standard, 391–394
  studying relief maps, 402–408
  three-dimensional maps, 405–408
  understanding map projections, 398–402

Math skills, application in social studies, 36–37
Media aids for instruction (*see* Instructional media; Learning aids)
Middle school, 40–42
  grounds for concern, 41–42
  improvements needed, 42
  purpose, 41
Minority groups, cultural backgrounds, 169–170
Mister Rogers' Neighborhood, educational television, 317
Moral education, stages in, 139, 141
Morality as teaching objective, 10
Motion pictures as instructional media, 305
Motivation:
  in children's learning, 97–99
  in learning effectiveness, 97–99
"Movies" as creative activity, 276
Multimedia kits as learning aids, 304–305
Murals as creative activity, 274–275
Museums in field trips, 296–298
Music and dance as creative activity, 276–277

National Geographic Magazine, 165
Native Americans:
  planning a unit on, 165–167
  See also American Indians
News in classroom discussion, 144–146
Newspapers:
  using adult newspapers, 146
  written for children, 145–146
Nongraded schools, 42–44
  purpose, 42–43
  social studies in, 43–44
  teaching problems, 43

Opaque and overhead projections as instructional media, 307–308
Open classroom:
  evaluation, 46
  learning centers in, 44–46
  teaching-learning methods, 44
Our Working World, curriculum program, 34, 61

Performance of pupils (*see* Pupil performance)
Pesticides in environmental studies, 181
Pictures as instructional media, 308–309
Political science, 6, 21–22
  conceptual structure, 6–7
  as social science, 6
  See also Government
"Postholing":
  curriculum content, 63
  type-study unit, 157
Practical writing, 369–370
Practice and review in children's learning, 102–103
Prejudice, probing, 137

Presidency, teaching about, 149
Presidents, learning about, 150
Previewing books and chapters, teaching
    reading comprehension, 354
Problem solving:
    promotion of, 213
    training in, 222–223
    See also Critical thinking
Programmed materials as instructional media,
    313–315
Psychology:
    as social science, 6
    of teaching social studies, 96–111
Published curriculum programs:
    components, 53
    dominant position, 53–54
    goals, 53
    scope and sequence, 54–55
    teacher's role, 69
Pupil background in creative thinking, 260
Pupil evaluation records:
    anecdotal records, 339–340
    cumulative records, 338
    file of pupil's paper work, 340–341
    See also Evaluating pupil performance
Pupil performance:
    evaluating, 325–347
    related to teaching objectives, 325
    testing (see Testing pupil performance)
Pupil's committee work (see Committee work)

Radiation in environmental studies, 180–181
Radio as instructional media, 311
Reading assignments, pupil preparation for,
    355
Reading to children, in stimulating reading,
    363
Reading comprehension, teaching of (see
    Teaching reading comprehension)
Reading plays together, in stimulating
    reading, 363–364
Reading skills, application in social studies,
    36
Reception and inquiry in children's learning,
    101–102
Recordings as instructional media, 310–311
Reference reading, in teaching reading
    comprehension, 360
Reinforcement in children's learning, 102
Report cards, reporting pupil performance to
    parents, 343–344
Reportorial writing, 367–368
Resource unit:
    collection, 118
    definition, 118
    See also Unit
Resources in environmental studies, 184,
    188–189

Rewards and punishment in classroom
    management, 109
Role playing:
    in affective education, 137–138
    children as bankers, 201–202
    children as entrepreneurs, 201–202
    in creative experiences, 266–268
Rules in classroom management, 108–109

School library as multimedia center, 300–301
Self-discipline in children's learning, 110
Sesame Street, educational television, 317
Silent Spring in environmental studies,
    181–182
Simulation games as instructional media,
    311–313
Skills as teaching objective, 10–11
Social psychology:
    curriculum programs, 21
    as social science, 6
Social Science Laboratory Units, curriculum
    program, 21, 60–61, 163
Social sciences, 5–8, 17–34
    basis for social studies, 5
    overlapping of, 6–7
    and social studies curriculum, 17–34
Social studies:
    aims of instruction, 8
    art activities, 273
    children's attitude toward, 79–82
    children's low interest in, 80–81
    combining with natural science, 184
    contributions of creative experiences,
        257–258
    curriculums, 55–57
    definition, 3
    derived from social sciences, 5
    evaluating pupil performance, 325–347
    field trips, 279–291
    formulating objectives, 14–16
    and the humanities, 8
    implications of children's characteristics,
        73–95
    importance of, 5
    improving reading comprehension in,
        351–366
    learning principles, 96–103
    math skills, 36–37
    middle school improvements, 42
    nature of, 4
    objectives, 8–11
    overcoming lagging interest, 81–82
    paper (published) curriculums, 67–68
    providing writing experiences, 367–377
    psychology of teaching, 96–111
    reading skills, 36
    testing in elementary school, 342
    trends in elementary education, 35–51

the unit, 115–133
using consultants, 292–294
using instructional media, 300–324
writing skills, 36–37
Social values, as teaching objective, 9–10
Sociodrama in creative experiences, 266–268
Solid wastes in environmental studies, 181, 188
State government, acquainting children with, 148–149
State legislation, example of children's experience with, 148–149
Stimulating love of reading, 362–364
Study prints as instructional media, 309–310
Sustained silent reading, in stimulating love of reading, 364

Taba Program in Social Science, curriculum program, 20, 57, 121
Teacher:
    planning role in classroom management, 109
    responsibility for classroom management, 107–108
    role in curriculum development, 69
Teacher behavior in promoting creative thinking, 259
Teaching competencies:
    citizenship and government, 153–154
    in committee work, 254–255
    in creative activity, 277
    culture studies, 173–174
    developing time concepts, 420
    environmental studies, 192–193
    evaluating pupil performance, 345
    field trips, 298
    improving reading comprehension, 364
    instructional media, 322
    products, work, and careers, 207–208
    in promoting critical thinking, 228–230
    providing writing experiences, 376
    social studies units, 132
    study of cultures, 173–174
    in unit teaching, 132–133
    using consultants, 298
    using maps and globes, 408–409
Teaching government, 146–151
Teaching Program in Human Behavior and Mental Health, A, curriculum program, 21
Teaching reading comprehension:
    clues to word meanings, 356
    difficult textbooks, 361–362
    flexibility, 355
    grasping paragraphs, 358–360
    neglect of, 352
    stimulating love of reading, 362–364
    teaching as part of social studies, 351–352
    team learning, 361–362
    techniques, 352–364

Teaching strategies, critical thinking, 213–231
Teaching Strategies for Ethnic Studies, 170
Teaching the unit (*see* Unit teaching)
Teaching units (*see* Unit)
Team learning in reading comprehension, 361–362
Team teaching:
    defined, 46
    how it works, 47
    in social studies, 47
Television, educational (*see* Educational television)
Television in children's political socialization, 144–145
Testing in elementary school social studies, 342–343
Testing pupil performance:
    criterion-referenced tests, 330–331
    informal teacher-constructed tests, 331–334
    norm-referenced (standardized) tests, 334–338
    See also Evaluating pupil performance
Textbook selection in teaching reading comprehension, 354
Thinking and communication, importance of concepts, 104
Time concepts:
    constructing time lines, 415–417
    development of, 411–421
    events, 412–414
    historical periods, 415
    separating events, 414–415
    stimulating development of, 418
    teaching, 412–415
    teaching through pictures, 420
Time units, mental images of, 412
Travel through Pictures, 165

Unit:
    assessing pupil background, 118–119
    concepts and generalizations in, 117
    content, 116–117
    defining scope of, 121
    definition, 115
    informal units in primary grades, 122
    introducing the class to, 120–121
    launching, 120–121
    method, 115–116
    packaged, 117–118
    planning the content, 118–120
    pupil input in planning, 121
    scope, 116
    teacher-created, 117–118
    teaching of, 122–123
    unity, 116–117
    See also Resource unit

Unit teaching:
  class planning sessions, 124–125
  concluding the unit, 130–131
  daily lesson plans, 123
  effectiveness, 131–132
  example, "The City," 125–130
  individual differences, 135
  overview, 122–131
  pupil record keeping, 125
  teaching competencies, 132–133

Values clarification:
  and affective education, 47–49
  in curriculum, 47–49

Water pollution in environmental studies, 180
Wildlife conservation in environmental studies, 182–183
Women, careers, for, 205–206
Women's rights, teaching sources, 170–171

Work, differentiating goods from services, 195
World government, teaching about, 153
World peace, teaching about, 152
Writing:
  choosing topics, 373
  dictated compositions, 370
  emphasizing content, 375
  imaginative, 368–369
  practical, 369–370
  preserving in notebooks, 374
  promoting writing experiences, 367–377
  reportorial, 367–368
  sharing works, 373–374
  teacher praise and criticism, 375–376
  team writing, 372–373
  trading ideas, 372
  types of experiences, 367–371
  ways of stimulating, 371–375
Writing skills, application in social studies, 36–37

Zoom, educational television, 317